A Worldview of Animal Law

AF718985

LAW LIBRARY
GOLDEN GATE UNIVERSITY

A Worldview of Animal Law

Bruce A. Wagman

Matthew Liebman

LAW LIBRARY

JUL 12 2011

GOLDEN GATE UNIVERSITY

Carolina Academic Press

Durham, North Carolina

Copyright © 2011
Bruce A. Wagman
Matthew Liebman
All Rights Reserved

Library of Congress Cataloging-in-Publication Data

Wagman, Bruce A.
A worldview of animal law / Bruce A. Wagman, Matthew Liebman.
p. cm.
Includes bibliographical references and index.
ISBN 978-1-59460-462-1 (alk. paper)
1. Animal welfare--Law and legislation. I. Liebman, Matthew. II. Title.

K3620.W34 2011
346.04'6954--dc22

2011005411

CAROLINA ACADEMIC PRESS
700 Kent Street
Durham, North Carolina 27701
Telephone (919) 489-7486
Fax (919) 493-5668
www.cap-press.com

Printed in the United States of America

Contents

Preface

There is much diversity of opinion and even angry disagreement over how we should treat the animals with whom we share the planet. At the same time, is there some level at which we all—worldwide—agree? Are there acts of cruelty to animals that almost every human thinks are unacceptable? What thread of human kindness to nonhumans touches all cultures and countries? In 2007, that notion of a universal foundation of cruelty got me thinking, as I struggled with the daily reality of brutality to which most animals on the planet are subjected. If we can identify that basic level of agreement, perhaps we can use it to move forward to a world in which animal interests are given greater weight in the decisions of individuals, states, countries, and international congregations. The concept gestated in conversations with colleagues from around the world. Four years later, this monumental project completed in early 2011. It was probably just denial, but I did not appreciate the magnitude of the undertaking until I was a few years into it—and even then, it just seemed too big to ever fully conquer. A large team of partners and participants contributed ideas, research, editing and structural advice.

Like some of the best aspects of animal law itself, the text is unconventional in a few notable ways. First, it is intentionally directed at a wider range of readers than most books about the law. We hope to satisfy the intellect of interested citizens of the world with no legal background, as well as practicing lawyers and official decision-makers. The desire to serve that broad readership means that the descriptions of legal doctrine may be too simplistic for some, and that parts of the book may be too specialized for others. We have done our best to tread the information level median on those issues so that everyone can benefit from and enjoy reading and considering what is here.

Second, this book does not, and was never intended to be, an exhaustive or detailed coverage of international law as it pertains to animals. There is already excellent and extensive scholarly discussion of the multitude of international agreements and their effects on animals worldwide. We wanted this project to be a supplement to that, but it is not a substitute, because its focus is decidedly different. Our approach is to look, from a bird's-eye view (or chimpanzee's, pig's, or dog's eye views) at popular issues and some legal constructs, and then at the manner in which the law and animals' interests correspond or clash, in different countries, around the world. We provide what we think are interesting and illustrative examples of the manner in which nations address the difficult intersections of animals and people through the use of the law. We do this to satisfy those first questions in this Preface, and to provide food for further thought. This is why our international animal law chapter is last; for this work, international treaties and agreements and organizations are not the leading reason for this book, nor the central theme. They are simply another set of examples of how things work in the world.

While there are some significant differences in the current legal protection for animals, our conclusions are that there is much similarity in the way animals are treated—and great room for improvement. Some countries may be lagging in developing particular protections in certain areas; others may have developed an intricate set of laws in a given area, but in the end still provide little in the way of meaningful standards that will have any value to individual animals. We are still at the beginning. For each animal has a beating heart and an active mind that must be considered in any evaluation of the laws governing their treatment. Certainly our deepest desire is that what we have written will stimulate positive change for them.

We hope that you, and the animals, are happy with the results.

BAW April 2011

Acknowledgments

The authors especially thank Michelle Maloney for her dedication and motivational work on the book, without which it would not have moved forward; and Elizabeth Brown for her devotion to the project in its latter half. We also thank the extensive team of students and volunteer researchers who gave their time to work on various aspects of the book in its early stages. And we pay tribute to the animals all over the world, whose minds and hearts stimulated the idea which was the genesis of the text.

Matthew thanks Sarah Kite and Tim Phillips for feedback on the animal research chapter; Vince Field, Agnes Tam, and Katya Mezek for assistance with research and translation; Bruce Wagman and Joyce Tischler for unparalleled mentorship; Richard, Ruthie, and Jeremy Liebman for unwavering support; Salena Copeland for constant companionship; and Ashleigh, Oliver, Emma, Spider, Anais, and Chaplin for joy and inspiration.

Bruce thanks Deborah for the patience she showed while I worked on this, and for constant support; Julius and Gloria Wagman for putting up with me all those years; my Schiff Hardin partners for their support; and my animal companions at home, who provided endless entertainment and insight. For Tamba and Paka, who were there at the beginning but not the end.

LIST OF TERMS

A "WORDVIEW" OF ANIMAL LAW

Acronym	Definition
A(SP)A	Animals (Scientific Procedures) Act [UK]
AEC	Animal ethics committees [Australia]
ALDF	Animal Legal Defense Fund
APA	Animals Protection Act [South Africa]
APAC	Animal Protection Act of Croatia
APAS	Sammarinese Association for the Protection of Animals
APHIS	Animal and Plant Health Inspection Service [US]
APO	Swiss Animal Protection Ordinance
ASEAN	Association of Southeast Asian Nations
ASEAN-WEN	Association of Southeast Asian Nations Wildlife Enforcement Network
ATS	Antarctic Treaty System
AWA	Animal Welfare Act [US]
AWBI	Animal Welfare Board of India
AWMA	Act on Welfare and Management of Animals [Japan]
BCTF	Bushmeat Crisis Task Force
BSE	Bovine Spongiform Encephalopathy, commonly known as "Mad Cow Disease"
BUAV	British Union for the Abolition of Vivisection
CAFO	Concentrated Animal Feeding Operations
CHRB	Council of Europe's Convention on Human Rights and Biomedicine
CIOMS	Council for International Organizations of Medical Sciences
CITES	Convention on International Trade in Endangered Species
CRW	Convention for the Regulation of Whaling

EC	European Community
ECJ	European Court of Justice
EEC	European Economic Community (EEC)
EPBC Act	Environment Protection and Biodiversity Conservation Act [Australia]
EPBCA	Environment Protection and Biodiversity Conservation Act 1999 [Australia]
ESA	United States' Endangered Species Act
ETIS	Elephant Trade Information System [CITES]
EU	European Union
FAAP	Federal Act of Animal Protection [Switzerland]
FAO	United Nations' Food and Agriculture Organization
FCI	Fédération Cynologique Internationale
GAPNZ	Great Ape Project New Zealand
GATT	General Agreement on Tariffs and Trade
HMSA	Humane Methods of Slaughter Act [US]
HSUS	Humane Society of the United States
IACLAM	International Association of Colleges of Laboratory Animal Medicine
IACUCs	Institutional Animal Care and Use Committees [US]
IAEC	Institutional Animals Ethics Committee [India]
IARW	International Agreement for the Regulation of Whaling
ICCVAM	Inter-Agency Coordinating Committee for the Validation of Alternative Methods [US]
ICJ	International Court of Justice
ICLAS	International Council of Laboratory Animal Science
ICRW	International Convention for the Regulation of Whaling
IGP	International Guiding Principles for Biomedical Research Involving Animals
ISO	International Organization for Standardization
IUCN	International Union for the Conservation of Nature and Natural Resources
IWC	International Whaling Commission
MIKE	Monitoring the Illegal Killing of Elephants [CITES]

MMPA	Marine Mammal Protection Act [US]
MMRs	Canadian Marine Mammal Regulations
MOU	Memorandums of Understanding
NAFTA	North American Free Trade Agreement
NAMMCO	North Atlantic Marine Mammal Commission
NAWAC	National Animal Welfare Advisory Committee [New Zealand]
NGO	Nongovernmental organizations
NIH	National Institutes of Health
NPC	National People's Congress [China]
NZAWA	Animal Welfare Act of 1999 [New Zealand]
OIE	World Organization for Animal Health
OIG	USDA's Office of Inspector General
OLAW	NIH's Office of Laboratory Animal Welfare
OSPCA	Ontario's Society for the Prevention of Cruelty to Animals Act [Canada]
PAWA	Philippine Animal Welfare Act
PCAA	Prevention of Cruelty to Animals Act [India]
PHS	Public Health Service [US]
PIMC	Primary Industries Ministerial Council [Australia]
PPA	European Convention for the Protection of Pet Animals
REACH	Registration, Evaluation, Authorisation and Restriction of Chemical Substances [EU]
RSPCA	Royal Society for the Prevention of Cruelty to Animals
SAVF	South African Veterinary Foundation
SPS Agreement	The World Trade Organization Agreement on the Application of Sanitary and Phytosanitary Measures
UDAW	Universal Declaration on Animal Welfare
UDHR	Universal Declaration of Human Rights
UN	United Nations
UN Convention	United Nations' Convention on the Law of the Sea
USDA	United States Department of Agriculture
WSPA	World Society for the Protection of Animals
WTO	The World Trade Organization

A Worldview of Animal Law

CHAPTER 1

INTRODUCTION

Overview: An Introduction to Comparative Animal Law

In the last fifty years, our relationships with the nonhuman sentient beings with whom we share the planet have undergone major revisions. These changes have in many ways been as radical and earth-shaking as the transformations that brought us from caves to cubicles, from the prehistoric to the postmodern. And these alterations—in law, in conduct, and in consciousness—have taken place in evolutionary seconds compared to the slow progression of the physical changes that our world and the species in it have experienced. Ethical, social, economic, and scientific changes in the last five decades have dramatically altered our relationships with animals. Although we continue to use and abuse animals in new and vastly expanded ways, never before have so many people been so focused on what (or whom) they are eating, wearing, or exploiting. At the same time that the industrial factory farming model moves around the globe, more and more people are turning to vegetarianism and veganism. While the luxuries and status symbols of the West continue to spread internationally, animal-derived fabrics (especially fur, but also leather and wool) have become targets of increased scrutiny and criticism. While the culture and entertainment industries continue to cater to our desire to view animals through the media and live exhibitions, a growing movement has battled the exploitation of primates and other animals in the entertainment industries. And while biotechnology produces human-animal chimeras and cloned animals (from sheep to dogs), the movement against vivisection has gone global.

The legal system is just beginning to feel the pressure of these heterogeneous movements as animal lawyers bring more lawsuits and legal issues involving animals receive more media coverage. Judges and lawmakers have begun to take seriously the sentience and consciousness of animals, as well as considerations of cruelty and humane treatment. We are in the midst of an era in which those concepts are gaining increased space in public dialogues, and the ultimate results have not yet been realized. There have been noteworthy changes in societies' interests in animal protection issues, and, of course, these drive many of the changes in the law. To many involved in defending animals, these alterations have been minimal and barely scratch the surface of the changes they hope to see. Yet these shifts have occurred in a split second compared to the millennia during which human societies have developed, refined, and codified the relationships we have with animals. It is possible that this rapid reordering is a harbinger of things to come.

This book notes those changes in a unique way—by addressing the multitude of human-animal relationships as they are mediated through law in the global community. The book presents concepts and doctrines anecdotally, with an eye towards an exegesis of the current state of animal law around the world. An essential step in the growth of the discipline of animal law is the examination of similarities and differences across borders both national and cultural. It is imperative upon those of us involved in the dialogue and practice of legal change for animals to consider our positions in the biggest picture—the international one. Given this imperative, we must reflect on the ways in which different communities articulate human-animal relationships through their legal systems. This project involves, at this nascent stage, an attempt to identify and qualify the facts and motivations underlying different nations' and peoples' treatment of animals within their legal structures.

The global community consists of countless component parts, including nation-states, tribal governments, supranational entities such as the World Trade Organization and the United Nations, non-governmental organizations, multinational corporations, individuals, and even the biotic community. In this book, we focus on the changes in individual nation-states (including their participation in international treaties) and their political subdivisions, because they are the entities that enact and enforce laws, and we keep an eye on the way all components of the global community influence and affect laws at the level of the nation-state. The ways in which these entities address questions of animal exploitation on a situational basis in each country contribute to global changes in practice, philosophy, and law.

Without any attempt at comprehensive coverage, we have surveyed the world's laws as they pertain to animals and selected those laws that present exemplary ideas and stimulate further thought. In order to facilitate the reader's ability to focus on concepts rather than doctrine, we have avoided excessive citation in the text and instead included chapter endnotes and appendices with the pertinent and cited laws. Our purpose is to glean a sense of international issues—both those on which nations (and their citizens) clash and those on which they agree.

Our examination of historical, cultural, and national distinctions and commonalities is intended to provide a genealogy of current thinking and to identify points of agreement and contention between nations and peoples. This will allow those who are working to improve the status of animals to incorporate the broadest scope of considerations into their decision-making processes, with the hope that such contemplation will lead to a more nuanced and productive effort to protect animals around the world. This collective consideration enables us to move forward in a cooperative and effective fashion. The similarities and the differences in the treatment of animals identified in this text should guide all interested in animal protection in the ongoing development of animal law concepts for the future. The text is intended to serve as a starting point for readers' further discussion and considerations of potential avenues of development. We aim to provide a solid basis for beginning to think comparatively about the interactions between laws and diverse human societies, with the hope that this will lead to proactive efforts of international collaboration.

This book has been intentionally structured to provide examples of those changes around the world. It is not exhaustive—but is a template for discussion and a starting place for those interested in further research into the field of comparative animal law. We hope to connect some of the dots between geographically and politically disparate legal systems. We encourage our readers to use this knowledge and take the next steps towards progress for animals.

Animals and the Law

Until fairly recently, most laws reflected the prevailing belief that animals had only instrumental value. Those animals who lacked economic exchange value were thus unprotected from cruelty and abuse. In the very recent past, for instance, dogs, cats, and the other species of animals with whom many humans now share their homes and hearts were considered worthless in every sense—without economic significance and lacking inherent value. Because dogs and cats lacked exchange value, they were excluded from most early anti-cruelty laws in the United States and England. As recently as the mid-1800s, the only animals who obtained any significant legal attention were those who had economic value—those we could buy, sell, or use for financial gain, such as cows, pigs, chickens or draft horses.[1] Those animals found their place in the law solely because they provided an economic advantage to humans. They were considered commodities of no worth greater than the financial benefit that they accorded their owners. Society recognized that animals had market value, but not that animals' sentience, physiology, and social cultures entitled them to ethical consideration.

Today, despite the relatively resistant (some might call it intransigent) nature of the written law, multiple opportunities have appeared for those working to improve the lives of animals. Some are shifts in doctrine, some involve new applications of old laws or traditional principles, and some involve discoveries of laws that were intended to help animals but had not been previously used. The relationship between law and society is bidirectional: as law defines society, so does it follow popular progression of thought, and that is what we are experiencing—worldwide. Changing concepts concerning the place of animals in the world have led to a tectonic shift that is generating a wave-like force against the traditional legal wall that separates humans and animals. These new thoughts have affected courts, legislatures, and law enforcement authorities in virtually every culture and society.

Four decades before this book's publication, few would have thought it possible that the incipient animal rights movement could synthesize its philosophy into a viable set of legal theories, principles, and laws focusing on the interests of animals. Nor did it seem possible that lawyers across the globe would begin practicing animal law to challenge practices they considered illegal or inhumane. Judges were not asked, as they often are today, to entertain the argument that an animal's interests should be given legal weight. The idea that animal protection could be written into national constitutions was unheard of.

Yet the past forty years have seen significant changes in animal protection issues. Throughout the world, legal scholars have taken up the challenge of evaluating our treatment of animals, and the public is becoming increasingly interested in these issues. Legislators are listening to their constituents (as well as to lobbyists from the animal industries); government heads are discussing animal welfare issues, even if they are still not the most important items on the agenda; law enforcement personnel are becoming aware of the connections between cruelty to animals and cruelty to human beings; and the public is increasingly sensitive to the plight of animals. Law schools around the world are adding animal law to their curricula, and a growing number of lawyers are devoting at least part of their practices to animal law issues. The field of animal law is still comparatively new and its development varies from country to country, and sometimes differs between jurisdictions within a given country as much as it does between countries. But the fact is—there *is* a field of animal law. And there is, even if we have not actively embraced and recognized it, a growing field of comparative animal law.

What Is Animal Law?

Under its broadest definition, animal law covers all aspects of the law—legislative, judicial, regulatory, executive—that deal with issues pertaining to nonhuman animals. A short list of these areas includes: criminal prosecution of perpetrators of animal cruelty, political and philosophical efforts to include specific animals within the group of fundamental legal rights-holders, civil litigation that challenges longstanding practices affecting animals, and laws that affects animals (such as legislation that protects animal farmers from liability for creating noxious environments, that increases penalties for animal cruelty, that restricts the species or breeds of animals allowed in a jurisdiction, or that provides heightened protection for certain species). Animal law includes regulatory and municipal control of the keeping of companion animals, as well as governmental regulation of animal experimentation, including the conditions of confinement and the types of research performed on animals. And it includes a wide variety of international arrangements, compacts, and treaties that affect how countries deal with animals within their borders, as well as those who may enter their borders on a transient basis. Animal law as we understand it is now a broad field with multiple sub-disciplines. Questions about the field are increasingly defined by the fact that the sentient nature of the animals at issue somehow impacts the analysis and application of law.

Practitioners of animal law work in a wide range of areas, likely covering much more ground than most people would expect. The field is quite broad at this point and includes (1) individual tort cases (such as veterinary malpractice and dog bite cases); (2) impact litigation (trying to change broad industry practices in agriculture and research); (3) animal control and sheltering issues; and (4) wills and trusts. Civil litigators address this extended list of potential actions. Prosecutors are seeing, and taking, a growing number of animal abuse cases; because anticruelty laws are prevalent—as is abuse of animals—this represents a significant amount of animal law cases that actually get to court. Government agencies and departments are adding animal law specialists to either litigate cases or provide analysis based on the growing body of law with respect to animals. Animal lawyers may be civil litigators and appellate practitioners who take cases on behalf of animal protection organizations or concerned individuals who seek to enforce animal protection laws. Or they may be criminal prosecutors who pursue punitive and rehabilitative measures against those who perpetrate animal cruelty. Animal lawyers may also be lobbyists or political campaign coordinators who attempt to convince legislatures to enact new laws, strengthen old ones, or allocate appropriate resources to enforce existing laws.

One type of litigation related to animal law involves activists who have been accused of violating the law while engaging in animal rights activism. Such criminal defense may involve actions of open civil disobedience (such as a sit-in or lockdown at a fur store) or clandestine direct action (such as breaking into a laboratory to liberate animals and sabotage equipment). In the last few years, the international animal rights movement has seen more and more people willing to take dramatic and sometimes illegal action to rescue animals or inflict economic injury on industries that use animals. Given the new spotlight on these activists in the media and by law enforcement, their trials have become battlegrounds in the public debate about animal protection.

Many animal lawyers focus on legislative change, lobbying for new animal protection laws or the amendment of existing laws. It takes a somewhat different set of skills from those of the litigator to excel in this area. Legislative advocates must have a diverse understanding of the process of lawmaking, not only the technical and procedural nuances of how to pass a law, but also the political climate and the individual personalities of the legislators and lobbyists. The legislatively-focused animal lawyer assists in the drafting of new laws, works to engender support from legislators and varied special interest groups, and educates legislators who vote on the laws so that they understand the importance of animal issues to their constituents. Legislative activism forges consensus and, by doing so, often generates public awareness of issues that most people had not even considered. Legislation is also incredibly important to litigators whose work includes enforcing the laws that animal law lobbyists have succeeded in getting passed.

Transactional lawyers—those who prefer to operate outside of courtrooms and legislatures—can also offer great value to animals and animal law. Business lawyers are indispensable advisors to animal protection organizations before and during their establishment. Often transactional lawyers can provide the expertise on nonprofit formation and incorporation laws, thus shepherding nongovernmental animal protection organizations through the daunting task of setting up their corporate structures in compliance with national and local laws—both in their home country and others where they may be soliciting donations and doing their work. Animal advocacy organizations are also regularly involved in contracts vital to promoting and carrying out their work, and the legal expertise corporate lawyers provide is necessary to avoid traps for the unwary.

Attorneys also provide important counseling to advocacy organizations wishing to effect change through lobbying efforts and public campaigns. For instance, an organization launching a campaign against a specific animal researcher may seek advice on defamation law and its potential liability for libel or slander. An organization pursuing an undercover investigation may seek advice on laws pertaining to videotaping at a facility without consent. Animal law attorneys who provide such advice are crucial to public education programs because they help protect the organizations from liability and also help to ensure the value of the information collected. Lawyers who are familiar with the potential for liability from such conduct help make possible the campaigns that shape the changing beliefs of society towards a more animal-friendly outlook.

What Is Comparative Animal Law?

Now that we have provided a general overview of animal law and the lawyers who serve as its backbone, we turn to the definition of "comparative animal law" for the purposes of this text. The field we address here entails a summary of laws and decisions, as well as analysis of the underlying cultural constructs that affect animals and delineate the legal constraints on human interactions with animals. This body of information covers individual relationships with animals (such as companion animals), and corporate use of animals (such as farming, clothing production, and research). For our purposes, comparative animal law includes all legal constraints and allowances and their supporting (whether obvious or unseen) doctrines and ideologies. It includes all theories and laws that support or restrict the control and use of animals in a given social system and country, and how that system affects animals there and around the world. Comparative animal law can be distinguished from "normal" animal law in a few ways. The most obvious difference is the scope of the field. Comparative animal law crosses borders and therefore encompasses not just domestic legal systems, but also the interactions and agreements, distinctions and consistencies, among the nations of the world. Comparative animal law includes a comparative survey of each nation's domestic law, and takes into account formal international agreements, such as the Convention on International Trade in Endangered Species (CITES), as well as international governing bodies such as the World Trade Organization. In addition to surveying formal laws, the comparative animal law approach recognizes the imperative of "thinking politics outside the confines of the sovereign territorial state."[2] The dialogue in this area incorporates the ways in which the social dimension of law migrates between nations and peoples and how domestic changes in one country may be the catalyst for changes in other nations. Laws that carry little or no weight outside of their borders may nevertheless, for our purposes, help define the big picture of comparative animal law.

Just as comparative animal law adds new questions to the field of animal law, animal lawyers who practice in multiple countries or deal regularly with international treaties need expertise in areas that may not be especially important to domestic animal lawyers. The variety of international agreements (only some of which are highlighted and discussed in this text) occasionally impact domestic animal lawyers. In contrast, those international agreements are an important focus for the comparative animal lawyer, because those agreements bind countries in ways that are different from domestic laws.

A second notable difference for the animal lawyer focused on international issues is a need to be comparative in her thinking. Comparative animal lawyers must be familiar with the laws of multiple countries and able to compare and contrast protections in order to help her clients understand where campaigns are likely to succeed or fail. This skill may arise in the context of interpretation of international agreements or in formulating agreements between nations. Without this comparative perspective, the lawyer working in the international forum will not be able to best serve clients whose work is affected by the laws and practices of multiple countries. For instance, an attorney representing an international whale protection organization will need to be familiar with not only the laws of whaling nations like Japan and Norway, but also the parameters of the current moratorium on whaling imposed by the International Whaling Commission. Such a comparative view will be crucial to searching out the most effective avenues for advancing animals' interests.

Comparative animal lawyers need to appreciate not only the *laws* of the various countries, but also the cultural and religious attitudes towards animals in those countries. Those ideas will be motivating forces, whether the lawyers are dealing with courts, legislatures, or public opinions. Animal attorneys within countries with diverse and heterogeneous cultures must be sensitive to cultural and religious differences extant domestically. This obligation is magnified in the international context, both because of the increased influence of cultural and religious principles in more homogenous societies, and because of the interplay of cultural and religious pressures which, in the international context is highlighted by cultural and national interaction.

Now that we have defined the "what" of comparative animal law, it may serve us to answer the corollary question—"Why should we consider the international scope of comparative animal law?" That is, what need do we hope this book will fulfill? Through conversations with other animal law practitioners from multiple countries, in classrooms, and at conferences devoted to the issues of animals and the law, we found that those involved in the field are interested in identifying commonalities across jurisdictions, as well as those differences that impede meaningful advancement of animal interests. Many people working on animal issues domestically are coming to realize that the globalization of capital, cultural exchange, and technology has internationalized animal industries. Globalization has forced these activists and attorneys to reckon with the state of animal law in other nations. For instance, United States lawyers and activists worked hard to institute a national ban on commercial horse slaughter for human consumption, but businesses consequently began shipping horses to Canada and Mexico, where horse slaughter is legal and where conditions may be even more atrocious than in the U.S.[3] Unless animal activism is to devolve into an ineffective provincialism that ascribes to an "out-of-sight, out-of-mind" philosophy, animal advocates cannot turn a blind eye to the effects their activism has internationally—and that international law may have on their activism. When multiple countries are involved in an animal welfare case, lawyers may need to have a broader perspective and approach. For example, when the Dallas Zoo announced it would ship its sole surviving African Elephant Jenny to a drive-through zoo in Mexico instead of to an elephant sanctuary in Tennessee, domestic animal lawyers were forced to turn to international law, specifically the treaties regarding import and export of endangered animals, to determine whether they could prevent the transfer. In the end, the Dallas Zoo changed its mind and decided to keep Jenny in Dallas, but attorneys were made acutely aware of the importance of an international perspective.[4]

We hope to open the dialogue among anyone and everyone involved with the treatment of animals—lawyers and philosophers, members of industry and members of parliaments, activists and judges—in order to increase understanding in all directions, and perhaps forge a way forward. It is certainly our desire to improve the treatment of animals throughout the world, and to put the spotlight on abuses and practices that cause pain and suffering. But it is also our desire to do that in an objective and academic fashion. To that end, this is a general text intended to reach a broad audience. It addresses the laws of countries across the world, but it is specifically not a legal casebook.

Even the most casual observer will recognize that the treatment of animals varies between countries, judicial systems, cultures, geographical regions, and religions, as well as across time. The same act may be condemned in one culture, era, or religion, and approved or even made sacred in another. Our purpose is not to condemn or judge, but to facilitate engagement with these tensions, which we hope will lead us to a new vision for the direction of animal law, one that recognizes and respects difference while searching for consensus.

Our process was somewhat limited by the absence of research on unwritten tribal laws and our own handicap of being fluent mainly in English, although we did our best to research outside of traditional law and to obtain translations of helpful foreign laws and texts. Even with those constraints, we believe the resulting set of illustrations of issues addresses the scope and breadth of cultural and legal ideas throughout the world. We endeavored to go off the track of American and European law as much as possible. Nevertheless, with the increased amount of legal attention given to animals in those areas of the world, as well as the accessibility of materials from those nations, their laws and issues still occupy a fair amount of the analysis. Yet this concentration does make us hesitant to ascribe universal status to the lessons we divine from those jurisdictions alone. We recognize that the act of mistaking Western particulars for universal imperatives is a form of colonialism that impedes the productive cross-cultural dialogue that is necessary if we are to forge a transnational movement for animal protection.

Our effort should be distinguished from those that focus more intensely on traditional instruments of international law—treaties, compacts, and committees. Although we do address those instruments in the course of our discussion, we take a more expansive view of the basic sets of rules and regulations in order to describe different ways of dealing with the interplay between animals, humans, and the law in varied cultures and parts of the world. Certainly, the focus of international species-specific agreements such as CITES provides insight into how member nations, in one collective group, view *some* animals, for some reasons. But we must place these protections and agreements in their broader context; we seek here to move towards an appreciation of animals of all species. Our inquiry canvasses general and specific laws and philosophies in Australasia, North America, South and Central America, Asia, the European Union, and Africa. As the book cannot cover every country or region, and just present examples, some issues may not be covered. Through that examination, we develop some ability to analyze the treatment of animals around the world, and hope to move forward from there in a positive direction towards a better world for all—a world with less cruelty, more compassion, and more of a shared vision for what is best for all species.

The field addressed here, and the topics covered, are in a state of change. While this book was being written there were noticeable shifts in thinking and law around the world. And certainly shortly after its publication some of the book's questions will be answered, and some of its provocations engaged. If nothing else, the world's treatment of animals, and the law that addresses that conduct, is in flux. It will be interesting for all involved to watch the development over the next few decades. The evolution is occurring largely because of a growing discomfort with the way modernity has turned animals into commodities without any consideration of their sentience, and the parallel recognition of the significance of that sentience. The backlash of feeling against that industrial development has stimulated a public outcry, which is being heard and felt in courtrooms and legislatures throughout the world.

Common Issues in Comparative Animal Law

In this section, we identify recurrent themes and questions that arise in comparing the animal laws of disparate jurisdictions. These issues come up throughout the book, both explicitly and implicitly, so we take this opportunity to frame them in a way that will facilitate later reflection. It goes without saying that different nations and cultures have different answers to these questions, which is precisely why this book exists.

Which animals are the subjects of laws and why are they privileged over other animals?

There are many ways of grouping the classes of animals that are the subjects of animal protection laws. For our purposes, we identify the following categories: wild animals (both endangered and not); domestic companion animals; animals exploited for profit as food, fiber, or entertainment; and animals used as research tools (with the type of research ranging from cognitive to cosmetic to biomedical).[5] Governments and societies attribute varying values to each of these classes of animals. A common question readers should have throughout this book is: what values or policies explain the laws' coverage of certain animals and not others? Why, for instance, do most international agreements protect endangered animals, but not common ones? Why do many countries' domestic laws protect companion animals but not farmed animals?

We first address the distinction between wild animals and domestic animals and the related distinction between endangered and non-endangered species. Although the organized humane movement had raised concerns about the suffering of individual animals as early as the 1820s,[6] it was not until the 1960s, with the rise of the modern environmental movement, that humans began to understand that they were capable of extinguishing entire species.[7] The environmentalists succeeded in bringing international attention to vanishing species, and, as a result, there now exist numerous international agreements that deal with endangered and wild animals.

Is there something about wild animals that makes their lives more worthy of protection than the lives of domesticated animals? Why do many societies consider a wolf more important than a dog or a bison more important than a dairy cow? Why do some consider the reverse to be true?

Some argue that wild animals have more autonomy than domesticated animals, that they exist independently from human beings and are therefore entitled to be left alone. Some view domesticated animals as human creations, "living artifacts ... [that] constitute yet another mode of extension of the works of man into the ecosystem," while wild animals arose through the biological process of natural selection.[8] They see domestic animals as unnatural and, in the case of non-native species, incompatible with the flourishing of the biotic community.[9] Under this view, privileging wild animals and providing them with special legal protection makes perfect sense.

On the other side, theorists argue that each individual animal matters, regardless of whether she is wild or domestic, so long as she is otherwise entitled to moral consideration. They argue that domestic animals' interests, while they may differ from those of wild animals, are no less worthy of consideration.[10] Some commentators contend that the arguments used to privilege wild animals perpetuate sexist and speciesist qualities at the expense of the holistic valuation of interrelationships.[11] They see a masculine bias in the privileging of ruggedness and autonomy over dependency and interconnectedness. Some critics also argue that the distinction between wild and domestic is increasingly tenuous (as in, for example, the case of feral cats) and is, in many cases, socially constructed by the segment of the human population that grants the privileges.[12]

A related controversy is that between endangered and non-endangered animals. By what criteria can we value an individual Pygmy Three-toed Sloth, which is critically endangered, above an individual Pale-throated Sloth, which is comparatively plentiful and non-endangered? Biologically, the animals are quite similar. So why should the legal protection of one be so prioritized over the protection of the other?

The response that "endangered species will disappear" is obvious enough. Those who favor special protections for endangered species believe that extinction is an evil in itself.[13] In other words, what is especially wrong about killing the Pygmy Three-toed Sloth is the fact that doing so pushes the species closer to the brink of extinction, an utterly final and irremediable harm. Under this value system, the harm exists at a species level, and not only an individual level. But what exactly is the harm in extinction? The anthropocentric answer is that species may hold value for human beings and that value may be lost if the species goes extinct. One sees this value system at play in arguments that we should preserve rainforests because they may hold within them undiscovered plants with untold medicinal properties. The nonanthropocentric answer is that each species has value in itself, regardless of its utility to humans; to put it another way, we have moral obligations to species *per se*, not just to individual members of species.[14] One might also view the loss instrumentally, but in a way that is still biocentric: there may be currently unknown values provided to the entire ecosystem (not just humans) by one or more "keystone" species—one that has a greater effect on the ecosystem and its environment than would be assumed based on its population numbers. As an example, the rainforest's contribution to global climate control is now known to be invaluable, and only when it is destroyed do we appreciate the full impact of its loss.

Other theorists argue that it is only the individual and not the species that matters. This theory coincides with the cornerstone of much animal rights theory—that one's species is a morally irrelevant characteristic, like race or sex.[15] Under this view, one cannot morally distinguish between the nearly extinct Pygmy Three-toed Sloth and the more common Pale-throated Sloth; it would be equally wrong to kill either of them. According to philosopher Tom Regan, who holds this view, "[t]hat an individual animal is among the last remaining members of a species confers no further right on that animal, and [her] right not to be harmed must be weighed equitably with the rights of any others who have this right."[16]

This is not a philosophy book *per se*, so we do not take sides in these debates. The practical issues that arise from those discussions will, however, be further addressed in the context of specific laws. We encourage our readers to independently investigate the philosophical nuances if they desire. But we do think it is important to raise these debates here as questions that readers should keep in mind as they reflect on those values that animate animal laws.[17] Like culture, the law cannot exist outside of ethics, and the philosophical considerations of our treatment of animals logically center on the ethics of our relationship with them. Ethical philosophy helps to explain what underlies the legal doctrines discussed in this book, and it is a necessary framework for discussing what could or should be done by legal systems wrestling with how to treat animals. In fact, it is probably the interplay between the two areas—philosophy and the law—that makes animal law such a compelling and interesting field.[18]

For example, many of these values come into focus when considering CITES, which is discussed in more detail in Chapter 6. Because CITES protects only species that are endangered or threatened, it clearly adopts an ethical system that ascribes higher value to those animals that have been deemed, by the prevailing combination of scientific knowledge and popular and political pressure, to be in the greatest danger of disappearing. Those species and individuals who do not get so classified merit limited attention, at least by CITES standards. One can also identify in CITES tensions about the reasons for protecting endangered animals: CITES' protection of species can be justified on both anthropocentric and nonanthropocentric grounds. The Convention's signatory countries recognize "that wild fauna and flora in their many beautiful and varied forms are an irreplaceable part of the natural systems of the earth which must be protected for this and the generations to come."[19] The CITES parties further state that they are "[c]onscious of the ever-growing value of wild fauna and flora from aesthetic, scientific, cultural, recreational and economic points of view."[20] Each of these values is at least partly based on human use of the animals for humans' benefit, but the fact that CITES acknowledges the aesthetic and cultural values of endangered species also suggests that species may have worth that is distinct from their utilitarian or exchange value. The aesthetic and cultural values that many people derive from animals may also be premised (at least in part) on their belief that these animals do in fact have some intrinsic value: that's what makes them culturally revered and aesthetically gratifying. At the same time, however, there is no doubt that much of CITES is premised on anthropocentrism: endangered species have economic and scientific value to member nations and their citizens.[21]

It is impossible to ascribe a single motivation to such international agreements, since different countries may assent to them for different reasons. One nation may wish to join CITES to help conserve animal species for their intrinsic value, while another may be motivated to be a party to CITES to preserve a valuable economic resource it wishes to exploit in perpetuity. Others may join for political reasons wholly unrelated to animal interests or the philosophical issues raised here. We cannot definitively answer the question of what values are embodied in international agreements because these agreements do not entail a single, particular value; we can only raise the question and identify the varied answers that may motivate different people and the nations they represent.

Having addressed the wild/domestic and endangered/non-endangered distinctions, we now turn to the distinctions drawn among domestic animals. In step with the broader ideological change in how people view animals, there is a definite trend of increasing appreciation of "companion animals." These animals who live in our homes, barns and pastures provide both instrumental, objectively quantifiable value (such as the mental health and noneconomic benefits of animal companionship) as well as their inherent value as sentient and conscious beings. That is, we appreciate the relationships we share with them and the pecuniary and nonpecuniary advantages of animal companionship. The media, the scientific community, the legal community, and society at large have all addressed and embraced this shift in recognition to varying degrees. The increased valuation of companion animals is certainly more marked in affluent countries, but the interspecies shift is occurring everywhere.

Not surprisingly, most countries' domestic laws protect only the animals who their societies regard as worthy of protection. Because some classes of animals are more highly regarded than others, those animals are protected while other animals whose exploitation is more institutionalized are left legally unprotected. In practice, this means that companion animals receive more protections than farmed animals or animals used in research. Why are companion animals such as dogs and cats privileged over cows, pigs, and mice?

Again there is an obvious, if scientifically unsound, answer on the surface—because companion animals live with us, and we believe them to be more "worthy" of our protection. But many animal protection advocates argue that there is no ethically or intellectually significant distinction between a dog and a pig. Scientists generally agree that pigs and dogs feel pain in the same way, experience joy and fear in the same way, and are similarly intelligent. Yet in the United States, dogs are protected from most forms of cruelty while more than 100 million pigs are slaughtered every year for food and receive very little protection from routine cruelty.[22] Although most people will not tolerate random or senseless cruelty to animals, they are willing to accept (or at least ignore) "routine" suffering that is incidental to human uses of animals, such as raising them for food.[23] Likewise, most nations and jurisdictions permit the mutilation of farmed animals without anesthesia (such as branding, debeaking, tail docking, and castration) because such practices are common in the industrial production of animals as food. In this sense, the animal laws tell us just as much about what a society is willing to tolerate as what it thinks should be criminalized.

The distinctions between companion animals and farmed animals that show up in many domestic cruelty laws are almost entirely attributable to market economics and convention, not to the fine points of ethical theory. Industrialized agriculture is made possible by a host of cruelties that enable corporations to facilitate the conversion of animals from sentient beings to "animal machines." These industrial practices are profitable, so those in the business spend large sums of money to ensure their practices are insulated from regulation as much as possible. Probably because of significant lobbying efforts, legislatures are generally hesitant to interfere with the production of animal products that are the result of industrialized farming. As a consequence, many statutes that prohibit cruelty to animals actually privilege companion animals over farmed animals.

International agreements may also be driven by species-specific interests related to commerce. Although international treaties reflect concern about the species themselves, these treaties are not solely aimed at safeguarding the animals as sentient beings who deserve protection. Rather, most were originally designed to preserve species so that they could be used for pleasure or profit. The effort to save certain animal species may be based on the potential for extinction, but we still have to ask why the international community wants to avoid that species' extinction; often the answer is that the species has commercial value and its extinction would be an economic blow to those countries who use the species commercially.

The controversy over the killing of whales is a classic example of this dilemma, and it illustrates the conflict between governments, indigenous peoples, and animal activists. The disputes often split these groups internally as well. The original intention behind the formation of the International Whaling Commission (IWC) in 1946 was to "provide for the proper conservation of whale stocks and thus make possible the orderly development of the whaling industry."[24] The goal was to increase the whales' populations to the point that commercial whaling, a profitable industry for hundreds of years, could continue indefinitely. The IWC thus originally embodied the "save to kill" version of ecological preservation. Over time, public sentiment shifted as science revealed more about the unique social lives and mental acuity of whales. As a result of public protest and scientific education, the IWC instituted a moratorium on commercial whaling in 1986 that continues today.[25] At the time of this writing, very few countries are still whaling, though the push to lift the ban on commercial whaling is as contentious as ever.[26] The frequent debates about the moratorium often invoke the conservation doctrines of "sustainable harvest" and "sustainable populations," in which scientists with different viewpoints provide estimates of the number of animals in a species necessary and sufficient to continue healthy reproduction and population growth and ultimately to provide for a stable population and increased genetic diversity. The goal of a sustainable number is often tied directly to the desire to hunt or otherwise exploit members of the species.

What is the relationship between social values about animals and the law?

Social, cultural, and religious views about animals are shot through the fabric of how any given society treats animals. The law grows out of those underlying beliefs and concepts, and at the same time it produces new beliefs and concepts. We believe that studying a society's animal laws will tell us much about that society's normative and ethical views about animals.

That said, we recognize that it is naïve to believe that law *necessarily* reflects widely-held social values. Law produces power and power produces law. The existence of a law shows only that some group was able to harness the machinery of government to effectuate its ends.[27] In both established and transitional governments, ruling classes cement their privilege through the legal system, judicially and legislatively. By establishing economic and social policies that favor the *status quo*, those in power may create laws that are contrary to the beliefs and desires of a majority of people within that society. The agribusiness lobby, for example, has enormous influence in the United States and abroad.[28] The existence of agricultural subsidies, corporate welfare, and farming exemptions from environmental and anti-cruelty laws do not necessarily reflect a social belief that factory farms are morally acceptable or deserving of economic reward. To the contrary, some studies suggest that large parts of society are opposed to the cruel ways that animals are used for food.[29] Yet many anticruelty laws continue to exempt farmed animals or permit practices known to cause intense suffering. This privileging of agribusiness more likely reflects not popular will, but rather the political power of a wealthy minority that has disproportionate influence on lawmaking bodies.[30]

Less nefariously, law may blindly follow trajectories established centuries or even millennia ago, even when those paths now clash with prevailing social beliefs. The most evident example is one with which we are intimately familiar: the fact that the law considers all animals to be property, despite the fact that most people consider at least some animals to be family members. This legal belief is rooted in millennia-old philosophies and cosmologies that much of society has now jettisoned. So while more than ninety-seven percent of companion animal guardians refuse to view their companions as property, the law persists in viewing them as such.[31]

These examples caution against using the law as a direct proxy for social beliefs. The law is often evidence of the prevailing values and ideologies of a society, and that is one of the theses of this book. At the same time, and especially in areas where ethical and commercial values may be in conflict, we must recognize that law is not necessarily a mirror of societal views or the consensus of a nation. The variations between popular opinion and the law also tell us much about legal culture and the kinds of thinking and values it embodies.

Is there a difference between "animal welfare laws" and "animal rights laws"?

For years, the animal protection movement has engaged in an internal debate about whether advocates should be involved in reforming animal industries to make them more "humane" or whether they should instead work to abolish those industries altogether. The conflict is framed as one between "regulationists" who seek to regulate how humans treat the animals they use, and "abolitionists," who seek to do away with all nonconsensual human uses of animals. This debate is also cast as one between two concepts: *welfare* on the one hand (that is, reducing the suffering of animals while continuing to use them for food, research, and entertainment) and *rights* on the other (that is, recognizing animals as rights-holders who may not be used without their consent, regardless of how humane the use). There are also others who deny that welfare and rights are opposing concepts; these advocates adopt the end goal of the abolitionists, but the strategic means of the welfarists. In other words, they seek to increase animal welfare as a pathway towards establishing animal rights.

There is also debate about what constitutes a right for animals. Some commentators argue that the anti-cruelty laws that exist in many countries provide animals a right not to be treated cruelly, while others argue that only "legal persons" can have rights, and because animals are property, even when protected by anti-cruelty laws, they cannot be said to possess legal rights.[32] If one adopts this latter understanding of legal rights, there are currently no countries that recognize any animals as having rights, because every legal system considers animals to be property.

Much has been written about these concepts, and we do not rehash those debates here. Instead, we identify how distinctions between welfare and rights arise in different countries' approaches to animal law and what such laws reveal about countries' underlying views of animals. Undoubtedly, the majority of the world's animal laws take a welfare approach, in that they regulate the specifics of animal use. Many countries have laws that set standards for the treatment of animals who are raised for food and used in medical research and product testing. Such laws accept the legitimacy of the underlying use of animals, that is, their use as food and as tools of research. In other words, welfare laws, by their very nature, tolerate the suffering that is inseparable from the practices involved in raising animals for meat or using them in scientific research.

In contrast to these welfare-based approaches, several countries have adopted laws that may signify steps towards legal rights for animals that would be consistent with a more robust understanding of what it means to have legal rights. Animal activists in Germany, Austria, and Spain have sought to establish basic legal rights for animals through legislation and litigation, with varying degrees of success.[33] What these activists seek is a legislative or judicial affirmation that at least some animals have all the relevant characteristics that entitle human beings to legal personhood. They therefore argue that these animals deserve the following basic fundamental rights: the right to life and the right to be free from torture. These efforts are discussed in more detail later in the book.

One of the most interesting case studies of the interplay between rights and welfarism occurred recently in New Zealand.[34] In the late 1990s, New Zealand decided to adopt a new Animal Welfare Act and undertook a comprehensive review of its animal welfare laws, which had not been updated since 1960. The reform was initially and primarily concerned with updating agricultural practices, which form a significant part of New Zealand's economy. But in 1998, the Great Ape Project New Zealand (GAPNZ) submitted a proposal to Parliament, suggesting it add a provision to the animal welfare bill granting legal rights to nonhuman hominids (chimpanzees, orangutans, bonobos, and gorillas). The submission garnered international media attention, and many heralded the development as a qualitative leap forward in the movement for animal rights. In the end, Parliament declined to affirmatively grant the proposed legal rights. In doing so, it recognized the split between rights and welfare. One lawmaker stated his belief that granting rights to nonhuman hominids was inappropriate in the context of this legislation because the Act "adopts an animal welfare rather than an animal rights philosophy."[35] In other words, the New Zealand Parliament was interested in regulating the commercial use of some animals (those used in agriculture), not in establishing rights for others (hominids). The new Animal Welfare Act has spurred the refinement of highly technical and detailed codes that regulate the minutiae of industrial animal agricultural practices.

Although it did not grant rights to any animals, the New Zealand Animal Welfare Act did forbid the use of nonhuman hominids in biomedical research, product testing, and teaching in all but the rarest cases.[36] Such a concession may have been intended to appease the Great Ape Project and to bolster New Zealand's desired reputation as an international leader in animal issues. And there is evidence this move worked: many have continued to praise New Zealand as a nation at the forefront of animal protection. Certainly the Act was "the first time that a parliament has voted in favor of changing the status of a group of animals so dramatically that the animal cannot be treated as a research tool."[37] The law is exceptional because it virtually bans the use of nonhuman hominids in research.

The New Zealand law demonstrates that inroads to change are often made in jurisdictions where opposition is limited or unlikely. When the law was passed, only thirty-four great apes lived in the country, and none of them was being used in ongoing research. For this reason, "it is highly probable that the Act's provisions specifically protecting non-human hominids will never be used in a New Zealand court of law."[38] So while some praise the law, others have cautiously asked what function such a law serves outside of its direct practical impact, which is, by all accounts, nonexistent. Peter Sankoff, an animal law professor in New Zealand, has suggested that the hominid issue has enabled the New Zealand government to tout itself as a leader in animal protection at a time when its welfare policies continue to permit practices that cause immense suffering to more than 100 million farmed animals annually.[39] This tension reflects another aspect of the competing frameworks of animal welfare and animal rights. New Zealand and the GAPNZ have sought to straddle both ideologies, granting welfare for some animals and limited rights for others.[40] Readers should reflect on which values and ideologies inhere in these positions.

How do nations' concerns about how they are perceived in the international community affect their animal laws?

Animal laws are not always motivated by altruistic motives of kindness to animals. As with any law, myriad considerations and factors affect decisions on animal policy issues. Throughout this book we will discuss some of the external pressures that may induce a country to adopt a law, sign a treaty, or stop an action affecting animals.

One reason a country may adopt animal protection laws is the hope that such laws will improve the country's image internationally. The aforementioned New Zealand reforms of the late 1990s were spurred by concerns about New Zealand's reputation internationally and its ability to sell its agricultural products in European markets.[41] Many European nations had welfare policies for farmed animals that exceeded those of New Zealand. According to one New Zealand commentator, "[w]hen this disparity, along with a veiled threat of tightening import restrictions, was pointed out by the European Union (EU) trade officials, the New Zealand agricultural community suddenly became a great deal more concerned with animal welfare."[42] In cases like this one, economic concerns may very well motivate welfare reforms. In the words of the country's ministry in charge of animal welfare policy, "[v]alue systems outside New Zealand … have a strong influence on animal welfare practices in this country. Throughout the world, consumers have become more sensitive to the way in which animals are raised for food and fibre."[43]

Sometimes this external criticism comes from citizens of other nations whose belief system elevates certain animals over others. For example, Australian animal activists have criticized the exportation of Australian greyhound dogs, who are products of the racing industry in Australia, to Asia for the creation of a dog racing industry in certain Asian countries.[44] Although dog racing is rife with cruelty wherever it exists (including in Australia), some perceive a greater concern in Asia, where retired dogs may be used for their meat or slaughtered and dumped at landfills.[45] Korea, Vietnam, and China, where little to no protection exists for dogs, have all imported greyhounds from Australia to establish a racing industry.

In the international arena, foreign condemnation of internal practices may have a variety of effects. In some cases, the criticism may shame the country into changing its practices, such as when the Chinese government prohibited the sale of dog meat during the 2008 Olympics, just as Korea had previously done.[46] That same criticism, however, may instead be seen as a form of species bias or, worse, cultural imperialism, and may solidify the practice as a point of nationalistic pride.

Both of these outcomes contribute to the ongoing controversy over dog meat in Korea, which is discussed in more detail later in the chapter and in Chapter 2.[47] In the early 1980s, the South Korean government banned dog meat throughout the capital of Seoul out of concern about its national image leading up to the 1988 Olympics in Seoul. This decision was obviously motivated more by concern over international reactions than a principled determination that eating dogs was for some reason wrong. It was likely also motivated by the anticipated negative response from foreign tourists—and how that might affect the amount of foreign money they would bring in to the country during the Olympics. Although the ban was enforced during the Olympics and remains on the books, it is now widely flouted and unenforced.[48] Many Koreans defend the use of dogs for food, pointing out that it is no more objectionable than eating any other mammal.

A nation's animal laws can also have an economic impact on other countries. For instance, most American states ban the sale of dog and cat fur. Animal protection groups have used these laws to attempt to block the importation of clothing from several Asian countries that they suspect contains dog and cat fur.[49] Whether or not such a ban would cause a change in the use of dogs and cats for fur or cause the industry to simply take such conduct further underground remains to be seen. Just as the Korean dog meat issue raises the question of why the consumption of dog is qualitatively different from the consumption of pigs or cows, the cat and dog fur issue raises the challenging question of why fur coats made of animals such as foxes or mink are legal, but dog and cat fur raises the ire of the public. Is it the fact that dog and cat fur is much cheaper, yet sold at traditional fur prices? Is it the quality of the fur? Or is it the sentiment connected with dog and cat fur that is most offensive and makes the sale of such fur both illegal and undesirable?

These examples illustrate the potential tensions that arise when activists and governments pressure other nations to change their practices.

Why are some issues dealt with on an international basis, while others are considered domestic issues?

Readers will notice that much of this book compares the domestic laws of different countries, while other parts discuss international agreements among countries. Why do some issues merit international treaties or conventions while others issues are handled on a country-by-country basis?

Issues may be international rather than domestic for either of two reasons: the nature of the *problem* or the nature of the *animals* at issue. Some problems are inherently international because they involve multiple countries and border crossings—such as trade in species or their products. These mandate international solutions. And some animals are transnational or migratory and thus require international treatment.

An example of an international problem that demands an international solution is the global trade in rare and endangered species, which is regulated by CITES. Consider an endangered elephant killed in South Africa whose ivory is sold to a manufacturer in China that makes a product that is in turn sold to a consumer in the United States. Or consider a rare Amazonian parrot who is smuggled from South America to a pet store in Texas. One method of stopping such exports and imports is to establish a multinational agreement prohibiting such trade. The agreement must include the country of origin as well as the recipient country in order to be effective. Because the nature of the problem is international, conventions such as CITES see the solution as international, encouraging all signatory nations to participate in stemming the trade in endangered species.

Just as international problems require international solutions, so too do "international animals." Geographic borders between nations are artificial human creations, produced by geopolitical shifts in power and cartography. Animals do not recognize or respect national boundaries, and their ranges may traverse these artificial constructs. Nations often quarrel over who these animals "belong" to or who has a right to exploit them as a resource. In order to settle these disputes, countries enter into international treaties governing the use (or protection) of such animals.[50] Other "international animals" are those who reside in the common areas of the planet that do not belong to any sovereign power. For instance, the International Whaling Commission (IWC) was established to govern whaling, which often takes place in international waters. Likewise the Antarctic Treaty System (ATS) covers unclaimed territories. The ATS is made up of the formal Antarctic Treaty (signed by forty-six countries) and various other treaties such as the Convention for the Conservation of Antarctic Marine Living Resources, the Convention for the Conservation of Antarctic Seals, the Agreed Measures for the Conservation of Arctic Fauna and Flora, and the International Agreement for the Protection of Polar Bears and Their Habitats.[51] These treaties are voluntary agreements between countries to protect and preserve the unique habitat of Antarctica and the species that live there.

Although all existing international animal laws focus on either international problems or international animals, there is one groundbreaking proposal for globalizing animal protection that relies on neither of these grounds: the Universal Declaration on Animal Welfare (UDAW). The UDAW, sponsored by the World Society for Protection of Animals (WSPA), is premised on the idea that all animals, even those who reside solely within national borders, are entitled to basic welfare protections.[52] In this sense, the UDAW models international human rights principles, which make human rights an international issue, even if the objectionable conduct, such as torture or religious persecution, occurs entirely within national borders.

The UDAW was proposed in 2000 as an ambitious campaign to create legal recognition of the need for animal welfare.[53] The document was modeled after similar statements of ethics and the policies embodied in the Universal Declaration of Human Rights and the Declaration of the Rights of the Child. WSPA has sought to gain the agreement of multiple countries to the UDAW with the eventual goal of gaining ratification by the United Nations (UN). As of 2011, over thirty countries were considering the Declaration for formal presentation to the UN's Economic and Social Council. Once ratified by the UN, the Declaration could be developed as a Convention on Animal Welfare, which would create an international body devoted to monitoring animal welfare issues worldwide. Several governments, including Sweden, New Zealand, Kenya, India, the Philippines, Costa Rica, Chile, Peru, and the Czech Republic, have officially backed the Declaration.[54] Other countries have expressed support for animal welfare principles, but have yet to officially sign on. As of September 2010, over 2.24 million individuals from 192 countries had signed the "Animals Matter to Me" petition, which endorses the UDWA. WSPA's goal is to get 2 million more signatures.[55]

The UDAW is a creative and animal-centric document—one that may have political and social value by attracting attention to the international animal welfare movement. By utilizing the rubric and rhetoric of the international human rights movement and the Universal Declaration of Human Rights, the UDAW advances the critique of speciesism, placing animal protection within the same sphere as human rights. Of course, even if the UDAW gained UN approval, it would not necessarily provide specific ways to improve animal welfare or restrict particular types of treatment. But it would signal a general affirmation that animal welfare issues are important to the global community. By making the well-being of all animals an international issue regardless of the nature of their exploitation or the range of their migration, the UDAW affirms the idea that animals are not the instruments or resources of the nation-states that lay claim to their habitats.

How does the fact that animals are considered property affect animal laws in different countries?

As mentioned above, in every legal system in which the issue has been addressed directly, animals have been deemed "property." This classification serves the economic interests of the *status quo.* Since the formation of agrarian societies, animals have been utilized as commodities. They have been bought and sold in commerce. In many cultures, a family's animals are its wealth: the richest person in town is the one with the most cattle. In the earliest agricultural societies, and still in many parts of the globe, animals perform work that cannot be performed by humans alone. In industrialized societies this role for animals has largely disappeared, but other ways of interacting with animals have replaced that role. Animals, wherever possible, are used as living machines, an important aspect of commercial society. Whether actually designated as property or not, the treatment of animals under the law of every country results in *de facto* status as property—generically defined as something that is owned, and including an aggregate of rights of ownership that are protected by the government. It is this status that in many ways controls the battle between those who want to disrupt the current treatment and status of animals and those who want to maintain it.

Commentators have long debated the advantages and disadvantages of this property classification. Some have argued that animals' status as property makes it essentially impossible to give their interests adequate and fair consideration.[56] Others have argued that the concept of property is malleable and can be stretched to allow major improvements in animal well-being.[57] Recent developments throughout the world suggest that significant progress in our legal and social treatment of animals may be possible without changing the property paradigm.

This debate becomes even more interesting in the international context, especially given the fact that different nations and cultures have varied ideas of what constitutes property and how it may be regulated. As a result, residents of these countries may be more tolerant of animal protection laws that interfere with the use of animal property. On the other hand, in countries such as the United States, which tends to exalt individual property rights as inviolable, one may find greater resistance to government regulation of how individuals use their property.[58] Property is an artificial, socially-constructed concept, and so one should expect to find cultural and attitudinal differences about how to regulate or treat animal property.

What role does science play in the formulation and enforcement of animal laws?

Throughout the course of this book, readers will notice that the role of the sciences arises in many different aspects of animal law: from farmed animal welfare to laboratory research to questions about how we know animals' experiences. Many of the laws that affect animals treat them as resources to be managed.[59] Accordingly, technical and scientific questions arise as to how to "sustainably harvest" animal populations. In the IWC, for example, much of the debate around the issue of whaling involves competing scientific claims about whether certain practices threaten whales with extinction. Those who wish to lift the moratorium on commercial whaling argue that science supports their position that a limited and regulated hunt would not threaten the continued survival of whale species. Those that wish to maintain the moratorium argue the opposite.

As many philosophers of science have observed, science is inseparable from politics and ideology.[60] This is not to say that science is completely socially constructed, but it is used and manipulated in the service of competing claims to "truth." So it should come as no surprise that nations that want to resume commercial whaling can come up with scientific evidence supporting their claims that resuming the hunt will not impact long-term survival. Just as easily, those who oppose commercial whaling can come up with scientific evidence supporting their claims. Science may also be used to provide cover for continued animal exploitation. Japan has justified its ongoing whaling in spite of the moratorium by claiming that it is complying with the exception for performing vital scientific research on whale populations that will help promote the health of the species. Others have argued that Japan's research is a pretext to continue its whaling for commercial purposes.

Science also plays a role in animal law to the extent decisions about animals are based on intelligence and sentience or other characteristics of animal societies. In many circumstances laws are driven or supported by scientific beliefs and conclusions. For example, the scientific community has almost unanimously concluded that the great apes share a large part of the genetic makeup and social structure of humans.[61] In response, both the public and lawmakers have acted to improve the conditions of treatment and legal protections for these particular animals. It is almost surely the scientific (biological, physiological, sociological) evidence that has spurred this heightened interest and special treatment. If the scientific evidence of culture and emotion in other species develops to the same degree, with the same level of similarity, increased protections may be more likely.

Some argue that our treatment of animals is an ethical issue that cannot be exhausted by appeals to the sort of calculative thinking that science privileges.[62] The issue of farmed animal welfare is an ideal example. There is an entire discipline known as welfare science that aims to reduce animal suffering to a technical problem that can be solved through more efficient construction of factory farms and slaughterhouses. Those who believe animals are not ours to kill or subject to farming practices eschew these scientific solutions and see them as a way of replacing ethics with production-line efficiency.

Comparative Animal Law in Practice

Most countries have adopted anticruelty laws at some level and in some form. Others, such as Iran, Lebanon, Iraq, Somalia, and Ethiopia, have failed to enact virtually *any* protections for animals. As a first concept, it is important to understand that there are no completely binding international laws, at least not in the same sense that laws of a country are binding on its citizens. Of course, there are other ways to compel conduct, and the international laws and treaties that set up economic sanctions or trade barriers for noncompliance may provide greater motivation than national or regional laws that carry fines or the potential for incarceration. Nevertheless, the structure of most international law—to the extent there is any compelling document or rule—comes by way of treaty or compact between multiple nations in the global community. Countries voluntarily enter into treaties. Often, in order to ensure that their citizens act consistently with those treaties, they enact supportive domestic laws.

The social and legal treatment of a given animal or species under these treaties and domestic laws is often dependent upon the species of animal involved, and may demonstrate human sensibilities across borders. For example, a longstanding controversy over the inclusion of polar bears on the list of threatened species under the United States' Endangered Species Act (ESA) focused the public eye on these symbols of the pristine Arctic landscape.[63] After overhunting brought severe survival pressure onto the species, protection of the polar bear began internationally with the 1973 signing of the International Agreement for the Conservation of Polar Bears in Oslo (the "Oslo Agreement").[64] All five countries that comprise the range territory of the polar bear (Canada, Russia, Denmark (Greenland), Norway, and the United States (Alaska)) are signatories to the Oslo Agreement, in which they agree to cooperate on research and conservation efforts throughout the polar bear's habitat range. Although the Oslo Agreement offers little protection to a species now threatened by climate change and loss of sea ice, the fact that such an agreement was reached by antagonistic nations during the Cold War is evidence of the sentimental attraction that the polar bear evokes. "For many years, the conservation of polar bears was the only subject in the entire Arctic that nations from both sides of the Iron Curtain could agree upon sufficiently to sign an agreement. Such was the intensity of human fascination with this magnificent predator, the only marine bear."[65] In May 2008, the U.S. Department of the Interior, through the Fish and Wildlife Service, finally listed the polar bear as a threatened species under the ESA.[66]

The cross-cultural dialogue that this type of issue engenders is an important part of the field of comparative animal law. Questions arise about whether there is any potential to establish international consensus concerning cruelty and compassion—and if so, that would be sufficient to force the global community to compel or prohibit conduct with respect to animals.

While the previous sections discussed common themes, questions, and examples that will arise throughout the book, the remainder of this chapter looks at how different nations approach animals and the law. These examples are not exhaustive: there are many countries we do not discuss here, and even those countries we do discuss are presented incompletely for the purpose of providing some examples. By selecting some countries and not others we do not mean to suggest the chosen countries are more important, only that they contribute something to the issues investigated.

The laws as they relate to animals are changing around the world, in different degrees and at different speeds. There is a slow movement towards meaningful change. The illustrations that fill the rest of this chapter make that clear. So we begin with this assumption: animal protection is a global concern. Throughout the world, regardless of the actions of governments, despite the absence of animal protection laws in some places or their under-enforcement in others, there is an underlying sentiment among a majority of humans that "cruelty" to animals is unacceptable. We recognize that definitions of "cruelty" and the determination as to what conduct is permissible vary greatly. But temporarily putting aside the important question of definition, most humans believe that unjustified cruelty to animals is unacceptable and a black mark on our species' moral status. In what follows, we move from continent to continent to provide some examples of how different countries and regions are approaching animal welfare issues. We hope this will promote discussion and initiate the cross-pollination of ideas about the treatment of animals under the law, across borders, cultures, and species, and that this process of intellectual analysis will stimulate consideration of the most effective means of legal change for animals.

Asia

China

According to Song Wei, a lawyer in China who has become an effective advocate for animals, China has typically resisted the enactment and enforcement of animal protection laws.[67] Although Chinese criminal law does prohibit injuring or slaughtering draft animals, it does so "in the same sentence in which it prohibits destroying machinery and equipment, demonstrating that the purpose of the law is to prevent the damaging of one person's property by another, not to protect animal welfare."[68] This law also requires the offender to have committed the slaughter "with the purpose of giving vent to spite, seeking revenge, or for other personal motives."[69] Such a showing of malicious intent would be nearly impossible in most cases and would also preclude prosecution for animal abuse that is routine, but not "spiteful," such as what occurs in factory farming. Nevertheless, historically, the anticruelty laws in America and the United Kingdom also were based in property concepts.[70] Over the last few hundred years the focus of these laws has turned towards a more humane-oriented approach. Although we recognize that there is no singular path of development,[71] perhaps China's laws will evolve in a way similar to that of U.S. anticruelty laws.

In 2010, an anticruelty law was introduced to the Chinese legislature. The law included bans on slaughter and consumption of dogs and cats; the feeding of live prey to large predators in zoos and safari parks; declawing and defanging of performing animals; dogfighting and cockfighting; and animal cruelty during the raising, handling, transport, and slaughter of animals used in commercial food production.

Despite China's history of relative inactivity in enacting national laws governing animal treatment, China did join CITES in 1981.[72] China then implemented its own wildlife protection laws[73] and regulations in order to meet CITES requirements. China prohibits its citizens from killing endangered animals and also prohibits the sale and purchase of such animals.

The Chinese wildlife law, as well as other national and provincial laws, sets out to protect endangered species, but the lack of enforcement and prevailing cultural norms have limited its efficacy.[74] For example, there are laws with harsh penalties that prohibit the killing of rhinoceros, whose horn and other body parts are considered valuable components for traditional Chinese medicine. All countries in which the rhinoceros is commercially valuable (with the sole exception of North Korea) have enacted domestic legislation prohibiting the import or export of the rhino horn. Following a meeting with CITES member nations in 1993, China prohibited the manufacture of medicines containing rhinoceros horn after those nations threatened to institute economic sanctions against China. The tension here—between a product invested with cultural significance, and the needs of a species in danger of extinction—is a good example of the conflicts between nations over animal treatment. Chinese medical textbooks today proffer both old and new uses for rhinoceros horn.[75]

Despite the absence of general anti-cruelty laws, there have been some moderately successful campaigns to reduce animal suffering in China. For example, the Chinese government has worked with Animals Asia, a group dedicated to ending the torture occurring on "bear farms." On these "bear farms," the highly-intelligent Moon Bears are trapped in tiny cages in which they can barely move in order to remove their bile, naturally produced by the bear's gall bladder. Like rhinoceros horn, bear bile is a component of traditional Chinese medicine.[76] Some forms of bear farming are technically illegal in China, but the laws are not enforced. The species of farmed bears are listed under the most critical category of endangerment under CITES, but the demand for bear bile and parts has created a consistent market for the products of the industry. As discussed in Chapter 6, CITES governs only international trade, so bear bile can be sold within Chinese borders with impunity.

Despite these obstacles, the work of Animals Asia highlights a hopeful example of change. China has responded to the group's pressure by signing international agreements with outside non-governmental animal welfare organizations agreeing to close certain farms.[77] Animals Asia has accomplished its startling successes through a determined process of negotiation and cooperation with both the Chinese government and the bear farmers themselves. By patiently and determinedly working with government officials, the group has rescued hundreds of bears from lives of suffering. Animals Asia also provides a compelling example of the need to foment and support internal, indigenous movements to protect animals. According to Jill Robinson, the founder of Animals Asia, what will end the practice of bear farming is "not some Westerner pointing ... this imperialistic finger ... and demanding that bear farming end. Absolutely not. It's the voice of the Chinese people here, and that is what is developing now."[78]

China presents a good example of a country trying to reconcile historical views about animals with the developing global animal welfare movement. China's use of endangered species for meat, medicine, and export in the illegal wildlife trade threatens the survival of these species of animals, and its growing companion animal population and increased reliance on factory farming all pose major challenges for the future. Both foreign and domestic activists have the potential to create major change in the Chinese government's move towards a more favorable climate for animals.

Japan

Animal welfare issues in Japan discussed in this book revolve around three main issues: companion animals, research, and whaling. Japan passed its first domestic animal protection law[79] in 1973 to coincide with a visit from Queen Elizabeth II of Britain, a country that maintains a reputation as being a world leader with respect to companion animal welfare.[80] Although the law may have been little more than "a cosmetic measure"[81] designed to protect humans from animal-borne diseases, it did criminalize animal cruelty. In 1999, recognizing that the 1973 law was ineffective and rarely enforced, Japan revised the law, adding increased penalties and more pro-animal rhetoric.[82] The law was revised again in 2005.[83] The current version of the Animal Protection and Control Act states that its purpose is "to engender a spirit for animal welfare among citizens and contribute to the development of a respect for life and sentiments of amity and peace."[84] In 2002, the new anticruelty law was put to the test after a man viciously tortured a stray cat and posted gruesome pictures of the crime online.[85] Public outrage was severe, with more than 3,000 people writing to the prosecutor to urge strict punishment.[86] The defendant pleaded guilty, but received only a six-month prison sentence, which the judge suspended.

Critics also point to inadequate animal control policies and gassing of dogs and cats in shelters as other areas in need of reform.[87] Euthanasia by gas, however, is still popular in most countries, and euthanasia remains a fact of life for shelters because of a rampant overpopulation of dogs and cats. These practices are developing in correlation with the increased attention paid to the care of companion animals. The issues of what the best practices are for housing and euthanizing homeless animals affect local jurisdictions, but the ramifications of how a country treats its companion animals may influence its standing in the international community as well.

As previously mentioned, Japan is also one of the few countries that continues to engage in regular and significant whaling practices. This issue will be examined in greater depth in Chapter 6, but suffice it to say that it is clear that Japanese whaling practices have remained controversial around the world. Article VIII of the International Whaling Convention allows countries to engage in whaling for the purposes of scientific research, and Japan insists that all its whaling is done under this exception to the general moratorium on whaling. Its critics contend that the research it is performing does not require it to kill the whales, and meat from the whales involved in this lethal research is sold in Japanese markets and restaurants—which is entirely permissible under international law. On the other side, supporters of whaling have claimed that the moratorium has been perpetuated in bad faith. Their arguments include the assertion that the whaling ban is impermissible under the treaty, because it was created to regulate, not abolish, whaling.[88] The U.S. has threatened to lead a "trade war" against Japan if it continues to disregard what it deems as the norms of the international community.[89] However, trade sanctions, which are really the only practicable form of control one country has over another country's actions (short of military action), can be difficult to undertake in light of international trade agreements. It is also unclear that the U.S. is willing to put its trade relations with Japan on the line over the whaling issue. This draws attention to the one of the central difficulties of international law: its force is only present when participants voluntarily adhere to it.

The Philippines

In 1998, the Philippines passed its Animal Welfare Act,[90] which provides significant coverage for animals in a variety of contexts. For example, the Philippine Animal Welfare Act (PAWA) may provide greater protection for farm animals than U.S. law in that it requires that all animals who are slaughtered be killed "humanely"[91]—whereas the U.S.'s Humane Methods of Slaughter Act does not cover chickens, turkeys, or other birds. Furthermore, "humane [killing] procedures shall mean the use of the most scientific methods available as may be determined and approved by the Committee. Only those procedures approved by the Committee shall be used in the killing of animals."[92] These provisions are also important because of the extent to which confinement methods in farming are becoming more prevalent in the country. The PAWA appears to provide protection to all animals, which may prove more and more necessary as industrialized farming methods expand into countries such as the Philippines. However, the PAWA does contain notable exceptions including a cultural practices exemption that allows animals to be killed when "it is done as part of the religious rituals of an established religion or sect or a ritual required by tribal or ethnic custom of indigenous cultural communities."[93]

South Korea

South Korea has had some form of animal protection law since 1991, but it added greater protections in 2007.[94] Then in 2010, public awareness of ongoing cruelty led to further revisions of the penalties for animal cruelty.[95] One ongoing issue (mentioned above) that has attracted much international attention is Korean consumption of dog meat—a practice also extant in China and the Philippines. Technically, the consumption of dog meat has been banned in the capital city of Seoul since South Korea hosted the Olympics in 1988.

Fearing disapproval and censure from Western nations, the city's government banned dog meat at that time.[96] However, twenty years later, there are an estimated two million dogs consumed each year in Korea.[97]

According to one poll, seventy-five percent of Koreans support those who eat dog meat and oppose a ban on dog meat, even though only a minority of Koreans actually eat it.[98] The practice is defended against external criticism on the grounds that it is a cultural tradition, and that those who criticize it are trying to impose their own cultural and personal beliefs on Koreans. The international complaints and conflict have resulted in a backlash: "[i]n the face of what are perceived as cultural imperialist threats, dog meat has been given status as a cultural symbol of nationalism."[99]

India

India is particularly interesting in the area of animal protection because of the frequent dichotomy between the cultural exaltation of some animals and the simultaneous inhumane use of them in practice—which parallels that of many other nations. For example, in America, dogs and cats are given a place of special treatment as companion animals, but are at the same time subjected to the rigors and torture of biomedical research. In India, cows are considered sacred according to majority religious beliefs, but are also subjected to extreme suffering in certain areas where the religious protections do not apply.

India's Prevention of Cruelty to Animals Act dates back to 1960, but an apparent lack of enforcement and a slow court system have prevented the Act from being an effective tool for animal protection. In accordance with Section 4 of the Act, India set up an Animal Welfare Board.[100]

Perhaps the most progressive aspect of Indian animal law is the Indian Constitution, which states: "It shall be the fundamental duty of every citizen of India ... to protect and improve the natural environment including forests, lakes, rivers and wild life, and to have compassion for living creatures."[101] The Indian judiciary has also recognized this legal duty to protect animals. In *Nair v. Union of India*, plaintiffs, who used animals in entertainment, challenged a new law that barred the training and exhibition of bears, monkeys, tigers, panthers, and lions. The High Court of Kerala upheld the law, noting that "[i]t is not only our fundamental duty to show compassion to our animal friends, but also to recognize and protect *their rights*."[102]

Perhaps most importantly, the court acknowledged animals' *rights*, rather than simply recognizing the need of humans to "show compassion to our animal friends." Recognizing the distinction between rights and compassion (or justice and kindness) is a very powerful declaration by any official body.[103] Cases like *Nair* could ultimately foretell a shift in judicial treatment of animals. This holding, centered in the interpretation of the Indian Constitution, is especially pertinent to Chapter 5, which focuses on the value of constitutions in shaping animal law.

Israel

Although Israel's Penal Code prohibited animal abuse in 1977, no enforcement provisions were provided. In 1994 the Israeli Parliament enacted two additional animal welfare laws: The Animal Protection Law[104] and the Animal Experimentation Law.[105]

The Animal Protection Law exempts animals in slaughterhouses and animal experimentation which is covered by the Animal Experimentation Law. Furthermore, municipal veterinarians are permitted to poison animals to control rabies and other animal-borne illnesses (zoonoses) pursuant to the Rabies Ordinance of 1934 or the Animal Disease Ordinance of 1985.[106] While the Animal Protection Law does, at least in principle, apply to farm animals, "the police rarely investigate allegations of animal abuse in the large factory-farm industry. The courts are also often hesitant to enforce the Law on the farm industry and other institutionalized animal abusers. Therefore, the Law remains largely on paper: in reality, it is enforced primarily on individuals who abuse animals, leaving institutionalized animal cruelty mostly unaffected."[107] This phenomenon is, of course, not limited just to Israel.

In a landmark 2003 decision, the Israeli Supreme Court banned the current method of production of *foie gras.*[108] *Foie gras* is fatty duck or goose liver that results from the force-feeding of these animals. The result is a pathologically large and diseased liver, which is a culinary delicacy around the world. While recent efforts to ban the production of *foie gras* in other jurisdictions have met with mixed success, the Israeli Supreme Court found the practice unacceptably cruel and in violation of the Animal Protection Act. At the time, Israel was one of the leading *foie gras* producers in the world, which makes the findings of the court especially impressive.

The Supreme Court declared: "no one denies that these creatures also feel the pain inflicted upon them through physical harm or a violent intrusion into their bodies."[109] The inhumanity of the process, the court held, could not be tolerated under Israeli law, even though the *foie gras* farmers' livelihoods and the "gastronomic delight of others" would be eliminated. The Court held the practice had "a price—and the price is reducing the dignity of [humankind]."[110] However, the Court ruled that the Israeli Parliament could allow *foie gras* production to continue if the Agriculture Ministry issued regulations that "would guarantee the use of means that would substantially reduce the suffering caused to the geese."[111]

As noteworthy as this case is, the issue of force-feeding was not immediately resolved. The illegal regulations remained in force until March 2005. Goose farmers filed a petition for injunction that would "stop the state from shutting down their operations until a more humane alternative to the feeding of geese for *foie gras* was found. However, the High Court ruled that the appeal did not contain a persuasive argument for justifying the requested delay. It confirmed its earlier deadline for ending the force-feeding of geese by April 2006."[112]

Africa

South Africa

South Africa has three laws that cover animal protection issues. The first was the 1935 Performing Animals Protection Act.[113] In 1962, the country enacted a general anticruelty law, the Animals Protection Act (APA), which has been amended several times, the most recent being in 1993.[114] The latter Act prohibits a broad range of cruelty against animals, using language similar to that found in American and British anticruelty laws.[115] The 1993 amendment explicitly prohibits animal fighting.[116] A separate law establishes enforcement power in South Africa's national network of societies for the prevention of cruelty to animals, known as the NSPCA.[117] In addition to enforcing the APA, the NSPCA's work covers a wide range of animal welfare issues, including animal research, animal agriculture, and companion animals.[118] The Animal Anti-Cruelty League is another South African animal welfare organization that aims to educate the general public on animal protection issues, provide animal sheltering services, and prosecute animal cruelty.[119]

Veterinarians' groups are usually supportive of general animal welfare legislation, but the South African Veterinary Foundation (SAVF) has had several specific criticisms of the coverage and structure of the South African laws.[120] It has also publicly stated its belief that the protections in the laws are not being realized because of a lack of government engagement, and because the central government has failed to comply with its mandate to enact a regulatory framework for the animal protection laws.[121] As of 2006, no regulations were in place, leaving law enforcement and animal control workers with little or no guidance on how to invoke the protections of the law on behalf of animals. The SAVF proposed a six-year program which would include the creation of codes and standards for various areas of human-animal interactions, a widely-disseminated and broad "Manual of Animal Care and Use," and ongoing modification and review of the corresponding regulations.

South African law also deals with numerous wildlife issues. Because of the historical and present-day popularity of Africa as a destination for hunters of "exotic" animals, there are a significant number of laws covering this area. In 2007, South Africa banned "canned hunting," a practice in which hunters pay for a guaranteed kill on a safari. In practice, canned hunting usually entails the killing of aged and sick zoo animals, captive-bred wild animals, or drugged wildlife in a confined space where the animal has no means of escape. The South African environmental minister stated that he was "sickened by wealthy tourists shooting tame lions from the back of a truck."[122] Both bow hunting and vehicle chases of wildlife are also banned.

In addition to South Africa's larger animal welfare organizations, there is also a burgeoning grassroots animal rights movement, led by Animal Rights Africa, which adopts an abolitionist, rights-based approach to animal protection.[123] Perhaps not surprisingly, many of South Africa's animal rights activists have their roots in the anti-apartheid movement and highlight the similarities they perceive between human and animal oppression in South Africa.[124] This is a prime demonstration of the notion suggested by some commentators that animal protection is the newest and currently most pressing social justice movement.

Egypt

Like many countries in the Middle East and North Africa, Egypt has very few laws that protect animals, and those that do exist are rarely enforced.[125] However, there are indigenous animal protection movements developing in many of these countries, often relying on the Qur'an's prohibition against cruelty to animals to persuade predominantly Muslim populations to adopt a more humane approach to the treatment of animals.[126] In Egypt, local animal welfare organizations are working with the government to reform the country's animal control policy, which consists of shooting stray dogs and poisoning them with strychnine.[127] Demonstrating the national attention these issues are attracting, former Egyptian president Hosni Mubarak demanded a report on the issue following international outcry over the killings.[128]

One of the most internationally contentious animal issues involving Egypt is the live export trade, in which animals are raised in one country and then shipped to another for slaughter. Animals suffer during transportation even on relatively short trips, but that suffering is magnified significantly when animals are transported overseas on trips that may take several weeks.[129] Until recently, Egypt imported tens of thousands of live sheep and cows from Australia, which is nearly 8,000 miles away.[130] In 2006, Animals Australia, an Australian animal protection group, released a video from an investigation that revealed extreme animal cruelty at an Egyptian slaughterhouse. Australia then halted all live exports to Egypt. A few months later, the Egyptian and Australian agricultural ministers signed a pair of Memorandums of Understanding (MOUs) to improve animal welfare during transportation and slaughter, and live exports resumed. Animals Australia then released another investigation depicting ongoing cruelty to sheep in violation of the MOUs, and Australia again halted live exports. In 2008, Australia announced its intention to resume shipments of sheep and cows to Egypt, but none have taken place yet, and animal activists in Egypt and Australia are continuing their campaigns against live exports.[131] Egypt recently hosted a meeting between regional political leaders and animal welfare advocates on the topic of live animal exports and the requirements of Islam. The parties all agreed that reform was necessary in order to bring current practices into accordance with international standards and Islamic teachings.[132]

North America

United States of America

The United States occupies a conflicted role when it comes to animal law. Although animal law as a discipline is more established in the United States than anywhere else in the world, the United States' animal protection laws lag behind those of many other industrialized nations.[133] And while the United States tends to have progressive policies for companion animals, it largely ignores the plight of farmed animals and is responsible for implementing the factory farming model that causes more global animal suffering than any other form of animal use. These tensions make studying animal law in the United States a complex and fascinating undertaking.

Most animal law issues in the United States are dealt with on a state-by-state basis. Each of the fifty states has its own set of statutes prohibiting some form of cruelty to animals. Forty-six states have declared some forms of animal cruelty felonies, reflecting the states' judgments that animal cruelty is a serious crime. Although each state is different, many of the anticruelty laws share common elements and provisions. For instance, many state judges can require defendants convicted of animal cruelty to undergo psychological counseling, and some allow courts to prohibit defendants from owning animals in the future.[134]

Many state laws provide exemptions for the most common commercial and recreational uses of animals, such as the production of animal-derived food products (meat, eggs, and dairy), the use of animals in research, and hunting.[135]

The U.S. federal government has also passed a multitude of animal protection laws, including laws governing animal research, animal exhibition, slaughtering procedures, animal fighting, and endangered species conservation.[136] Animal advocates have criticized some of these laws for leaving too much animal suffering unregulated. For example, the Humane Methods of Slaughter Act exempts birds, who comprise more than ninety percent of the animals slaughtered for food in the United States.[137] The Animal Welfare Act, which regulates animal experimentation, exempts rats, mice, and birds, who comprise more than ninety percent of the animals used in research.[138]

There has also been a wide variety of animal protection litigation in the United States.[139] Organizations such as the Animal Legal Defense Fund and the Humane Society of the United States have brought numerous lawsuits in state and federal courts to protect animals. Some of these cases seek to enforce existing laws, such as the Animal Welfare Act and the Humane Slaughter Act, while others utilize more creative and unconventional arguments to attempt to challenge animals' current property status.[140] An example of this latter type is animal custody cases. These cases involve competing claims to possession of an animal, such as a divorcing couple's dispute over who gets to keep a companion animal who previously occupied the communal home. Such disputes are normally resolved through a formal legal analysis of who owns the animal, and the animal is apportioned like any other piece of shared property. But animal lawyers in America are increasingly arguing that as sentient beings, animals have interests that are distinct and superior to those of inanimate property. Those lawyers often urge judges to treat animals differently than other property, and to consider the animals' best interests, much as judges do in child custody cases. Such cases challenge the traditional legal conception of animals as mere property, and may lead to a shift in judicial reasoning and a consideration of animals as a unique type of property that should be treated in a unique way under the law.[141]

South America

Brazil

The Brazilian Constitution expressly requires the government to "prohibit[] ... all practices [that] ... cause the extinction of species or subject animals to cruelty."[142] Pursuant to this provision, the Brazilian Supreme Court has banned cockfighting, as well as a traditional Brazilian practice known as "Ox Feast," in which an ox is tortured and beaten with stones and sticks by an entire village.[143]

The Brazilian judiciary was also among the first in the world to begin grappling with the challenging issue of animal personhood. In 2005, Brazil made international news when lawyers filed a petition for a writ of habeas corpus to have a chimpanzee named Suíça freed from a zoo and sent to a sanctuary.[144] Habeas corpus is the traditional writ used to release a prisoner from unlawful imprisonment, and legal scholars are now proposing its applicability to captive great apes.[145] While the court allowed the issue to be considered with respect to Suíça, she died before the issue was finally resolved, and the case was dismissed as moot.[146] This kind of rights-based litigation, and the Brazilian courts' reception to the arguments, demonstrates a shift in opinions about the place of animals in the courts and society. It also suggests that perhaps some of the areas most fertile for truly radical change lie outside of the more traditional approach to animal welfare seen in the Anglo-American traditions, which typically promote humane treatment to the extent that does not conflict with traditional commercial or personal uses of animals.

Brazil also has an active grassroots animal protection movement that has had a significant impact on animal laws in that country, primarily at the state and local level. In the wake of extensive public education about the use of wild animals in circuses, four states and forty-one municipalities have banned animal circuses, and the federal government is considering a similar ban.[147] Activists contend that such a ban is necessary because animals in circuses are not only physically abused to force them to "perform," but also because the very fact of their captivity is incompatible with the needs of wild animals. There is widespread public support in Brazil for this position and a federal ban on animal circuses appears imminent.

Brazil is also likely to become a central site in the debates about the treatment of farmed animals. Many factory farms are relocating to Brazil and other South American countries after being driven out of the United States and Europe by increasing regulation of farmed animals.[148] At the same time, there is a burgeoning vegetarian movement in Brazil that aims to combat these factory farms.[149]

Ecuador

In 2007, Ecuador convened a constitutional assembly to rewrite its constitution, which provided a platform for environmentalists and animal advocates to lobby for the inclusion of environmental rights and animal protection in the Ecuadorian constitution. Animal advocates initially proposed an article that would have required "[t]he state [to] protect and defend the life of every animal species, banning all kinds of illegal traffic and cruel treatment against them."[150] After animal industry organizations learned of the proposed language, they mobilized opposition and successfully lobbied the assembly to propose a substitute animal welfare article, which provided that "[t]he law will regulate the conditions for animal welfare. This protection cannot be claimed to ban or restrict ancestral rights or cultural practices."[151] The latter clause in this amended article would have immunized bullfighting, cockfighting, and religious animal sacrifices from regulation. Ecuadorian animal advocates refused to support the new article and in fact actively worked to remove it. They felt that it was better to have no animal welfare provision in the constitution than to have one that exempted common practices that cause animal suffering. In the end, the Ecuadorian constitution was ratified without any animal protection clause.[152]

The constitution, however, does grant rights to nature. Article 71 states, "Nature or Pacha Mama [an indigenous term for Mother Earth], where life is reproduced and exists, has the right to exist, persist, maintain and regenerate its vital cycles, structure, functions and its processes in evolution." Article 71 permits "[e]very person, people, community or nationality ... to demand the recognition of rights for nature before the public bodies." The article further requires the state to "promote respect for all the elements that form an ecosystem," which would presumably include wild animals.[153] Article 73 further commits the state to restricting activities that risk species extinction.[154]

In this regard, the Ecuadorian constitutional experience raises interesting questions related to the themes discussed above. It grants rights to inanimate elements of ecosystems such as trees and rivers, but not to sentient, domestic animals such as bulls and roosters. Readers should consider what philosophies and values underlie such a distinction.

Europe

European Union

The European Union (EU) is a political and economic community comprised of twenty-seven member states. The countries share a common body of standardized laws, including animal welfare and anticruelty laws. Although the EU's animal laws still lack strict enforcement provisions, they are a vast improvement on laws elsewhere.

In June 1999, the EU passed a directive[155] on the welfare of hens involved in the egg laying industry, which required egg producers to phase out conventional "laying cages" (also called "battery cages") by 2012.[156] The enriched cages that the directive requires will provide more room and better conditions than previously available, and better than those in most U.S. facilities. Traditional industry practice for egg-laying hens in America has been that each hen receives less than 67 square inches of individual space.[157] Even the voluntary guidelines developed by the American industry group United Egg Producers still prevent hens from turning around or stretching their limbs. In the EU, the enriched cage systems that will be permitted must allow a minimum of 116.25 square inches of space per bird. The EU directive also requires that cages include nests, litter, and perches, which are not seen in most U.S. operations.[158] Although these larger cages are an improvement over battery cages, animal advocates argue that enriched cages still fail to meet the basic needs of hens. According to a report by Compassion in World Farming, "[t]he space and facilities provided in 'enriched' cages are so inadequate that this system deprives hens of the ability to meaningfully fulfill natural behaviours, leading to abnormal behaviours, frustration, suffering and body degeneration."[159]

The EU has also addressed animal welfare during transportation. The Convention for the Protection of Animals During International Transport provides measures intended to avoid animal suffering during transit. The Convention has specific sections regarding veterinary inspections and treatment, provision of food and water, space and ventilation, loading animals into transport vehicles, and sanitation.[160] The Convention applies to all horses, livestock, pets, nondomestic birds and mammals, and cold-blooded animals.

United Kingdom

The United Kingdom has exhibited one of the most rapid courses of change in the area of animal protection. Its populace has spurred policymakers to institute a series of laws aimed at improving the lives of animals, especially those used in agriculture and food production. The UK experience also confirms the value of sustained grassroots campaigning for animal rights. For example, following a fifteen-year campaign in England and Wales, the Fur Farming (Prohibition) Bill banned fur farming on the basis of "public morality."[161] Scotland soon followed England and Wales' lead, passing a similar ban.[162] The Scottish bill demonstrates the moral imperative behind such laws. At the time of adoption of the ban, Scotland did not have any fur farms. The law's adoption there thus serves two roles—it declares Scotland's unity of thought with England and Wales on this issue and it prevents fur farmers put out of work in other parts of the UK from moving their operations to Scotland. What is especially noteworthy about the fur farm ban is the fact that it is truly a rights-based law that completely eliminates an abhorrent practice, rather than a welfare-based law that seeks to regulate it.[163] At the same time, like the New Zealand ban on great ape research, it had no direct impact on any animals in Scotland, and so did not engender as much objection as if it had been attempted in a country with a large fur farm industry.

Germany

In 2002, Germany amended its Constitution to declare that "[t]he State, in a spirit of responsibility for future generations, also protects the natural living conditions and the animals within the framework of the constitutional rules through the legislation and as provided by the laws through the executive power and the administration of justice."[164] From a legal perspective, these are significant developments; such a change in a country's basic integral document can change the legal landscape dramatically and facilitate the passage of new protective laws. From a symbolic and social viewpoint, these constitutional provisions are evidence of the continued success of the animal protection movement's efforts to strengthen the basis for safeguards for nonhumans. Germany had an extensive and detailed animal protection law, the *Tierschutzgesetz*, before the adoption of the constitutional amendment. At its core, this law prohibited injury or suffering "without sound reason."[165] This ambiguous term was subject to varied interpretation and could be easily redefined depending on the circumstances of an act. Nevertheless the *Tierschutzgesetz* was imbued with an ethical concern for animal welfare—subject, of course, to human justification and the constitutional rights to carry out professional activities and artistic expression, either of which may in some cases conflict with animal welfare.

Italy

Like most members of the European Union, the bulk of Italy's animal welfare laws simply represent an incorporation of the EU provisions. Italy has independently had a general anticruelty law on the books for nearly 100 years, and in July 2004, its parliament strengthened protections specifically directed at the human-animal bond formed with companion animals.[166] "In Italy, an important section of the regulation of man's relationship with companion animals is contained in the 'State-Regions Agreement on Companion Animal Welfare and Pet Therapy,' which was recognised by the Council of Ministers in DCPM 28th February 2003."[167]

Since the national law was enacted, local governments have added to the body of animal welfare law with laws applicable only in their jurisdiction. For example, Rome's municipal government passed a statute in 2005 ordering better treatment for all companion animals.[168] This law included:

1. A ban on "choke chains" and electric shock collars, two types of collars used to discipline dogs through the use of a tightening of a metal collar around the dog's neck, or the issuance of a small electric shock;
2. A requirement for daily walks for dogs;
3. A ban on the nontherapeutic docking (surgical removal) of dogs' ears and tails, and cats' claws;
4. A ban on round goldfish bowls, because of problems they apparently may create for the goldfish.[169]

Croatia

In 2007, the Animal Protection Act of Croatia (APAC) was adopted.[170] This extensive (thirty-four pages) statute represents an omnibus coverage of animal protection issues. It touches on nearly every way in which humans and animals interact. The Croatian law articulates "the responsibilities, obligations, and duties of natural and legal persons" with regard to a variety of animal welfare issues including transportation, experimentation, slaughter, zoos and circuses, and companion animal care.

The law is discussed in further detail elsewhere in this text, but some of its most notable sections prohibit: (1) "rais[ing] animals in a way that causes them pain, suffering and fear"; (2) ear cropping and tail docking of dogs and declawing of cats, (3) animal fighting; and (4) circus performances where animals are forced to act "unnaturally" or are subject to pain, suffering, injury, or fear. Under the APAC, anyone who injures an animal must provide help to the animal. The law also establishes a government "Ethics Committee" to provide guidance on ethical and animal protection issues, and creates a centralized enforcement regime with penalties for violations of each provision of the APAC. The APAC does have some significant limitations. As one example, it covers only vertebrates, and has an exemption for hunting and fishing.

Slovakia

The Slovak Republic, or Slovakia, is a member of the EU and so is subject to all the rules issued by its governing body. But Slovakia also has an active animal welfare community, which has campaigned for and obtained a ban on cosmetic and tobacco testing on animals, and addressed issues involving school dissection, slaughterhouse practices, and the care for animals in municipal shelters.[171] Active since the country's shift from a communist government, the citizens' groups have been able to motivate significantly greater protections than the EU regulations provide for animals in some areas. Freedom of Animals, founded in

1992, addresses the treatment of animals in virtually every area they are used, and also runs a rescue and rehabilitation shelter for homeless animals.[172]

Australasia

It is fairly well accepted that "[a]nimals have played an integral role in shaping Australian and New Zealand society since these countries were first colonized. Today, farmers raise several hundred million animals for slaughter every year, and animal-based industries producing meat, dairy products, eggs and wool form a key part of [their] economies."[173] Australians and New Zealanders of course keep animals as companion animals as well. The live export of animals to other countries, for use as food, has attracted much attention because of the treatment of the animals subjected to those trips.

Australia

In Australia, each State and Territory has created its own anti-cruelty legislation, with variations among the different governmental entities.[174] Both state and local government officials and officers in the Royal Society for the Prevention of Cruelty to Animals (RSPCA) have the authority to arrest violators and enforce the laws. Most prosecutions are begun by the RSPCA.[175] The RSPCA is largely a charitable organization, though it has official government support and sanction, but it has a notable limitation on its ability to handle larger cases, or to address all violations of the statutes.[176] Nevertheless, prosecutions regularly do occur with respect to basic violations. For example, in *Royal Society for the Prevention of Cruelty to Animals v. Stojcevski*,[177] the defendant's dog had a fractured leg, which went untreated. Stojcevski was arrested and tried for the commission of animal cruelty for failing to provide care to his dog (who was seized and then euthanized). The evidence established the dog had a severely broken leg that was untreated, and the South Australia Supreme Court affirmed the dismissal because the criminal "beyond reasonable doubt" standard was not met.[178]

The law at issue in *Stojcevski* was the standard anticruelty law but the charge was not that the defendant had hurt the dog but only that he had "failed to take reasonable steps to alleviate any pain suffered by the animal ..."[179]

Anti-cruelty prosecutions also tend to disregard farmed animals who "ultimately fall largely outside the protective reach of the law, despite the presence of a detailed regulatory framework which purports to address their welfare."[180] Australian states and territories adopt "Codes of Practice" relating to animal welfare,[181] which are "usually based on Model Codes of Practice, developed by the Primary Industries Ministerial Council (PIMC), comprised of federal, State and Territory primary industry ministers.... [However,] a number of States and Territories have developed their codes in the same topic area, inconsistent as between themselves and with the Model Codes adopted by the remaining jurisdictions."[182]

One area of animal welfare governed by Australia's federal laws is the export of live animals for food,[183] also discussed in the section on Egypt. The Australian Federal Government has enacted legislation under the trade and commerce power of the Commonwealth Constitution.[184] This complex legislation is discussed in greater detail in Chapter 2. Aside from animal welfare concerns inherent in live export, the "other major cruelty issue ... is the fate of the animals in the importing country."[185] Reports of horrific cruelty in Egyptian slaughterhouses resulted in a two-year suspension of live export trade to Egypt.[186]

Australia is notable for an especially active animal law community comprised of groups and individuals who have pushed legal change in the courts and the legislatures, and highlighted specific concerns in public presentations. Australian law schools have provided an increasing number of animal law courses, and groups like "Voiceless, the Fund for Animals" and others have supported scholarly and broad-based educational efforts which are slowly alerting the Australian people to common practices and problems inherent in the commercial uses of animals.

New Zealand

In New Zealand, the Animal Protection Act 1960 was replaced with the Animal Welfare Act 1999, which came into force January 1, 2000.[187] The Animal Welfare Act 1999 lays out general guidelines for animal protection and also provides for codes of welfare that create minimum standards for specific animal industries.[188] Although New Zealand has made some notable progress on the animal welfare front, industry participation in welfare code writing has also hampered welfare advances in the context of farmed animals; for example, "the pig Code of Welfare was written by the New Zealand Pork Industry Board."[189] All codes are ultimately formulated or reviewed by the National Animal Welfare Advisory Committee (NAWAC),[190] which is intended to provide a buffer zone between the direct influence of those who are involved in commercial animal production and those who are regulating treatment in that industry. Because New Zealand is "a nation that relies primarily upon agricultural production for economic viability,"[191] it is clear that economic and political pressures come to bear in determining the degree to which the industry is regulated.

Perhaps New Zealand's most noteworthy animal welfare provision is Section 85 of the Animal Welfare Act, which has garnered much international attention.[192] This section (discussed in greater detail in Chapter 4) puts significant restrictions on the use of non-human hominids in research, testing and teaching. While laudable on many levels, it must also be noted that, on a practical level, only thirty-four great apes resided in New Zealand at the time the Animal Welfare Act was enacted and not one of them was being used in research, testing, or teaching.[193]

Conclusion

The preceding discussion of animal laws in illustrative locations is far from exhaustive and demonstrates just a fraction of the multitude of ways in which countries are attempting to incorporate animals into their legal systems, both as chattel and as subjects of protection. In what follows, we discuss how different countries are regulating various commercial uses of animals for food, fiber, and entertainment (Chapter 2); how animals are incorporated into the criminal laws of nations (Chapter 3); how countries regulate the use of animals in scientific and cosmetic research (Chapter 4); how animals are affected by international treaties and other agreements that regulate conduct between nations (Chapter 6); and how and why animals are incorporated into the constitutions of some countries (Chapter 5).

Notes

1. David Favre & Vivien Tsang, *The Development of Anti-Cruelty Laws During the 1800's*, 1993 Det. C.L. Rev. 1, 7–8 (Spring 1993).

2. Thom Kuehls, Beyond Sovereign Territory: The Space of Ecopolitics 37 (1996). As Kuehls observes, "[t]he politics of ecology exceeds the limits of the state; and we need to allow theory to exceed the state model as well." *Id.* at 37–38. Yet this expanded theory cannot simply jettison the "striated space of the state" in favor of the "smooth space of the not-state." *Id.* at 42. Rather, "the two spaces in fact exist only in mixture." *Id.* at 42 (quoting Gilles Deleuze and Félix Guattari, A Thousand Plateaus: Capitalism and Schizophrenia 474 (1987)). Our hope is that this project highlights the mixture between arboreal state-based animal laws and the more rhizomatic exchanges of ideologies in international animal politics.

3. The commercial use of horses for food, as well as the U.S. ban on horse slaughter, is discussed in greater depth in Chapter 2.

4. James C. McKinley, Jr., *What to Do With Traumatized Elephant Stirs Up Dallas*, N.Y. Times, Aug. 14, 2008, *available at* http://www.nytimes.com/2008/08/15/us/15elephant.html; Joanna Cattanach & Rudolph Bush, *Jenny to Stay at Dallas Zoo With New Friend, New Digs*, Dallas Morning News, Aug. 22, 2008, *available at* http://www.dallasnews.com/shared content/dws/news/localnews/stories/082108dnmetjenny.170b37fc.html.

5. These groups overlap, as in the cases of endangered animals exploited for fur or wild-caught animals sold for scientific research or to zoos.

6. DIANE BEERS, FOR THE PREVENTION OF CRUELTY: THE HISTORY AND LEGACY OF ANIMAL RIGHTS ACTIVISM IN THE UNITED STATES 22 (2006).

7. *See generally*, RACHEL CARSON, SILENT SPRING (1962).

8. J. Baird Callicott, *Animal Liberation: A Triangular Affair, in* IN DEFENSE OF THE LAND ETHIC 15, 30 (1989); *but see* J. Baird Callicott, *Animal Liberation and Environmental Ethics: Back Together Again, in id.* at 49 (reappraising the potential of a coalition between the environmental and animal rights movements).

9. Callicott, *Triangular Affair, supra* note 8, at 30–32.

10. Jennifer Everett, *Environmental Ethics, Animal Welfarism, and the Problem of Predation: A Bambi Lover's Respect For Nature*, 6 ETHICS & ENV'T 42, 54 (2001) ("[A]lthough all subjects-of-a-life (both human and nonhuman, wild and domestic) are equally bearers of inherent value and equally deserving of respectful treatment, the principle of respect does not entail that all of the rights we possess are equivalent.").

11. Karen Davis, *Thinking Like a Chicken: Farm Animals and the Feminine Connection, in* ANIMALS & WOMEN: FEMINIST THEORETICAL EXPLORATIONS 192 (Carol J. Adams & Josephine Donovan eds., 1995); Marti Kheel, NATURE ETHICS: AN ECOFEMINIST PERSPECTIVE 1–35 (2008).

12. BARNEY NELSON, THE WILD AND THE DOMESTIC: ANIMAL REPRESENTATION, ECOCRITICISM, AND WESTERN AMERICAN LITERATURE (2000); Glen Elder, Jennifer Wolch, & Jody Emel, Le Pratique Sauvage*: Race, Place, and the Human-Animal Divide, in* ANIMAL GEOGRAPHIES: PLACE, POLITICS, AND IDENTITY IN THE NATURE-CULTURE BORDERLANDS 72 (Jennifer Wolch & Jody Elem eds., 1998).

13. Holmes Rolston, III, *Environmental Ethics: Values in and Duties to the Natural World, in* THE BROKEN CIRCLE: ECOLOGY, ECONOMICS, ETHICS 73, 85 (F. Herbert Bormann & Stephen R. Kellert eds., 1991) ("A shutdown of the life stream is the most destructive event possible.... Every extinction is a kind of superkilling. It kills forms (*species*), beyond individuals. It kills 'essences' beyond 'existences,' the 'soul' as well as the 'body.'").

14. *Id.*

15. *See, e.g.*, PETER SINGER, ANIMAL LIBERATION 19 (revised ed., Avon Books 1990) ("To avoid speciesism we must allow that beings who are similar in all relevant respects have a similar right to life—and mere membership in our own biological species cannot be a morally relevant criterion for this right.").

16. TOM REGAN, THE CASE FOR ANIMAL RIGHTS 359 (1983).

17. For a discussion of how different environmental ethical theories may lead to different policies, *see* Mikael Stenmark, *The Relevance of Environmental Ethical Theories for Policy Making*, 24 ENVIRONMENTAL ETHICS 135 (2002).

18. We should note that the philosophical questions that animal law raises are not limited to ethical or moral ones. Animal law also implicates questions of ontology (what, if anything, is exceptional about being human?), epistemology (how can we know other beings?), philosophy of mind (what counts as a "person"?), philosophy of language (do animals have language, and if so, does that entitle them to protection?), and political philosophy (what is the source and nature of legal rights?).

19. CONVENTION ON INTERNATIONAL TRADE IN ENDANGERED SPECIES OF WILD FAUNA AND FLORA, Mar. 3, 1973, preamble, 27 U.S.T. 1087, 993 U.N.T.S. 243.

20. *Id.*

21. ROBERT GARNER, THE POLITICAL THEORY OF ANIMAL RIGHTS 119–20 (2005); Kyle Ash, *Why Managing Biodiversity Will Fail: An Alternative Approach to Sustainable Exploitation for International Law*, 13 ANIMAL L. 209, 211 (2007).

22. National Agricultural Statistics Service, United States Department of Agriculture, Livestock Slaughter 2007 Summary 1 (2008) (stating that commercial hog slaughter for 2007 totaled 109.2 million head). For a discussion of the lack of laws regulating treatment of farmed animals, *see* David J. Wolfson & Mariann Sullivan, *Foxes in the Hen House: Animals, Agribusiness, and the Law: A Modern American Fable*, *in* Animal Rights: Current Debates and New Directions 205 (Cass R. Sunstein & Martha C. Nussbaum eds., 2004).

23. In this sense, what anticruelty statutes aim to eliminate is *gratuitous* suffering, or suffering that serves no socially-accepted purpose. Darian M. Ibrahim, *The Anticruelty Statute: A Study in Animal Welfare*, 1 J. Animal L. and Ethics 175, 183 (2006).

24. International Convention for the Regulation of Whaling, Dec. 2, 1946, preamble, 62 Stat. 1716, 161 U.N.T.S. 72. The International Whaling Commission is discussed in greater detail in Chapter 6.

25. International Whaling Commission Schedule, para. 10(e).

26. *See, e.g.*, Bob Holmes & Duncan Graham-Rowe, *Pressure is on to Lift Whaling Ban*, New Scientist, June 20, 2005, *available at* http://www.newscientist.com/article/mg186 25043.900.

27. "Sovereignty does not regulate everything that exists within its territory. There is a beyond, an outside, that exists within the geopolitical walls of the sovereign state..., but *outside* its apparatus...." Thom Kuehls, Beyond Sovereign Territory: The Space of Ecopolitics 41 (1996). In other words, every territory has within its borders constituencies that are not represented or mapped by the politics of the sovereignty that claims to speak for those within its territory.

28. According to the Center for Responsive Politics, a nonpartisan organization that monitors the influence of money on elections and policymaking in the United States, the agribusiness lobby spent more than $102 million on federal lobbying in 2008. *Lobbying Spending Database Agribusiness 2008*, Center for Responsive Politics, *available at* http://www.opensecrets.org/lobby/indus.php?lname=A&year=2008. In addition to the millions spent lobbying Congress, agribusiness contributed more than $64.9 million to candidates for federal offices during the 2008 election cycle. *Agribusiness: Long-term Contribution Trends*, Center for Responsive Politics, *available at* http://www.opensecrets.org/industries/indus.php?ind=A. Specifically, the livestock industry contributed $3 million, the dairy industry contributed $4.8 million, the poultry and eggs industry contributed $1.5 million, and the meat processing industry contributed $1.7 million to federal legislators' election campaigns. *Id.* (These figures do not include lobbying or campaign contributions at the level of state legislatures, which constitute much more significant and influential forums for governing the treatment of farmed animals.) For a critical assessment of the role of the agribusiness lobby in federal food policy, see Editorial, *A Disgraceful Farm Bill*, N.Y. Times, May 16, 2008, *available at* http://www.nytimes.com/2008/05/16/opinion/16fri3.html?ref=opinion (referring to the federal Farm Bill as "an inglorious piece of work tailored to the needs of big agriculture" and excoriating legislators who "cannot resist the blandishments and power of the farmers"). *See also* David Wolfson, *Beyond the Law: Agribusiness and the Systemic Abuse of Animals Raised for Food or Food Production*, 2 Animal L. 123, 145–46 ("The power of the farming industry in the United States must be recognized in order to fully understand the conflict that such a simple subject as the prevention of cruelty to animals raises and the difficulties facing any attempted reform.... These industry giants are extraordinarily powerful and efficient lobbyists, and they are primarily concerned with profit.").

29. Consider these statistics reported by a leading American animal lawyer:

> More than two-thirds of Americans find it unacceptable that there are no federal laws that protect the welfare of animals on the farm. More than four-fifths believe there should be effective laws that protect farm animals against cruelty. And nearly three-quarters of Americans believe there ought to be federal inspections of farms to ensure humane treatment.... [A] national poll found that the vast majority of Americans favor humane slaughter methods for chickens, turkeys, and ducks who are raised for food, as opposed to current U.S. Department of Agriculture policy allowing these animals to be slaughtered without first rendering them insensible to pain. So there is undoubtedly a gap, and a quite large one, between the current cruelties visited upon animals and where society is ready to go in terms of reform.

Jonathan Lovvorn, *Animal Law in Action: The Law, Public Perception, and the Limits of Animal Rights Theory as a Basis for Legal Reform*, 12 ANIMAL L. 133, 137–38 (2006) (citing numerous polls).

30. Evidence of this influence could be seen in 2004 when Joe Roberts, a New Jersey legislator, blocked a widely-supported bill that would have banned the practice of keeping veal calves in small crates that prevent them from turning around. Gene Baur, the president of Farm Sanctuary, an animal rights group that supported the legislation, stated:

> This legislation has widespread support throughout New Jersey, and it is very frustrating that a couple of Assembly members aligned with agribusiness could block the bill at the last minute. By refusing to allow a vote, Assemblyman Roberts has served the narrow interests of the factory farming industry to the detriment of broader popular concerns and basic human decency.

Press Release, Farm Sanctuary, *Bill to Prevent Cruelty to Veal Calves Killed by Agribusiness Lobby, Popular Humane Legislation Stopped at Last Minute on Assembly Floor* (Jan. 9, 2004), *available at* http://www.farmsanctuary.org/mediacenter/2004/pr_vealbill_04.html.

31. *See Human-Animal Bond Boosts Spending on Veterinary Care*, JAVMA NEWS, Jan. 1, 2008, *available at* http://www.avma.org/onlnews/javma/jan08/080101a.asp (recounting results of survey that found that 49.7 percent of guardians viewed their companion animals as "family," while another 48.2 percent considered them "companions," and that only 2.1 percent viewed them as property).

32. *Compare* Cass R. Sunstein, *The Rights of Animals*, 70 U. CHI. L. REV. 387, 389 (2003) ("If we understand 'rights' to be legal protection against harm, then many animals already do have rights...."), *with* Gary Francione, *Reflections on Animals, Property, and the Law and Rain Without Thunder*, 70 LAW & CONTEMP. PROBS. 9, 36 (2007) ("A right to 'humane' treatment and to be free from 'unnecessary' suffering is no 'right' at all in that it prohibits only those actions that do not benefit humans and would, in any event, not be committed by rational property owners.").

33. *Germany Votes for Animal Rights*, CNN, May 17, 2002, *available at* http://archives.cnn.com/2002/WORLD/europe/05/17/germany.animals; Adam Cohen, *What's Next in the Law? The Unalienable Rights of Chimps*, N.Y. TIMES, July 14, 2008, *available at* http://www.nytimes.com/2008/07/14/opinion/14mon4.html; Martin Roberts, *Spanish Parliament to Extend Rights to Apes*, REUTERS, June 25, 2008, *available at* http://www.reuters.com/article/scienceNews/idUSL256586320080625.

34. The authors relied on the following articles for this discussion: Paula Brosnahan, *New Zealand's Animal Welfare Act: What Is Its Value Regarding Non-human Hominids?*, 6 ANIMAL L. 185 (2000); Rowan Taylor, *A Step at a Time: New Zealand's Progress Toward Hominid Rights*, 7 ANIMAL L. 35 (2001); and Peter Sankoff, *Five Years of the "New" Animal

Welfare Regime: Lessons Learned from New Zealand's Decision to Modernize Its Animal Welfare Legislation, 11 ANIMAL L. 7, 8–9 (2005).

35. John Luxton, Minister for Food, Fibre, Biosecurity, and Border Control, quoted in Brosnahan, *supra* note 34.

36. The law permits the Director General of the Ministry of Agriculture and Forestry to approve such use if she finds that doing so "is in the best interests of the individual non-human hominid" or "is in the interests of the species to which the non-human hominid belongs and ... the benefits are not outweighed by the likely harm to the non-human hominid." Animal Welfare Act, 1999, § 85 (NZ).

37. Peter Singer, Canadian Fed'n. of Humane Societies, *Legislative Breakthrough for Great Apes in New Zealand*, 15 CARING FOR ANIMALS (newsletter of the Canadian Federation of Humane Societies) 6 (Winter 2000), *available at* http://www.cfhs.ca/CaringForAnimals (quoted in Sankoff, *supra* note 34, at 8–9).

38. Brosnahan, *supra* note 34, at 191.

39. Sankoff, *supra* note 34, at 9.

40. Rowan Taylor, information officer for the Great Ape Project New Zealand, praised the Act for "singling out great apes [and] mark[ing] them as being different from other animals. Labels are important. Hominid rights are more likely to win acceptance if they are seen as applying only to beings like us...." Taylor sees animal rights as an "obstacle" to the Great Ape Project, stating that "GAPNZ makes a clear distinction between hominid rights and animal rights...." Taylor, *supra* note 34, at 39, 41. Kyle Ash sees an implicit speciesism in Taylor's statements. Ash contends that although the New Zealand great ape law "may be considered a breakthrough in some ways, it may also indicate an implied reluctance to recognize legal entitlement to other nonhuman animals. [The law] may have passed because it represents an expansion of legal entitlement 'only to beings like us....'" Kyle Ash, *Why "Managing" Biodiversity Will Fail: An Alternative Approach to Sustainable Exploitation for International Law*, 13 ANIMAL L. 209 (2007) (quoting Rowan Taylor).

For a general critique of the argument that animals deserve moral consideration because they are similar to humans, *see* Taimie L. Bryant, *Sacrificing the Sacrifice of Animals: Legal Personhood for Animals, the Status of Animals as Property, and the Presumed Primacy of Humans*, 39 RUTGERS L. J. 247 (2008); *see also* Taimie L. Bryant, *Similarity or Difference as a Basis for Justice: Must Animals Be Like Humans to Be Legally Protected from Humans?*, 70 LAW & CONTEMP. PROBS. 207 (2007); *see generally* JACQUES DERRIDA, THE ANIMAL THAT THEREFORE I AM (Marie-Louise Mallet ed. & David Wills trans., 2008).

41. Sankoff, *supra* note 34, at 12–13.

42. *Id.*

43. Ministry of Agric. & Forestry, *MAF's Animal Welfare Mission* 74 (Nov. 1999) (quoted in Sankoff, *supra* note 34, at 13).

44. Alison G. Jones, *Australia's Damaging International Trade Practice: The Case Against Cruelty to Greyhounds*, 14 PAC. RIM L. & POLICY J. 677 (2005).

45. Lorna Edwards, *Hounded to Death*, SYDNEY MORNING HERALD, Oct. 25, 2004, *available at* http://www.smh.com.au/articles/2004/10/24/1098556290613.html.

46. *China Bans Dog From Olympic Menu*, BBC NEWS, July 11, 2008, *available at* http://news.bbc.co.uk/2/hi/asia-pacific/7501768.stm.

47. *See generally* Rakhyun E. Kim, *Dog Meat in Korea: A Socio-Legal Challenge*, 14 ANIMAL L. 201 (2008).

48. *See generally id.*

49. *See, e.g.*, Press Release, Humane Society of the United States, *Bill Would End Sale of Raccoon Dog Fur in New York* (June 11, 2007), *available at* http://www.hsus.org/furfree/news/press_releases/ny_raccoon_dog_fur_ban_bill_introduced.htm.

50. *See, e.g.*, International Agreement on the Conservation of Polar Bears and Their Habitats, Nov. 15, 1973, 4 U.S.T. 3918, T.I.A.S. No. 8409.

51. *See generally Antarctic Treaty Secretariat*, Secretariat of the Antarctic Treaty, *available at* http://www.ats.aq/index_e.htm.

52. *See, e.g.*, *About the UDAW Campaign*, AnimalsMatter, *available at* http://www.animalsmatter.org/en/campaign.

53. For the text of the UDAW, *see* http://www.animalethics.org.uk/i-ch-appendix2.html.

54. *See Explore the Map*, Animals Matter, *available at* http://www.animalsmatter.org/en/map.

55. *See Support Grows in Latin America for a UDAW*, AnimalsMatter, *available at* http://news.animalsmatter.org/.

56. Gary L. Francione, Animals, Property and the Law (1995); Gary L. Francione, Rain Without Thunder: The Ideology of the Animal Rights Movement (1996).

57. Cass Sunstein, *Introduction: What Are Animal Rights?*, *in* Sunstein & Nussbaum, *supra* note 22, at 3, 11; David Favre, *A New Property Status for Animals: Equitable Self-Ownership*, in Sunstein & Nussbaum, *supra* note 22, at 234; Robert Garner, *Political Ideology and the Legal Status of Animals*, 8 Animal L. 77 (2002).

58. *See generally* Joseph William Singer, Entitlement: The Paradoxes of Property (2000).

59. Kyle Ash, *Why "Managing" Biodiversity Will Fail: An Alternative Approach to Sustainable Exploitation for International Law*, 13 Animal L. 209 (2007).

60. *See generally* Donna J. Haraway, Primate Visions: Gender, Race, and Nature in the World of Modern Science (1990); Thomas S. Kuhn, The Structure of Scientific Revolutions (1962); Paul Feyerabend, Against Method (1975); Sandra Harding, The Science Question in Feminism (1986).

61. "Great apes" include gorillas, chimpanzees, orangutans, and bonobos.

62. *See generally*, Ariel Tsovel, *The Untold Story of a Chicken and the Missing Knowledge in Interspecific Ethics*, 19 Science in Context 237 (2006).

63. *See, e.g.*, Marsha Walton, *Polar Bear Now Listed as 'Threatened Species,'* CNN.com, May 14, 2008, *available at* http://www.cnn.com/2008/TECH/science/05/14/polar.bears.listing/index.html. "The Center for Biological Diversity was one of three environmental groups, including Greenpeace and the Natural Resources Defense Council, that sued the federal government to force a decision on the status of the polar bears." *Id.* The U.S. Fish and Wildlife Services provides a timeline of this polar bear action on its website, *available at* http://www.fws.gov/home/feature/2008/polarbear012308/pdf/Timeline.pdf.

64. International Agreement on the Conservation of Polar Bears and Their Habitats, Nov. 15, 1973, 4 U.S.T. 3918, T.I.A.S. 8409.

65. Ian Stirling, *Foreword* to Norbert Rosing, The World of the Polar Bear (1996).

66. *See Endangered and Threatened Wildlife and Plants; Determination of Threatened Status for the Polar Bear* (Ursus Maritimus) *Throughout Its Range*, 73 Fed. Reg. 28, 212–303 (May 15, 2008) (to be codified at 50 C.F.R. pt. 17).

67. Song Wei, *Traditional Chinese Culture Poses Difficulty for New Animal Welfare Laws*, Animal Legal & Historical Center (2004), *available at* http://www.animallaw.info/articles/archsongculture2004.htm.

68. Betsy Tao, *Note, A Stitch in Time: Addressing the Environmental, Health, and Animal Welfare Effects of China's Expanding Meat Industry*, 15 GEO. INT'L ENVTL. L. REV. 321, 352 (2003).

69. *Id.* (quoting Criminal Code art. 276 (P.R.C.).

70. *See generally*, David Favre & Vivien Tsang, *supra* note 1 at 1–22.

71. *See, e.g.*, Anne McClintock, *The Angel of Progress: Pitfalls of the Term "Post-colonial,"* 31/32 SOCIAL TEXT 84 (1992) (exploring the politics of linear narratives of progress and development).

72. Charu Sharma, *Chinese Endangered Species at the Brink of Extinction: A Critical Look at the Current Law and Policy in China*, 11 ANIMAL L. 215 (2005).

73. *Law on the Protection of Wildlife* (promulgated by Standing Comm. Nat'l People's Cong., Nov. 8, 1988, effective Mar. 1, 1989), *translated in Animal Law in China*, ANIMAL LEGAL & HISTORICAL WEB CENTER, *available at* http://www.animallaw.info/policy/pocnindex.htm.

74. Sharma, *supra* note 72, at 231–32.

75. Julie Cheung, *Implementation and Enforcement of CITES: An Assessment of Tiger and Rhinoceros Conservation Policy in Asia*, 5 PAC. RIM L. & POL'Y J. 125, 135 (1995).

76. Tao, *supra* note 68, at 345.

77. Jill Robinson, *Ending Bear Farming in China*, *in* A GLOBAL PERSPECTIVE ON ANIMALS IN THE LEGAL SYSTEM, International Animal Welfare Law Conference, California Western School of Law (2004).

78. *Animals Asia Foundation: Sanctuary and the Struggle to End Bear Bile Farming*, Interview by Lauren Corman with Jill Robinson, founder and CEO, Animals Asia Foundation (Animal Voices, CIUT radio broadcast, July 15, 2008), *available at* http://www.animalvoices.ca/shows/jill_robinson.

79. Law Concerning the Protection and Control of Animals, Law No. 105 of 1973.

80. Michael H. Fox, *Japan's Animal Protection Law: A Bark Without A Bite?* 7 (July 6, 2006) (unpublished conference paper).

81. *Id.*

82. The "[n]ame of the law was changed with a strong intention of Animal Welfare. The old law was named 'Law Concerning the Protection and Management of Animals'. While name of the amended law by directly translation is 'the Law for Animal AIGO and Management'. 'AIGO' is a very common Japanese [term] being defined in the dictionary that it mean to think a great deal of with love and is specifically used for animals in such a way as 'Animal AIGO'. As no English term equivalent to this Japanese is found, English name of this law will be, if we dare to translate the meaning, 'the Law for the Humane Treatment and Management of Animals'. Although we have a Japanese term 'Fukushi' equivalent to 'Welfare', it was not used for this law to avoid a possible confusion between human welfare and animal welfare." Akira Takeuchi, Amendment of Legislation for Animal Welfare in Japan, Address at the 28th Congress of the World Small Animal Veterinary Association (Oct. 24–27, 2003), *available at* http://www.vin.com/proceedings/Proceedings.plx?CID=WSAVA2003&Category=&PID=6490&O=Generic.

83. Act on Welfare and Management of Animals, Law No. 105 of 1973, revised by Law No. 68 of 2005, translated at http://www.cas.go.jp/jp/seisaku/hourei/data/AWMA_2.pdf.

84. *Id.*

85. *Mutilated Cat Pics Posted on Top Site*, MAINICHI DAILY NEWS, May 9, 2002, *available at* http://www.dearkogenta.com/e/news.htm.

86. Cat-Killer Spared After Privacy "Invaded," JAPAN TIMES ONLINE, Oct. 22, 2002, *available at* http://search.japantimes.co.jp/cgi-bin/nn20021022a6.html.

87. Abolitionist Online, *Japan, It's* [sic] *Gas Chambers, Pet-Shops and the Terrible Cruelty Inflicted Upon Japanese Animals, available at* http://www.abolitionist-online.com/interview-issue04_SASA.japan-lydia.tanab.shtml (interview with Lydia Tanabe, spokesperson, Small Animals Support Association Japan).

88. *See, e.g.*, William C.G. Burns & Geoffrey Wandesforde-Smith, *The International Whaling Commission and the Future of Cetaceans in a Changing World*, 11(2) Rev. of Eur. Community and Int'l Envtl. L. 199–210 (2002).

89. *See, e.g.*, Reuben B. Ackerman, *Japanese Whaling in the Pacific Ocean: Defiance of International Whaling Norms in the Name of "Scientific Research," Culture, and Tradition*, 25 B.C. Int'l & Comp. L. Rev. 323 (2002). "In September, 2000, the United States attempted to pressure Japan into ceasing its illegal whaling by restricting Japanese fishing rights within the U.S. exclusive economic zone (EEZ). More importantly, the United States even has contemplated, although not yet imposed, trade sanctions as a more potent measure to stop Japanese whaling." *Id.* at 324.

90. Republic Act No. 8485 of 1998 (English translation *available at* http://www.internationalwildlifelaw.org/phil_animal_act.html).

91. *Id.* §6(7). "In all the above mentioned cases, including those of cattle, pigs, goats, sheep, poultry, rabbits, carabaos, horses, deer and crocodiles the killing of the animals shall be done through humane procedures at all times."

92. *Id.* §6(7).

93. *Id.* §6(1).

94. *See Korea's Animal Protection Law*, International Aid for Korean Animals, *available at* http://www.koreananimals.org/animals/apl/2007apl.htm.

95. *See S. Korea Plans Tough Pro-Animal Laws*, Daily Nation, Aug. 11, 2010, *available at* http://www.nation.co.ke/News/world/S.%20Korea%20plans%20tough%20pro-animal%20laws/-/1068/975022/-/k0kpsc/-/index.html.

96. *See id.* For a history of Korea's involvement with eating dog, *see The History of Korea's Dog Meat Industry*, Korea's Animal Rights Advocates, *available at* http://animalrightskorea.org/dog-meat-issue/the-history-of-koreas-dog-meat-industry.html.

97. Rakhyun E. Kim, *Dog Meat in Korea: A Socio-Legal Challenge*, 14 Animal L. 201, 202 (2008).

98. *Id.* at 230.

99. *Id.* at 233.

100. *See* Animal Welfare Board of India, *available at* http://www.awbi.org/funct.htm.

101. India Const. art. 51-A(g). The Indian Constitution is discussed in detail in Chapter 5.

102. *Nair v. Union of India*, (Kerala H.C. June 6, 2000) No. 155/1999, at 38 (quoted in Martha C. Nussbaum, *Animal Rights: The Need for a Theoretical Basis*, 114 Harv. L. Rev. 1506, 1547 n.148 (2001) (book review)).

103. The distinction between kindness and justice is a cornerstone of the analytic philosophical justification for animal rights. *See* Tom Regan, *supra* note 1b, at 199 ("Kindness is not justice, and to the extent that animals are owed just treatment, we cannot look to the injunction that we be kind to animals as a principle that accounts ... for this dimension of our duties to animals."); *see also id.* at 280 ("It is not an act of kindness to treat animals respectfully. It is an act of justice."); Martha C. Nussbaum, *Beyond "Compassion and Humanity": Justice for Nonhuman Animals, in* Animal Rights: Current Debates and New Directions 299 (Cass R. Sunstein & Martha C. Nussbaum eds., 2004).

104. Animal Protection Law, 5754-1994, amended 2005, *available at* http://www.vetserveng.moag.gov.il/NR/rdonlyres/7D36399D-4659-4247-8466-021A5D25FD32/868/CrueltytoAnimalsLaw.pdf.

105. *See The Animal Experimentation Law,* CHAI ONLINE, *available at* http://www.chai.org.il/en/compassion/legislation_experimentation.htm.

106. "In practical terms ... municipal veterinarians who poison stray dogs and cats cannot be prosecuted under the Animal Protection Law, so long as their actions were made in an effort to prevent rabies or other zoonoses (animal diseases that can be transmitted to humans). Clause 4 specifically allows poisoning animals with the slow-acting, painful neurotoxic compound strychnine if authorized by the Head of the Veterinary Services in the Ministry of Agriculture, the government agency responsible for the control of rabies—the same agency that is responsible for enforcing the Animal Protection Law." *Animal Legislation in Israel, The Animal Protection Law*, CONCERN FOR HELPING ANIMALS IN ISRAEL (CHAI), *available at* http://chai-online.org/en/compassion/legislation_protection.htm [hereinafter CHAI].

107. *See id.*

108. HCA 9232/01, Noah (the Israeli Federation of Animal Protection Organizations) v. Attorney General, Minister of Agriculture, Egg and Poultry Board, Moshe Benishty and 31 Colleagues [2003], *available at* http://www.animallaw.info/nonus/cases/cas_pdf/Israel2003case.pdf.

109. *Id.*

110. *Id.*

111. *Id.*

112. Israel Ministry for the Environment, *High Court of Justice Rejects Appeal to Continue Force-Feeding of Geese* (Feb. 23, 2006), *available at* http://www.environment.gov.il/bin/en.jsp?enPage=e_BlankPage&enDisplay=view&enDispWhat=Object&enDispWho=News%5El2884&enZone=e_news.

113. Performing Animals Protection Act (Act 24 of 1935).

114. Animals Protection Act (Act 71 of 1962).

115. *Id.*

116. Animal Matters Amendment Act 42 of 1993.

117. Societies for the Prevention of Cruelty to Animals Act, 1993 (Act. No. 169 of 1993); Animals Protection Act, Act 71 of 1962, §8.

118. NATIONAL COUNCIL OF SPCAS, STATEMENT OF POLICY, *available at* http://www.nspca.co.za (follow "About Us" hyperlink; then follow "Statement of Policy" hyperlink).

119. *About Us*, ANIMAL ANTI-CRUELTY LEAGUE, *available at* http://www.aacl.org.za/index.php/about.

120. *See generally* SOUTH AFRICAN VETERINARY ASS'N, REVIEW OF ANIMAL CARE LEGISLATION IN SOUTH AFRICA (2006), *available at* http://www.savf.org.za/Documents/Animal%20Care%20Legislation%20Review.pdf.

121. *Id.*

122. *South Africa Puts Limits on Hunting*, LOS ANGELES TIMES, Feb. 21, 2007, *available at* http://articles.latimes.com/2007/feb/21/world/fg-hunters21.

123. *Animal Rights Africa: Activism & Witness*, Interview by Lauren Corman with Michele Pickover and Steve Smit, Animal Rights Africa (Animal Voices, CIUT radio broadcast, Sept. 25, 2007), *available at* http://www.animalvoices.ca/shows/michele_pickover.

124. *Id.*

125. For an explanation of existing Egyptian animal laws, *see* http://www.sparelives.org/index.pl/the_laws.

126. For a discussion of Islamic perspectives on animals, see Martin Forward & Mohamed Alam, *Islam*, *in* THE ANIMAL ETHICS READER 235 (Susan J. Armstrong & Richard G. Botzler eds., 2003).

127. *See, e.g.*, Nadia Abou el Magd, *Animal Rights Movement Starting to Stir in Egypt*, NATIONAL (Abu Dhabi), Nov. 24, 2008, *available at* http://thenational.ae/article/20081124/FOREIGN/90341144/0/ART/; *see also Rescue, Rehabilitation, and Advocacy in Egypt*, Interview by Lauren Corman with Mona Khalil, Secretary General, Society for the Protection of Animal Rights in Egypt (Animal Voices, CIUT radio broadcast, Dec. 12, 2006), *available at* http://animalvoices.ca/2006/12/12/rescue-rehabilitation-and-advocacy-in-egypt.

128. Abou el Magd, *supra* note 127.

129. *See generally* LONG DISTANCE TRANSPORT AND WELFARE OF FARM ANIMALS (Michael C. Appleby *et al.* eds., 2008).

130. Egypt's role in the live import trade is minuscule compared to Kuwait and Saudi Arabia, which each import approximately one million live sheep each year, and Indonesia, which imports more than half million live cows each year. *Meat & Livestock Australia*, FAST FACTS 2008: AUSTRALIA'S SHEEPMEAT INDUSTRY 2 (2008), *available at* http://www.mla.com.au/NR/rdonlyres/8A977FC3-0C2E-48F7-B289-6214F83239CE/0/SheepmeatFastFacts2008.pdf; MEAT & LIVESTOCK AUSTRALIA, FAST FACTS 2008: AUSTRALIA'S BEEF INDUSTRY 2 (2008), *available at* http://www.mla.com.au/NR/rdonlyres/7AF99822-A1E3-4F30-B94A-454CAEF1B138/0/BeefFastFacts2008.pdf.

131. *Egypt Live Trade Announcement Ignores Catalogue of Shame*, ANIMALS AUSTRALIA (May 9, 2008), *available at* http://www.liveexport-indefensible.com/news/media_release.hp?press=98; Jane Bardon, *Egypt Live Cattle Export Ban Lifted*, ABC RURAL QUEENSLAND (May 9, 2008), *available at* http://www.abc.net.au/rural/qld/content/2007/s2240355.htm.

132. *Egypt Hosts Meeting on Animal Transport*, WORLD SOCIETY FOR THE PROTECTION OF ANIMALS (Oct. 24, 2008), *available at* http://www.wspa-international.org/latestnews/2008/egypt_meeting_animal_transport.aspx.

133. According to a 2007 study by Peter Sankoff, eighty percent of the world's animal law classes are taught in the United States, and "animal law remains primarily an American subject of study." Peter Sankoff, *Charting the Growth of Animal Law in Education*, 4 J. ANIMAL L. 105, 116, 118 (2008). For an analysis of the weaknesses of American animal laws compared to those of other countries, see David J. Wolfson & Mariann Sullivan, *Foxes in the Hen House: Animals, Agribusiness, and the Law: A Modern American Fable*, *in* ANIMAL RIGHTS: CURRENT DEBATES AND NEW DIRECTIONS 205 (Cass R. Sunstein & Martha C. Nussbaum eds., 2004); Jessica Braunschweig-Norris, Note, *The U.S. Egg Industry—Not All It's Cracked Up to Be for the Welfare of the Laying Hen: A Comparative Look at United States and European Union Welfare Laws*, 10 DRAKE J. AGRIC. L. 511 (2005); Laura Donnellan, *Animal Testing in Cosmetics: Recent Developments in the European Union and the United States*, 13 ANIMAL L. 251 (2007).

134. *See generally* Pamela D. Frasch *et al.*, *State Animal Anti-Cruelty Statutes: An Overview*, 5 ANIMAL L. 69 (1999).

135. *See* BRUCE A. WAGMAN, SONIA S. WAISMAN & PAMELA D. FRASCH, ANIMAL LAW: CASES AND MATERIALS 92–93, 420–21 (4th ed. 2010).

136. Animal Welfare Act, 7 U.S.C. §§2131–2159, 18 U.S.C. §49 (animal research, exhibition, and fighting); Humane Methods of Slaughter Act, 7 U.S.C. §§1901–1906 (livestock slaughter); Endangered Species Act, 16 U.S.C. §§1531–1544 (endangered and threatened species conservation).

137. *See* Darian M. Ibrahim, *A Return to Descartes: Property, Profit, and the Corporate Ownership of Animals*, 70 LAW & CONTEMP. PROB. 89, 103–04 (2007); Jeff Welty, *Humane Slaughter Laws*, 70 LAW & CONTEMP. PROB. 175, 198–201 (2007).

138. Animal Welfare Act, 7 U.S.C. §2132(g); Darian M. Ibrahim, *Reduce, Refine, Replace: The Failure of the Three R's and the Future of Animal Experimentation*, 2006 U. CHI. LEGAL F. 195, 214.

139. *See generally* Joyce Tischler, *The History of Animal Law, Part I (1972–1987)*, 1 STAN. J. ANIMAL L. & POL'Y 1 (2008), *available at* http://sjalp.stanford.edu/pdfs/Tischler.pdf.

140. Many of these cases are collected in WAGMAN, WAISMAN & FRASCH, *supra* note 135.

141. Barbara Newell, *Animal Custody Disputes: A Growing Crack in the "Legal Thinghood" of Nonhuman Animals*, 6 ANIMAL L. 179 (2000).

142. C.F. art. 225, ¶1, §VII.

143. "In 1997, the Supreme Court ruled, in a public civil action against the state of Santa Catarina (Recurso Extraordinario n.153.531/SC;RT 753/101), that although it is the duty of the state to guarantee to all people the expression of cultural rights, this can not happen without observing the constitutional norm of the article 225, which forbid any practice that submits animals to cruelty." Lane Azevedo Clayton, *Overview of Brazil's Legal Structure for Animal Issues*, ANIMAL LEGAL & HISTORICAL CENTER (2003) *available at* http://www.animallaw.info/nonus/articles/ovbrazil.htm.

144. *Suica—Habeas Corpus*, No. 833085-3/2005 (Oct. 4, 2005) (Carlos de Paula, trans.), *Suica—Habeas Corpus*, ANIMAL LEGAL & HISTORICAL CENTER, *available at* http://www.animallaw.info/nonus/cases/cabrsuicaeng2005.htm.

145. Steven M. Wise, *The Entitlement of Chimpanzees to the Common Law Writs of* Habeas Corpus *and* De Homine Replegiando, 37 GOLDEN GATE U.L. REV. 219 (2007).

146. *Habeas Corpus for a Zoo Chimpanzee is Ordered in Brazil*, GREAT APE PROTECTION (Dec. 17, 2009), *available at* http://www.greatapeproject.org/en-US/noticias/Show/2665, habeas-corpus-for-a-zoo-chimpanzee-is-ordered-in-brazil.

147. *ProAnima: Animal Rights Lessons From Brazil*, Interview by Lauren Corman with Simone de Lima, founder, ProAnima (Animal Voices, CIUT radio broadcast, Nov. 25, 2008), *available at* http://www.animalvoices.ca/shows/simone_de_lima.

148. TONY WEIS, THE GLOBAL FOOD ECONOMY: THE BATTLE FOR THE FUTURE OF FARMING 20 (2007).

149. *Animal Rights in Brazil*, Interview by Lauren Corman with Marly Winckler, president, Brazilian Vegetarian Society (Animal Voices, CIUT radio broadcast, Sept. 27, 2005), *available at* http://www.animalvoices.ca/shows/marly_winckler.

150. *AnimaNaturalis: Helping Animals in Ecuador and Beyond*, Interview by Lauren Corman with Paula Gilbert, AnimaNaturalis (Animal Voices, CIUT radio broadcast, Aug. 5, 2008), *available at* http://www.animalvoices.ca/shows/paula_gilbert.

151. *Id.*

152. Article 281 does require that farmed animals be healthy and raised in healthful surroundings, but, based on its placement and context, this requirement appears aimed at promoting human health rather than animal welfare. CONSTITUCIÓN DE LA REPÚBLICA DEL ECUADOR art. 281. Article 57 protects collective indigenous rights, including the right to traditional medicinal practices, which includes "the right to recover, to promote, and to protect ritual and sacred places, as well as plants, animals, minerals and ecosystems." *Id.* art. 57. This article is aimed at protecting indigenous cultural rights rather than animal welfare (though the two may coincide).

153. Constitución de la República del Ecuador art. 71. The authors have relied on their own translations of the original Spanish, as well as the translation provided by the Community Environmental Legal Defense Fund. Press Release, Community Environmental Legal Defense Fund, Ecuador Approves New Constitution: Voters Approve Rights of Nature (Sept. 28, 2008), *available at* http://celdf.org/article.php?id=302.

154. Constitución de la República del Ecuador art. 73.

155. The EU uses three different types of legal instruments to pass laws. A "regulation" is binding law upon all member states and prevails over conflicting domestic law. "Directives" bind the governments of the member states without becoming national law. Member states then pass individual domestic laws in compliance with the directives. "Decisions" are rendered by the European Council, and EU member states must comply with such decisions.

156. Directive 1999/74/EC1 ends battery cages, but it does not end confinement of laying hens. *See* http://eur-lex.europa.eu/LexUriServ/LexUriServ.do?uri=CELEX:31999L0074:EN:HTML.

157. *See, e.g., Factory Egg Farming is Bad for the HENS...*, Wesleyan University, *available at* http://www.wesleyan.edu/wsa/warn/eon/batteryfarming/hens.html; *see also Cage-Free vs. Battery-Cage Eggs: Comparison of Animal Welfare in Both Methods,* HSUS (Sept. 1, 2009), *available at* http://www.humanesociety.org/issues/confinement_farm/facts/cage-free_vs_battery-cage.html.

158. *See Protection of Laying Hens,* Europa, *available at* http://europa.eu/legislation_summaries/food_safety/animal_welfare/l12067_en.htm.

159. Philip Lymbery, Compassion in World Farming, Laid Bare: The Case Against Enriched Cages in Europe 5 (2002).

160. *See generally* European Convention for the Protection of Animals During International Transport (Revised), *available at* http://conventions.coe.int/Treaty/en/Treaties/Html/193.htm.

161. Fur Farming (Prohibition) Act 2000 c. 33.

162. Fur Farming (Prohibition) (Scotland) Act 2002 (asp 10).

163. Prior to the ban, the UK's Farm Animal Welfare Council refused to issue welfare regulations for fur farming out of fear that doing so would legitimate the practice. The FAWC's chairperson stated, "We have decided against drawing up a Welfare Code for mink and fox farming to avoid giving it the stamp of approval which a Government-backed Welfare Code would imply." Quoted in Andrew Linzey, *The Ethical Case for European Legislation Against Fur Farming,* 13 Animal L. 147, 152 (2006).

164. *Id.*

165. *Id.* at 288.

166. *See generally* A. Passantino, *"Companion Animals: An Examination of Their Legal Classification in Italy and the Impact On Their Welfare,"* 4 J. Animal L. 59 (2008).

167. *Id.* at 60, 80, 80 n.41.

168. *See* http://news.bbc.co.uk/2/hi/europe/4376612.stm.

169. *See id.* According to different reports, the round bowls may make the goldfish lose their eyesight, or deprive them of oxygen.

170. Text of the Act is available in English translation at http://www.prijatelji-zivotinja.hr/index.en.php?id=470.

171. *See* http://www.ru.org/artareas.html.

172. *See* http://www.slobodazvierat.sk.

173. Peter Sankoff & Steven White, *Introduction in* ANIMAL LAW IN AUSTRALASIA 1 (Peter Sankoff & Steven White eds. 2009). This book is recommended to all those interested in a scholarly examination of the animal law movement in Australasia.

174. Katrina Sharman, *Animal Law in Australia*, ANIMAL LEGAL AND HISTORICAL WEB CENTER (2004), *available at* http://www.animallaw.info/nonus/articles/ovaustrailia.htm.

175. Peter Sankoff & Steven White, *supra* note 173, at 51–52.

176. *See generally* DEBORAH CAO, ANIMAL LAW IN AUSTRALIA AND NEW ZEALAND 174–76 (Thomson Reuters 2010).

177. (2002) 134 A Crim R 441, 2002 WL 228890 (Feb. 15, 2002).

178. *Id.* at sec. 37.

179. *Id.*

180. Katrina Sharman, *Farm Animals and Welfare Law: An Unhappy Union, in* ANIMAL LAW IN AUSTRALASIA 35 (Peter Sankoff & Steven White eds. 2009).

181. "Due to constitutional limitations the Commonwealth is generally not able to legislate in the area of animal welfare. States and Territories have adopted varying approaches to the development, content and significance of codes of practice." Arnja Dale, *Animal Welfare Codes and Regulations: The Devil in Disguise?, in* ANIMAL LAW IN AUSTRALASIA 176 n.9 (Peter Sankoff & Steven White eds. 2009).

182. *Id.* at 176–77. "[D]ue to the lack of federal legislation governing animal welfare, there has so far been no successful attempt to bring a rational and uniform approach to the development and adoption of the Codes of Practice." *Id.* at 177.

183. *See* Malcolm Caulfield, *Live Export of Animals, in* ANIMAL LAW IN AUSTRALASIA 35 (Peter Sankoff & Steven White, eds., 2009). "Australia is the world's largest exporter of live animals, accounting for 33% of global exports of sheep and 10% of global cattle exports in 2003.... During the 2006–07 voyages from Australia, 37,428 sheep and 1101 cattle died. The focus by regulators and reporters on mortalities under-emphasises the extent of the animal welfare problem, as it is evidence that many more animals suffer in many respects while on-board ship, yet survive." *Id.* at 154–55.

184. *Id.* at 157.

185. *Id.* at 172.

186. Jane Bardon, *Egypt Live Cattle Export Ban Lifted*, ABC RURAL QUEENSLAND, May 9, 2008, *available at* http://www.abc.net.au/rural/qld/content/2007/s2240355.htm.

187. *See* CAO, *supra* note 176, at 95–96.

188. Greater detail is provided by Arnja Dale, *Animal Welfare Codes and Regulations—The Devil in Disguise?*, in ANIMAL LAW IN AUSTRALASIA, *supra* note 181, at 174–78.

189. ANIMAL LAW IN AUSTRALASIA, *supra* note 173, at 184.

190. *Id.* at 178.

> The NAWAC was established as a way of ensuring that the creation of Codes of Welfare would not fall exclusively to the government, as there was concern that wider consultation was required to ensure that animal interests were protected.... It is viewed as an 'expert' body, primed to consider science, ethical standards and other relevant concerns. The membership of NAWAC consists of primary industry stakeholders, educators, veterinarians, animal welfare advocates, animal welfare and livestock scientists, lay people and others. The body's composition is intended to represent diverse interests, including animal welfare groups ... and also a healthy contingent of members representing commercial farmers and other industry-friendly bodies.

Id. at 179. However, "many believe that animal industries dominate the process." *Id.* at 187.

191. Peter Sankoff, *Five Years of the "New" Animal Welfare Regime: Lessons Learned from the New Zealand's Decision to Modernize Its Animal Welfare Legislation*, 11 Animal L. 7 (2005).

> New Zealand is a country whose economy relies heavily upon the production of meat products, and consequently, the killing of animals. At any given time, there are at least ten sheep for every human in New Zealand, and the iconic portrayal of the country as a place where livestock range freely across the landscape has some basis in reality. The solitary farmer, herding his sheep and making do without the interference of "accursed Green Townies" remains a popular icon, idolized in literature and advertising campaigns and generally admired by the populace.

Id. at 10.

192. See Rowan Taylor, *A Step at a Time: New Zealand's Progress Toward Hominid Rights*, 7 Animal L. 35 (2001).

193. Paula Gerber, *Scientific Experimentation on Animals: Are Australia and New Zealand Implementing the 3Rs? in* Animal Law in Australasia 212, 222 (Peter Sankoff & Steven White eds., 2009).

CHAPTER 2

Commercial Uses of Animals for Food and Entertainment

Chapter Overview

To understand the significance of the relationship between animals and commerce, one need only consult etymology. The word "buck," which is slang for a U.S. dollar, derives from "buckskin," the hide of a male deer. Buckskins were used as currency in trading in the 1800s.[1] The word "pecuniary" (involving money) derives from the Latin *pecunia* or *pecus*, which means property in cattle.[2] Similarly, the word "fee" (ownership, usually in land) derives from the Old English *feoh* and the Old High German *fihu*, both of which also mean cattle.[3] Animal references and metaphors pervade how we talk about economics: a rising market is termed a "bull" market, while a falling one is a "bear" market.[4] When Western economists speak of the economies of other nations, they often personify them with animal metaphors: the economies of Taiwan, South Korea, Singapore, and Hong Kong are termed the "Asian Tigers," and the economies of China and India have been referred to as "Pandas" and "Elephants."[5]

It should come as no surprise, then, that animals, whether wild or domesticated, are the subjects of commerce all over the world. The uses of animals are vast in scope. This chapter focuses on a few of those areas, and primarily on the use of animals for food and for entertainment. Without question, the largest numbers of animals are used as sources of food. An estimated sixty billion land animals are killed globally each year for food production, ten billion in the United States alone.[6] The companies and individuals in the agribusiness industry are involved in the production of the flesh and organs of animals for human (or animal) consumption, as well as the production of milk and eggs produced by animals. ("Agribusiness" refers to the enormous industry involved in the production of animal-related food products.) We also include here the extraction of bodily fluids (such as bile from bears) and the removal of body parts (such as the horns of rhinoceroses) for use in medicines, as well as the commercial use of animal skin, wool, and furs for clothing.

The second area we address is the commercial use of animals for entertainment. Animals are involuntary participants in a broad range of activities, such as the use of animal "actors" in television, film, and live performances (including circuses); exhibitions such as dog and cat shows; and the use of animals in sport (including cockfighting, bullfighting, dog fighting, hunting, and fishing). We save for Chapter 4 a third major commercial use of animals: biomedical research involving scientific testing for disease prevention and cures, and animal testing of cosmetics and other products to determine toxicity and irritancy. A fourth commercial use of animals, the international wildlife trade, is covered in Chapter 6.[7]

There is a large body of law that touches on areas involving animals but that we will not discuss because those laws regulate humans involved in any business. These laws address the commercial and individual interests of those involved in the business of raising animals and using them to generate profit. They may address the financial arrangements of businesses; govern employee relations and human resources concerns; impose restrictions on trade, transport or sales issues; or focus on human health and safety with respect to animal-related products. These laws generally provide no protection for animals, although they may impact the way animals are treated. Because of this tangential connection to animals and their welfare, we have omitted them from the discussion here.

We do not address the laws that implicate animals after their deaths, such as laws that require proper hygiene in the treatment of animal products used for food, or that, for example, limit the time in which slaughtered animals may be kept without refrigeration. Such laws are not designed to afford better treatment for the animals who are being used; they are intended to protect the ultimate consumers of the products, and thus fall outside the scope of this book.[8]

Animals Used for Food

This section is primarily organized by species, in contrast to the structure of most of the book, which organizes the law by countries within each chapter's topic. For each species, we discuss the common industry practices, as well as various laws that govern those practices in different countries. As we explain throughout the book, our goal was not to be exhaustive, but to provide examples of how different countries regulate the treatment of animals—in this chapter, those animals used for food and entertainment.

Our discussion of the international use of animals for food begins with the widespread practice of "factory farming." The term "factory farming" refers to the modern industrial practice of raising animals under intensive confinement, and using housing, feeding and management techniques that minimize labor costs and maximize output and profit. Factory farming is associated with the use of Concentrated Animal Feeding Operations (CAFOs). CAFO is the term used by United States regulatory agencies (as well as producers) for facilities in which animals are confined without access to grazing or range land. CAFOs are an integral part of the agribusiness model in countries with high levels of food production and have, in many places, almost completely replaced the traditional family farm. The evolution from family farm to CAFO is a contemporary fact in the production of food from animals in the United States and other countries with significant agribusiness concerns. Intensive confinement practices are now seen in many parts of the world, including Mexico, the Philippines,[9] Poland,[10] and beyond.[11] The growing number of CAFOs has increased both the numbers of animals raised internationally and the global concerns about humane treatment of those animals. Thus, an important focus for this chapter, and for anyone concerned about the welfare of animals, must be farmed animals.[12]

In addition to the animal welfare concerns that are discussed in detail below, large-scale animal farming operations generate massive environmental impacts. According to the United Nations' Food and Agriculture Organization (FAO), "[t]he livestock sector emerges as one of the top two or three most significant contributors to the worst environmental problems, at every scale from local to global.... Livestock's contribution to environmental problems is on a massive scale.... The impact is so significant that it needs to be addressed with urgency."[13] These environmental impacts can be classified into five different categories: threats to public health, pollution of air and water, depletion of natural resources, emission of greenhouse gases, and diminution of biodiversity. Because these impacts are not directly related to animal welfare, we discuss them only briefly to familiarize the reader with the environmental effects of factory farms.

First, factory farms create significant threats to public health because the confinement of tens or hundreds of thousands of animals increases the potential for disease. Confining animals in close, often filthy, quarters raises the likelihood that animals will spread diseases, some of which are zoonotic (transmissible from animals to humans). One study found a variety of public health concerns associated with industrial farmed animal production, including

> heightened risks of pathogens (disease- and nondisease-causing) passed from animals to humans; the emergence of microbes resistant to antibiotics and antimicrobials, due in large part to widespread use of antimicrobials for nontherapeutic purposes; food-borne disease; worker health concerns; and dispersed impacts on the adjacent community at large.[14]

Second, factory farms pollute the air and water as animals generate endless amounts of solid, liquid, and gaseous wastes, all of which override the natural environment's ability to process these products or the results of their breakdown. According to the FAO, "[l]ivestock excreta contain a considerable amount of nutrients (nitrogen, phosphorous, potassium), drug residues, heavy metals and pathogens. If these get into the water or accumulate in the soil, they can pose serious threats to the environment."[15] The waste from pigs "contains a host of [] toxic substances: ammonia, methane, hydrogen sulfide, carbon monoxide, cyanide, phosphorous, nitrates and heavy metals. In addition, the waste nurses more than 100 microbial pathogens that can cause illness in humans, including salmonella, cryptosporidium, streptococci and giardia."[16] Factory farms pollute the air as well as the water. Emissions from factory farms include such pollutants as carbon monoxide, chlorofluorocarbons, ammonia, nitrogen oxides, sulfur dioxide, and volatile organic compounds, "many of which degrade the quality of the air for all terrestrial life."[17]

Third, factory farms use significant amounts of resources, including water and grain. Animals drink significant water as a physiological requirement, and their intensive confinement also necessitates the use of large amounts water for a variety of tasks, such as cleaning machinery, hosing off animals, and flushing out production areas. According to the FAO, "[l]ivestock's use of water and contribution to water depletion trends are high and growing. An increasing amount of water is needed to meet growing water requirements in the livestock production process, from feed production to product supply."[18] Intensive confinement operations also require large amounts of purchased grain input because the factory farmed animals cannot engage in normal activities such as foraging or grazing. Thirty-five percent of the grain grown worldwide goes to feed livestock.[19] The expansion of factory farming has exacerbated land degradation and contributed to widespread deforestation and desertification.[20]

Fourth, factory farms contribute substantially to global climate change. Intensive confinement methods of farmed animal production contribute large amounts of carbon dioxide, methane, and nitrous oxide—the three most significant greenhouse gases—to the atmosphere.[21] The FAO describes animal agriculture's contribution to climate change as "enormous."[22] Livestock production contributes more greenhouse gases "than the transportation sector worldwide. Livestock contribute about 9 percent of total carbon dioxide emissions, but 37 percent of methane and 65 percent of nitrous oxide."[23] Thus, the implications of raising and slaughtering animals on such a colossal scale have significant repercussions globally. Even countries not engaged in large-scale factory farming will be affected when the global ecosystem is significantly damaged by climate change.

Finally, factory farms undermine biological diversity by facilitating the destruction of natural habitat, emitting pollution, accelerating climate change, introducing invasive species, and overexploiting natural resources. The FAO reports that "[l]ivestock play an important role in the current biodiversity crisis, as they contribute directly or indirectly to all these drivers of biodiversity loss, at the local and global level."[24] These major interventions in the global environment, such as the clear-cutting of rainforests to grow grain for livestock, have pushed numerous species to the brink of extinction.[25]

Many countries have laws governing each of these environmental dangers. Such laws can protect the public health, regulate pollution, limit resource use, cap greenhouse gas emissions, and protect threatened and endangered species.[26] These areas are often the subject of complex regulatory structures and detailed scientific debate. Regulations and statutes delineate the degree to which factory farms can permissibly discharge animal wastes, based on the amount and concentration of the strongest and most harmful components of the waste products. Large factory farms often cannot comply with the regulations, simply because the volume of waste (solid and gaseous) produced far exceeds current ability to disseminate or spread it over any area.

These environmental laws may be used to shut down or modify the practices of factory farms that are unable to safely manage their waste. For example, in the state of New York, the Humane Society of the United States (HSUS) successfully sued a *foie gras* producer, alleging that it violated the federal Clean Water Act more than 1,000 times by discharging disease-laden duck manure into local rivers and streams.[27] HSUS has also sued egg farms for polluting the air and water.[28] If punishment is meted out for these violations, it could send a message to industry that the current methods of mass production are unacceptable. Thus, if these actions are successful there will be an indirect impact on the welfare of the animals involved, but ultimately there may not be a significant effect on the way the animals are treated. That is the case because a successful legal challenge may simply result in an abatement of the waste, not necessarily a change in how the facility processes and manages the animals under its care. If the problems are bad enough and the penalties high enough, however, cases like these may force producers to move away from the most restrictive confinement models. Such suits also serve as a good platform for educating the public—and legislators—about the cruelty inherent in the common practices that are not often unknown and even invisible to the public.[29]

As discussed above, greenhouse gas emissions from factory farms are a serious contributor to climate change, and countries have been looking at ways to curb these emissions through various creative strategies. In order to meet its obligations under the Kyoto Treaty,[30] New Zealand considered a "gas tax" on sheep and cattle farmers for the amount of noxious gases emitted by their animals. Agricultural gas emissions, in the form of methane gas expelled by sheep and cows, have been measured to comprise about eighteen percent of dangerous greenhouse gases worldwide.[31] The percentage of greenhouse gases varies from country to country. As of 2005, "[l]arge-scale livestock production operations [were] responsible for twenty-five percent of methane emissions in the United States."[32] In New Zealand, livestock contributes "fifty percent of the country's total greenhouse gas emissions and ninety percent of its methane emissions."[33]

Outside of the environmental laws, there has been a growing trend to change the laws governing the actual treatment of animals in agriculture production. There is some public resistance to this movement based in part on a false sense of security regarding the state of the law affecting animals. Most people believe that animals are already given sufficient protections under the law, and that those safeguards should alleviate any concerns. This is categorically not true and in fact the opposite is generally the case. In the United States, farmed animals are subjected to acts that would clearly constitute animal cruelty if committed upon other animals. Yet there are no federal laws specifically governing the welfare of the animals who are being raised for food or clothing. Each American state has a general anti-cruelty law, governing the treatment of animals, but in over thirty of the fifty American states, those laws do not apply to animals used for commercial purposes. Thus, the international dichotomies and contrasts which represent a theme throughout this text are also seen *intra*nationally, between different species and based on cultural and societal taboos, morals and decisions ingrained in the popular consciousness. Rather than being based on a scientific distinction, such as a determination that a given species or group of animals does not feel or experience pain or does not suffer, the differential treatment is based almost solely on the notion that humans' desire to use these animals justifies the hardships they might experience in order to provide the products for which they are intended.

There has a been a concerted effort to add new laws protecting farmed animals, remove the existing exemptions for them, or utilize preexisting laws (whether anticruelty laws or others) in order to change or challenge the practices of the animal agriculture industry. The objective is to obtain better treatment for all animals, particularly those subjected to the most severe abuses.

The most active efforts have been made in the United States, the United Kingdom, and the European Union (EU). The widest-ranging actualized changes have been put in place by the EU and its member countries. The EU has actually established a binding Protocol that recognizes animals as sentient beings.[34] As a corollary to that declaration, the Protocol requires that the EU and its member states "pay full regard" to issues of animal welfare when implementing animal agricultural, transport and research policies.[35]

In contrast, in the United States, as of 2011 the only federal laws that even touch on farmed animals were the Humane Methods of Slaughter Act (HMSA)[36] and the "Twenty-Eight Hour Law."[37] Advocates work to change practices through legislation, and such efforts are occasionally promising (see discussion of horse slaughter for human consumption *infra*), as is the litigation frequently employed in the U.S. to address the treatment of animals in agribusiness.

Transport

The European Convention for the Protection of Animals During International Transport[38] covers the treatment of all commercially-transported vertebrates who are transported to or from countries outside of the EU. (This Convention does not cover intra-EU transport.) The Convention's rules, revised in 2006, provide a set of standards for travel that are aimed at ensuring efficient transport and some degree of protection for animals. At the same time, the rules allow for practices the drafters deemed appropriate for the industry, including the use of electric prods and other devices. Animals can still be subjected to extended transport that may cause them pain and suffering. Many of the provisions leave much discretion to the transporters or may be extremely difficult to enforce.

These treaties combine and form part of the EU law, discussed in greater detail later in the chapter, that governs farmed animals, beginning with their lives on the farm, going through transport and slaughter. Typically targeted practices internationally include "battery cages" for egg-laying hens, crates for veal calves, and gestation crates for pregnant sows.

Chickens

A variety of species are raised for commercial use in the United States, but roughly ninety percent of the animals killed are birds, particularly chickens, who are used for both meat and egg production. A similar breakdown in percentage is seen around the world.

Laying Hens[39]

Chickens used in egg production on factory farms endure a level of suffering that is great in magnitude and intensity. Worldwide, approximately five billion hens are used for egg production, at least three billion of whom are confined to "battery cages."[40] Battery cages are a form of high-volume, extreme confinement. The standard battery cage houses up to ten chickens, who live their entire lives on barren wire; each hen has approximately sixty-seven square inches of space, less than a letter-sized sheet of notebook paper.[41] At the typical factory farm, battery cages are stacked side by side, several cages high in long rows in windowless buildings. Tens of thousands of chickens can occupy a single building, and a single factory farm may contain millions of laying hens.[42]

These crowded conditions prevent hens from even turning around or spreading their wings. They are deprived of virtually every aspect of natural behavior: battery cage hens never see the outdoors and never walk on the ground. They cannot hunt for food, "dust bathe," establish social relationships, or build nests, all of which hens will do in the wild or when liberated from battery cages to sanctuaries. Battery caged chickens are almost completely restricted in their ability to move, and get so little exercise that they suffer from severe physical abnormalities due to lack of exercise. There are unquestionably severe psychological effects from the confinement as well.

The close confinement of hens in battery cages disturbs the natural pecking order that hens establish in wild social groups. In an open space, a hen who is lower on the pecking order can escape the pecking of a higher hen by fleeing the conflict. Flight from conflict is not an option in a small wire cage, though, so battery cage hens often peck each other to death or resort to cannibalism.[43] To avoid these pecking deaths, the beaks of female chicks are "trimmed" on factory farms—a process by which ⅓ to ⅔ of a hen's beak is sliced off with a hot blade without anesthesia.[44] Chickens' beaks contain sensitive nerve endings and sensory receptors so that removing the beak tip is exceedingly painful.[45] In addition to the acute pain of slicing off a hen's beak, the practice of debeaking eliminates her ability to eat normally and severely impairs her ability to touch, taste, perceive temperature, and pick up objects.[46] For these reasons, this technique leads to a lifetime of physical and mental problems.[47]

"Forced molting" is another common practice in the egg industry. Molting is the natural process of losing feathers that birds undergo annually, usually in the fall. This process enables wild birds to replace their feathers and to time their egg-laying in a way that increases the likelihood of their chicks' survival. This biological process is manipulated on factory farms, where "forced molting" is used to gain control of hens' reproductive systems. Forced molting stimulates a new cycle of egg-laying and increases the commercial quality and quantity of eggs. The forced molting process consists of depriving chickens of all food, and often light and water, for up to two weeks. Food deprivation shocks hens' systems and light deprivation induces instinctual confusion about the seasons, thus forcing the flock to molt simultaneously.

Some countries have begun to address these conditions. In 1981 Switzerland established new requirements for the housing of chickens.[48] By law, Swiss farmers must give groups of forty or more hens "access to perches and nest boxes and a minimum of 120 square inches of wire-grid floor speech each."[49] These requirements, which went into effect in 1991, effectively eliminated battery cages in Switzerland and have made aviaries the most common method of raising hens in Switzerland.[50]

The European Union has also taken steps to improve the welfare of laying hens by changing their housing conditions under the Hens Directive, which it passed in 1999.[51] The Directive reflects the European Commission's conclusion "that the welfare conditions of hens kept in current battery cages and in other systems of rearing are inadequate and that certain of their needs cannot be met in such cages."[52]

The Hens Directive distinguishes three rearing systems for laying hens: non-enriched cages, enriched cages, and non-cage systems (referred to as "alternative systems"). Non-enriched cage systems consist of barren wire cages, but the Hens Directive requires that these cages provide at least 550 cm^2 per hen. By January 2012, these systems must be phased out completely.[53] Enriched cage systems are marginally better than battery cages, and must provide each laying bird at least 750 cm^2 of cage space, a nest, litter for pecking and scratching, unrestricted access to a feed trough, and perching space of fifteen centimeters per hen.[54] Alternative or non-cage systems must have a stocking density no greater than nine hens per square meter of usable space and must provide adequate perches and at least one nest for every seven hens.[55] A separate directive requires all egg producers to label their egg cartons to identify the method of production used.[56]

Although the Hens Directive generally prohibits mutilation of hens, it does not prohibit debeaking; in fact, it explicitly permits states to authorize the practice on hens who are younger than ten days old.[57] In England, implementing regulations for this Directive originally allowed beak trimming up to December 31, 2010, at which point a complete ban was supposed to be in effect.[58] Subsequently, an independent government advisory body suggested the ban should be indefinitely delayed, citing the potential for "injurious pecking."[59] The ban on debeaking was ultimately delayed, and is now scheduled to go into effect in 2016.[60]

In November 2008, citizens of the state of California passed the Prevention of Farm Animal Cruelty Act, which bans the use of battery cages for chickens, as well as the confinement of pigs in gestation crates and calves in veal crates.[61] The law, which goes into effect in 2015, actually makes the use of battery cages a criminal offense.[62] Battery cages have been the subject of proposed legislation in several other American states.

Litigation involving battery cages has taken various forms in the U.S. In California, a lawsuit was brought challenging the state's involvement with the use of battery cages. Plaintiffs alleged that the state of California provided tax subsidies to factory farms for the purchase of battery cages and alleged that this conduct was an illegal use of state funds.[63] In the state of Pennsylvania, humane agents (officials working for animal control agencies) initiated a criminal case against an egg producer for animal cruelty after an undercover investigation documented laying hens in cruel and inhumane conditions. The defendant was ultimately acquitted of all charges.[64]

Australia and New Zealand have also reformed the battery cage industry and have effected some minimal change. The Australian State and Territory governments increased the minimum cage size by 100 cm^2 in 2000; the same was done in New Zealand in 2007, increasing the cage size from 450 to 550 cm^2.[65] Further changes are also possible, including a possible elimination of battery cages at some point.[66]

Broiler Chickens

Consumption of chicken meat in the United States has skyrocketed in the past half century.[67] It has been reported that in 2000 "the average American was eating over a hundred times more chicken" than in the 1920s.[68] The same growth has occurred throughout the world. Global production and consumption of chicken meat has increased drastically in the last few decades. The number of chickens slaughtered for meat (known as "broilers") jumped from approximately seven billion in 1962 to more than fifty billion in 2007, a six-fold increase.[69] In the 1950s in Great Britain, the average person consumed less than a kilogram (2.2 pounds) of chicken each year; now the average person eats almost two kilograms each month—for a total of approximately twenty-three kilograms per year.[70] In China, chicken consumption quadrupled between 1987 and 1995, and in 2007, China slaughtered 7.7 billion chickens, making China the world's second leading broiler producer, after the United States.[71] Significant increases in broiler production have also occurred in Brazil, Indonesia, and India.[72]

The chicken industry is a prime example of the transition from small farms to factory farms. In the United States, "[t]he broiler industry has evolved from millions of small backyard flocks of dual-purpose (eggs and meat) chickens in the early 1900s to less than 50 highly specialized, vertically integrated agribusiness firms."[73] The United States Department of Agriculture (USDA) has called the broiler industry "one of the success stories in American agriculture during the last century and is an example of how the use of technology, improvements in production practices, and product marketing can change the basic structure of agriculture."[74] In fact, "[t]he broiler industry set the blueprint for the vertical and horizontal integration that occurred in the egg industry in the 1960s and more recently in the pork and beef industries."[75] Australia followed a similar trajectory after it "embraced the United States' broiler integration model" in the 1950s.[76] In the decades since then, "the Australian industry [has] swiftly transformed from a system of backyard producers and family farms to intensive highly mechanized commercial operations," with only three companies controlling eighty percent of the broiler market.[77]

The same practices lauded by the USDA have resulted in severe compromises of animal welfare.[78] Selective breeding has resulted in birds who cannot, and do not, live without pain. The genetic selection engaged in by industry scientists has led to chickens who grow so quickly that the parts of their bodies destined to become meat (such as their breasts) overwhelm other sensitive tissue and organs, causing suffering and injury.[79] This accelerated growth means that broiler chickens live less than two months, as opposed to the six to seven year natural lifespan of a chicken. These animals are slaughtered when they reach six or seven *weeks* of age.[80] Many broilers die of various diseases during production as a result of this genetic manipulation.[81] The facilities in which broilers are raised also compromise their welfare. These "grower houses" are long, warehouse-like sheds, usually windowless, where up to 20,000 birds are tightly confined, sometimes with no more room than battery cage hens.[82] Like battery cage facilities, grower houses prevent broiler chickens from engaging in natural behaviors such as foraging or even stretching their wings.[83] The accumulation of chicken waste in grower houses creates high levels of toxic ammonia gas, which damages the chickens' acute sense of smell and injures other sensitive membranes, including birds' eyes and respiratory systems.

Broilers suffer greatly during transport from the farm to the slaughterhouse, which can take as long as several days. Chickens are loaded onto trucks with little regard for their welfare; birds are grabbed, inverted, and thrown into crates, often carelessly and in a manner that causes them both fear and physical pain.[84] Once they are loaded onto trucks or railcars, they are transported long distances, usually exposed to extreme weather and the stress of busy highways. Many chickens do not survive transport.

Once they arrive at the slaughterhouse, broilers are shackled upside down, passed through an electric stunning tank that immobilizes them but may not render them unconscious, and then have their throats slit, bleeding to death. Every stage of this process can cause significant physical and psychological suffering.

Despite (or perhaps because of) the staggering number of broiler chickens slaughtered in the world (fifty billion) and the severe suffering they endure, there are very few laws that protect the welfare of these birds anywhere in the world.

In the United States, there are essentially no limits on how farmers can treat the broilers on their farms. Broilers are excluded from the minimal protections afforded to other farmed animals during transportation and slaughter. Although federal law requires anyone transporting "animals" to unload them for food, water, and rest every twenty-eight hours, the United States Department of Agriculture (the agency tasked with enforcing the law) takes the position that chickens are not "animals" and are therefore not covered by the law.[85] Similarly, chickens are not considered "livestock" for purposes of the Humane Methods of Slaughter Act, which means they do not have to be "rendered insensible to pain" before they are slaughtered.[86] As a result, chickens receive almost no legal protection at the time of their slaughter when they are part of the meat or egg production process.

Broilers in the EU are covered by the Broilers Directive, enacted in 2007, which set some standards for the confinement of these chickens.[87] The Directive does not apply to facilities with less than 500 chickens, or those that house only breeding chickens or hatchlings and eggs.[88] The drafters of the Directive recognized the "[un]satisfactory level of animal welfare and health" caused by the fast growth strains of chickens being used for meat, as well as the problems created by poor indoor climate conditions and housing.[89] The Directive sets a maximum "stocking density" to limit crowding. The Directive allows a range of 33 to 42 kilograms per square meter of chickens.[90] In other words, the broilers are considered in terms of their maximum weight (which is usually about 2.2 kilograms at the time of slaughter), and the number of chickens that can be placed in a space is based on that weight and the space they are allocated. Factory farm owners are allowed to increase the stocking density if they can keep the mortality rate of chickens down.

The Directive also places some requirements on other conditions for the chickens' treatment. For example, there must be a period of rest with the lights off; fresh litter must be placed on a regular basis, and their housing must be properly ventilated to reduce the chance of toxic reactions to the ammonia fumes. Seriously injured birds must be treated or humanely euthanized. The

Directive also established a set of training and certification requirement for all those in the broiler business. Detailed records focused on animal welfare must be kept, and twice-daily checks on the animals are required.[91]

Chickens receive minimal protection, even compared to other animals. One reason is their species: there is a general societal belief that birds are different than other animals, and that they do not experience pain and suffering in the same way (despite scientific evidence to the contrary). Regardless of the veracity of this belief, many people simply do not have the sympathy for chickens that they have for cows or pigs. Another reason for the paucity of legal protections for chickens is economic. Given the enormous number of chickens used for their eggs and meat, establishing meaningful regulations would significantly affect the industry's bottom line. In the United States alone, ninety percent of the animals slaughtered are chickens who are exempted from animal protection laws; regulating these birds' lives and deaths would costs vast amounts of money, and the agribusiness lobby has worked hard to keep these animals legally uncovered. There are also international issues at stake: as discussed in Chapter 6, countries who are parties to international trade agreements such as the WTO worry that refusing animal product imports that do not meet humane standards may subject them to trade sanctions.[92] For example, the Broilers Directive was weaker than it otherwise might have been because of "the widely held belief that WTO rules prevent the EU from restricting imports on welfare grounds."[93] The EU was also concerned that "if EU farmers were compelled by law to meet good welfare standards, they would be undercut by lower welfare imports."[94]

Ducks and Geese

Ducks and geese are raised for their meat, fat, and feathers. Those uses are generally governed by the same laws that govern chickens and other birds. In the United States, for example, ducks and geese are excluded (like chickens) from the laws that protect animals during transportation and slaughter. There is one area, however, in which ducks and geese have received significant attention: the production of *foie gras*, which is the fattened liver of a duck or goose.

Foie gras is produced by fattening geese or ducks through a prolonged process of daily force-feeding, also known as "gavage." Force-feeding is performed by inserting a funnel attached to a feeding tube into the bird's throat. The food, typically a corn mash, is then deposited directly into the bird's crop, where food is stored prior to deposit in the stomach. Depending on the size and species of the bird, gavage is performed two to four times a day for a period of ten days to five weeks. Eventually, the birds' livers become grossly enlarged, swelling to as much as twelve times normal size. The birds are then slaughtered, and the livers are sold commercially.[95]

Force-feeding causes the development of liver disease, decreased liver function, a pathologically enlarged liver, and excessive weight gain in the bird's abdomen, which may prevent the animals from being able to move around normally.[96] The insertion of the feeding tube and the gavage practice may also scratch and wound the bird's esophagus, causing infection and, in some cases, death.[97] In 1992, birds seized from a U.S. *foie gras* facility had chronic heart disease, trauma to the esophagus, liver disease and related catastrophic health problems. Dead birds were removed from the facility with food filling their throats and spilling out of their mouths and nostrils.

The consumption of *foie gras* may jeopardize human health as well; one study linked *foie gras* consumption with rheumatoid arthritis and tuberculosis.[98]

There is no ban on *foie gras* under French law, and its supporters view the food as an important aspect of French culinary and cultural tradition. They also deny that the gavage method is cruel.[99] Migratory waterfowl such as ducks and geese naturally ingest a large amount of food and gain weight before their migrations. *Foie gras* defenders contend that force-feeding merely mimics this natural process[100]; they also argue that the force-feeding process is not uncomfortable or painful for geese and ducks because they lack a gag reflex and have a large flexible esophagus.[101] Producers claim they have a right to farm and engage in a livelihood and insist on the consumer's right to *foie gras*.[102]

Other countries in the European Union have recommended against the use of force-feeding techniques. The European Convention for the Protection of Animals Kept for Farming Purposes, an agreement among EU nations, states that "[n]o animal shall be provided with food or liquid in a manner ... which may cause unnecessary suffering or injury."[103] In 1999, the Standing Committee of this convention recommended that EU nations refrain from initiating *foie gras* production in countries where no industry exists, but it exempts countries that had production facilities at the time.[104] It recommends "[c]ountries allowing *foie gras* production [to] encourage research on its welfare aspects and on alternative methods which do not include gavage."[105] The Recommendation has been ratified by thirty countries (including France) and the European Union.[106]

Force-feeding has been banned in many individual European Union countries. Poland,[107] Denmark,[108] Sweden,[109] Norway,[110] Finland,[111] Switzerland,[112] Luxembourg,[113] the Czech Republic,[114] Germany,[115] Italy,[116] and the United Kingdom[117] have all either enacted explicit provisions prohibiting force feeding or interpreted their general animal protection laws to prohibit force feeding for non-medical purposes. Of Austria's nine provinces, six have explicitly banned force feeding.[118] However, because the vast majority of these countries have never produced *foie gras*, the bans have not had a significant impact on reducing the number of ducks and geese raised for *foie gras* production. *Foie gras* is still commercially produced in Belgium, Bulgaria, Spain, France, and Hungary.[119]

Foie gras has proved controversial in other parts of the world as well. In 1999, Israeli animal advocacy organizations petitioned the High Court for a ruling that the force-feeding of geese was forbidden under Israeli law.[120] At the time, Israel was the world's fourth-largest producer of *foie gras*, with its industry generating more than five hundred tons every year.[121] "According to industry sources, at least 600 families depended on *foie gras* production for their livelihoods."[122] *Foie gras* was a state-supported enterprise with significant cultural importance and economic benefits. Despite these barriers, the Israeli Supreme Court held that the force-feeding of geese was unjustifiably cruel, with one justice opining that the practice constituted a "degradation of man's own dignity."[123]

Like their Israeli counterparts, animal advocates in the United States have used litigation to challenge *foie gras* production. Although the United States has not historically been a large *foie gras* producer, this has been changing. In 2003, it produced an estimated 340 tons of *foie gras*.[124] Total American consumption was estimated to be 420 tons that year.[125] As of 2008, there were reportedly two main producers in the United States: Hudson Valley Foie Gras in New York and Sonoma Foie Gras in California.[126]

In 2006, the Humane Society of the United States (HSUS) sued the state of New York, seeking to compel the state's agricultural agency to declare *foie gras* an adulterated (and therefore illegal) food product.[127] A New York state food safety law requires the classification of food as "adulterated" if it is from a diseased animal.[128] The trial court dismissed HSUS' complaint, holding that HSUS did not have standing and had not properly stated a legal claim.

This was just one of several actions brought by HSUS with respect to *foie gras* in New York. As mentioned earlier in the chapter, it also sued Hudson Valley *Foie Gras* directly for violating the federal Clean Water Act, alleging more than 1,100 documented violations.[129] These violations resulted from a "manure lagoon" that contained fecal excrement from the 250,000 ducks who were warehoused at the farm.[130] In response, New York fined the facility for hundreds of violations of the Clean Water Act. HSUS also sought to have another New York *foie gras* producer, La Belle, criminally prosecuted for animal cruelty; the local authorities refused to pursue criminal charges, despite extensive documentation of animal suffering.

At the federal level, HSUS, along with the Animal Legal Defense Fund, Farm Sanctuary, and New York University Law School's Student Animal Legal Defense Fund, filed a similar "adulteration" complaint with the United States Department of Agriculture's Food Safety and Inspection Service, asking the agency to declare *foie gras* adulterated because it is a diseased food product.[131] The USDA had not yet responded to the petition when this book went to press.

Animal advocates have pursued litigation in California as well. In 2003, after activists filmed and rescued suffering birds from Sonoma Foie Gras, both sides filed legal actions. The activist groups argued that *foie gras* production violated the state's anticruelty law and sought to stop the production; the *foie gras* producer alleged that the activists had trespassed on his property and harassed him and his family, and sought criminal and civil remedies. While these lawsuits were pending, the California legislature passed a bill to ban the production and sale of *foie gras* in the state, beginning in 2012.[132] The controversy surrounding the issue made it unlikely that the bill would have passed without incorporation of this "grace period." The bill also included a provision that immunized Sonoma Foie Gras from lawsuits related to animal cruelty, thus nullifying the pending lawsuit.[133]

Foie gras legislation has also passed at the local level. In 2006, the City Council of Chicago, Illinois enacted an ordinance banning the sale of *foie gras* by Chicago restaurants, supermarkets, or other vendors.[134] While some claimed the ban was a significant step forward for animal welfare in general and for Chicago as a model for humane legislation, the ordinance provoked predictable outrage from the Chicago restaurant community. Soon after enactment of the ban, opponents sued, alleging that the city had exceeded its authority under the Illinois Constitution and violated the Commerce Clause of the United States Constitution.[135]

The city of Chicago defended the ordinance by asserting that it was offering optimal dining options while honoring concerns about ethical treatment of animals.[136] The court upheld the ordinance because it reflected "the City Council's judgment that banning the sale of *foie gras* would benefit the City and advance the morals of the community."[137] It was therefore legal as a valid exercise of the city's home rule powers under the Illinois Constitution because it regulated food served and sold in the city. The court also found no violation of the federal Constitution. On May 14, 2008, two years after it had voted to ban *foie gras*, the Chicago City Council voted to repeal the ordinance.[138]

Pigs

Every year more than one billion pigs are slaughtered for food worldwide.[139] Most of these pigs are raised in intensive confinement on factory farms, and we discuss some of these conditions below. But we begin our discussion of the use of pigs by focusing on the conditions of confinement for female pigs (sows) used for breeding. In the United States alone, six million breeding sows are confined in "gestation crates" and "farrowing crates." These crates, also known as "sow stalls," are seven-foot-by-two-foot enclosures with cement floors and metal bars on the ends and sides. The sows cannot turn around, walk forward or backward, or engage in natural and instinctive activities such as foraging, rooting, and nest building. These barren crates provide sows with no stimulation or enrichment, and as a result, the sows suffer from the constant boredom that afflicts any intelligent species when confronted with such deprivation. The documented effects of gestation crate confinement include depression and other psychological problems, which can be manifested by behaviors such as biting of the bars of their enclosures, prolonged repetitive waving of their heads, obsessive licking, and "vacuum chewing" where the animals simulate chewing for extended periods of time.[140] In addition to these psychological problems, confinement in gestation crates can also result in physical problems, especially given the large size of the sows' bodies and their complete lack of exercise.

These breeding sows are kept in a constant state of repeated reproduction, with each pregnancy cycle followed by the nursing and weaning period, followed by another pregnancy cycle, in order to produce the maximum yield of piglets in the shortest amount of time. For the entirety of the pig's adult life she is confined to a crate, giving birth an average of 2.5 times a year.[141] Shortly before giving birth, the sows are moved from gestation crates to farrowing crates. Slightly wider, farrowing crates contain small areas outside the crate where piglets can nurse. During the farrowing period, the sows are denied all normal nurturing and mothering behaviors, with the sole exception of nursing. The piglets are able to access only the nipples of their mother, who lies on her side in the farrowing crate. Once the young pigs are weaned, they are shipped off to other facilities to grow into pigs of sufficient size for slaughter, or as replacement breeding sows. Their mothers are returned to the cycle of reproduction until they reach their maximum breeding age at which point they too are killed.

Non-breeding pigs who are raised for meat also endure a variety of procedures aimed at facilitating their industrial use. For example, the practice of "tail docking," the removal of unanesthetized piglets' tails, is standard industry practice.[142] The reasons for tail docking are similar to those for debeaking battery hens: close confinement encourages aggression and eliminates the subordinate animal's ability to escape. As a result, closely confined pigs will bite each others' tails, which can cause painful injuries and potential infection if untreated.[143] Some animal husbandry experts justify the practice by claiming that it is necessary to spare pigs the pain and suffering that tail-biting causes. Animal welfare experts respond that it is the intensive confinement, and the concomitant restrictions of pigs' natural behaviors, that causes tail-biting in the first place.[144] Other significant industry practices include unanesthetized needle teeth trimming,[145] tusk trimming of boars,[146] ear notching,[147] and castration of newborn pigs.[148]

Some countries are beginning to address the concerns about the welfare of pigs raised for meat. In 1991, the European Union issued its first directive to substantively deal with the issue.[149] The 1991 Directive required pig farmers to provide pigs with adequate heating, ventilation, lighting (artificial or natural), food, water, and veterinary care.[150] It required that each pig be able to "lie down, rest and stand up without difficulty; have a clean place in which [he or she] can rest; [and] see other pigs."[151] The Directive prohibited the construction of new facilities that tether sows, and banned tethering outright, effective in 2006.[152]

In 2001, the EU amended the Directive to more specifically address gestation crates. The Directive explicitly acknowledged that "[s]ows prefer to have social interactions with other pigs when provided with freedom of movement and environmental complexity" and that this fact made it necessary to prohibit "[t]he current practice of keeping sows in continuous close confinement."[153] The Directive prohibited the construction of new gestation crate facilities after 2002, but it gave the pork industry until 2013 to phase out most uses of gestation crates.[154] Group housing is required for all sows as of that point in time. Sows may still be confined to gestation crates during the first four weeks of their pregnancies and during the week before they give birth.[155]

The 2001 amendments to the Directive also required that pregnant sows be given high-fiber and high-energy foods to ensure adequate nutrition during this period of increased need, and that they must have access to the food, even when competitors are present.[156] In addition, it mandated that each pregnant sow must have at least 1.3 square meters of continuous solid floor as part of their housing and 2.25 square meters of floor area in which she can move.[157]

In a separate 2001 amendment to the 1991 Directive, the EU addressed conditions for non-breeding pigs, establishing more objective and measurable welfare requirements and rearticulating the 1991 requirements pertaining to noise, light, feeding, and housing.[158] The amendments also acknowledged that "[t]ail docking, tooth clipping and tooth grinding are likely to cause immediate pain and some prolonged pain to pigs" and that "[c]astration is likely to cause prolonged pain which is worse if there is tearing of the tissues."[159] Accordingly, the amendments prohibited non-therapeutic procedures that "result[] in damage to or the loss of a sensitive part of the body," including routine tail docking and clipping of teeth.[160] The amendments did not completely ban these practices, however; tail docking and teeth reductions may be performed "where there is evidence that injuries to sows' teats or to other pigs' ears or tails have occurred" and after the producer has considered alternatives to these practices.[161] Producers are prohibited from castrating or tail-docking pigs who are older than seven days unless they use anesthetics. The amendments also paid at least some consideration to pigs' natural behavior by requiring they be given "permanent access to a sufficient quantity of material to enable proper investigation and manipulation activities."[162]

In 2008, the EU superseded the 1991 Directive by incorporating and codifying all the amendments into a single document, which is currently the operative Directive.[163]

These changes in acceptable practices in the EU may create pressure to change welfare standards in other countries, particularly countries which depend on the EU economically. For example, "recently the pork industry [in Australia] initiated a review of the Pig Code based on their concern over changes to welfare practices and especially the continued acceptability of sow stalls in the European Union, the United Kingdom and in New Zealand."[164] It will still take some time to determine whether the EU's reforms will actually have a broader effect in other countries.

New Zealand's Pork Industry Board was involved in the preparation of its welfare code for pigs. Welfare codes play an important role in animal cruelty law in New Zealand because they provide exemptions to the Animal Welfare Act's general prohibition of animal cruelty, and thus the codes act against animals' best interests. When welfare codes adopt standard industry practices, as has been done for pigs in New Zealand, they sanction a wide variety of practices that would otherwise be considered cruel under the law. The Pig Code of Welfare, for example, allows for the use of gestation and farrowing crates.[165] Despite the inherent problems of these confinement systems, New Zealand has defended this decision by stating that "current alternatives to these systems do not guarantee better welfare for pigs and may, in fact, reduce the welfare of the sows and/or their piglets."[166]

Although gestation crates are widely used in the U.S., a trend has begun to end their use. In 2002, Florida voters approved an amendment to the state constitution to "limit the cruel and inhumane confinement of pigs" by prohibiting the use of gestation crates in the state.[167] The ban, which had a six-year phase-in period, passed by a wide margin, with fifty-five percent of voters approving the measure. In 2006, Arizona became the second state to ban gestation crates (and the first to ban veal crates for calves).[168] The Arizona measure, which also has a six-year phase-in period, passed with an overwhelming sixty-two percent of the vote. And in 2008, California voters approved a ban on gestation crates (as well as veal crates and battery cages).[169] This ban, which goes into effect in 2015, passed with more than sixty-three percent of the vote. While the Florida, Arizona, and California bans resulted from popular ballot initiatives, state legislatures have also acted to eliminate gestation crate use: in 2007, Oregon banned gestation crates, and in 2008 and 2009 respectively, the Colorado and Maine legislatures banned both gestation crates and veal crates.[170]

Litigation has also been used to challenge gestation crate confinement. Prior to the California vote, litigation played a significant role in shutting down the state's last gestation crate facility. In *Animal Legal Defense Fund v. Clougherty Packing Co.*, an animal protection organization and three consumers of pork sued the owner and operator of Southern California's Corcpork gestation crate facility and a pork producer and seller.[171] The suit alleged that the confinement of pregnant and nursing sows at the facility violated the state anti-cruelty law, which requires that confined animals be provided "with an adequate exercise area."[172] The case settled when the defendants agreed to close their facility and halt their use of gestation crates in California.

Outside of the legal context, the pig industry seems to be responding to a growing popular consensus opposed to cruelty. In January 2007, Smithfield Foods, America's largest pork producer, and Maple Leaf Farms, Canada's largest pork producer, announced that they would phase-out gestation crates over a ten-year period.

Cows

Cows are subjected to a number of commonly-challenged practices. A brief summary is provided here as an overview. Most of these practices are also discussed in more detail in this section.

1. Calves who are used for the production of veal are kept in restrictive confinement their entire lives;
2. Veal calves are also given special diets to assure the quality of their flesh for meat;
3. Infant dairy calves are removed from their mothers at birth and often shipped to other facilities for the first part of their lives, where they are kept in solitary confinement in order to manage their intake of food and drugs[173];
4. Cows are often given subtherapeutic levels of antibiotics in order to limit the potential spread of disease;
5. The intensive milking and crowding of dairy cows may lead to painful diseases such as mastitis and other infections;

6. Cows in production may receive regular injections of artificial growth hormones[174];
7. Tail-docking, which is painful when performed and during the healing period, is done without anesthesia. Once their tails are amputated, cows may be unable to protect themselves from insects;
8. Cropping (cutting) of cows' ears is done without anesthesia, despite the pain of performing the procedure as well as the pain of recovery;
9. Castration of male calves is performed routinely without anesthesia;
10. Cattle are branded with different techniques, all of which are painful;
11. Cows are transported for long periods in trucks without rest, water or food; and
12. Slaughterhouse practices cause extensive fright, pain and suffering—especially with respect to downed animals who cannot move, either because they are too sick, injured or fatigued to stand.

Veal Calves

Like all mammals, cows produce milk to feed their young, and they tend not to lactate unless they have recently given birth. Accordingly, in order to enable their dairy cows to continue producing the milk for human consumption, dairy farmers must force their cows to give birth every year. The female calves are retained as replacement dairy cows, while the male calves are sold to veal farmers.[175] "Unwanted" male calves are sent to auction or directly to slaughter.[176]

"White veal" calves are kept in the most stringent confinement conditions and receive the most unhealthy and unsupportive diet.[177] They are tethered in small wooden crates that prevent them from making virtually any movement or developing any muscle mass; the lack of normal muscle tissue makes the calves' flesh especially tender when they are killed and eaten. Most veal calves' diets are similarly devised to maintain white flesh; calves are fed a milk replacement formula deficient in iron that often causes them to become clinically anemic. The diet produces a lack of hemoglobin, a critical component of red blood cells (which would make the meat pink). The calves are given a steady stream of prophylactic, subtherapeutic antibiotics to ward off any potential opportunistic bacteria.[178] "Pink" or "red" veal calves are provided with a modified, slightly less restrictive confinement and a different diet, which gives their body tissue a healthier look and tone, producing a darker color.

In 1990, the United Kingdom banned the use of veal crates.[179] This ban, however, led UK calf farmers to export live calves to other European countries with lower standards of welfare.[180] This made a regional approach necessary. In 1997, the EU acknowledged "that calves should benefit from an environment corresponding to their needs as a herd-living species" and that "they should be reared in groups."[181] It therefore prohibited the new construction of veal crates, and provided a ten-year phase-out period for those crates then already in use.[182] In 2007, the directive's prohibition came into effect, and all veal crates were banned, subject to a few exceptions. The law still allows farmers to isolate calves in individual pens for the first eight weeks of their lives, but once the calves reach eight weeks of age, they must be kept in groups.[183] Since 1998, the deficient diet traditionally fed to veal calves (to keep their flesh white) has been prohibited by EU law.[184]

In the United States, Arizona, Colorado, and California, Maine, and Michigan have banned veal crates.[185] As with the pig industry, some of the large veal producers have also agreed to voluntarily phase-out veal crates.[186] In the 1980s, animal advocates tried to use litigation to put a stop to the use of veal crates and expose industry practices. In *Animal Legal Defense Fund [ALDF] Boston, Inc. v. Provimi Veal Corp.*, ALDF claimed that the defendant, a veal producer and seller, was engaging in animal cruelty, as well as misleading and confusing consumers by not disclosing the manner in which veal calves were raised.[187] ALDF sought an order directing Provimi Veal to inform consumers of the exact way in which it treated its calves. The court ruled against ALDF, holding that the organization lacked standing to enforce the anti-cruelty laws and that ALDF's attempt to force Provimi to change its labels was preempted by the federal labeling scheme for meat products.[188]

Cows Used for Dairy Products

In 2007, there were 245 million dairy cows in the world.[189] These animals are treated in a variety of ways, but animal welfare advocates have identified a subset of these practices that raise concerns with industrialized and traditional methods of raising cows for their milk. These include: tail docking, separation of infant calves and their mothers, prolonged tethering, serial pregnancies, branding,[190] and the use of subtherapeutic levels of antibiotic drugs to maintain health.[191] Additionally, dairy cows' flesh is used as meat once their milk productivity slows down. Thus, many of the welfare concerns associated with how cows are transported and slaughtered apply equally to dairy cows.

In the United States, it is increasingly common for dairy farmers to send their young dairy cows to be raised at "calf ranches." As discussed above, male calves are usually sold for veal, whereas female calves are often used to replenish the dairy herd once older cows' milk production decreases. These future dairy cows (and sometimes their male siblings) are taken from their mothers within a day of birth so that the milk that is intended for them can be sold for human consumption. The calves are trucked to the calf ranches, where they are denied all access to other cows and all ability to socialize and interact in a normal fashion. At these facilities, young calves (one to two days old) are isolated in highly restrictive enclosures for an extended period of time (60 to 180 days). According to the industry, this is done so that the calf ranchers can raise and "grow" the calves in the quickest and most efficient way, without concern for their social or mental development. Confinement allows specific monitoring of the calves' intake and output of food and supplements; keeps them from getting "injured" as a result of play behavior; and reduces the possibility of contagion transmission.

In *Animal Legal Defense Fund v. Mendes*, ALDF challenged the legality of the intensive confinement at one of these calf ranches in order to establish the illegal cruelty occurring on a daily basis.[192] As in *Animal Legal Defense Fund v. Clougherty Packing Co.*, the aforementioned gestation crate case, ALDF alleged that Mendes Calf Ranch confined calves (like the sows in *Clougherty Packing Co.*) in crates that violated California's requirement that enclosed animals have "an adequate exercise area."[193] The consumer-plaintiffs in the *Mendes* case also claimed that the milk producers had committed consumer fraud by selling a product that was the result of illegal conduct and not telling the consumers about that conduct. The plaintiffs had assumed that the products they purchased were produced in compliance with state laws, especially those related to the treatment of the animals whose products they were purchasing. Plaintiffs requested that the court order that the illegal conduct be stopped. Without ruling on the question of whether the intensive confinement of calves was illegal, the trial court held that ALDF and the individual consumer-plaintiffs did not have standing—the right to sue. The California Court of Appeals affirmed, and the California Supreme Court denied further review. This case is a good example of the outcome in many animal law cases; that is, the merits and substance of the alleged cruelty were never evaluated because the defendants were able to have the case dismissed on a strictly procedural basis.

India provides a good contrast to other countries in terms of its treatment of animals in general and cows in particular. India is home to a significant percentage of the world's human and livestock population. India's relationship with animals, particularly cows, is exceedingly complex, from both a spiritual/religious/cultural viewpoint as well as a legal one. There are many laws regarding the protection and treatment of its animals. As discussed in more detail in Chapter 6, India's Constitution provides protection for animals, making it "the fundamental duty of every citizen of India ... to have compassion for living creatures."[194]

India's legal protection of cows is usually assumed to be attributable to the historical protection provided by followers of Hinduism. A variety of laws have been enacted at the federal, state and local levels intended to ensure humane treatment. For example, Article 48 of the Indian Constitution recommends administration of "agriculture and animal husbandry on modern and scientific lines ... and prohibit[s] the slaughter of cows...."[195] Section 12 of the federal Prevention of Cruelty to Animals Act of 1960 prohibits any practice used to artificially stimulate milk production, in an effort to have more natural practices govern the animals.

The Indian Prevention of Cruelty to Animals Rules of 1978 also require commercial operations involving cows to register with the government. Registration is withheld unless the "registering authority is satisfied that ... the welfare of the cattle is adequately secured and that they are not likely to undergo any unnecessary suffering."[196] Furthermore, if the cows are being kept specifically for milk, the owner is required to prominently display a copy of the law Section 12, described above, regarding stimulation of milk production.[197]

Cows Used for Meat

Worldwide, approximately 300 million cows are slaughtered for meat each year.[198] There are numerous aspects of the beef production process that raise animal welfare issues, such as husbandry practices, long-distance transportation, and slaughter. These laws vary widely by country, and we discuss some of them below.

A large portion of India's population supports a prohibition on the killing of cows, but there are segments of Indian society that do wish to participate in the use of cows for beef (and dairy) practices. The Indian Constitution allows states to prohibit the slaughter of cows, even where failure to slaughter would impinge on individuals' rights to work and pursue a profession.[199]

Most states in India have passed laws prohibiting the slaughter of cows; for example, the Andhra Pradesh Prohibition of Cow Slaughter and Animal Preservation Act of 1977 specifically forbids the slaughter of cows and their calves.[200] Penalties for violations of the Act include up to six months imprisonment, or up to a 1,000 rupee fine, or both.[201] The Assam Cattle Preservation Act similarly forbids the slaughter of cattle in most cases.[202] Religious exemptions do exist, however: the Assam Act is "not [] applicable to slaughter of any cattle on the occasion of Id-uz-Zuha festival on such conditions as the State Government may specify."[203] The Delhi Agricultural Cattle Preservation Act of 1994 prohibits slaughter of cows as well as transport, purchase, sale or disposal of cows from Delhi for slaughter.[204] Even possession of the flesh of cows is prohibited.[205]

Although there is a nearly national ban, slaughter is not prohibited in the Indian states of West Bengal and Kerala. Therefore, cows and bulls raised across the country are herded or shipped by train to these states for slaughter. Specific laws cover this practice as well. The Transport of Animals Rules[206] apply specifically to the transport by rail of cattle; however, reports and footage demonstrate that these laws are not being followed or enforced.[207] Similarly, The Prevention of Cruelty to Animals Rules of 2001 include a section on herding transport which requires that animals be moved in typical social groups[208] and prohibit the use of whips or sticks during transport.[209] In addition to the illegal herding of cattle to slaughterhouses in Kerala and West Bengal, illegal slaughterhouses exist across the country.[210]

India is unique, with its legal proscriptions reflecting the prevailing religious rules, and actually prohibiting cow slaughter in some cases. In all other countries that have regulations regarding the transport and slaughter of animals, slaughter is not prohibited, but instead is regulated, as discussed elsewhere, based on concerns for human health and to some degree for animal welfare.

In the United States, slaughter is governed by the Humane Methods of Slaughter Act (HMSA), discussed above, which makes it "the policy of the United States that the slaughtering of livestock and the handling of livestock in connection with slaughter shall be carried out only by humane methods."[211] Despite its welfare-oriented title, the language of the HMSA indicates the law was motivated mainly by food and worker safety concerns. It aims to "prevent[] needless suffering" of animals killed for food, but its primary effect is apparently to protect workers and meat-eaters because "humane" killing "results in safer and better working conditions for persons engaged in the slaughtering industry; brings about improvement of products and economies in slaughtering operations; and produces other benefits for producers, processors, and consumers which tend to expedite an orderly flow of livestock and livestock products."[212]

When the HMSA was enacted, most animals covered by the law (including cows) were killed in the following way: first, the animal's rear legs were shackled with handcuff-type restraints. The animal was then raised by cables attached to those shackles and suspended upside down, head pointed towards the floor. (The animals are hoisted for sanitary purposes in order to keep their bodies, which will eventually be turned into meat, from mixing with the fluids that collect on slaughterhouse floors.) The animal was then slaughtered with a quick cut of the carotid artery, which leads to death within seconds. When an animal is hoisted, her weight may force hip dislocation, and conscious animals may struggle in terror and pain while hanging upside down, causing them to swing erratically in a way that endangers workers as well as causing immense pain to the animal.[213]

With that in mind, and presumably understanding the pain and terror of the shackling and hoisting process, the HMSA's first provision requires that the animal be "rendered insensible to pain by a ... means that is rapid and effective, before being shackled, hoisted, thrown, cast, or cut."[214] This is usually accomplished by a "captive bolt gun." The gun plunges a metal bolt, attached to the gun, into the brain of the animal and, if correctly used, will cause unconsciousness in the animal.[215] If the process does indeed render them unconscious, the animals are unable to feel pain, fear, or stress, and if the rest of the process is followed, are killed very shortly after the captive bolt procedure. Animal advocates have raised serious concerns, however, that in practice, slaughter causes immense suffering.[216] Slaughter workers report having to use the captive bolt gun as many as ten times before a cow collapses into unconsciousness.[217] And many "stickers," the workers who slit cows' throats, often receive cows at their stations who are still conscious and moving.[218]

Paradoxically, slaughter of animals has also been declared to be humane under subsection (b) of the HMSA even if animals are *not* rendered unconscious before they are shackled and hoisted—as long as the animals are slaughtered "in accordance with the ritual requirements of the Jewish faith or any other religious faith."[219] Although not expressly mentioned in the statute, "kosher slaughter"—the ritual slaughter carried out under Jewish law—requires that an animal be fully conscious when she is slaughtered. Thus, this section of the statute declares that it is humane to hoist and shackle animals *without* rendering them insensible to pain—based on the recommendations of religious leaders who testified before Congress during the writing of this law. Despite the apparent desire in section (a) of the statute to ensure that animals are insensible to pain, section (b) approves a situation in which the animals are fully aware of all the events leading up to their death.

In 1974, in one of the American animal law movement's first lawsuits, plaintiffs challenged the aspect of the HMSA that effectively provides an exemption to the requirement that animals must be rendered unconscious before being shackled and hoisted.[220] The plaintiffs[221] in *Jones v. Butz* argued that section (b) violated both the purpose of the law (to provide humane methods of slaughter) and the federal First Amendment, which prohibits the government from either establishing a religion or interfering with an individual's free exercise of her own religious beliefs.[222] The court rejected these arguments because Congress had held hearings and made a factual determination—which the court refused to question—that kosher slaughter (which prohibits the slaughter of unconscious animals) was "humane." Unwilling to contradict the findings of the legislature, and finding no conflict with the requirement that church and state be separate (because the secular purpose of "humane slaughter" was being satisfied), the court upheld the law.[223]

Like the ostensible requirement in the U.S. law, "[m]ost developed and many developing countries have legislation that requires pre-slaughter stunning."[224] The European Union has adopted similar requirements, with similar exceptions, to the American law: animals must be rendered insensible unless a "religious rite" requires otherwise.[225] This requirement is not universal; one study indicated that as many as half of the animals slaughtered in "developing" countries are not stunned before slaughter.[226] Thus, between the exception under many laws for kosher and ritual slaughter, and other countries that do not even have a stunning requirement, billions of animals annually are hoisted and shackled and slaughtered while fully conscious. And as a matter of practical application, they are also forced to watch the slaughter of many other animals who are being killed at the same time. Finally, even when animals are stunned, the methods may still cause animal suffering, as when manual percussive means are used, such as sledge hammers or poleaxes.[227]

The practice of using "downed animals" for meat production has been challenged and changed in America as well, especially with respect to cows, because of the potential that such meat can cause Bovine Spongiform Encephalopathy, commonly known as "Mad Cow Disease" (BSE). For cows, BSE is a "fatal neurodegenerative disease that affects the central nervous system of adult cattle" who have been fed ground up cow parts.[228] BSE can lead to a progressive and fatal disease (a variant of Creutzfeldt Jakob Syndrome) in humans who consume the meat of infected animals.[229] As of March 16, 2009, the United States Department of Agriculture had banned the slaughter of all downed cows for human consumption.[230] Under federal law, other downed animals, who "collapse for unknown reasons and are too ill to walk or stand prior to slaughter,"[231] may be examined and eventually slaughtered if they can pass a federal inspection.

In New Zealand, the Animal Welfare Act provides for basic protection from cruelty for all animals, with a lofty and progressive approach to coverage. This grant is then delimited by "Codes of Welfare" addressing each area of animal-related business and activity in the country.[232] Once the Codes are written and applied, the treatment of animals in agriculture is similar to that seen elsewhere, although the country has some particular characteristics that may influence both the legislative treatment of the issues and their practical application. The significant amount of New Zealand's economy dedicated to animal production drives the decisions made regarding the treatment of farmed animals. "It is accepted that animal welfare is important, so long as it does not interfere too much with farming and economic concerns."[233] Where financial interests could impact production, they may indeed trump animal welfare decisions.[234] As of 2007, there was no specific Code prepared that applied to cows used for meat, although the basic Animal Welfare Act provisions applied. The Codes that had been prepared by that point applied to pigs, broiler chickens, laying hens, zoos, rodeos, circuses, companion cats, deer, and painful husbandry procedures, which applies to cows as well as all other animals.[235] In February 2010, the Code of Welfare for Dairy Cattle was issued, which sets out specific guidelines and refers to the painful husbandry code for discussion of those issues. In June 2010, the code for cows used for meat and sheep was also issued.[236]

Horses

Horses have long been portrayed in the poetry, songs, and traditions of the western world. An old Spanish proverb declares, "A horse is worth more than riches." In the United States, the horse figures hugely in the nation's history. Much of Latin America relies heavily on horses for transportation, cattle herding, and various types of farm labor. As one Texas judge put it, "[t]he lone cowboy riding his horse on a Texas trail is a cinematic icon. Not once in memory did the cowboy eat his horse, but film is an imperfect mirror for reality."[237]

While many cultures have developed a gastronomic aversion to horsemeat, it is regularly eaten elsewhere. In 2007, about five million horses were slaughtered for human consumption worldwide.[238] In France, where horsemeat has been legal since 1866, it is commonly sold in the supermarket.[239] It is also consumed in Italy, Austria, (where it is most commonly seen served in fast food shops), and Belgium. Japan, Canada, Iceland, Kazakhstan, Poland, Malta, Mongolia, Sweden, Russia, and Switzerland. All are known to have horsemeat on their menus and several of these countries consider horsemeat to be part of their national heritage and a dietary staple.[240]

In the United States, the slaughter of horses for human consumption has generated both laws and lawsuits. Until 2007, three slaughterhouses in the United States killed horses for human consumption; two were located in Texas, and one in Illinois. Based on public sentiment that this practice was cruel (because of documented stories of the struggles that horses put up going to slaughter), Illinois banned the slaughter.[241] The Texas law had been in effect for many years, but the slaughterhouse owners had continued the slaughter. The slaughterhouse owners sued the states in two separate lawsuits (in 2005 in Texas and 2007 in Illinois).[242]

The producers' main argument in both cases was that the Federal Meat Inspection Act[243]—which governs some aspects of slaughterhouse practices—prevented the states from prohibiting horse slaughter for human consumption. In 2007, two different federal appellate courts ruled in favor of the states and upheld the laws.[244] The Illinois court set out the general principle in America that each state possesses the right to make determinations about animal cruelty within its borders:

> [A] state is permitted, within reason, to express disgust at what people do with the dead, whether dead human beings or dead animals. There would be an uproar if restaurants in Chicago started serving cat and dog steaks, even though millions of stray cats and dogs are euthanized in animal shelters.[245]

Given the nature of the challenge by the producers, the court needed to find only that the ban on slaughtering horses for human consumption had some rational justification and served some legitimate purpose.[246] The states' "interest in prolonging the lives of animals that their population happens to like" was strong enough to support the prohibition.[247] The court would perhaps have ruled differently if the Illinois law significantly affected international relations (which is uniquely the prerogative of the federal government)—for example, if Belgium could only get horse meat from Illinois.[248] The court found that the ban did not intentionally discriminate against countries with populations that do consume horsemeat; instead the law was merely indifferent to these countries.[249]

The horse slaughter cases and legislation arose because Americans are generally uncomfortable with the notion of eating horses.[250] This cultural taboo is found throughout the United States,[251] the United Kingdom,[252] Australia,[253] Peru, and Brazil.[254] The three slaughterhouses in the United States discussed above operated huge businesses. Cavel International, Inc. operated the Illinois facility, which had over sixty employees and $20 million in annual revenues.[255] Over 130 employees worked at the two Texas slaughterhouses, which had approximately $39 million in sales in 2001.[256] Over 100,000 horses were killed each year.[257] Although the closure of those operations prevented the slaughter of horses for human consumption in the United States, horses were subsequently exported to slaughterhouses just across the border in Mexico and Canada, where horse slaughter remains legal.[258] Pending legislation in the U.S. Congress would prohibit the export of horses for the purpose of slaughter.[259] At the same time, the state of Montana passed a law (on May 1, 2009) which allowed the slaughter of horses for human consumption to begin in that state.

Bushmeat

An area that has gained a significant amount of international support is the attack on the "bushmeat" trade.[260] The term "bushmeat" has been used generally to refer to flesh of any wild-caught animals (even legally hunted animals).

The use of the term for our purposes, and the major focus of animal protection groups currently, is the black market trade in the meat of great apes (especially chimpanzees, bonobos, and gorillas),[261] other nonhuman primates, and a variety of endangered or threatened species including elephants, forest antelopes (duikers), crocodiles, porcupines, bush pigs, cane rats, pangolins, monitor lizards, and guinea fowl.[262] The practice of killing and selling these animals for meat is an ongoing problem in Africa, Asia, and Central and South America.[263] Whether disguised as something else or expressly labeled, bushmeat is available in many open markets, where laws regulating the sale and possession of wildlife are not strictly enforced.

Government officials have reportedly been involved in the killing of great apes. This demonstrates the diminished concern for these animals in the very countries where they are occupying the limited habitat remaining. In March 2008, Honore Mashagiro, formerly a top Republic of the Congo conservation official overseeing the park where the mountain gorillas live, was arrested and charged with planning and helping to carry out the slaughter of ten mountain gorillas. The slaughter was allegedly planned in order to aid the illegal charcoal trade that depends on free access to the bush to continue its progress; to intimidate park rangers; and to discredit another conservation official for his efforts to protect the gorillas and shut down the charcoal trade.[264] Notably, the gorillas were not killed as part of the bushmeat trade, although some reports attempted to make that connection. Their bodies were left intact, and the orphaned infants were not taken and sold as pets,[265] but instead left to starve to death.[266] While not specifically a bushmeat issue, this incident highlights the vulnerability and fragility of wild species involved in the bushmeat trade as well.

Because of a generalized lack of legislation, funding, and political capacity, "[t]he bushmeat crisis is a complex issue that Central African governments will not be able to address adequately without strong U.S. and international support."[267] Across the world individuals concerned about the sale of all bushmeat have been taking their concerns to the public in an attempt to motivate legislative bodies to enact laws that would impact those profiting from the bushmeat trade. For example, the Bushmeat Crisis Task Force (BCTF) is a "consortium of conservation organizations and scientists dedicated to the conservation of wildlife populations threatened by commercial hunting for sale as meat."[268] A global organization comprised of many zoos and nongovernmental animal protection organizations,[269] the BCTF has brought attention to the severity of the bushmeat problem—both as an animal and human crisis. If weapons are not used to kill the animals, the method of trapping is usually wire snares, which cause extreme and prolonged pain and suffering. Animals are not always killed outright, but sometimes suffer amputations or severe injuries. Trapping can also cause death by starvation if the animal is unable to find or forage for food, or death by infection. Another consequence of the bushmeat trade is that when species become extinct through unregulated and expanded markets, this loss threatens livelihoods of rural communities dependent on the meat of the animals for their survival.[270] Additionally, "bushmeat consumption is increasingly linked to deadly diseases like HIV/AIDS, Ebola, and Foot and Mouth disease."[271]

For these reasons, and unlike many other animal protection issues that often create controversy and raise many debates, the bushmeat trade is generally condemned by anyone who is not directly involved. Many groups are working to stop the problem at every level, although some are willing to accept the fact of the trade and simply regulate it to prevent the extinction of species. For example, the Convention on International Trade in Endangered Species (CITES) (discussed in detail in Chapter 6) enacted the Bushmeat Working Group to promote awareness and action in order to achieve better and sustainable management of the bushmeat trade.[272] Despite the fact that most of the bushmeat trade is domestic, CITES member countries found the problem compelling enough to create the Bushmeat Working Group and task it with "identifying solutions that can be willingly implemented by [countries] where bushmeat is a problem."[273]

In West and Central Africa, very little was done to control the bushmeat trade until the 1990s, when wildlife populations reached crisis levels. The international response, including CITES' Bushmeat Working Group and the BCTF, has increased population levels and drawn attention to the situation. In 2008, the bushmeat crisis remained a significant threat to biodiversity in Central Africa. Extensive logging and development operations collude in the extinction of many species—and make the hunting of deep forest dwelling species possible at a greater rate than ever.[274]

A significant problem also exists in East and Southern Africa. In March 2008, Kenyan officials reported that poaching for bushmeat was at an all-time high and could spell the end of small game in the area around (and outside of) Tsavo National Park.[275] While officials increased their patrols, as well as their efforts to get local ranchers involved in the prevention program, the poachers developed new methods of avoiding those efforts.[276] The bushmeat trade from West and Central Africa alone could exceed one billion USD each year.[277] And it is clear that the problem of bushmeat mushrooming from a small subsistence form of hunting to a full-scale commercial trade commodity is not just a West or Central African problem.[278]

Imports of bushmeat into the United States and Europe have also raised concerns—both for human health and species conservation reasons. Heathrow Airport in London estimates that five tons of bushmeat were smuggled into England in 2000 alone.[279] Worldwide, bushmeat is also part of wildlife trade in Asia and Latin America, and exports to North America and Europe are a growing concern.[280] The issue of exports has gained some interesting transnational legal attention in potentially unexpected places. A December 2007 article in the New York Times[281] discussed a criminal prosecution that arose after a Liberian citizen, living in America, attempted to import bushmeat that included two protected species:

> In a case now pending in a federal court in Brooklyn, Mamie Manneh of Staten Island stands accused of having brought smoked bushmeat—known colloquially as "monkey meat"—into the United States without proper permits, in violation of CITES. Ms. Manneh's defense is that in her religion the eating of bushmeat has both a cultural and a spiritual significance. In an affidavit, 17 of her co-religionists declared, "We eat bushmeat for our souls." Manneh's lawyer, Jan Rostal, has analogized the African-based practice to the consumption at a Passover seder of foods like bitter herbs "that might have some reference to the Exodus." In a motion to dismiss, Rostal said that the case, while apparently novel, "represents the sort of clash of cultural and religious values inherent in the melting pot that is America."

The federal court rejected Ms. Manneh's argument, based mainly on the fact that she had not applied for the proper importation permits, and that applying for such permits would not place a substantial burden on her religious practice.[282] The *Manneh* bushmeat case's narrow holding is simply that, whether or not a religious exemption applies to limits on the importation of bushmeat, Ms. Manneh was required to complete the necessary paperwork to import the bushmeat. The court never reached the issue of whether the prohibition on importation of endangered species could be overridden by the desire to participate in a religious practice—and in fact expressed doubt as to whether Ms. Manneh would be allowed to import bushmeat even with a religious claim to the meat.[283]

The *Manneh* case represents a potential example of a legal issue caused by different cultures' relationships with animals and their animal welfare paradigms. Most relevant here, it also represents a culture clash with international law. That is, the *Manneh* case arose because CITES prohibits (without a proper permit) the importation of two of the primates whose body parts were in Ms. Manneh's shipment. In Africa and other less industrialized societies in proximity to forests, the hunting and eating of primates has been and remains a traditional means of subsistence.[284] "[W]ild animal meat … remains a major source of protein for millions of people in West and Central Africa."[285] Even after the formation of large cities led to movement away from rural life, the craving for bushmeat is constantly cited as a reason for the cultural significance of bushmeat.[286] This aspect of comparative laws and principles requires careful consideration when devising programs and strategies to protect animals who, in some cultures, may be an important part of a longstanding lifestyle.

Dogs—As Food

Dogs truly illustrate the duality of animal treatment across the globe. In most parts of the world, dogs are treated as close companions and even nonhuman family members. In the United States alone, billions of dollars each year are spent on their care and comfort.[287] However, in a variety of countries, dogs—while still treated by some people as companions—are commercially used as food and for their fur.[288] Dogs thus obtain a complex range of protections, depending on who owns them, and the purposes for which they are being used. This varied legal treatment exemplifies the international split personality over animals.

Dogs raised for their meat on farms are typically kept in wire cages, crowded with many other dogs, for their entire lives.[289] Methods of slaughter include beating, pouring boiling water over the animals, blowtorching, and bone breaking prior to death by stabbing, drowning, strangulation, or throat slitting.[290] These methods of "preparing" the animal increase adrenalin, which is thought to improve the taste of the meat and to increase strength and boost virility.[291] In Nigeria, dog meat is consumed and is commonly thought to give immunity to different diseases.[292]

Traditionally, some segments of some Asian countries have long sanctioned consumption of dog meat. At the same time, dogs and cats have been kept as companion animals, among citizens and royalty, for thousands of years. In more recent years, several Asian countries have enacted bans on selling and eating dog meat, despite vocal objection by the populace. For example, the sale of dogs for commercial food purposes has been banned in the Philippines since 1998, although weak penalties and enforcement have allowed the trade to continue.

As discussed in Chapter 1, in 2001, the Taiwanese Parliament passed a law banning the consumption of dog meat.[293] The legislation further banned the use of the meat and fur of "pets" from being used for economic purposes.[294] Violations of the law can result in a fine of roughly 300 USD.[295] In South Korea, the sale and eating of dog meat was made illegal during the 1988 Olympics.[296] Just before the 1988 Olympics, which took place in Seoul, government officials feared that selling and eating dog meat (and snake meat) would result in negative international publicity and enacted the ban.[297] This, rather than a popular consensus against eating dog meat, was the stimulus for the law.

Interestingly, there is a current movement to re-legalize the trade in dog meat by classifying the dogs as livestock—both for the animals' protection and in the interest of human health. That is, as an illicit substance, dog meat is not currently subject to any humane slaughter restrictions or health inspections.[298] Of course, South Korea also has the option of enforcing its Animal Protection Act of 1991,[299] which bans cruelty to all animals, and using that to protect cats and dogs in the dog meat industry. In 2011, the law was reportedly not enforced, with many people insisting that eating dog meat was no better or worse than eating any other mammal.[300]

The controversy over dog meat represents a matter of cultural confrontation between Korea and the West. For Koreans, accepting the practice of eating dog meat may be less about personal culinary preference or economic rationales, and more about standing up to outside judgments. This is another good example of the distinction between countries and cultures in their choices of what they do with various animals.[301]

It was reported that in 2007 there were sixty Taiwan restaurants that had dog meat on their menus.[302] Despite the prevalence of consumption of dog meat in the Philippines and South Korea[303] and lack of enforcement, the existence of cruelty laws and bans on dog meat in those countries is in significant contrast to China and Vietnam, where no laws exist to regulate the treatment of animals in the dog and cat meat industry.[304] In both countries, dogs are increasingly commercially raised on farms for their meat, although animal welfare groups report that some of the animals slaughtered are former pets.[305] Certain breeds are especially coveted and imported from other countries for breeding.[306]

Notably, even where consumption of dog meat is not a preferred practice and considered taboo, it may still be legal. For example, sale and consumption of dog meat is legal in Canada, as long as it is properly inspected.[307] This may be due more to a lack of perceived need to ban the practice than an official sanction of it.

Fur

Dogs and Cats—As Clothing

Despite their place as the two most popular companion animal species, dogs and cats are used for their fur as well as their meat. Dog and cat fur are components of many articles of clothing, often without full disclosure by the sellers. So while laws prohibiting dog and cat fur in clothing or requiring accurate labeling do exist, they may not be a sufficient deterrent because the fur is often put into clothing fraudulently. The use of dog and cat fur has been well documented,[308] so much so that in 2000, the United States Congress enacted the Dog and Cat Protection Act of 2000.[309] The Act set penalties of up to $10,000 for each item in one's possession containing dog or cat fur.[310] Repeat offenders may be barred from selling *any* fur products whatsoever.[311] The Act also required United States Customs to publish a list of businesses and individuals known to trade in dog and cat fur.[312] Subsequently, bills have been introduced to the U.S. Congress that would add labeling requirements for fur imported into the United States.[313] The Dog and Cat Fur Prohibition Enforcement Act was introduced in an effort to strengthen the existing prohibitions, and to protect consumers and animals by outlawing import of fur from "raccoon dogs," and requiring all garments trimmed with fur to be labeled, identifying any fur products used.[314] The Act was finally passed, after extensive campaigning and legislative efforts by the Humane Society of the United States, near the end of 2010.

In 2004, the federal Australian government banned the import and export of dog and cat fur.[315] The law did not ban the use of fur within the country, however, and allowed limited imports for several purposes, including pet taxidermy, research purposes, and fur historical displays.[316] The visceral reaction the companion animal issues raised was evident with respect to the interest in this legislation, as over 70,000 Australians signed the petition to enact the law.[317]

In 2006, the European Commission adopted a proposal to ban the import, export and sale of cat and dog fur in the EU.[318] The ban took effect January 1, 2009.[319] Prior to this proposal, many individual European countries, including Italy, Denmark, France, Greece, and Belgium, had already enacted similar laws.

> There is evidence that cat and dog fur is being placed on the European market, usually undeclared as such or disguised as synthetic and other types of fur. The vast majority of the cat and dog fur is believed to be imported from third countries, notably China where the rearing of these animals for this purpose is practiced. Many Member States have introduced their own specific legislation against cat and dog fur in response to the strong opposition of EU consumers to the trade of fur from these animals. However, as these national bans are divergent, they may cause disruption to the internal market. The proposed Regulation adopted today addresses EU citizens' concerns and creates a harmonised approach, prohibiting all production, marketing and imports and exports of cat and dog fur in the EU. It also establishes a system of information exchange on the detection of cat and dog fur.[320]

In June of 2007, the European Parliament voted unanimously for a complete ban on the import, export, and trade in cat and dog fur in all twenty-seven Member States.[321] The ban took remains in effect.

Fur Seals

In several countries around the world, seals are killed for their skins. Canada has the largest commercial sealing industry, followed by Namibia, Russia, Norway and Greenland.[322] Commercial seal hunting also occurs off the coasts of the United States, Britain, Finland and Sweden.[323] The annual seal killing in Canada, which predominantly kills infant harp seals, is the largest slaughter of marine mammals in the world. The killing is conducted under the Canadian Marine Mammal Regulations (MMRs).[324] Vocal opposition to the practice from around the world has not been successful in stopping the killing.

The primary method of killing the seal pups is clubbing. The MMRs regulate the methods of killing: "(1) No person shall fish for seals, for personal or commercial use, in any of Sealing Areas 4 to 33 except with: (*a*) a round club … [,] (*b*) an instrument know as a hakapik … [,] (*c*) a rifle and bullets that are not full metal-jacketed … ; or (*d*) a shotgun.…"[325] Further regulations addressing the manner in which seal pups are killed include: crushing the cranium and the subsequent palpation of the cranium to confirm it has been crushed when using a club or hakapik; palpating the cranium to confirm it has been crushed following a contact shot when using a firearm; and immediately striking the seal following cranium palpation that confirms the cranium is not crushed.[326] The MMRs also prohibit skinning seals before the cranium has been crushed and require a one minute waiting period before skinning, following the severing of the seal's two axillary arteries.[327]

In 2001, a report by an independent team of veterinarians who studied the hunt concluded that governmental regulations regarding humane killing were neither being respected nor enforced, and that the seal hunt failed to comply with Canada's basic animal welfare standards. The veterinarians found that in 42 percent of the cases they studied, the seals had likely been skinned alive while conscious.[328] The report also documented "79 per cent of cases where sealers did not check to ensure that the seals were dead prior to skinning them."[329]

Fisheries and Oceans Canada attempts to monitor the killing of seals via annual Total Allowable Catches (TAC) quotas. The TAC for 2009 was set at 280,000 for harp seals, 8,2000 for hooded seals and 50,000 for grey seals.[330] The quotas do not necessarily reflect the number of seals actually killed. For example, fatally-injured seals may escape and die out in the sea. Many of these fatally-wounded seals are abandoned due to multiple shots to their bodies, decreasing the value of their pelt, or because the seals fall back into the open waters and the killers do not search for them. The Canadian seal industry is worth tens of millions of dollars annually.[331]

South Africa also slaughters seals for fur in large numbers. In 1977, a case was brought in U.S. courts that focused on the methods of killing in South Africa while examining the propriety of a federal agency's regulations regarding the importation of sealskins. In *Animal Welfare Institute v. Kreps*,[332] animal and environmental protection groups challenged the decision by the United States Fish and Wildlife Services agency to waive the federal Marine Mammal Protection Act's (MMPA) moratorium on taking or importing marine mammals, so as to permit importation of baby fur seal skins from South Africa. The court ultimately determined that the waiver was invalid because the regulations were in violation of some of the prohibitions of the MMPA.

Many countries, including the United States, Belgium, Hungary, Czech Republic, the Netherlands, Italy, Austria, Croatia, Slovenia, Switzerland, Germany, Panama and Mexico, have enacted or are in the processing of enacting legislation addressing the concerns with the inhumane slaughtering of seals. The enactment of the American MMPA in 1972 resulted in a ban on the importation of all seal products. Seal pelts are banned in Croatia, Belgium, Italy and the Netherlands while Canadian seal pelts are banned in Greenland and Denmark.[333] The commercial markets for seal fur are "primarily in Norway, Russia, Eastern Europe, China and Japan."[334]

In 2007, Belgium banned the import of seal products.[335] The law prohibits the use and sale of seal parts or products, with limited exceptions.[336] This Belgium ban of seal products was the first adopted by a European Union nation, and has been challenged by Canada as an improper discrimination on international trade.[337]

In March 2009, the most effective legislation aimed at curtailing the seal hunt began in Russia, when the Russian government banned the killing of all seals less than one year old.[338] This ban would effectively eliminate the hunting of seals for fur in Russia, because the fur of older seals is commercially undesirable due to its coarseness. However, the Russian government has yet to clarify whether the ban would extend to the importation and selling of seal products.

In May 2009, the European Union took things one step further and banned the importation of seal products, with limited exceptions for noncommercial reasons such as "personal use."[339] This ban would significantly impact the industry, and so the Canadian government, citing the argument that the ban improperly discriminated against Canadian products, stated that it would be attacking the ban in a formal manner before the World Trade Organization.[340] At the same time, Canadian Senator Mac Harb has introduced legislation to amend The Fisheries Act, which would "effectively [end] the commercial seal hunt while respecting treaty obligations and protecting the rights of Canada's aboriginal people" to continue hunting seals.[341]

Other Animals, Other Uses

Bears

The use of bear parts across Asia has created serious welfare issues for bears around the world. The Asiatic black bear, also known as the Moon Bear for the distinctive V-shaped marking across the chest, has been the focus of an international campaign to end the farming of bears in Vietnam and China. Closely related to the American black bear, the Moon Bear is one of the most endangered species of bear in the world; only a few thousand remain in the wild.[342] The bears are listed under Appendix I of CITES (discussed in Chapter 6), which prohibits all trade in the species; captive-bred members of Appendix I species are designated as Appendix II species under CITES, which are given significant legal protection.

Despite their endangered status, Moon Bears were illegally hunted in China—almost to extinction—in efforts to obtain their gallbladders and bile.[343] In traditional Chinese medicine (TCM), the bear's gallbladder and bile have a variety of uses, including treatment of patients with diseases of the liver.[344]

As an alternative to hunting the bear to extinction, government-sanctioned bear farms have been in existence for years in China and Vietnam in order to satisfy market demand. Bears on the farms are often kept in individualized "crush" cages in which they cannot stand up or sometimes even move at all. This allows easier access to bears' gall bladders so that their bile can be "milked."[345] There are several methods of bile extraction, each of which inflicts unending pain and suffering on the bears.[346] Some producers put metal "jackets"—instruments of great torture and suffering—on bears who are milked. Bears may be forced to wear the weighty jacket for years at a time.

Crush cages also can be employed with a metal catheter.[347] This method is thought to more effective for milking, because the bears are forced into a flat position, unable to move, sometimes for years at a time. The most "humane" method is the "free drip," which requires a permanent hole to be placed in the bears' abdomens—then the bile can drip out of the open wound. Investigations by an animal protection group in Vietnam revealed new techniques being used, including abdominal surgery, and ultrasound location of the gall bladder on a routine basis. These practices can result in slow and painful deaths from infections related to the procedures.[348]

Despite medical alternatives, bear farming has continued and it is estimated that 12,000 bears are captive in Asian farms.[349] Since that time, no new farms have started and at least forty farms have been shut down.[350] Strict Chinese wildlife laws[351] prohibit the hunting of wild bears, and the Chinese government estimates that one farmed bear can produce enough bile over a five year period to save 220 wild bears from poaching. Chinese law does allow the sale of bear bile extracted from live bears on the government-sanctioned farms, but has banned the sale of other bear parts. Taiwanese law also bans the sale of bear parts[352]; unfortunately, much like the situation in China, the law is not actively enforced. In 1992, China stopped commercial export of products containing bear bile.[353] The government also stopped the issuance of licenses for the construction of new bear farms.[354] Elsewhere in Asia, the laws of countries where bear parts are used, like South Korea and Japan, do not address the trade in bear parts.

Some independent groups, utilizing law and politics, are able to make changes for animals by direct contact with national governments. Animals Asia Foundation, a Hong Kong-based animal welfare organization, was founded in 1998 to "to improve the lives of all animals in Asia, end cruelty and restore respect for animals Asia-wide."[355] In this effort, Animals Asia has worked to end the farming of bears in China and Vietnam, creating rescue centers for farmed bears,[356] and bringing awareness of the issue to the rest of the world:

> In July 2000, Animals Asia signed a landmark agreement with the Chinese Authorities to rescue 500 suffering Moon Bears in Sichuan Province, to work towards the future elimination of bear farming in China and to promote the herbal alternatives to bear bile. This historic agreement was the first accord between the Chinese Government and any outside animal welfare organization.[357]

Animals Asia has also worked with the Vietnamese government to rescue bears, end breeding of captive bears, and phase out bear bile farms altogether. In 2005, in response to the efforts of Animals Asia, the World Society for the Protection of Animals, and other animal protection groups, the Vietnamese Government made a firm commitment to phase out bear farming.[358] Although it has been illegal to poach or "use" endangered bears in Vietnam since 1992,[359] certain loopholes existed that allowed second generations of endangered bears to be used.[360] Recent legislation has closed these loopholes,[361] but concerns over enforcement still clearly exist.[362]

International response to this problem, which was originally limited to a small set of countries, demonstrates the widespread effect of concern over the treatment and survival of certain species. For example, as a result of the demand for bear products in Asia, North American bears have been poached in increasing quantities. The international trade in bear parts and bile in Asia has increased damage to such a degree that Russian and North American bears are being killed for their gallbladders, bile, and paws.[363] Resulting laws in the United States and Canada outlaw poaching of most North American bears and the sale of bear bile and gallbladders. However, as of 2011 at least five U.S. states did not ban the practice, fueling the interest and supplying the market.[364] The U.S. response has been generally comprised of a patchwork of bear protection laws.[365] Various Bear Protection Acts have been introduced into the U.S. Congress which would prohibit import, export and interstate trade in bear viscera—as well as products containing, or labeled or advertised as containing—bear viscera.[366] The Bear Protection Act of 2008,[367] as introduced, would also have amended the federal Lacey Act and extended its protections to bears illegally harvested for their viscera in the same manner as with respect to prohibited wildlife species.[368] Neither this bill nor the subsequent version passed into law.

Entertainment—Hunting, Competition, Fighting, and Exhibitions

"Entertainment" in its broadest sense (and for purposes of this text) refers to "amusement or diversion provided especially by performers" or "something diverting or engaging."[369] Animals have been an integral part of human entertainment as long as humans have watched them move through the same world as we do. Their involvement in entertainment has increased over the years, and we remain fascinated and continue to utilize them to entertain us.

With that broad definition, here is a nonexhaustive but extensive list of specific types of entertainment involving animals that might be affected or questioned by court cases, and regulated or legislated by government bodies:

1. Viewing wildlife;
2. Spending time with a companion animal;
3. Attending or participating in a companion animal show;
4. Visiting a zoo;
5. Attending or participating in a live animal exhibition, including circuses and rodeos and shows at private parks;
6. Participating in interactive events with captive animals, such as "swim with the dolphin" programs, and personal interactions with captive exotic animals at private facilities;
7. Hunting or fishing;
8. Viewing a film or television program involving animals (including broadcasts of any of the above instances);
9. Attending or participating in an animal fighting venture, such as dogfighting, cockfighting, bullfighting, or hog-dog fighting.[370]

Before addressing the (limited) law that applies to some of these forms of animal entertainment, it is important to recognize that the broad range of activities listed above covers some that most people consider innocuous and others that many people consider reprehensible. Perhaps even more divided than the world's view of what animals should and can be eaten is the world's view on the use of animals in entertainment.

The Law on Entertainment

Unlike the descriptions of standard farming practices, most of the listed items do not need detailed explanation as to their particulars. Where specifics may be helpful or where the targeted practices are ones which do not often become public, the text will provide informative explication in order to provide the necessary background.[371] In keeping with the general themes of this book, the idea is to provide some sense of the legal challenges faced when animals are used in entertainment.

The focus of this section is on the relevant laws specific to entertainment issues. As in virtually every other area of the book, there are laws of general application that may impact the use of animals in various forms of entertainment, but that are not focused or directed particularly at the entertainment aspect of the behavior. By way of example, a law that prohibits individuals from entering a government-run park or reserve during certain times would impact the ability to view or hunt the animals in that park, but it is not the type of law considered here.[372] Conversely, a law that restricted the number of animals one could kill while hunting, or a law that governed the distance visitors must keep between themselves and resident animals in a park, would be laws relating to the entertainment activity.

Companion Animals

There may be healthy debate regarding whether companion animal issues fall within the entertainment realm. No one who has spent time with companion animals, however, can deny that they are "diverting" and "engaging," and so we include them here. Special laws exist in many jurisdictions with respect to companion animals. Some of the laws are intended to protect the public as well as the animals and address the eventualities and potential problems that arise by virtue of animals' incorporation into so many aspects of modern society. In many jurisdictions, dogs must be licensed to their owner and must have certain vaccinations on a regular schedule. There are also laws governing animals' movement, such as "leash laws" and those prohibiting animals running at large. Extensive regulations and ordinances address how we deal with stray, homeless and abandoned animals. Animal shelters in many communities may be subject to special rules, and most jurisdictions have official animal control departments that deal with the problems that arise in connection with the management and ownership of companion animals. Animal control officers are usually primarily responsible for the laws regarding maintenance and care of all animals in a jurisdiction; they often share investigative and enforcement duties with local police. Local or regional animal control departments are usually exclusively responsible for rescuing and receiving stray and abandoned animals, and with the humane euthanasia of abandoned, unwanted or unclaimed animals. They also must euthanize animals that are suffering and untreatable. They promote licensing of companion animals, and usually encourage and offer sterilization services to their community, at the shelters that they maintain to house the abandoned dogs and cats.

A fact of modern life is that millions of animals are killed in these shelters every year—euthanized because there are no homes for them and insufficient space in the shelters.[373] State or local laws often govern the allowable methods of euthanasia as well as the minimum requirements for government-run shelters.[374]

The companion animal overpopulation problem is one of national concern in America and elsewhere. At least part of the blame for the problem rests on the large industry in breeding companion animals, because breeders logically compete in the marketplace that would otherwise be filled solely by homeless animals in shelters who are killed because they are not adopted. For every dog produced for profit by a breeder and sold to an individual, an otherwise adoptable dog is euthanized by shelters that cannot manage to adopt out all of the stray and abandoned animals they receive.

A related phenomenon is that of the breeder who also qualifies as an animal "hoarder" or "collector." A hoarder/collector is generically defined as someone who (1) has more animals than she can care for, (2) creates, through neglect, conditions in which the animals suffer physically and psychologically, and (3) is in denial of the suffering she causes. Many breeders who are also hoarders run facilities colloquially known as "puppymills." These individuals breed and sell large numbers of puppies (sometimes in the thousands) to a public that is unaware that the vendor runs a large operation in which hundreds of animals are severely neglected, suffer from or are exposed to a variety of diseases, and often live in chronic pain in toxic environments and are unable to escape their own filth.[375] There are limited legal resources to attack these problems. The most logical approach is prosecution under the anticruelty laws, which are generally enforced under the criminal law by government prosecutors. Unfortunately, for a variety of reasons the anticruelty laws are only occasionally used to prosecute breeders or hoarders. Civil actions may be brought by animal protection groups utilizing specific laws that provide for challenges to these practices, or through the use of consumer protection laws intended to protect an unsuspecting public from being fooled by dishonest businesses.[376]

Individuals who breed companion animals for sale organize in groups specific to the particular breed on which they focus, as well as larger umbrella groups like the American Kennel Club and the Fédération Cynologique Internationale (FCI).[377] Each breed usually has specific criteria for entry into the public exhibitions in which these animals are shown to the general public. The requirements of some of the breed groups may involve some form of mutilation of the animals. "Tail docking" and "ear cropping" are the most common; in both situations the tail/ears must be partially surgically removed in order to satisfy the appearance and criteria standards set by the groups.

It is difficult to challenge such practices. One lawsuit, brought in New York City, was dismissed because the plaintiff had no procedural right to bring an action invoking the anticruelty laws, since that right is reserved to the state prosecutor.[378]

Legislation targeting specific breeds or species of animals, and restricting or prohibiting their presence within a given jurisdiction (city, county or other municipality), has generated great public interest and controversy for many years.[379] The broad category of "pit bulls" was targeted around the world in the 1990s and the first decade of the twenty-first century, in part because of their use by criminals involved in dog fighting activities, because of their connection to others involved in the drug trade, and also because of their involvement in a series of highly-publicized biting incidents. Anecdotal and statistical data regarding attacks led, in the 1990s especially, to a series of local laws prohibiting their ownership or presence in identified areas.

A related area of international interest is the social and legislative viewpoint as to which species are properly owned as companion animals. Although dogs and cats are generally accepted (with the exception of the occasional breed bans just mentioned), many jurisdictions restrict ownership of "exotic" animals—species that are normally wild and that, even when captive, are deemed close enough to their wild origins, or inherently dangerous enough, to never be safe as companion animals.[380] Not all jurisdictions have limitations or proscriptions on such ownership, however, and current data indicates that in the United States alone, millions of wild animals—especially monkeys, chimpanzees, big cats (tigers, lions, and ligers), and bears—are kept by private individuals.[381] Both federal and state laws in America regulate the possession and ownership of these animals, but the laws are not absolute and do not cover all areas or all exotic species.[382] In the European Union, a formal declaration has been made that "the keeping of specimens of wild fauna as pet animals should not be encouraged."[383]

More specific laws, focusing solely on companion animal treatment, are also on the rise. Increasing scientific data reports a connection between human-animal violence and human-human violence.[384] These studies demonstrate that people who are discovered committing acts of cruelty on animals are also likely inclined to do the same to people. This has triggered increased attention on the problem of animal cruelty. For example, American courts may include companion animals in restraining orders involving violent spouses who have threatened to harm both their spouses, children, and any companion animals.[385] An increasing number of American jurisdictions have enacted specific laws authorizing such an order.[386]

In the European Union, the European Convention for the Protection of Pet Animals, also know as the Pet Protection Treaty, directed special focus on the welfare of companion animals, because of a recognition that humans have "a moral obligation to respect all living creatures and bearing in mind that pet animals have a special relationship" with those people with whom they live.[387] The Treaty is based on the premise "that a basic common standard of attitude and practice which results in responsible pet ownership is not only a desirable, but a realistic goal."[388] Under the Treaty, docking of tails and ears, debarking, declawing, and defanging are all banned. The treaty applies to any animal "kept or intended to be kept by man ... for private enjoyment and companionship."[389]

Zoos

Around the world, zoological parks flourish, and people visit them in large numbers. In most countries there are no laws specific to zoos that affect the way in which animals are treated, exhibited or housed. Nevertheless, there are many layers of laws, from local to state to national, that do impact and control the way zoos operate and the way they treat their animals.

As one limitation, zoos and the animal handlers in zoos are often subject to the prohibitions in animal cruelty statutes. Elephants, perhaps due to their large size and difficulty managing them, have been the victims in a few criminal cruelty cases of note.[390] In the United States, the federal Animal Welfare Act sets minimum requirements for "handling, housing, feeding, watering, sanitation, shelter [and] adequate veterinary care by exhibitors, including zoos."[391] Zoos fall within this coverage, and so this law is one (limited) control on the maintenance of animals in zoos.[392] There are slightly different standards for great apes than for other animals, including a requirement that they be provided with some mental stimulation and some undefined program of psychological enrichment.[393]

As discussed elsewhere in the text, if an animal is on a government's list of endangered species, and/or included in the Convention on International Trade in Endangered Species, there may be certain additional restrictions on treatment that are not applicable to other animals. At the same time, those laws may establish permitting processes that allow zoos to exhibit animals where it would otherwise be illegal to keep them. For example, under the American Endangered Species Act (ESA),[394] it is illegal to purchase or have endangered animals unless the importing entity is granted a permit pursuant to the restrictions of the ESA—a permit available to most zoos and even some circus groups. Groups and individuals who are concerned about the treatment of zoo animals can occasionally use those laws to try to improve the conditions under which animals are kept, or to prevent importation of protected animals.[395] However, if a zoo engages in educational and conservation efforts with respect to the endangered animal, it can be entitled to both exhibit and breed the animals in captivity.

Zoos have industry groups that adopt certain requirements for treatment and protocols—but without the force of law and without full consensus or participation by a country's facilities. In America, the Association of Zoos and Aquariums audits and provides accreditation to qualifying member zoos. It is self-regulating and its power lies almost solely in its ability to exclude or expel institutions that do not meet its standards.[396] On the international front, the World Association of Zoos and Aquariums acts as an "'umbrella' organisation for the world zoo and aquarium community. Its members include leading zoos and aquariums, and regional and national Associations of Zoos and Aquariums, as well as some affiliate organisations, such as zoo veterinarians or zoo educators, from all around the world." Its mission is "to guide, encourage and support the zoos, aquariums, and like-minded organisations of the world in animal care and welfare, environmental education and global conservation."[397]

Live Exhibition (Circuses, Rodeos, Television, and Film)

The live entertainment industry covered by this heading is generally considered to be one that treats its participant animals badly, both in and out of the public eye. Nevertheless, it has few legal constraints, like most businesses using animals for profit, and may even have effective legal approval (through judicial sanction or statutory exemption from the anticruelty laws) in many areas. This makes the coverage (other than international treaties discussed elsewhere in the book, such as CITES) somewhat limited on a country-specific basis.

In many countries, there are simply no laws regulating the treatment of animals used in entertainment. In America, many state anticruelty laws have specific exemptions, either for entertainment in general or specific events, such as rodeos.[398] Even where there are clear violations, they are rarely discovered or addressed. This is in part because of the transient nature of the events, with many public exhibitors moving from one location to another in rapid succession. The inability to identify instances of cruelty also stems from the fact that much of the preparation for the events occurs in areas not open to the public, so that legal violations are hard to observe and therefore difficult to prove as well. Concerns about abuse of performing animals have been raised for years, but there has been very little legislative, law enforcement, or judicial action.

The facts that do get reported in cases involving circuses suggest that animals involved in this industry are mistreated on a regular basis. Tom Rider, a former elephant trainer, sued Ringling Brothers & Barnum and Bailey Circus for the abuse it approved and encouraged with respect to its treatment of elephants used in the circus. According to the lawsuit, "[e]mployees of Ringling Bros. beat the elephants with sharp bull hooks, kept the elephants in chains for long periods of time, and forcibly removed baby elephants from their mothers at an earlier age than they could normally be weaned in the wild."[399] The lawsuit was dismissed in December 2009, when the court found that Mr. Rider did not have standing to challenge the alleged practice.[400]

India has taken a step to decrease the supply of animals in entertainment with its Prevention of Cruelty to Animals Act,[401] previously discussed in Chapter 1. Chapter 5 of that law covers "performing animals." Pursuant to the Act, Performing Animal Rules were adopted that, among other things, prohibit the training or exhibition of bears, monkeys, tigers, panthers, and lions—all animals who are used in circuses and by some wild animal exhibitors. When the law's restriction on the common practices of training animals was challenged, an Indian court upheld the prohibition on practices that are typical in circuses, ruling that the Act imposes a fundamental duty of compassion towards animals and therefore, no exceptions were allowed.[402] The statute clearly covers all types of exhibition, including circuses and street performances, and so the practices were banned:

> [W]e hold that circus animals are being forced to perform unnatural tricks, are housed in cramped cages, subjected to fear, hunger and pain, not to mention the undignified way of life they have to live, with no respite.... Though not homo sapiens, they are also beings entitled to dignified existence and humane treatment sans cruelty and torture.[403]

The Indian judiciary has also affirmed bans on ox racing and camel joy rides.[404] India even has special rules for films involving animals, and the Cinematograph Act of 1952 requires "[t]he Board of Film Certification [to] ensure that scenes showing cruelty to, or abuse of, animals, are not presented needlessly."[405] While anticruelty laws generally apply to the use of animals in entertainment, this is a very rare law that specifically directs its prohibitions at the film industry.

China has had several traditions at its zoos which look more like the things seen at traditional western circuses. For example, zoos have exhibited lions riding on the backs of horses, and a regular feature of Chinese zoos was the feeding of live animals to lions, tigers and other big cats. Zoo guests could purchase chickens, goats, cows and horses, and put them in with the cats to kill and eat. In a groundbreaking law, in January 2011 the Chinese government banned these practices in the roughly 300 hundred state-run zoos. There may, however, be many private zoos that are not affected by the new law.[406] In 2009, Bolivia became the first country in the world to ban the use of all animals in circuses. The ban followed undercover investigations by Animal Defenders International that exposed egregious practices and suffering in travelling circuses.[407] Brazil and Peru are considering similar bans.[408]

Animal Fighting

Animal fighting, another popular class of entertainment utilizing animals, has obtained notoriety, especially in America, where the practices of cockfighting and dog fighting are now prohibited in every state. Cockfighting, in which two roosters fitted with metal spurs are placed in a small ring and allowed to "fight" until one of them is no longer able to stand, is a practice with varying support around the world. Cockfighting was still legal in the American states of Louisiana and New Mexico until 2008; those states finally outlawed the "sport" that year. Each American state makes its own laws that address the events. And despite the prohibition on the act of making two cocks fight, the practice continues, in part because the laws may not address all the related activities that are inextricably intertwined with cockfighting. For example, in the state of Texas, it is *not* illegal to attend a cockfight, to raise fighting cocks, or to have any of the paraphernalia necessary for cockfights. Thus, none of the supporters who come to cockfights and thereby generate the industry's ability to survive are breaking the law, leaving a very large hole in law enforcement's ability to stop the illegal conduct.[409]

The legal prohibition and social criticism of cockfighting is not universal. While it is illegal in much of Europe and the United Kingdom, it is an open, legal, public event in many countries including Mexico, the Philippines, Guam, Bali, and parts of India and Indonesia.[410] In some countries the cruelty is justified by assertions that it is a part of indigenous peoples' cultures and therefore should not be considered illegal or inhumane. Even in the unincorporated American territory of Puerto Rico, the practice is condoned. Puerto Rico's anticruelty statute specifically exempts cockfighting from the law's animal fighting prohibition.[411] In 2007, cockfighting was recognized as an official sport of the commonwealth.[412] Participation in the practice has been recognized as a cultural right to all Puerto Ricans.[413]

Dog fighting usually involves two dogs who are usually one of the "bully breeds" commonly known as "pit bulls," although other breeds may be used. Dog fights do not usually go to the death of one of the participant, but are staged and regulated on a more stringent set of rules that govern when a fight is over.

The international distaste for dog fighting is stronger and more consistent than for cockfighting, though it is still not absolute. That is, in most of the world, dog fighting is criticized as unacceptable cruelty, again demonstrating a common distinction made on a species-wide basis—between birds (or at least chickens) and dogs. Nevertheless, in some countries dog fighting is both condoned and legal. But even where it is illegal, dog fighting goes on. For example, in America, the large majority of the public (as well as the law) strongly condemns dog fighting as unacceptable animal cruelty. Despite that, the incidence of arrests and discoveries of dog fighting rings in America is disturbingly high.

The same cross-cultural disparity that occurs with the consumption of dog meat occurs with this practice. Some countries allow this form of entertainment to continue. In others, dog fighting may occur because there are no laws specifically outlawing it, though there are the general laws that prohibit cruelty to animals that could and should apply. The question then becomes whether the organizer of a dogfight, or the owners of fighting dogs, are committing illegal animal cruelty when they simply place two dogs in a ring together.[414] This is a question that, while it may seem to most readers to be a clear "yes," may not trigger the same response in all countries, all communities, or all cultures.

Perhaps the most well-known and generally accepted animal fighting exhibitions is bullfighting, which pits a man against a bull, in a large ring, in front of large groups of people. The practice is a very popular national event in many countries in Latin America, South America, and Europe, and is banned in many others. Rather than focus on the different prohibitions, versus the promotions, that bullfighting draws, we simply note again the cultural and national disparity in the practice. Its supporters claim bullfighting is a noble and valiant interplay between humans and animals, citing the potential for danger to the human participant. Its detractors complain about the mistreatment of the animals before the fights and the frightening and often extreme suffering they receive in the ring.

Animal racing (most commonly using horses, and sometimes dogs) is a practice that also impacts the health and welfare of animals but is, like most entertainment, generally exempt from government regulation and subject only to industry rules. In India, the use of traditional whips in horse racing has risen to the level of legislation. In 2001, a law was passed requiring only specialized "air-cush" whips to be used.[415] A group of jockeys claimed that traditional whips caused no harm. A court stayed the enforcement of the law, finding that the national government had exceeded its constitutional authority in enacting the law.[416] In response, the government subsequently amended the law and mandated the use of a new kind of whip. India's jockeys protested again and the national debate continued.[417]

Conclusion

This survey of laws concerning the commercial uses of animals for food, fur, and entertainment demonstrates the ways in which animals' welfare tends to suffer when they are made objects of economic transactions. Intensive confinement of pigs, hens, and cows is directly related to the need to increase production in ways that produce large profits; fur products cannot be produced without the deaths of animals; and animal circuses require the repression of wild animals' instincts. How the law mediates between the welfare interests of animals and the commercial interests of humans has been the topic of this chapter. In some cases, as in the Bolivian circus ban and the Israeli *foie gras* decision, animal interests prevail; in others, as in the prevalence of farming exemptions from animal cruelty statutes and the ongoing demand for fur products, commercial interests prevail. As the disparate examples in this chapter demonstrate, which side wins out depends on too many factors to warrant any kind of absolutist statement about who will win the balancing act between animal interests and human interests. The sympathies of a particular judge, the balance of power within a legislative body, the size and influence of a protest movement, and the existence of social and cultural trends all influence whether or not commercial interests will prevail over the welfare interests of animals.

Notes

1. Robert A. Palmatier, Speaking of Animals: A Dictionary of Animal Metaphors, 40 (1995).
2. John Taylor, An Essay on Money, Its Origin and Use 10–11 (3d ed. 1844).
3. Merriam-Webster Online Dictionary, entry for "fee," *available at* http://www.merriam-webster.com/dictionary/fee.
4. Palmatier, *supra* note 1, at 20, 50.
5. Andrew Leonard, *Fun with Developmental Economics Animal Metaphors*, Salon.com (Sept. 18, 2006), *available at* http://www.salon.com/tech/htww/2006/09/18/panda/.
6. Compassion in World Farming, Cracking Factory Farming: Annual Review 2007–2008 7 (2008), *available at* http://www.ciwf.org.uk/includes/documents/cm_docs/

2008/a/annual_review_0708.pdf (sixty billion land animals slaughtered annually for food worldwide) [hereinafter CRACKING FACTORY FARMING]. For specific statistics by country and species, *see* UNITED NATIONS, FOOD AND AGRICULTURE ORGANIZATION, *FAOSTAT: Livestock Primary*, *available at* http://faostat.fao.org/site/569/default.aspx#ancor [hereinafter FAO]. For United States slaughter statistics, *see* Taimie L. Bryant, *Sacrificing the Sacrifice of Animals: Legal Personhood for Animals, the Status of Animals as Property, and the Presumed Primacy of Humans*, 39 RUTGERS L. J. 247, 250–51 n.27 (2008) (ten billion land animals slaughtered annually for food in the United States); *see also* NATIONAL AGRICULTURAL STATISTICS SERVICE, UNITED STATES DEPARTMENT OF AGRICULTURE, LIVESTOCK SLAUGHTER 2008 SUMMARY 3 (2009), *available at* http://usda.mannlib.cornell.edu/usda/current/LiveSlauSu/LiveSlauSu-03-06-2009.pdf (35.5 million cows and calves, 116.6 million pigs, and 2.7 million sheep slaughtered in the U.S. in 2008); NATIONAL AGRICULTURAL STATISTICS SERVICE, UNITED STATES DEPARTMENT OF AGRICULTURE, POULTRY SLAUGHTER 2008 ANNUAL SUMMARY 3 (2009), *available at* http://usda.mannlib.cornell.edu/usda/current/PoulSlauSu/PoulSlauSu-02-25-2009.pdf [hereinafter POULTRY SLAUGHTER 2008 ANNUAL SUMMARY] (9.1 billion chickens, 271.2 million turkeys, and 24 million ducks slaughtered in the U.S. in 2008).

7. *See generally* WILDLIFE LAW: A GLOBAL PERSPECTIVE (Raj Panjwani ed., 2008).

8. For example, the Poultry and Poultry Products Inspection Act, 21 U.S.C. §451 *et seq.*, governs inspections of poultry traveling in interstate commerce, but it does not consider the safety of the animals—only the quality of the food they will become.

9. > "Not only do small farmers have to compete with the three big companies that control white chickens in the Philippines, but they must also be content with pressure from the World Trade Organization (WTO) to open up trade. In the last two decades the Filipino poultry production system has transitioned from mainly backyard farms to a huge industry."

Danielle Nierenberg, *Factory Farming in the Developing World*, WORLD WATCH, Vol. 16, No. 3 (May/June 2003).

10. Tom Garrett & Dr. Agnes Van Volkenburgh, *Animals on the Farm, A Polish Story*, Proceedings from the 2004 International Animal Welfare Law Conference 137 (2004), *available at* http://www.animallaw.info/policy/pobowelfareconf2004.htm.

11. *See, e.g.*, Joyce D'Silva, *Factory Farming and Developing Countries, A Compassion in World Farming Trust Briefing* (Jan. 2000), *available at* http://www.ciwf.org.uk/includes/documents/cm_docs/2008/f/factory_farming_and_developing_countries_2000.pdf. "Worldwide, the big names in livestock breeding and pork and poultry production, the big seed companies and the agro-chemical giants are moving into the rapidly expanding intensive livestock industries in Asia and South America. Governments—increasingly concerned about feeding their growing urban populations—appear more than willing to ease the way for such ventures." *Id.* at 12.

12. We use the term "farmed animals" instead of "farm animals" because the animals described are being actively manipulated (farmed) for commercial purposes, and because the process of being used for food is not in the animals' nature, except to the extent their nature has been altered so that they can be used for production.

13. Livestock, Environment and Development Initiative, United Nations Food and Agriculture Organization, *Livestock's Long Shadow: Environmental Issues and Options* xx (2006), *available at* ftp://ftp.fao.org/docrep/fao/010/a0701e/A0701E00.pdf [hereinafter "*Livestock's Long Shadow*"].

14. Pew Comm'n on Indus. Farm Animal Prod., *Putting Meat on the Table: Industrial Farm Animal Production in America* 11–13 (2008).

15. *Livestock's Long Shadow*, *supra* note 13, at 136.

16. Jeff Tietz, *Boss Hog*, ROLLING STONE, Dec. 14, 2006, *available at* http://www.rollingstone.com/politics/story/12840743/porks_dirty_secret_the_nations_top_hog_producer_is_also_one_of_americas_worst_polluters.

17. *Livestock's Long Shadow*, *supra* note 13, at 83.

18. *Id.* at 128.

19. Brian Halweil, *Grain Harvest Sets Record, But Supplies Still Tight*, WORLD WATCH INSTITUTE, Dec. 12, 2007, *available at* http://www.worldwatch.org/node/5539; *see also* Richard Schwartz, *Abolishing Intensive Livestock Agriculture: A Global Imperative*, in A PRIMER ON ANIMAL RIGHTS 195 (Kim W. Stallwood ed., 2002) [hereinafter "Stallwood"].

20. *Livestock's Long Shadow*, *supra* note 13, at 29–31.

21. *Id.* at 82–83.

22. *Id.* at 272.

23. *Id.*

24. *Id.* at 182.

25. *Id.* at 373–74 (App. 2, Table 16).

26. *See, e.g.*, India's Environmental (Protection) Act, the Wildlife and Countryside Act 1981 in the United Kingdom, Federal Government of Nigeria's Water Resources Decree No. 101 of August 1993, or Japan's Law No. 91 of 1993, which creates basic environmental policies.

27. *Humane Society of the United States v. HVFG, LLC*, 2010 WL 1837785 (S.D. N.Y. May 6, 2010) (granting summary judgment); *see also* http://www.humanesociety.org/news/press_releases/2010/05/HVFG_050610.html.

28. One case, in California, was set to proceed to trial in the spring of 2011. *See, e.g.*, http://www.humanesociety.org/news/press_releases/2010/08/olivera_081210.html.

29. *See* Cecilia Isaacs-Blundin, *Why Manure May Be the Farm Animal Advocate's Best Friend: Using Environmental Statutes to Access Factory Farms*, 2 J. ANIMAL L. & ETHICS 173 (2007).

30. "The Kyoto Protocol is a legally binding agreement under which industrialized countries will reduce their collective emissions of greenhouse gases by 5.2% compared to the year 1990." Kyoto Protocol, *available at* http://unfccc.int/kyoto_protocol/items/2830.php.

31. *Livestock Impacts on the Environment*, FAO (2006), *available at* http://www.fao.org/ag/magazine/0612sp1.htm.; *see also supra* note 23 and text.

32. A. Hatchett, *Bovines and Global Warming: How the Cows are Heating Things Up and What Can Be Done to Cool Them Down*, 29 WM. & MARY ENVTL. L. & POL'Y. REV. 767 (Spring 2005).

33. *Id.* at 780.

34. Protocol on Protection and Welfare of Animals, 1997 OJ C 340, *available at* http://eur-lex.europa.eu/en/treaties/dat/11997D/htm/11997D.html#0110010013.

> The High Contracting Parties, desiring to ensure improved protection and respect for the welfare of animals as sentient beings, have agreed upon the following provision which shall be annexed to the Treaty establishing the European Community, In formulating and implementing the Community's agriculture, transport, internal market and research policies, the Community and the Member States shall pay full regard to the welfare requirements of animals, while respecting the legislative or administrative provisions and customs of the Member States relating in particular to religious rites, cultural traditions and regional heritage.

Id.

35. *Id.*

36. 7 U.S.C.A. §§1901, 1902, 1904, 1906, 1907.

37. 49 U.S.C. §80502(a)-(b). The Twenty-Eight Hour Law requires that animals must be taken out of the "vehicle" transporting them (trucks or trains), provided food and water, and given at least five hours of rest for every twenty-eight hours of interstate travel. Until 2006, the United States Department of Agriculture interpreted the word "vehicle" so that it excluded trucks, and included only trains. This rendered the law virtually meaningless because more than ninety-five percent of farm animals are transported by truck. In response to a petition by the Humane Society of the United States, the USDA finally agreed that the law covered truck transport, but stubbornly refused to apply it to birds (who represent over ninety percent of the animals used in America for food production). *See* Bruce Wagman, Sonja Waisman & Pamela Frasch, Animal Law: Cases and Materials 420 (4th ed. 2010).

38. The European Convention for the Protection of Animals During Transport, 1968; ETS 65, *available at* http://www.coe.int/t/e/legal_affairs/legal_co-operation/biological_safety, _use_of_animals/Transport.

39. *See generally.* Jessica Braunschweig-Norris, *The U.S. Egg Industry—Not All It's Cracked up to Be for the Welfare of the Laying Hen: A Comparative Look at United States and European Union Welfare Laws*, 10 Drake J. Agric. L. 511 (2005); Michael C. Appleby, *The European Union Ban on Conventional Cages for Laying Hens: History and Perspectives*, J. Applied Animal Welfare Science 6(2), 103 (2003).

40. *The World Egg Industry—A Few Facts and Figures*, International Egg Commission, http://www.internationalegg.com/corporate/eggindustry/details.asp?id=18&cid=19 (4.93 billion egg-laying hens); Cracking Factory Farming, *supra* note 6, at 6 (three billion caged hens).

41. *See, e.g., Cage-Free vs. Battery-Cage Eggs: Comparison of Animal Welfare in Both Methods*, HSUS (Sept. 1, 2009), *available at* http://www.humanesociety.org/issues/confinement_farm/facts/cage-free_vs_battery-cage.html.

42. *See, e.g.*, Holly Zacharia, *Much Rests on State Hearing for Egg Farm*, The Columbus Dispatch, Dec. 15, 2010, *available at* http://www.dispatch.com/live/content/local_news/stories/2010/12/15/much-rests-on-state-hearing-for-egg-farm.html (discussing hearing for a single Ohio facility that would house six million birds).

43. Rick Callahan, *Agriculture: Big Pens Breed Chicken 'Cannibalism' on Egg Farms*, North County Times, May 10, 2010, *available at* http://www.nctimes.com/business/article_a5e05c26-cd08-5f8a-ba31-7b31eb5610d3.html.

44. R.C. Newberry, *Cannibalism*, *in* Welfare of the Laying Hen (G.C. Perry ed., 2004); *Id.* at 1–2. *See also* Ian J. H. Duncan, *Animal Welfare Issues in the Poultry Industry: Is There a Lesson to be Learned?*, 4(3) Journal of Applied Animal Welfare Science 207 (2001).

45. *Id.*

46. *Id.*

47. W. Kuenzel, *Neurobiological Basis of Sensory Perception: Welfare Implications of Beak Trimming*, 86 Poultry Science 1273 (2007). *See also* J. Mench, *The Welfare of Poultry in Modern Production Systems*, 4 Poultry Science Review 112 (1992).

48. BV 1992 §24; Stephanie J. Engelsman, *"World Leader"—At What Price? A Look at Lagging American Animal Protection Laws*, 22 Pace Envtl. L. Rev. 329, 361 (2005) (quoting Karen Davis, *The Battery Hen*, *in* Stallwood, *supra* note 19, at 188, 194); *see also Switzerland—Swiss Animal Protection Ordinance 1981*, Animal Legal & Historical Center (2010), *available at* http://www.animallaw.info/nonus/statutes/stchapo1981.htm.

49. *Id.*

50. David J. Wolfson & Mariann Sullivan, *Foxes in the Hen House: Animals, Agribusiness, and the Law: A Modern American Fable*, *in* ANIMAL RIGHTS: CURRENT DEBATES AND NEW DIRECTIONS 205, 222 (Cass R. Sunstein & Martha C. Nussbaum eds., 2004) (discussing Swiss law). There is some concern that the elimination of battery cages in Switzerland has increased imports of battery cage eggs from other countries. *See* Darian M. Ibrahim, *A Return to Descartes: Property, Profit, and the Corporate Ownership of Animals*, 70 LAW & CONTEMP. PROBS. 89, 108 (2007) (suggesting that the ban has led Swiss consumers to purchase imported eggs from caged hens); *but see* Gaverick Matheny & Cheryl Leahy, *Farm-Animal Welfare, Legislation, and Trade*, 70 LAW & CONTEMP. PROBS. 325, 353, 358 (2007) (stating that Swiss shell eggs from uncaged hens have increased their market share since the ban and that overall per capita egg consumption has decreased).

51. Council Directive 1999/74/EC of 19 July 1999, *Laying Down Minimum Standards for the Protection of Laying Hens*, 1999 O.J. (L 203/53) [hereinafter Hens Directive]. *See also* Peter Stevenson, *European Union Law on the Welfare of Farm Animals,* Proceedings from the 2004 International Animal Welfare Law Conference 165 (2004), *available at* http://www.animallaw.info/policy/pobowelfareconf2004.htm.

52. Hens Directive, *supra* note 51, at preamble (7).

53. *Id.* at art. 5.

54. *Id.* at art. 6.

55. *Id.* at art. 4. Commentators have criticized enriched cage systems as well. *See, e.g.*, Engelsman, *supra* note 48, at 352–53 (enriched cage "requirements are still too meager to enable hens to engage in natural behaviors. In recognition of this fact, Germany has prohibited 'enriched' cages as of 2012) (footnotes and citations omitted).

56. Commission Regulation (EC) No 557/2207 of 23 May 2007 laying down detailed rules for implementing Council Regulation (EC) No 1028/2006 on marketing standards of eggs [2007] OJ L 132 p 5–20, annex I.

57. Hens Directive, *supra* note 51, at annex (8).

58. *The Welfare of Farmed Animals (England)* AMENDMENT REGULATIONS 2002 (SI 1646).

59. *See Opinion on Beak Trimming of Laying Hens* (Nov. 2007), FARM ANIMAL WELFARE COUNCIL, *available at* http://www.fawc.org.uk/pdf/beak-trimming.pdf. "The purpose of the written opinion was [t]o advise the Government of the implications for the welfare of laying hens of the proposed ban on beak trimming, which is due for implementation by 31 December 2010 in England, Scotland and Wales." *Id.* at 1.

60. http://www.parliament.uk/briefingpapers/commons/lib/research/briefings/snsc-01367.pdf.

61. The statute reads: "[A] person shall not tether or confine any covered animal, on a farm, for all or the majority of any day, in a manner that prevents such animal from: (a) Lying down, standing up, and fully extending his or her limbs; and (b) turning around freely." CAL. HEALTH & SAFETY CODE § 25990 (2008). The term "covered animals" means "any pig during pregnancy, calf raised for veal, or egg-laying hen who is kept on a farm." The law defines "egg-laying hen" as "any female domesticated chicken, turkey, duck, goose, or guinea fowl kept for the purpose of egg production." The phrase "[f]ully extending his or her limbs" means "fully extending all limbs without touching the side of an enclosure, including, in the case of egg-laying hens, fully spreading both wings without touching the side of an enclosure or other egg-laying hens." "Enclosure" is defined as "any cage, crate, or other structure (including what is commonly described as a 'gestation crate' for pigs; a 'veal crate' for calves; or a 'battery cage' for egg-laying hens) used to confine a covered animal." *Id.* § 25991.

62. *Id.* §25993 ("Any person who violates any of the provisions of this chapter is guilty of a misdemeanor, and upon conviction thereof shall be punished by a fine not to exceed one thousand dollars ($1,000) or by imprisonment in the county jail for a period not to exceed 180 days or by both such fine and imprisonment.").

63. The case was dismissed with the court finding that the plaintiff did not adequately connect the cruelty with the government's activity. *Humane Society of the United States v. California Board of Equalization*, 152 Cal. App. 4th 349 (2007).

64. *Commonwealth v. Musser*, NT 12-80/06 (D.J.C., Lancaster Co.). *Pennsylvania Court Finds that Animal Abuse on Egg Factory Farm Is Legal,* Compassion Over Killing (June 4, 2007), *available at* http://www.cok.net/inthenews/releases/?pr=pennsylvania-court-finds-that-animal-abuse-on-egg-factory-farm-is-legal.

65. Katrina Sharman, *Farm Animals and Welfare Law: An Unhappy Union, in* Animal Law in Australasia 54 (Peter Sankoff & Steven White eds., 2009).

66. *Id.* at 54 n.106 (National Welfare Advisory Committee (2000) *Guide to Layer Hens Code as amended by Amendment Notice 2007*, p. 21).

67. Indeed, consumption of all animal products has grown enormously. "Americans are downing close to 200 pounds of meat, poultry and fish per capita per year (dairy and eggs are separate, and hardly insignificant), an increase of 50 pounds per person from 50 years ago." Mark Bittman, *Rethinking the Meat-Guzzler*, N.Y. Times, Jan. 27, 2008, *available at* http://www.nytimes.com/2008/01/27/weekinreview/27bittman.html?_r=1.

68. Steve Striffler, *Chicken: The Dangerous Transformation of America's Favorite Food* 32 (2005). More than 9.1 billion chickens are slaughtered for food each year in the United States. Poultry Slaughter 2008 Annual Summary, *supra* note 6, at 3.

69. FAO, *supra* note 6. This 600 percent increase cannot be attributed to human population growth, as the human population increased by only 117 percent between 1960 (3 billion) and 2005 (6.5 billion). Department of Economic and Social Affairs, Population Division, United Nations, *World Population Prospects: The 2008 Revision*, http://esa.un.org/unpp. This means the global broiler population is more than seven times that of the global human population.

70. *Farm Animals, Chickens, Meat Chickens,* Compassion in World Farming, *available at* http://www.ciwf.org.uk/farm_animals/poultry/meat_chickens/default.aspx.

71. Paul W. Aho, *The World's Commercial Chicken Meat and Egg Industries, in* Commercial Chicken Meat and Egg Production 3, 7–8 (Donald D. Bell & William D. Weaver, Jr. eds., 5th ed. 2001); FAO, *supra* note 6.

72. Aho, *supra* note 71, at 8.

73. Susan Brehm, *From Red Barn to Facility: Changing Environmental Liability to Fit the Changing Structure of Livestock Production*, 93 Cal. L. Rev. 797, 801 n.17 (May 2005) (citation omitted).

74. *Id.*

75. William Reppy, Jr., Jeff Welty, *A Return to Descartes: Property, Profit, and the Corporate Ownership of Animals*, 70 Law & Contemp. Probs. 89, 96 (Winter 2005).

76. Sharman, *supra* note 65, at 38.

77. *Id.*

78. *See, e.g., Broiler Chickens Bred For Fast Growth Are Having Difficulty Walking,* ScienceDaily (Feb. 7, 2008), *available at* http://www.sciencedaily.com/releases/2008/02/080206090505.htm.

79. *Id.* Broilers' tissues related to meat production, such as their muscles and fat, grow much faster than their bones. They get to a point where their bones, especially their legs, cannot support the weight of their bodies, leading to deformities and lameness. One study found that 26 percent of broiler chickens develop bone disease and extended pain in the last phase of their lives because of the rapid growth. S.C. Kestin, T.G. Knowles, A.E. Tinch, and N.G. Gregory., *Prevalence of Leg Weakness in Broiler Chickens and its Relationship with Genotype*, 131(9) The Veterinary Record 190 (1992). *See also* R.J. Julian, *Rapid growth problems: Ascites and Skeletal Deformities in Broilers*, 77 Poultry Science 1773, 1780 (1998), *available at* http://www.poultryscience.org/ps/paperpdfs/98/ps981773.pdf.

80. http://www.ciwf.org.uk/farm_animals/poultry/meat_chickens/default.aspx.

81. *Welfare Issues for Meat Chickens* , Compassion in World Farming, *available at* http://www.ciwf.org.uk/farm_animals/poultry/meat_chickens/welfare_issues.aspx [hereinafter *Welfare Issues*] ("Because they cannot move easily, the chickens are not able to adjust their environment to avoid heat, cold or dirt as they would in natural conditions. The added weight and overcrowding also puts a strain on their hearts and lungs. In the United Kingdom alone, up to 19 million chickens die in their sheds from heart failure each year. Across the EU, this figure could be as much as 121 million.").

82. *Id.*

83. A chicken needs 138 square inches to stretch one of her wings, 178 square inches to preen, 197 square inches to turn around, and 291 square inches to flap her wings. *Animal Suffering in the Broiler Industry*, Compassion Over Killing, *available at* http://www.chickenindustry.com/cfi/broilerindustryreport/confinement/ (citing M.S. Dawkins & S. Hardie, *Space Needs of Laying Hens*, 30 British Poultry Science 413, 413–16 (1989)).

84. *Welfare Issues*, *supra* note 81.

85. 49 U.S.C. § 80502(a) ("[A] rail carrier, express carrier, or common carrier ... may not confine animals in a vehicle or vessel for more than 28 consecutive hours without unloading the animals for feeding, water, and rest."); Letter from Ron DeHaven, Deputy Administrator, USDA Veterinary Services, to Peter Brandt, Attorney, Humane Society of the United States (Sept. 22, 2006) ("The Twenty-Eight Hour Law was never construed as being applicable to poultry, and ... USDA does not intend to change this longstanding interpretation of the statute.").

86. 7 U.S.C. § 1902(a) (requiring that "livestock" be "rendered insensible to pain by a single blow or gunshot or an electrical, chemical or other means that is rapid and effective, before being shackled, hoisted, thrown, cast, or cut").

87. Council Directive 2007/43/EC of 28 July 2007, *Laying Down Minimum Rules for the Protection of Chickens Kept for Meat Production*, 2007 O.J. (L 182/19).

88. *Id.* art. 1, § 1, p. 2.

89. *Id.* at p. 1.

90. *Id.* art. 3(2). "Stocking density" refers to the maximum live weight that can be within a square meter of space. *Id.* art. 2.

91. *Id.* annex 1.

92. *See, e.g.*, P.L.M. van Horne & N. Bondt, *Impact of EU Council Directive 99/74/EC 'Welfare of Laying Hens' on the Competitiveness of the EU Egg Industry*, Agricultural Economics Research Institute: The Hague (2003), *available at* http://ageconsearch.umn.edu/bitstream/29126/1/rr030204.pdf.

93. Stevenson, *supra* note 51, at 313.

94. *Id.*

95. *See Welfare Aspects of the Production of Foie Gras in Ducks and Geese,* Report of the SCIENTIFIC COMMITTEE ON ANIMAL HEALTH AND ANIMAL WELFARE (hereinafter "*Foie Gras Welfare*"), adopted Dec. 16, 1998, *available at* http://ec.europa.eu/food/fs/sc/scah/out17_en.pdf.

96. *See, e.g., id.* at 33–50, 61–63.

97. *Id.*

98. Alan Solomon *et al., Amyloidogenic Potential of Foie Gras,* 104 Proceedings of the National Academy of Sciences of the United States of America 26 10998–11001 (June 26, 2007), *available at* http://www.pnas.org/content/104/26/10998.full.pdf+html.

99. *See, e.g., Animal Welfare,* FOIEGRAS-FACTSANDTRUTH.COM, *available at* http://www.foiegras-factsandtruth.com/goose-duck-welfare.html, which claims, "No scientific surveys have established that goose or duck fattening generates direct consequences for animal behaviour. According to published conclusions, a normal fattening approach does not generate any stress or pain for ducks and geese."

100. *See, e.g., Facts about Foie Gras,* ARTISAN FARMERS ALLIANCE, http://www.artisanfarmers.org/factsaboutfoiegras.html, citing Guémené *et al., Force Feeding: An Examination of Available Scientific Evidence,* NATIONAL INSTITUTE OF AGRONOMIC RESEARCH (2006).

101. *Id.*

102. *See* ARTISAN FARMERS ALLIANCE, http://www.artisanfarmers.org/home.html.

103. Council Directive 1998/58/EC of 20 July 1998, *Concerning the Protection of Animals Kept for Farming Purposes,* 1998, O.J. (L 221). "Animals must be fed a wholesome diet which is appropriate to their age and species and which is fed to them in sufficient quantity to maintain them in good health and satisfy their nutritional needs. No animal shall be provided with food or liquid in a manner, nor shall such food or liquid contain any substance, which may cause unnecessary suffering or injury." *Id.* annex 14.

104. Standing Committee of the European Convention for the Protection of Animals Kept for Farming Purposes, Recommendation Concerning Muscovy Ducks (*Cairina Moschata*) and Hybrids of Muscovy and Domestic Ducks (*Anas Platyrhnchos*), adopted by the Standing Committee on June 22, 1999, *available at* http://www.coe.int/t/e/legal_affairs/legal_co%2Doperation/biological_safety%2C_use_of_animals/farming/Rec%20Muscovy%20ducks%20E%201999.asp ("Until new scientific evidence on alternative methods and their welfare aspects is available, the production of *foie gras* shall be carried out only where it is current practice and then only in accordance with standards laid down in domestic law.").

This Recommendation entered into force on December 22, 1999. *Id.* art. 24.2.

105. *Id.* art. 24.1.

106. List of signatories available at the Council of Europe website, *available at* http://conventions.coe.int/Treaty/Commun/ChercheSig.asp?NT=087&CM=1&DF=&CL=ENG.

107. The text of the Poland Animal Protection Act of August 21, 1997 is available in English at http://www.internationalwildlifelaw.org/PolandAnimalProtectionAct.html. "[F]eeding and watering an animal by force" is considered a cruel method of animal rearing and production and is not allowed. *Id.* art. 4, §8.

108. Danish Act on the Protection of Animals 1991, part 1, §5: "[A]nimals shall not be forcibly fed unless this is required to treat the animal for disease."

109. Swedish Animal Welfare Act (SFS 1988:534), as last amended by SFS 1998:56 of Feb. 19, 1998. *See* a summary and English translation of the act, *available at* http://www.animallaw.info/nonus/statutes/stseawa1998.htm. *See also* Helen Striwing, *Animal Law and Animal Rights on the Move in Sweden,* 8 ANIMAL L. 93 (2002).

110. The Norwegian Animal Welfare Act, Code 750.000 (June 16, 1995), *available at* http://www.animallaw.info/nonus/statutes/stnoapa1995.htm. "It is forbidden … [t]o force feed animals." *Id.* at §8(4). The act also imposes an affirmative duty to help animals:

> Should a person happen upon an animal which is obviously sick, injured, or helpless, he must help it as far as possible. Should it prove impossible to give assistance or sufficient help, and the animal in question is a domestic animal, tame reindeer, or large game animal, he shall, as soon as possible, inform the owner or the person in charge of the animal, or the nearest police authority.

Id. at §6.

111. Finland's Animal Welfare Act, 247/1996: "Animals may not be fed by force for fattening purposes or to increase their production." *Id.* §11(1). Unofficial translation into English is *available at* http://www.finlex.fi/fi/laki/kaannokset/1996/en19960247.pdf.

112. In Switzerland, the Swiss Federal Act on Animal Protection of March 9, 1978 (as amended in 1981), *available at* http://www.animallaw.info/nonus/statutes/stchapa1978.htm, does not explicitly prohibit force-feeding, but the Swiss government has since deemed force feeding to be inconsistent with this law. The annual report of the federal Counsel on the activities of Switzerland to the Counsel of Europe in 1999 of January 12, 2000 states: "During the vote of the last three recommendations [regarding raising domestic ducks, muscovy ducks and domestic geese], Switzerland abstained and justified its position in details, stating that the fattening of poultry is contrary to the protection of animals." *Id.* §3.5.

113. Luxembourg Animal Welfare Act of 1965 prohibits the forcible feeding of poultry by hand or machine.

114. In the Czech Republic, Act No. 246/1992 Coll., *On the Protection of Animals Against Cruelty*, as amended (Animal Welfare Act), defines force feeding as cruelty to animals.

115. Germany's Animal Welfare Act of 1993, Federal Law Gazette I, p. 1094, states: "It shall be prohibited to force feed an animal save for essential health reasons." *Id.* art. 3, §9. Germany has had legislation against force-feeding since 1936. The current text of the law is *available at* http://www.animallaw.info/nonus/statutes/stdeawa1998.htm (text in German at http://bundesrecht.juris.de/tierschg/__3.html).

116. Legislative Decree March 26, 2001, n. 146, *Accomplishment of the Executive One 98/58/CE Relevant to the Protection of the Animals*, published in the official Gazzette n. 95 of April 24, 2001. "As of January 1 2004 the use of force-feeding for ducks and geese and the plucking of live birds is forbidden." *Id.* art. 2, §1(b).

117. *See* Carol McKenna, *Forced Feeding: An Inquiry Into the Welfare of Ducks and Geese Kept for the Production of Foie Gras*, Report prepared for WSPA and Advocates for Animals (Feb. 2000), *available at* http://www.wspa.org.uk/Images/FoieGrasReport_tcm9-2611.pdf. "*Foie gras* is not produced in the UK and there are no specific laws regarding *foie gras* production or force feeding. However, successive Ministers of Agriculture have stated that anyone proposing to start *foie gras* production would be prevented from doing so."

118. *Id.* at 24.

119. *See, e.g., Foie Gras Production*, RSPCA Farm Animals Information (June 2008), *available at* http://www.rspca.org.uk/servlet/BlobServer?blobtable=RSPCABlob&blobcol=urlblob&blobkey=id&blobwhere=1166616307705&blobheader=application/pdf.

120. Mariann Sullivan & David J. Wolfson, *What's Good for the Goose … The Israeli Supreme Court, Foie Gras, and the Future of Farmed Animals in the United States*, 70 Law & Contemp. Probs. 139, 143 (2007).

121. *Id.*

122. *Id.* at 143–44.

123. *Id.* at 152 (quoting Justice Eliezer Rivlin). The full opinion is *H.C.A. 9232/01,* Noah (the Israeli Federation of Animal Protection Organizations) v. Attorney General, Minister of Agriculture, Egg and Poultry Board, Moseh Benishty and 31 Colleagues, *available at* http://www.animallaw.info/nonus/cases/cas_pdf/Israel2003case.pdf.

124. Hearings Before the Subcommittee on Livestock, Dairy, and Poultry of the House Committee on Agriculture, 110th Cong. 1st Sess (2007) (testimony of Guillermo Gonzalez, Artisan Farmers Alliance).

125. Thomas J. Shepstone, *The Economic Importance of the New York State Foie Gras Industry* (March 2004), *available at* http://www.shepstone.net/economicreport.pdf. By comparison, France's annual consumption of *foie gras* totals more than 17,500 tons. *Id.*

126. *Welfare Implications of Foie Gras Production*, American Veterinary Medical Association (Sept. 24, 2007), *available at* http://www.avma.org/reference/backgrounders/foie_gras_bgnd.asp#references.

127. *Humane Society of the United States v. Brennan et al.*, RJI No. 01-06-ST7184 (Mar. 18, 2008).

128. *See* N.Y. Agric. & Mkts. Law § 200.

129. *Humane Society of the United States v. HVFG, LLC,* 2010 WL 1837785 (S.D. N.Y. May 6, 2010) (granting summary judgment); *see also* http://www.humanesociety.org/news/press_releases/2010/05/HVFG_050610.html.

130. *Id.*

131. Press Release, *Animal Legal Defense Fund, Animal Protection Groups File Legal Petition Asking USDA to Declare Foie Gras Unfit for Human Consumption* (Nov. 28th, 2007), *available at* http://www.aldf.org/article.php?id=482.

132. Cal. Health & Safety Code § 25984(c). "It is the express intention of the Legislature, by delaying the operative date of provisions of this chapter pursuant to subdivision (a) until July 1, 2012, to allow a seven and one-half year period for persons or entities engaged in agricultural practices that include raising and selling force fed birds to modify their business practices."

133. *Id.*

134. Ordinance PO-05-1895 became effective on August 23, 2006.

135. *See Illinois Restaurant Assoc. v. City of Chicago*, 492 F. Supp. 2d 891 (2007).

136. *Id.* at 894 (citing the First Amended Complaint, Ex. 1).

137. *Id.* at 896.

138. Wagman,Waisman & Frasch, *supra* note 37, at 481–82.

139. FAO, *supra* note 6.

140. Morris, Hurnik, Friendship, Buhr & Allen, *The Behavior of Gestating Swine Housed in the Hurnik-Morris System,* 71 Journal of Animal Science 3280 (1993).

141. Reun, Dial, Polson & Marsh, *Breeding and Gestation Facilities for Swine: Matching Biology to Facility Design*, 8(3) The Veterinary Clinics of North America: Food Animal Practice 475 (1992).

142. *See, e.g.*, National Pork Producers Council, Swine Care Handbook 9–10 (1996), *available at* http://www.porkboard.org/swinecarehandbook/chapter1.pdf. "Tails may be docked. Tail docking should be done shortly after birth because the piglet is small, easy to hold and the procedure is less stressful." *Id.*

143. *See, e.g.*, Humane Farm Animal Care, Animal Care Standards: Pigs 7, 17–18 (2005), *available at* http://www.certifiedhumane.org/pdfs/2004-Std04.Pigs.3A.pdf.

144. *See, e.g.*, Morris *et al.*, *supra* note 140; The Expert Committee on Organic Agriculture (ECOA) Animal Welfare Task Force review of the Canadian standards for organic production (CAN/CGSB 32.310-2006 Organic Production Systems General Principles and Management Standards):

> Tail docking is not necessary and should not be allowed. Tail biting is related to welfare deficiencies such as overcrowded pens with no bedding to direct foraging and chewing behaviours, or discomfort caused by ventilation problems and temperature fluctuations. Tail biting can be prevented by providing a behaviourally appropriate and comfortable environment; the provision of bedding and sufficient space is most important. Eliminate slatted floors and provide good balanced nutrition.

145. Press Release, *Universities Federation for Animal Welfare, The Downside of Cutting Piglets' Teeth* (undated) (citing *Hay et al.*, *Long-term Detrimental Effects of Tooth Clipping or Grinding in Piglets: A Histological Approach*, 13 Animal Welfare 27–32 (2004)), *available at* http://www.ufaw.org.uk/pdf/impact-tooth-clipping.pdf.

> [R]esearchers say most of the effects they found on examining the teeth after slaughter—including fractures, haemorrhages and abscesses—"appeared sooner and were of greater magnitude after clipping than after grinding. Because most ... are known to cause severe pain in humans, it is likely that tooth resection—even when achieved through grinding—induces severe pain in piglets. Thus the rationale of this practice should be re-evaluated." But they conclude that tooth-cutting has implications for husbandry as well as for welfare: "Shortening of piglet teeth ... induces major lesions. These lesions are likely to induce pain and to cause health disorders. Therefore, the use of this practice in commercial piggeries needs to be objectively assessed...."

Id.

146. K. Bovey, J. DeLay, T. Widowski & P. Lawlis, *Trim Boar Tusks With Care*, National Hog Farmer (Dec 17, 2008), *available at* http://nationalhogfarmer.com/behavior-welfare/trim-boar-tusks-with-care.

> Boars continually grow tusks that pose a safety hazard to human handlers and other pigs. To remove the danger, tusks are sometimes trimmed once or twice a year. Tusks can be removed using hoof nippers or bolt cutters. Less frequently used—but the recommended method—is orthopedic wire is used as a "saw" to cut off tusks. Tusks are generally trimmed very close to the gum line without the use of painkillers or sedation. The majority of boar tusks have pulp extending above the gum line. The pulp contains nerves. Therefore, trimming may cause pain and leave the tusk open to infection.

Id. The South African Pig Welfare Code states: "The breaking or cutting or sawing of boars' teeth at any time is prohibited, except when performed by a veterinarian with appropriate anaesthesia."

147. Primary Industries Standing Committee, Model Code of Practice for the Welfare of Animals, Pigs, Third Edition, PISC Report 92, 5.6.17–18.

> Where it is necessary to mark pigs for permanent identification, the ear may be tattooed, tagged, notched or punched, or the body may be tattooed or a microchip implanted. Ear notching should be avoided where possible. Where ear notching is performed, it should be carried out before the piglets are seven days of age.

Id.

148. "It is recommended that piglets be castrated after two days of age, after they have established their suckling order, and before seven days of age. When pigs 8–21 days of age are castrated, appropriate and effective restraint is necessary." *Id.* at 5.6.7. "Surgical castration of male pigs older than 21 days or surgical procedures that render a male pig over 21 days of age sterile must be performed under anesthesia and by a veterinary practitioner." *Id.* at 5.6.2.

149. Council Directive 91/630/EEC of 19 November 1991, *Laying Down Minimum Standards for the Protection of Pigs*, 1991 O.J. (L 340) 33.

150. *Id.* annex, Ch. 1, §§(3), (5), (12)–(14).

151. *Id.* annex, Ch. 1, §(8).

152. *Id.* art. 3, §2.

153. Council Directive 2001/88/EC of 23 October 2001, preamble (5), 2001 O.J. (L 316) 1.

154. *Id.* art. 1, §1 (amending Council Directive 91/630, art. 3, §§4(a), 9).

155. *Id.*

156. *Id.*

157. *Id.*

158. Commission Directive 2001/93/EC of 9 November 2001 amending Directive 91/630/EEC laying down minimum standards for the protection of pigs, *available at* http://ec.europa.eu/food/animal/welfare/farm/pigs_en.htm.

159. *Id.* preamble, §4.

160. *Id.* annex, ch. 1, §8.

161. *Id.*

162. *Id.* annex, ch. 1, §4.

163. Council Directive 2008/120/EC of 18 December 2009, *Laying Down Minimum Standards for the Protection of Pigs*, 2009 O.J. (L 47/5).

164. Arnja Dale, *Animal Welfare Codes and Regulations—The Devil in Disguise? in* ANIMAL LAW IN AUSTRALASIA 176 n.9 (Peter Sankoff & Steven White eds., 2009) (quoting Geoff Neumann & Associates, *Model Codes of Practice for the Welfare of Animals* (2005)).

165. Animal Welfare (Pigs) Code of Welfare No. 3 (2005), *available at* http://www.biosecurity.govt.nz/files/regs/animal-welfare/req/codes/pigs/pigs-code-of-welfare.pdf.

166. National Animal Welfare Advisory Committee's Guideline 10: Phasing Out One Management System in Favour of Another, BIOSECURITY NEW ZEALAND, *available at* http://www.biosecurity.govt.nz/animal-welfare/nawac/policies/guideline10.htm.

167. FLA. CONST. art. 10, §21 ("It shall be unlawful for any person to confine a pig during pregnancy in an enclosure, or to tether a pig during pregnancy, on a farm in such a way that she is prevented from turning around freely.").

168. ARIZ. REV. STAT. §13-2910.07.

169. CAL. HEALTH & SAFETY CODE ANN. §§25990–94.

170. 7 M.R.S.A. §§1039, 4020 (effective date Jan. 1, 2011); OR. REV. STAT. §600.150. The Oregon law states: "A person commits the offense of restrictive confinement of a pregnant pig if the person confines a pregnant pig for more than 12 hours during any 24-hour period in a manner that prevents the pregnant pig from: (a) Lying down and fully extending [her] limbs; or (b) Turning around freely." *Id.* §2. COLO. REV. STAT. §§35-50.5-101–03. The Colorado law states: "A gestating sow shall be kept in a manner that allows the sow to stand up, lie down, and turn around without touching the sides of [her] enclosure until no earlier than twelve days prior to the expected date of farrowing. At that time, a gestating sow may be kept in a farrowing unit." COLO. REV. STAT. §35-50.5-102(1)(b).

171. *Animal Legal Defense Fund. v. Clougherty Packing Co.*, Tulare County Superior Court, No. SCV 240050 (filed September 7, 2006).

172. CAL. PENAL CODE § 597t.

173. Julie Morrow-Tesch, *Environmental Enrichment for Dairy Calves and Pigs*, ANIMAL WELFARE INFORMATION CENTER NEWSLETTER, Winter 1996/1997, Vol. 7, No. 3–4, *available at* http://www.nal.usda.gov/awic/newsletters/v7n3/7n3morro.htm.

> Under typical management practices, dairy calves are weaned from the dam within 24 hours of birth and then housed in individual pens of varying design. Dairy calves are not group-housed because these animals tend to look for something to suckle on or nurse on after being removed from the cow.

Id.

174. Challenges to this practice will be discussed in the WTO section in Chapter 6.

175. *Industry Information: Frequently Asked Questions*, THE VEAL FARM, *available at* http://vealfarm.com/industry-info/faqs.asp.

176. C. W. Arave & J. L. Albright, *Animal Welfare Issues: Dairy*, ANIMAL WELFARE INFORMATION CENTER BULLETIN, Fall 1998, Vol. 9, no. 1–2, *available at* http://www.nal.usda.gov/awic/newsletters/v9n1/9n1arave.htm.

177. "White veal" can be distinguished from "pink veal" by its color, which is a direct result of the method of confinement and the diet fed to the calves. *See generally Animal Legal Defense Fund Boston, Inc. v. Provimi Veal Corp.*, 626 F. Supp. 278, 279–81 (D. Mass. 1986) (referring to "red" veal).

178. *See generally id.*

179. Calf welfare is now covered by The Welfare of Farmed Animals (England) Regulations 2007 No. 2078, Schedule 6.

180. *See* C. Barclay, *The Export of Farm Animals Bill: Bill 20 of 1999–2000*, Research paper 00/11, House of Commons, London (2000).

> The introduction of higher animal welfare standards in the UK than in other EU countries naturally increased the import into the UK of meat from animals reared to standards that would be illegal in the UK.... [The] animal welfare effect was even worse, in that many calves have been sent from the UK to Continental countries where they have gone into veal crates. In some cases, the resulting veal was then imported into the UK.

181. Council Directive 2008/119/EC of 18 December 2008, *Laying Down Minimum Standards for the Protection of Calves*, 2008 O.J. (L 010), Preamble.

182. Council Directive 97/2/EC of 20 January 1997 amending Directive 91/629/EEC, *Laying Down Minimum Standards for the Protection of Calves*, 1997, O.J. (L 025), 0 0024–0025, art. 3(3).

183. Council Directive 2008/119/EC of 18 December 2008, *Laying Down Minimum Standards for the Protection of Calves*, 2009 O.J. (L 10), art. 3(a)(1).

> [N]o calf shall be confined in an individual pen after the age of eight weeks, unless a veterinarian certifies that its health or behaviour requires it to be isolated in order to receive treatment. The width of any individual pen for a calf shall be at least equal to the height of the calf at the withers, measured in the standing position, and the length shall be at least equal to the body length of the calf, measured from the tip of the nose to the caudal edge of the tuber ischii (pin bone), multiplied by 1,1. Individual pens for calves (except those for isolating sick animals)

> must not have solid walls, but perforated walls which allow the calves to have direct visual and tactile contact.

184. Commission Decision 97/182/EC of 24 February 1997 amending the Annex to Directive 91/629/EEC, *Laying Down Minimum Standards for the Protection of Calves,* 1997 O.J. (L 076), p 0030–0031, para 11. The annex now reads:

> All calves must be provided with an appropriate diet adapted to their age, weight and behavioural and physiological needs, to promote good health and welfare. To this end, their food must contain sufficient iron to ensure an average blood haemoglobin level of at least 4.5 mm/litre, and a minimum daily ration of fibrous food must be provided for each calf over two weeks old, the quantity being raised from 50 g to 250 g per day for calves from eight to 20 weeks old. Calves shall not be muzzled.

Council Directive 2008/119/EC of 18 December 2008, *Laying Down Minimum Standards for the Protection of Calves*, 2009 O.J. (L 10), annex I, ¶ 11.

185. ARIZ. REV. STAT. § 13-2910.07; COLO. REV. STAT. §§ 35-50.5-101–03; CAL. HEALTH & SAFETY CODE ANN. §§ 25990–94; ME. REV. STAT. ANN. tit. 7, § 4020; ME. REV. STAT. ANN. tit. 17, § 1039; MICH. COMP. LAWS § 287.746.

186. *See, e.g., Marcho Farms to Phase Out Veal Crates,* FARM SANCTUARY (Jan. 31, 2007), http://www.farmsanctuary.org/actionalerts/alert_marcho.htm (discussing 2007 announcement by Marcho Farms, one of the largest American veal companies, that it intended to end the use of veal crates).

187. *See generally, Provimi Veal, supra* note 177, 626 F. Supp. 278.

188. *Id.* at 281, 284.

189. FAO, *supra* note 6.

190. *See Humane Soc. of Rochester and Monroe County for Prevention of Cruelty To Animals, Inc. v. Lyng,* 633 F.Supp. 480 (W.D.N.Y. 1986). In this lawsuit, plaintiffs challenged a government-subsidized program that required participating dairy ranchers to use a hot iron to brand cows' faces in order to identify them for the program. Plaintiffs included the local humane group, which was authorized to enforce the anticruelty laws and dairy farmers who would be required to apply the brands. Plaintiffs claimed the procedure was painful and unnecessary and constituted cruelty to the cows. The court accepted testimony from veterinarians. While the testimony was somewhat in conflict, the court agreed with the statements of plaintiffs' witnesses, who testified that the branding was inhumane. *Id.* at 482. The court criticized the government for not considering the interests of the cows and the pain the procedure might inflict, and found that the practice would likely violate the state anticruelty laws. *Id.* at 486–87. Based on this finding, the program was enjoined.

191. C. W. Arave & J. L. Albright, *supra* note 176.

192. *Animal Legal Defense Fund v. Mendes,* 160 Cal. App. 4th 136, 72 Cal. Rptr. 3d 553 (Cal. Ct. App. 2008).

193. CAL. PENAL CODE § 597t.

194. INDIA CONSTIT. art. 51(g).

195. INDIA CONSTIT., art. 48. In other countries, dairy cows are routinely slaughtered for meat after they have stopped producing significant amounts of milk.

196. The Prevention of Cruelty to Animals Rules of 1978, § 5.

197. *Id.* § 9. The practices of "phooka" and "doom dev," used to stimulate the internal reproductive tracts and organs of milk cows and which supposedly increase milk production, are expressly prohibited by this provision. *Id.*

198. FAO, *supra* note 6.

199. India Const. art. 48 (states' rights to ban cow slaughter) with India Const. art. 41 (states to secure right to work).

200. The Andhra Pradesh Prohibition of Cow Slaughter and Animal Preservation Act of 1977, § 10.

201. *Id.*

202. The Assam Cattle Preservation Act, preamble.

203. The Assam Cattle Preservation Act, § 13.

204. The Delhi Agricultural Cattle Preservation Act of 1994, §§ 4–5, 7.

205. *Id.* § 8–9.

206. The Transport of Animals Rules, §§ 48–55.

207. *See, e.g.*, Visakha Society for Protection and Care of Animals, *available at* http://www.vspca.org/issues/transport.php; India Together www.indiatogether.org/reports/peta.htm.

208. Prevention of Cruelty to Animals Rules of 2001, *Transport of Animals on Foot*, § 6.

209. *Id.* § 11.

210. *See, e.g.*, Visakha Society for Protection and Care of Animals, *supra* note 199.

211. 7 U.S.C. § 1901.

212. *Id.*

213. While there has been some modernization of techniques, this is still a permissible method of slaughter.

214. 7 U.S.C. § 1902(a).

215. Jeff Welty, *Humane Slaughter Laws*, 70 Law & Contemp. Probs. 175, 176–77 (2007).

216. *See* Gail A. Eisnitz, Slaughterhouse (revised ed. 2007); *see also* Sue Coe, Dead Meat (2006). It is important to note that animal rights advocates argue that even if slaughter could be made painless and "humane," it would still be unacceptable because it deprives animals of their lives. *See, e.g.*, Tom Regan, The Case for Animal Rights 344 (1983) (arguing that treating animals well before killing them for food "would not remove the fundamental injustice endemic to the practice").

217. Eisnitz, *supra* note 216, at 43.

218. *Id.* at 117–34. One union official reported having "seen live animals shackled, hoisted, stuck, and skinned. Too many to count. Too many to remember.... I've seen shackled beef looking around before they've been stuck." *Quoted in id.* at 132–33. Another worker reported having "seen thousands and thousands of cows go through the slaughter process alive." *Quoted in id.* at 296. Other slaughterhouse workers told Eisnitz that "[w]orkers ... cut off the feet while the cow is breathing. It [sic] makes noise. It's looking around.... Cows can get seven minutes down the line and still be alive.... Sometimes they go pretty far. Sometimes they have all the skin out and they're all peeled. Sometimes you can tell they're alive because when you look at their eyes, you can see the tears of a cow. And their eyes are moving and everything. But mainly they just make a lot of noise and are trying to kick." *Quoted in id.*

219. 7 U.S.C. § 1902(b).

220. *Jones v. Butz*, 374 F. Supp. 1284 (S.D. N.Y. 1974).

221. Plaintiffs were "six individuals and three organizations having in common a professed commitment to 'the principle of the humane treatment of animals' and to 'the principle of the separation of church and state.'" *Id.* at 1287.

222. *Id.*

223. *Id.* at 1291.

224. United Nations Food and Agricultural Organization, Regional Office of Asia and the Pacific, Guidelines for Humane Handling, Transport and Slaughter of Livestock 55, *available at* ftp://ftp.fao.org/docrep/fao/003/x6909e/x6909e02.pdf (hereinafter FAO Guidelines).

225. Council Directive 1993/119/EC of 22 December 1993, *On the Protection of Animals at the Time of Slaughter or Killing*, 1993 O.J. (L 340), Article 5.

226. Neil Trent *et al.*, *The State of Meat Production in Developing Countries: 2002*, *in* THE STATE OF THE ANIMALS II: 2003 175, 175 (Andrew N. Rowan & Deborah J. Salem eds., 2003) (cited in Welty, *supra* note 213, at 178 n.16).

227. Welty, *supra* note 215, at 178; *see also* FAO Guidelines, *supra* note 222, at 68–73, *available at* ftp://ftp.fao.org/docrep/fao/003/x6909e/x6909e03.pdf (discussing inhumane slaughter methods used in "developing" countries).

228. *Baur v. Veneman*, 352 F.3d 625, 628 (2d Cir. 2003).

229. *Engler v. Winfrey*, 201 F.3d 680, 682 (5th Cir. 2000).

230. 9 C.F.R. §309.3(e).

231. *Baur v. Veneman*, *supra* note 228.

232. Arnja Dale, "*Animal Welfare Codes and Regulations*," in P. SANKOFF & S. WHITE, eds., ANIMAL LAW IN AUSTRALASIA 182.

233. *Id.* at 189.

234. *Id.*

235. *Id.* at 182 n.46.

236. http://www.biosecurity.govt.nz/files/regs/animal-welfare/req/codes/dairy-cattle/dairy-cattle.pdf; http://www.biosecurity.govt.nz/files/regs/animal-welfare/req/codes/sheep-beef-cattle/sheep-beef-cattle-code-2010.pdf.

237. *Empacadora de Carnes De Fresnillo, S.A. De C.V. v. Curry*, 476 F.3d 326, 328 (5th Cir. 2007).

238. FAO, *supra* note 6.

239. Apparently this taste for horsemeat dates back to the French revolution, where the starving revolutionaries killed and ate the horses of the aristocracy. *See* MARVIN HARRIS, *Good to Eat: Riddles of Food and Culture* (1998). "While the legalization of horsemeat for human food in 1866 was justified primarily on socioeconomic grounds—horsemeat was a ready and cheap source of protein for those in need—the consumption of horse remained a controversial idea because of the complex and conflicting affections horses inspired." Kari Weil, *They Eat Horses, Don't They? Hippophagy and Frenchness*, GASTRONOMICA, Spring 2007, Vol. 7, No. 2, 44–51, *available* at http://caliber.ucpress.net/doi/abs/10.1525/gfc.2007.7.2.44.

240. *See, e.g.*, C.J. Chivers, *A Sure Thing for Kazakhs: Horses Will Provide*, N.Y. TIMES, Dec. 26, 2005, *available at* http://query.nytimes.com/gst/fullpage.html?res=9401E3DD1230 F935A15751C1A9639C8B63&sec=&spon=&pagewanted=2. ("Horse meat, horse fat, horse entrails and mare's milk are principal ingredients in the national cuisine [of Kazakhstan]....); Michael Johnson, *Hungry for Horsemeat*, N.Y. TIMES, June 19, 2008, *available at* http://www.nytimes.com/2008/06/19/opinion/19iht-edjohnson.1.13829773.html.) ("In Siberia, the Yakut horse, bred mainly for its fatty flesh and its high caloric content, is an important part of the local diet."); *Japan Has a Yen for Canadian Horse Meat*, ASIAN PACIFIC POST, Sept. 13, 2006, *available at* http://classifieds.southasianpost.com/portal2/ff80808 10d8f7410010da8a1ef51007b.do.html ("Some 90,000 horses were slaughtered last year with almost all the meat exported to Japan, France or Belgium.... There is a strong horse-meat consumer market in Quebec.").

241. The Illinois legislature banned the slaughter of horses for human consumption in 2007. Illinois Horse Meat Act, 225 ILL. COMP. STAT. 635/1.5 (2007). The Texas legislature pro-

hibited the sale of horsemeat for human consumption in 1949, but the state did not enforce the prohibition until 2002, when the Texas Attorney General issued an opinion stating that Texas law prohibited horse slaughter for human consumption. TEX. AGRIC. CODE §§149.001–.007; *Empacadora, supra* note 237, 476 F.3d at 329–30.

242. *Empacadora*, 476 F.3d 326; *Cavel Int'l v. Madigan*, 500 F.3d 551 (7th Cir. 2007).

243. 21 U.S.C. §601 *et seq*.

244. *Empacadora, supra* note 237, 476 F.3d at 328–29; *Cavel*, 500 F.3d at 559.

245. *Cavel, supra* note 242, 500 F.3d at 557.

246. *Id.* at 556–57.

247. *Id.* at 557.

248. *Id.* at 558.

249. *Id.*

250. *See* Alvin E. Roth, *Repugnance as a Constraint on Markets*, 21 J. OF ECON. PERSPECTIVES 37 (Summer 2007).

251. Although taboo, horsemeat consumption in the U.S. has not always been illegal.

252. Although the sale and consumption of horsemeat is "perfectly legal" in Great Britain, there is a pervasive cultural aversion to the practice. *See* Tom Rawstone, *The English Horses Being Sent to France to be Eaten*, THE DAILY MAIL, May 19, 2007, *available at* http://www.dailymail.co.uk/news/article-455953/The-English-horses-sent-France-eaten.html.

253. "There are around 1.2 million horses in Australia, including approximately 400,000 feral horses. Between 30,000 and 40,000 horses are processed for human and pet consumption annually. Meat for human consumption is exported because it cannot be sold for this purpose in Australia." AUSTRALIAN GOVERNMENT, DEPARTMENT OF AGRICULTURE, FISHERIES, AND FORESTRY, HORSE INDUSTRY BACKGROUND, *available at* http://www.daff.gov.au/agriculture-food/meat-wool-dairy/ilg/industries/horses. "Horses are not farmed specifically for meat in Australia and horsemeat generally comes from failed or retired sport horses as well as feral horses. Therefore there is no code of conduct for the farming of horses." *Id.* In 2006, export of horsemeat generated approximately $10 million, down from $26.4 million in 1998/99. *Id.* Most of the meat is exported to Japan and Russia. *Id.*

254. Sale of horsemeat is illegal in Peru and Brazil. In April 2007, Peruvian police seized ten tons of horsemeat from a factory in Lima and arrested the factory workers. The factory intended to sell the meat in the market as beef. Wolfy Becker, *Police Seize 10 Tons of Horse Meat to be Sold as Beef*, JOURNAL PERU, Apr. 16, 2007, *available at* http://journalperu.com/lima-peru-police-seize-10-tons-of-horse-meat-to-be-sold-as-beef.

255. Brief of Plaintiffs-Appellants at 9, *Cavel Int'l, Inc. v. Madigan*, 500 F.3d 551 (7th Cir. 2007) (No. 07-2658).

256. Amended Complaint at 8, *Empacadora de Carnes de Fresnillo, S.A. de C.V. v. Curry*, No. 4-02CV0804-A, 2005 U.S. Dist. LEXIS 18261 (N.D. Tex. Jan. 8, 2003).

257. *See Horse Slaughter Statistics*, ANIMAL WELFARE INSTITUTE, *available at* http://www.awionline.org/ht/d/sp/i/14227/pid/14227 (numbers of horses slaughtered).

258. "Since all three U.S. horse slaughter operations were ordered closed last year, the number of horses exported to Mexico for slaughter has exploded. As of Dec. 20, 2007, 44,475 horses had been shipped to Mexico for processing for human consumption compared with 10,783 shipped at the same time in 2006—a 312 percent increase." *U.S. Horse Slaughter Exports to Mexico Increase 312%*, AMERICAN VETERINARY MEDICAL ASSOCIATION (Jan. 15, 2008), *available at* http://www.avma.org/onlnews/javma/jan08/080115a.asp.

259. HR 503/Senate Bill 727—the Conyers-Burton Prevention of Equine Cruelty—would prohibit exportation of horses to slaughter plants in foreign countries.

260. *See generally* Andrew E. Kohn & Heather E. Eves, *The African Bushmeat Crisis: A Case for Global Partnership*, 30 ENVIRONS ENVTL. L & POL'Y J. 245 (2007); DALE PETERSON, EATING APES (2003).

261. Although the bushmeat trade in great apes is generally considered to comprise less than one percent of the worldwide trade, the eating of great apes—with their striking similarities to humans—draws a great deal of attention. *See* PETERSON, *supra* note 260. "[T]he act of eating apes is itself distinctly destructive because of who they are. They are our sibling species, who share with us between 96 and 99 percent of their genetic code." *Id.* at i.

262. *What is the Bushmeat Crisis?*, BUSHMEAT CRISIS TASK FORCE, *available at* http://www.bushmeat.org/bushmeat_and_wildlife_trade/what_is_the_bushmeat_crisis. The BUSHMEAT CRISIS TASK FORCE lists wildlife species threatened by the bushmeat trade at http://www.bushmeat.org/bushmeat_and_wildlife_trade/wildlife_affected.

263. *See, e.g.*, Claudia A. McMurray, *Wildlife Trafficking: U.S. Efforts to Tackle a Global Crisis*, 23 NAT. RESOURCES & ENV'T 16 (2009); Kohn & Eves, *supra* note 257; Charu Sharma, *Chinese Endangered Species at the Brink of Extinction: A Critical Look at the Current Law and Policy in China*, 11 ANIMAL L. 215 (2005).

264. Mark Jenkins, *Who Murdered the Virunga Gorillas*, NATIONAL GEOGRAPHIC MAGAZINE, July 2008, at 34. "'Mashagiro had the gorillas killed to discredit Paulin,' says a conservation researcher familiar with the case, who requested anonymity out of fear for his life. 'This wouldn't have been difficult. You can have someone killed for a crate of beer in Congo.'" *Id.*

265. "Bushmeat hunting, especially for apes, is inextricably tied to the pet trade: the majority of live primates offered for sale in markets are infants orphaned when their mothers were killed for food. Current estimates suggest that for each orphaned chimpanzee, bonobo or gorilla entering the pet trade, at least 10 other individuals will have died." *Hunting Methods, Animal Welfare & Primate Sanctuaries*, BUSHMEAT CRISIS TASK FORCE, *available at* http://www.bushmeat.org/bushmeat_and_wildlife_trade/key_issues.

266. *Id.*

267. Kohn & Eaves, *supra* note 260, at 273.

268. BUSHMEAT CRISIS TASK FORCE, *available at* http://www.bushmeat.org.

269. Some member groups are the Jane Goodall Institute, the Dian Fossey Gorilla Fund, the Humane Society of the United States/Humane Society International, the African Wildlife Foundation, and the American Society of Primatologists.

270. BUSHMEAT CRISIS TASK FORCE, *supra* note 265.

271. *Id.*

272. *Bushmeat*, CONVENTION ON INTERNATIONAL TRADE IN ENDANGERED SPECIES (CITES), *available at* http://www.cites.org/eng/prog/bushmeat.shtml. CITES is discussed at length in Chapter 6.

273. *Interpretation and Implementation of the Convention—Other Themes and Issues: Bushmeat*, CONVENTION ON INTERNATIONAL TRADE IN ENDANGERED SPECIES, Twelfth Meeting of the Conference of the Parties, Santiago (Chile), Nov. 3–15, 2002, *available at* http://www.cites.org/eng/cop/12/doc/E12-62.pdf.

274. The increased demand for bushmeat fuels an industry of hunters, which compounds the concerns because of health issues. That is, "[i]n addition to destroying large swaths of critical habitat, the human invasion has sparked a lethal traffic in pathogens affecting humans and nonhuman species." Jim Chen, *Webs of Life: Biodiversity Conservation*

as a Species of Information Policy, 89 Iowa L. Rev. 495 (2004). *See also* Peter D. Walsh *et al.*, *Catastrophic Ape Decline in Western Equatorial Africa*, 422 Nature 611, 613 (2003); John Whitfield, *Ape Populations Decimated by Hunting and Ebola Virus*, 422 Nature 551 (2003).

275. *Kenya: Bushmeat Poaching Hits Alarming Levels*, AllAfrica.com (March 26, 2008), *available at* http://allafrica.com/stories/200803251145.html.

276. *Id.*

277. *See Economics, Food Security & Sustainability*, Bushmeat Crisis Task Force, *available at* http://www.bushmeat.org/bushmeat_and_wildlife_trade/key_issues/economics_food_security_and_sustainability.

278. *See generally* Kohn & Eaves, *supra* note 260.

279. *See, e.g.*, Michael McCarthy, *Fear of Imported Disease as Tons of Smuggled Food Seized from Luggage*, The Independent, Feb. 25, 2000, *available at* http://www.independent.co.uk/news/uk/home-news/fear-of-imported-disease-as-tons-of-smuggled-food-seized-from-luggage-661996.html.

280. "Reliable statistics are hard to come by, but Heather E. Eves, director of the Bushmeat Crisis Task Force ... estimated that more than 15,000 pounds of bushmeat come to market in the United States every month, of which only a tiny fraction is intercepted." Ellen Barry, *A Taste of Baboon and Monkey Meat, and Maybe of Prison, Too*, N.Y. Times, Nov. 17, 2007, *available at* http://www.nytimes.com/2007/11/17/nyregion/17meat.html.

281. *Id.*

282. *U.S. v. Manneh*, Memorandum Opinion, Case No. 06 248 (RJD) (E.D. N.Y. Dec. 31, 2008).

283. *See id.* at 28.

284. Peterson, *supra* note 260, at 39. "In many parts of Africa, traditional subsistence hunting of apes, hunting without guns, has gone on for longer, probably much longer, than anyone can remember."

285. *Id.* at 24. *See also* John Whitfield, *Bushmeat: The Law of the Jungle*, 421 Nature 8 (2003) (describing the dependence of some of the poorest communities in Asia, Africa, and South America on bushmeat).

286. Schenck, M., E. Effa Nsame, M. Starkey, D. Wilkie, K. Abernethy, P. Telfer, R. Godoy & A. Treves, "*Why People Eat Bushmeat: Results From Two-Choice, Taste Tests in Gabon, Central Africa*," 34 Human Ecology 433 (2006).

287. According to the American Pet Product Manufacturers Association Industry Statistics, \$41.2 billion dollars was spent on the pet industry in a single year. According to the 2007–2008 National Pet Owners Survey, 63% of U.S. households include a companion animal, which equates to 71.1 million homes.

288. Dogs and cats are also commercially bred and sold, shown in dog and cat shows, and used in various forms of entertainment.

289. *Id.*

290. *Id.*

291. Brian Lee, *The End of a Korean Dog's Life*, Asia Sentinel, Apr. 15, 2008, *available at* http://www.asiasentinel.com/index.php?itemid=194&id=1151&option=com_content&task=view.

292. Senan Murray, *Dogs' Dinners Prove Popular in Nigeria*, BBC News, Mar. 6, 2007, *available at* http://news.bbc.co.uk/2/hi/africa/6419041.stm. "For Mr. Nnkwo ... an Igbo from south-eastern Nigeria, eating dog meat is a question of culture. 'I hear they eat frogs in certain parts of the world. But I tell you, no matter how you cook or dress a frog, I can never eat it. But dog is different. So, eating dog meat is a question of culture for me.'"

293. *See Taiwan Bans Dog Meat*, BBC NEWS, Jan. 2, 2001, *available at* http://news.bbc.co.uk/2/hi/asia-pacific/1097823.stm.

294. *Id.*

295. *Id.*

296. *See generally*, Rakhyun E. Kim, *Dog Meat in Korea: A Socio-Legal Challenge*, 14 ANIMAL L. 201 (2008).

297. "On June 8, 1984, the Ministry of Health and Society formally institutionalized the ban on the sale of dog meat, or more specifically bosintang and gaesoju, when it classified those items, along with numerous others, as disgusting foods (or "unseemly food" or "foods deemed unsightly") in the Operational Rule relating to the Ministerial Ordinance of the [Food Safety Act], and prohibited the sale of such disgusting foods." *Id.* at 210.

298. *See Seoul Government to Reclassify Dog Meat*, THE CHINA POST, April 3, 2008, *available at* http://www.chinapost.com.tw/asia/korea/2008/04/03/150124/Seoul-gov't.htm.

299. The 1991 Act lacked sufficient force to effectively prevent or punish cruelty to animals. Kim, *supra* note 296, at 213–16. Ten years after its enactment, the first person sentenced under the law was fined the equivalent of 100 USD. *Id.* at 214. However, the Animal Amendment Protection Act of 2007 increased penalties, significantly improved enforcement by creating a provision to require the training of animal protection inspectors as law enforcement officials with the power to seize abused animals, and clarified the language of the law. *Id.* at 216–20. "The first-ever Animal Protection Law (a skeletal, incomplete document, and un-enforced) was passed less than two decades ago, in 1991." INTERNATIONAL AID FOR KOREAN ANIMALS, *available at* http://www.koreananimals.org. This website also includes links to unofficial English translations of the 1991 law and the 2007 law, as well as the Reasons for Revision and Key Points of the New Law (from Ministry of Agriculture and Forestry) and comparison of and commentary on the laws.

300. Kim, *supra* note 296, at 210.

301. *Id.* at 232–33.

302. Elly Maynard & Deidre Bourke, *Fighting the International Dog Meat Trade*, DOGMEATTRADE.COM, *available at* http://www.dogmeattrade.com/library_articles/international_dmt.html.

303. For example, it is estimated that between two and four million dogs are slaughtered and eaten in South Korea every year. The fact that the industry is illegal and non-regulated means that accurate numbers are difficult to ascertain. *See Anger as Seoul Aims to Reclassify DogMeat*, ABC NEWS, Apr. 2, 2008, *available at* http://www.abc.net.au/news/stories/2008/04/02/2206458.htm.

304. The exception is Hong Kong, where the consumption of dog meat has been banned since 1950. Maynard & Bourke, *supra* note 302.

305. *China's Dog Meat Trade: The Shocking Truth That Shames the Olympic Hosts*, ANIMAL RIGHTS KOREA REPORT (January 2008), *available at* http://animalrightskorea.org/files/chinese_dog_report.pdf. "[A] major undercover investigation in China by One Voice suggests that dogs being killed for meat are increasingly likely to be one-time pets or strays supplied piecemeal from various sources—indeed, some of these tragic animals are still wearing collars."

306. Maynard & Bourke, *supra* note 302. The authors claim that New Zealand dog breeders are being targeted as a source of dogs for human consumption in Asia. "The most sought after dogs being Saint Bernards and other large European breeds, such as German Shepherds, Dalmatians, Newfoundlands and Leonbergers." *Id.* More information is available at WWW.DOGMEATTRADE.COM.

307. *Dog Meat Legal, Health Inspector Says*, CBC NEWS, Nov. 7, 2003, *available at* http://www.cbc.ca/news/story/2003/11/07/dog_meat031107.html.

308. *See, e.g.*, *A Shocking Look Inside Chinese Fur Farms*, PETA ASIA-PACIFIC, *available at* http://www.petaasiapacific.com/feature-chinese-furfarms.asp; *Fur Free Campaign*, HSUS, *available at* http://www.hsus.org/furfree/. A variety of organizations have conducted investigations into false labeling and the use of dog and cat fur in products sold in the U.S.

309. 19 U.S.C. § 1308 (2000), Pub L. No. 106-476, 114 Stat. 2101.

310. *Id.* at § 1308(c)(1)(A).

311. *Id.* at § 1308(c)(1)(B), which reads:

> The designated authority may prohibit a person from importing, exporting, transporting, distributing, manufacturing, or selling any fur product in the United States, if the designated authority finds that the person had engaged in a pattern or practice of actions that has resulted in a final administrative determination with respect to the assessment of civil penalties for knowing and intentional or grossly negligent violations of any provision of this section or any regulation issued under this section.

312. *Id.* at § 1308(d), which reads:

> The designated authorities shall, at least once each year, publish in the Federal Register a list of the names of any producer, manufacturer, supplier, seller, importer, or exporter, whether or not located within the customs territory of the United States or subject to the jurisdiction of the United States, against whom a final administrative determination with respect to the assessment of a civil penalty for a knowing and intentional or a grossly negligent violation has been made under this section.

313. *Truth in Fur Labeling Act*, H.R. 891/S. 3610, 110th Cong. (2008).

314. *Id.*

315. *See Dog and Cat Fur Trade*, HUMANE SOCIETY INTERNATIONAL, *available at* http://www.hsi.org.au/?catID=160.

316. *RSPCA Knowledgebase*, RSPCA, *available at* http://kb.rspca.org.au/Is-the-use-of-cat-or-dog-fur-legal_280.html.

317. *See Dog and Cat Fur Trade*, *supra* note 315.

318. Press Release, *European Commission, Cat and Dog Fur: Commission Proposes Total EU Ban* (Nov. 20, 2006) (hereinafter "*Commission Proposes Ban*"), *available at* European Union's official website: http://europa.eu/rapid/pressReleasesAction.do?reference=IP/06/1586.

319. *EU Ban Dog and Cat Fur Trade*, D FOR DOG, *available at* http://www.dfordog.co.uk/events_2009_fur_trade_ban.htm.

320. *Commission Proposes Ban*, *supra* note 318.

321. Regulation (EC) No 1523/2007 of the European Parliament and of the Council of 11 December 2007 banning the placing on the market and the import to, or export from, the Community of cat and dog fur, and products containing such fur, *available at* http://eur-lex.europa.eu/smartapi/cgi/sga_doc?smartapi!celexplus!prod!DocNumber&lg=en&type_doc=Regulation&an_doc=2007&nu_doc=1523.

322. A.G. Sulzberger, *Russia to Ban Hunting of Baby Seals*, N.Y. TIMES, March 18, 2009, *available at* http://www.nytimes.com/2009/03/19/world/europe/19seal.html?ref=world.

323. Michael Comte, *Canada Seeks EU Approval for Hunting Code,* March 24, 2009, *available at* http://news.yahoo.com/s/afp/20090324/sc_afp/canadaeuanimalsealpolitics.

324. The text of the regulation is available at Canada's Department of Justice website: http://laws.justice.gc.ca/eng/SOR-93-56/page-1.html.

325. *See id.*
326. *Id.*
327. *Id.*
328. *See* Andrew Linzey, *An Ethical Critique of the Canadian Seal Hunt and an Examination of the Case for Import Controls on Seal Products*, 2 J. ANIMAL L. 87 (2006), *available at* http://www.animallaw.info/articles/arus2journalanimallaw87.htm ("[I]n 42 percent of cases [] there was not enough evidence of cranial injury to guarantee unconsciousness at the time of skinning.") A text of the Veterinary Report, Canadian Commercial Seal Hunt (March 2001) is *available at* http://www.scandinaviananantisealingcoalition.org/Reports/Vet%20report%20march%202001.pdf.
329. Linzey, *supra* note 328, at 87. "The majority of hunters did not assess the level of consciousness prior to skinning or hooking; 79 per cent did not perform the 'blinking reflex' test 'indicating that many of these seals could have been skinned or hooked alive.'" *Id.* at 91.
330. *Minister Shea Announces 2009 Measures for the Atlantic Seal Hunt*, FISHERIES AND OCEANS CANADA (March 20, 2009), *available at* http://www.dfo-mpo.gc.ca/media/npress-communique/2009/hq-ac06-eng.htm.
331. *See, e.g.*, "*Economics of Canadian Sealing Industry*," *available at* http://www.antisealingcoalition.ca/resources_library.php; *see also* Robert Galantucci, *Compassionate Consumerism Within the GATT Regime: Can Belgium's Ban on Seal Product Imports Be Justified Under Article XX?*, 39 CAL. W. INT'L. L.J. 281, 285 (Spring 2009) ("[I]n 2006 the value of the seal hunt was $33 million.").
332. 561 F.2d 1002 (D.C. Cir. 1977).
333. SEA SHEPHERD, *available at* http://www.seashepherd.org/seals/seals-faq.html#07.
334. *Id.*
335. *Belgium Becomes First EU Country to Place a National Ban on All Seal Product Imports*, INTERNATIONAL FUND FOR ANIMAL WELFARE (Jan. 25, 2007), *available at* http://www.ifaw.org/ifaw_united_states/media_center/press_releases/1_25_2007_41392.php.
336. *See EU Rejects Appeal for Ban on Canadian Seal Products*, CBC NEWS, Jan. 26, 2007, http://www.cbc.ca/world/story/2007/01/26/seal-hunt.html.
337. *See, e.g.*, *Canada Lobbies Against EU Seal Ban*, THE STAR, Apr. 2, 2008, *available at* http://www.thestar.com/article/409116; THE GENERAL AGREEMENT ON TARIFFS AND TRADES (July 1986) *available at* http://www.wto.org/english/docs_e/legal_e/gatt47_e.pdf; AGREEMENT ON TECHNICAL BARRIERS TO TRADE, *available at* http://www.wto.org/english/docs_e/legal_e/17-tbt.pdf. The issue of trade discrimination, and the clash with animal welfare policies, is discussed in Chapter 6 and elsewhere in the text.
338. Michael McKiernan, *Russia's Seal-Hunt Ban Pushes Canada Further Into Isolation*, NATIONAL POST, March 18, 2009, *available at* http://www.nationalpost.com/news/canada/story.html?id=1403213.
339. Press Release, *MEPs Adopt Strict Conditions for the Placing on the Market of Seal Products in the European Union* (May 5, 2009), *available at* http://www.europarl.europa.eu/news/expert/infopress_page/063-54953-124-05-19-911-20090504IPR54952-04-05-2009-2009-true/default_en.htm.
340. *See* Chapter 6 for a discussion of the World Trade Organization.
341. Senator Mac Harb, SENATE OF CANADA, *available at* http://sen.parl.gc.ca/SenWeb/custom/?lang=en&sen=57&cust=114.
342. *See, e.g.*, www.moonbears.org.

343. *See id.*; *see also* Jane E. Brody, *Boom in Poaching Threatens Bears Worldwide*, N.Y. Times, May 1, 1990, *available at* http://www.nytimes.com/1990/05/01/science/boom-in-poaching-threatens-bears-worldwide.html.

344. *See The Bear Bile Business: Bear Bile Production and Price,* AnimalsAsia.org, *available at* http://www.animalsasia.org/index.php?UID=G7C61FB6ZY89. "Bear bile is a prized ingredient of Traditional Medicine with a 3,000-year history of usage. The bile liquid within bear gall bladders is classed as a "bitter, cold" medicine with the function of expelling heat in the body. It is used to treat heat-related illnesses such as high temperatures, liver complaints and sore eyes."

345. *Bear Bile Farming, China: Bear Bile Extraction Techniques*, AnimalsAsia.org, *available at* http://www.animalsasia.org/index.php?UID=FFFUD5EP49V5.

346. *Id.*

347. *Id.*

348. *See, e.g.*, *Inside a Bear Bile Farm in Laos*, The Telegraph Aug. 19, 2010, *available at* http://www.telegraph.co.uk/news/worldnews/asia/laos/7950161/Inside-a-bear-bile-farm-in-Laos.html. Both Animals Asia and the World Society for the Protection of Animals have focused on bear farming and had significant successes with the Chinese and Vietnamese governments. *See, e.g.*, http://www.wspa-international.org/wspaswork/bears/bearfarming/default.aspx (discussing WSPA's memorandum of understanding with Vietnam to end bile farming).

349. http://www.wspa-international.org/wspaswork/bears/bearfarming/insidebear farms.aspx.

350. "Since October 2000, over 40 bear farms have been closed down by the Government and over 193 bears released into the care of Animals Asia at our Moon Bear Rescue Centre in Sichuan." *China Bear Rescue,* International Organization for Animal Protection, *available at* http://www.oipa.org/vivisection/campaign/bile/bears.html.

351. *Law on the Protection of Wildlife* (promulgated by Standing Comm. Nat'l People's Cong., Nov. 8, 1988, effective Mar. 1, 1989) *translated in Animal Law in China,* Animal Legal & Historical Web Center, *available at* http://www.animallaw.info/ policy/pocnindex.htm. In 1981, the People's Republic of China joined CITES and then implemented its own wildlife protection laws and regulations in order to meet CITES requirements. The wildlife law prohibits PRC citizens from killing endangered animals and also prohibits the sale and purchase of such animals. "[I]llegal hunting, catching, or destruction of wildlife" is prohibited, but possession of protected wildlife is not. *See Animal Law in China,* Animal Legal & Historical Center, *available at* http://www.animallaw.info/ policy/pocindex.htm. Penalties for violations of the PRC's wildlife law can be severe. In 1992, a defendant who was convicted of hunting and killing a panda received the death sentence. *See* discussion of criminal laws in Chapter 3.

352. *See Wildlife Conservation Law* [Taiwan, Republic of China] of 1989, as amended Oct. 29, 1994 (English translation *available at* http://www.internationalwildlifelaw.org/taiwan-wildlife.pdf).

353. Press Conference on Animal Welfare, Sponsored by the State Council Information Office, Speech by Wang Wei, Deputy Director of Department of Wildlife Conservation Under State Forestry Administration (Jan. 12, 2006), *available at* http://www.chinese-embassy.org.uk/eng/xw/t231011.htm.

354. *Id.*

355. *About AAF, Our Mission*, AnimalsAsia.org, *available at* http://www.animalsasia.org/index.php?module=9&lg=en.

356. This report is from the Animals Asia website:

> This spring, on 31 March 2008, 28 more moon bears arrived at AAF's Moon Bear Rescue Centre in Chengdu, bringing to 247 the total number of bears saved from lives of torture on cruel bile farms in China. But already, 11 are dead, the victims of a barbaric industry. One emaciated bear brought to the AAF rescue centre in Chengdu was dead on arrival, his body still warm. One died of prior injuries and nine more have been euthanized. Each was riddled with chronic liver cancer, as well as a litany of other agonizing ailments. All were in impossibly small cages, all skeletal, wounded in various ways, and terrified of what would happen in this next stage of their lives. Some are blind, some have shattered teeth and grotesquely ulcerated gums, some have shocking necrotic wounds their flesh literally rotting down to the bone. Most arrived with open wounds in their abdomens from the free-drip method of bile extraction, with some leaking bile, blood and pus. The number of bears in such an atrocious condition was unprecedented.

China Bear Rescue Campaign, AnimalsAsia.org, *available at* http://www.animalsasia.org/index.php?module=2&menupos=2&lg=en.

357. *Id.*

358. *WSPA Urges Vietnam to Stay on Track to End Bears Suffering in Bear Farms*, World Society for the Protection of Animals (May 23, 2008), *available at* http://www.wspa-international.org/latestnews/2008/vietnam_bearfarm.aspx. *See also Vietnam, Vietnam Bear Rescue*, AnimalsAsia.org, *available at* http://www.animalsasia.org/index.php?UID=2G1CCMSL7NY9.

359. Council of Ministers Decree 18 (1992). *See also Bear Bile Farming, Vietnam*, AnimalsAsia.org, *available at* http://www.animalsasia.org/index.php?UID=8KAPV0KR5PM ("Since 1992, it has been illegal to poach, exploit or utilise Asiatic black bears (moon bears) or sun bears in Vietnam under Ministerial Decree 18."); Vu Ngoc Thanh, *Biodiversity and Biodiversity Loss*, Seminar on Environmental and Development in Vietnam (Dec. 6–7, 1996), *available at* http://coombs.anu.edu.au/~vern/env_dev/papers/pap02.html.

360. "However at the time Asiatic Black Bears were listed in Group II of Vietnam's legislation and a grey area existed which stated that 'live animals from the second generation may be used for other purposes.' In September 2002 Asiatic Black Bears were finally elevated to Group IB, which in effect closed the loophole and made bear farming an illegal practice." *Vietnam, Vietnam Bear Rescue*, *supra* note 358.

361. *Id.*

362. Bear farming has backfired in many ways. The original idea was to end poaching and the capture of wild bears by replacing the supply of bile with farmed bears. But when the market was opened up, demand increased as well. More bears were needed to supply more bile for new consumers interested in the product. Poaching increased both to meet this demand and because there is a belief that wild bear bile is more potent than captive bear bile. Breeding programs for captive bears were not as successful as expected, and the suspicion is that wild bears are being caught to meet the market demand. *Id.*

363. Adam M. Roberts & Nancy V. Perry, *Throwing Caution to the Wind: The Global Bear Parts Trade*, 6 Animal L. 129 (2000).

364. *See, e.g.*, http://www.wildlifeextra.com/go/news/bear-bile011.html#cr, describing efforts to pass a bill in New York state to end bear hunting and the sale of bear bile or gallbladders.

365. *Id.* at 140. According to the commentators,

> The current approach of trying to regulate the legal bear parts trade on a state-by-state basis in the United States and on a country-by-country basis globally has failed, and has actually facilitated the illegal trade. It is time to recognize the usefulness, if not the necessity, for national legislation uniformly prohibiting commercialization of bear viscera.

Id. at 129.

366. In 2002, the Bear Protection Act passed the U.S. Senate as an amendment to the Farm Bill, S. 1731, but did not become law because the U.S. House of Representatives did not include it in its voting. The House developed its own law, the Bear Protection Act of 2001, H.R. 397, but that law also failed to pass. In 2007 H.R. 3029, the Bear Protection Act of 2007, suffered the same fate, as did the 2008 version, H.R. 5534.

367. H.R. 5534, 110th Congress (2008), *available at* http://www.govtrack.us/congress/bill.xpd?bill=h110-5534.

368. *See* Kim Todd, *Bear Market*, 2002 Legal Aff. 54 (2002). Commenting on American controls, the author states:

> [The Lacey Act is] a federal law banning international and interstate traffic in illegally taken wildlife. Passed in 1900 to protect wildlife from another slaughter like that of the buffalo, the act makes it a crime "to import, export, transport, sell, receive, acquire or purchase any fish or wildlife or plant taken, possessed, transported or sold in violation of any law, treaty or regulation of the United States." It extends the reach of state laws—the primary laws governing game animals—and gives them added force. For instance, New Jersey might lose control of a bear shot out of season once its gallbladder is shipped to Manhattan, but the truck driver, shop owner, or buyer can be prosecuted under the Lacey Act. A trafficker shipping bear bile crystals to Hong Kong without the permit required by the CITES treaty could also be arrested under the act.
>
> The Lacey Act, however, relies heavily on state laws that are wildly inconsistent. If a hunter wants to convert bear parts into cash, his chances of being arrested vary depending on where he attempts the sale. In Idaho, for example, he's free to sell a gallbladder from a bear he shoots legally in state. In New Hampshire, he could sell the paws, but not the gallbladder, claws, or teeth. In Arkansas, he could sell the gallbladder, but only from a bear killed legally in a different state. Four states —Hawaii, Illinois, Indiana, and Iowa—have no black bear trade laws, and no black bears either. Traders often smuggle bear parts harvested from states with tough restrictions into these unregulated states. Once parts have been moved, law enforcement officials have a tough time proving their origin.

Id. at 55–56.

369. Merriam-Webster Online Dictionary, *available at* http://www.merriam-webster.com/dictionary/entertainment.

370. "Hog-dog fighting" is a recent addition to the list of animal fighting exhibitions seen in America. Dogs are released to attack a captive pig, and the dogs are ranked based on the fierceness of their attack. The hogs, who have tusks, are usually badly injured, and the dogs may be gored by the hogs' tusks.

371. For example, most activities of concern in the zoo and circus contexts occur behind closed doors, in private areas limited to those in control of the animals. Likewise, the abuse that has been documented in connection with the use of animals in television and films

is only uncovered by investigations behind the scenes in places that are generally hidden from public view.

372. The general anticruelty laws can sometimes be used to protect animals from harm in entertainment situations, and so those laws may be considered to that extent. Additionally, statutes that identify specific groups for protection can be the basis for lawsuits addressing alleged cruelty. *See, e.g., American Society for the Prevention of Cruelty to Animals v. Ringling Brothers & Barnum & Bailey Circus*, 317 F.3d 334 (D.C. Cir. 2003) (using Endangered Species Act in action against circus for abuse of elephants).

373. The American Humane Association estimates that currently 9.6 million animals are euthanized in the United States every year. *Animal Shelter Euthanasia*, American Humane Association, *available at* http://www.americanhumane.org/about-us/newsroom/fact-sheets/animal-shelter-euthanasia.html. The numbers are unclear, though, because there is no uniform, consistent reporting process from shelters.

374. Regulations on euthanasia of shelter animals range from the general to the specific. For example, Article 12(7) of the recently amended Taiwanese law prohibits killing companion animals, but excludes "[a]nimals kept in animal shelters or in the places designated by the competent authorities of the special municipalities, counties or cities that are not claimed, adopted or well taken care of by anyone after a notice or a public announcement is made after more than 7 days." Article 13 further provides that the death of the animals shall be killed "in a humane way and their pains be reduced to a minimum." The only specific federal requirement regarding euthanasia of animals kept in shelters is that the euthanasia be performed by or under the supervision of a veterinarian. Taiwan Animal Protection Act Article 13(3). *See Taiwan Animal Protection Law*, Animal Legal & Historical Law Center, *available at* http://www.animallaw.info/nonus/statutes/sttaapl1998.htm. On the other hand, states like California have very specific prohibitions on euthanasia:

> (a) No person, peace officer, officer of a humane society, or officer of a pound or animal regulation department of a public agency shall kill any animal by using any of the following methods:
>
> (1) Carbon monoxide gas.
>
> (2) Intracardiac injection of a euthanasia agent on a conscious animal, unless the animal is heavily sedated or anesthetized in a humane manner, or comatose, or unless, in light of all the relevant circumstances, the procedure is justifiable.
>
> (b) With respect to the killing of any dog or cat, no person, peace officer, officer of a humane society, or officer of a pound or animal regulation department of a public agency shall use any of the methods specified in subdivision (a) or any of the following methods:
>
> (1) High-altitude decompression chamber.
>
> (2) Nitrogen gas.

California Penal Code Section 597(u), *available at* http://law.onecle.com/california/penal/597u.html.

375. *See, e.g., Animal Legal Defense Fund v. Woodley*, 640 S.E. 2d 777 (N.C.App. 2007). Animal hoarders come in several types; not all are breeders, and not all breeders are hoarders. Hoarding constitutes one of the most significant problems facing companion animals in America, and is an international problem.

376. *See, e.g., id.* (utilizing North Carolina statute that allows private enforcement of civil anticruelty laws, including transfer of ownership of abused animals).

In another legal approach, the Humane Society of the United States supported the plaintiffs in a class action against Wizard of Claws, an alleged Florida seller of hundreds of sick puppies. Plaintiffs were purchasers of sick puppies. Just before the case went to trial in 2009, Wizard of Claws declared bankruptcy, and HSUS worked with other groups to rescue all of the dogs in Wizard of Claws' possession at that time. After payment of a $26,000 fine, Wizard of Claws was back in business in the latter half of 2010. In a similar vein, HSUS helped represent plaintiffs suing Petland, a nationwide chain of stores, based on allegations that Petland was selling puppies who had known congenital and other diseases before they were sold to unknowing consumers.

377. *See* Federation Cynologique Internationale: For Dogs Worldwide, *available at* http://translate.google.com/translate?hl=en&sl=fr&tl=en&u=http%3A%2F%2Fwww.fci.be%2F. It has eighty-six members that are part of an international coalition that contributes breeding standards and pedigree qualifications. *Id.*

378. *See Hammer v. American Kennel Club*, 803 N.E.2d 766 (N.Y. 2003) (plaintiff sued the American Kennel Club after he was penalized in a show competition because his Brittany Spaniel did not have his tail docked, which requirement plaintiff claimed was animal cruelty).

379. *See, e.g., American Dog Owners Association v. City of Yakima*, 113 Wash. 2d 213 (1989), in which the state of Washington's supreme court ruled that Yakima's ordinance banning "dogs known by the owners to be pit bulls" was a constitutional exercise of the city's power. A similar decision upheld a ban in a city in the American state of New Mexico on "American Pit Bull Terriers." *Garcia v. The Village of Tijeras*, 108 N.M. 116 (1988). *See also* Amy Cattafi, *Breed Specific Legislation: The Gap in Emergency Preparedness Provisions for Household Pets*, 32 Seton Hall Legis. J. 351, 365 n.15 (citing Linda S. Weiss, Linda S., Breed Specific Legislation in the United States (2001)).

Some jurisdictions even restrict the availability of homeowners insurance based on the breeds the homeowner owns. *See Dogbite Liability*, Insurance Information Institute, *available at* http://www.iii.org/media/hottopics/insurance/dogbite.

Other countries have also dealt with "dangerous dogs" by enacting breed specific legislation. Great Britain's Dangerous Dogs Act 1991 (1991 c. 65), adopted in 1991 and amended as recently as 2010, was enacted in response to identified attacks by certain breeds known for fighting, including the "pit bull terrier" and "Japanese tosa." *Id.* 1(a)–(c). The Act makes it illegal to own the identified breeds without exemption, and even the exempted dogs were subject to strict controls. The Act is in force in England, Wales, and Scotland. *Dangerous Dog Act 1991*, UK Statue Law Database, *available at* http://www.statutelaw.gov.uk/content.aspx?activeTextDocId=1540384.

Northern Ireland has a similar law entitled The Dangerous Dogs (Northern Ireland) Order 1991 (No. 2292 (N.I. 21)). *The Dangerous Dogs (Northern Ireland) Order 1991*, The UK Statute Law Database, *available at* http://www.statutelaw.gov.uk/content.aspx?LegType=All+Legislation&title=dangerous+dogs&searchEnacted=0&extentMatchOnly=0&confersPower=0&blanketAmendment=0&sortAlpha=0&TYPE=QS&PageNumber=1&NavFrom=0&parentActiveTextDocId=1009700&ActiveTextDocId=1009700&filesize=31262.

In Australia, the restrictions are generally made on a citywide basis. For example, the city of Rockingham provides for identification—by way of a special striped collar—of all dogs who are deemed dangerous.

380. In *City of Rolling Meadows v. Kyle*, 145 Ill. App. 3d 168 (1986), the Kyles kept a monkey as a pet for many years. The court examined a local ordinance that banned "any

bees, goats, sheep hogs, cattle, fowl, reptile or serpent, spider, or other animal normally wild, dangerous to life or carnivorous in nature, other than domestic house pets...." The court decided that because of the monkey's adaptation to life with the Kyles, she was a domestic pet.

381. "Millions of wild animals, including reptiles, large felines, nonhuman primates, and others, are kept in private possession in the U.S. The trade in exotic animals is a multi-billion-dollar-a-year industry." *Ten Fast Facts About Exotic Pets,* Born Free, *available at* http://www.bornfreeusa.org/facts.php?p=439&more=1.

382. For a summary of American state laws regulating exotic pets see *Summary of State Laws Relating to Private Possession of Exotic Animals,* Born Free USA, *available at* http://www.bornfreeusa.org/b4a2_exotic_animals_summary.php.

383. European Convention for the Protection of Pet Animals, 1987, Europ. T.S. No. 125.

384. See Caroline Forell, *Using A Jury of Her Peers to Teach About the Connection Between Domestic Violence and Animal Abuse,*" 15 Animal L. 53, 55–57 (2008) (information and statistics linking domestic violence, animal abuse, and the varied levels of impact both types have on the family members)*; see also* Diana Wempen, *Four Footed and Largely Forgotten: Exploring the Connections Between Animal Abuse and Domestic Violence, available at* http://www.abanet.org/domviol/enewsletter/vol8/expertWempen.html (Summer 2007) (maintaining that domestic pets and animals hold a very intimate place in the lives of their families, and this position is oftentimes a channel for acts of domestic violence targeted at certain family members).

385. *See* Regina Cabral Jones, *Chapter 205: Including Pets in Domestic Violence Protective Orders,* 39 McGeorge L. Rev. 469 (2008) (including animals in protective orders will require state agencies to work together to stop the cycle of domestic violence against children and animals).

386. *See, e.g.,* Cal. Family C. §6320(b); Me. Rev. Stat. tit. 19-A, §4007(1)(N); N.Y. Crim. Proc. Law §530.12(1)(f); Vt. Stat. Ann. tit. 15, §1103(c)(7).

387. European Convention for the Protection of Pet Animals, 1987, Europ. T.S. No. 125.

388. *Id.*

389. *Id.*

390. *See* Wagman, Waisman & Frasch, *supra* note 37, at 150–51, describing cases in Washington state and California in which elephants were pierced with sharpened bullhooks, sodomized, and beaten repeatedly with ax handles. In both cases the courts found no liability; in the latter case it was because the beatings were the standard in the industry and approved by other professionals at other zoos. *Id.* In response to the California incident, a new law was adopted, making it a crime to discipline an elephant through the use of deprivation, electricity, "physical punishment resulting in damage, scarring, or breakage of the skin" or "insertion of any instrument into any bodily orifice"; and other physical abuse. Cal. Penal Code §596.5.

391. 7 U.S.C. §2143 (a)(2)(A).

392. 7 U.S.C. §2143 (a)(2)(A).

393. 7 U.S.C. §2143 (a)(2)(B).

394. 16 U.S.C. §1538 *et seq.*

395. For example, in *Born Free USA v. Norton*, 278 F. Supp. 2d 5 (D.D.C. 2003), *vacated as moot*, 2004 U.S. App. LEXIS 936 (D.C. Cir. Jan. 21, 2004), plaintiffs challenged the importation of eleven African elephants to two zoos in America, relying on the ESA, CITES

and the National Environmental Policy Act, 42 U.S.C. §4321 *et seq*. Plaintiffs sought a preliminary injunction preventing the importation of the elephants. The court denied that request and subsequently, the appellate court dismissed the case as moot because the elephants were already in the zoos.

396. Founded in 1924, the Association of Zoos and Aquariums (AZA) is a nonprofit organization dedicated to the advancement of accredited zoos and aquariums in the areas of animal care, wildlife conservation, education and science. The AZA is America's leading accrediting organization for zoos and aquariums and accredits only those institutions that have achieved rigorous standards for animal care, education, wildlife conservation and science. Association of Zoos and Aquariums, *available at* http://www.aza.org/.

397. World Association for Zoos and Aquariums, *available at* http://www.waza.org/home/index.php?main=home.

398. The U.S. federal Animal Welfare Act, 7 U.S.C. §2132(h), also specifically exempts rodeos from the definition of "exhibitors" covered under the AWA. Guidelines published by the United States Department of Agriculture Animal and Plant Health Inspection Service define rodeos as "[c]ompetitive events featuring only farm animals and horses [that] are exempt from both the Animal Welfare Act and the Horse Protection Act. Two examples would be bull riding and barrel racing. Circus-type acts performed at rodeos are not exempt and must be licensed as exhibitors." *Licensing and Registration Under the Animal Welfare Act: Guidelines for Dealers, Exhibitors, Transporters, and Researchers*, *available at* http://www.aphis.usda.gov/animal_welfare/downloads/aw/awlicreg.pdf.

399. *See, e.g.*, *American Society for the Prevention of Cruelty to Animals v. Ringling Brothers & Barnum & Bailey Circus*, 317 F.3d 334, 335 (D.C. Cir. 2003). In another case involving Ringling Brothers, plaintiff alleged the neglect and death of a young lion after plaintiff's supervisors refused to stop a train to provide water to the lions who were traveling through the desert in railroad cars. *Hagan v. Feld Entertainment, Inc. d/b/a Ringling Bros. and Barnum & Bailey Circus*, 365 F. Supp. 2d 700 (E.D.Va. 2005). *See also People for the Ethical Treatment of Animals v. Bobby Berosini, Ltd.*, 111 Nev. 615, 620 (1995) (involving videotape in which animal handler Berosini is "shown, immediately before going on stage, grabbing, slapping, punching and shaking [orangutans] while several handlers hold the animals in position. The tape also shows Berosini striking the animals with a black rod....").

400. *ASPCA v. Feld Entm't, Inc.*, 677 F. Supp. 2d 55 (D.D.C. 2009).

401. The Prevention of Cruelty to Animals Act, 1960.

402. *See* Wildlife Law, *supra* note 7, at 115–16, citing *N.R. Nair v. UOI AIR*, 2000 Kerala 340; Maneka Gandhi, Ozair Hussain & Raj Panjwani, Animal Laws of India 699–715 (3d ed. 1996).

403. *Id.*

404. *Id.* at 684–90.

405. The Cinematograph Act, 1952 (37 of 1952); Gandhi, *supra* note 397, at 252, 837–42.

406. *See, e.g.*, http://www.telegraph.co.uk/news/worldnews/asia/china/8266563/China-bans-animal-circuses.html; http://www.scmp.com/portal/site/SCMP/menuitem.2c913216495213d5df646910cba0a0a0/?vgnextoid=e838daa5a32cd210VgnVCM100000360a0a0aRCRD&vgnextfmt=teaser&ss=Columns+%26+Insight&s=Opinion.

407. *Bolivia Bans All Circus Animals*, Guardian, July 31, 2009, *available at* http://www.guardian.co.uk/world/2009/jul/31/bolivia-bans-circus-animals.

408. Press Release, Animal Defenders International, *One Positive Step Forward for the Ban on Animals in Circuses in Brazil* (Nov. 12, 2010), *available at* http://www.ad-international.org/

animals_in_entertainment/go.php?id=2015&ssi=10; Press Release, *Animal Defenders International, Peruvian Congress Considering Ban on Animals in Circuses* (June 24, 2010), *available at* http://www.businesswire.com/news/home/20100624006470/en/Peruvian-Congress-Ban-Animals-Circuses.

409. *See, e.g.*, Brandi Grissom, *Cockfighting Outfits Evades the Law, and Continue to Prosper*, NY Times, Dec. 23, 2010, *available at* http://www.nytimes.com/2010/12/26/us/26tt cockfighting.html?_r=1&pagewanted=1&partner=rss&emc=rss.

410. *See, e.g.*, *Cockfights in Mexico*, GuideMexico, *available at* http://www.guidemexico.info/articles/108 (describing the "popular" and "common occurrence" all through Mexico).

411. 2008 P.R. Laws 154.

412. P.R. Laws Ann. Tit. 15, § 3212 (2007).

413. *See id.*

414. *See, e.g.*, *Amores Perros, Dogfighting in Argentina*, The Argentina Independent, May 11, 2009, *available at* http://www.argentinaindependent.com/socialissues/urbanlife/amores-perros-dog-fighting-in-argentina-/ (discussing total ban on dogfighting in Latin America since 1954, but prevalence of continued illegal fighting.

415. *See, e.g.*, http://www.indiarace.com/Archives/whipstories/Jockeyswins.htm.

416. *Id.*

417. *See, e.g.*, http://www.indiarace.com/Archives/whipstories/whipstories.htm.

CHAPTER 3

Criminal Law

Animal Cruelty as a Crime

The anticruelty laws are the most prevalent, popular, and well-known laws relating to the treatment of animals; this chapter addresses their nature in some detail in accord with the book's overriding purposes described in Chapter 1. As a general (and universal) matter, the anticruelty laws are criminal (as opposed to civil) in nature, and this distinction is discussed. There are many other criminal laws that affect and incorporate human interactions with animals, but the focus here is on the anticruelty laws because they directly address the issue of animal abuse and society's response to it. In that way, they embody the law's implicit (though restricted) recognition of animal sentience by their efforts to protect animals to some degree.[1] Before engaging in a more detailed evaluation of various countries' anticruelty laws, it is important to appreciate how anticruelty laws fit within the fabric of the law overall.

Two initial facts are important. First, because of the limited focus of this chapter, it is crucial that all readers understand the distinction between the *criminal* law as contrasted with the *civil* law. Second, because of the nature of animals, and the fact that the crime committed in the anticruelty context often has multiple victims (the animal(s) as well as the humans who care for or own them), the anticruelty laws stand separate in some ways from other criminal laws. And while many will already know the difference between civil and criminal law, it bears emphasizing that this chapter is limited to a side of the law to which most animal protection advocates have little or no meaningful access.

Civil versus Criminal Law

Most domestic jurisdictions, national, state and local, operate under a dual system of laws—defined as civil and criminal. Some scholars and commentators may break down these general areas into further subcategories, but these are the two basic classifications in most countries and most systems of law.

Both types of laws are created in the same two ways. First, they may be adopted by the lawmaking body of a country, state, or smaller locality. Once codified by the appropriate process, they bind all citizens of the jurisdiction, subject to defenses or exemptions that may prevent application to certain actors or certain acts. Second, in many countries, law is created by reliance on prior "precedent"—decisions and rules found in judicial opinions issued by courts resolving active lawsuits. In such jurisdictions, the decisions of appellate courts directly mandate the results of courts that are inferior to the appellate courts in an established official hierarchy. That is, if a decision has been made on a specific issue in a controlling appellate court, and that issue arises again in a court that is required to follow the decisions of the appellate court, the appellate court's determination will be controlling and the lower court must follow that decision. This is the concept of "binding precedent."

Precedent may also be persuasive (as opposed to binding), or simply instructive with no effect at all—but can still be considered by a court faced with a legal issue it has not previously addressed. In animal law especially, many courts face issues that require novel applications of law to the facts of a case, and the questions raised may not have been previously analyzed by higher courts. Judges in other jurisdictions within the country (or in other countries), however, may have considered the issue in question. Although those other courts do not directly control the decisions of an unrelated court, judges may review and give some degree of consideration to the noncontrolling jurisdiction—and often do on novel issues.

Both areas (criminal and civil) include those laws adopted by legislatures and created by courts. The civil law governs the majority of activities and interactions undertaken by and between individuals and business entities, and the relationships among those groups. It establishes the basis for many liabilities and obligations within society. Its scope ranges from interpersonal conflicts (such as liability for physical or emotional harm caused by others) to corporate management (governing issues of competition, business relationships, employment, and intellectual property) to government regulation (environmental, business-related and regulatory issues). Lawsuits and other legal disputes between private individuals and businesses, and between government and individuals/businesses, are usually founded on the civil law. Governments may also have their own obligations under civil laws and may be required or entitled to enforce the duties and proscriptions of law on members of society under the civil law. In essence, the civil law forms the basis for most lawsuits and legal actions where private interests are involved. Finally, the civil law generally provides the mechanism for parties to obtain compensation for financial losses and to control the conduct of individuals and businesses related to legal disputes.

The one thing for which the civil law does not provide (with some limited exception) is punishment, whether in the way of incarceration or penalties and fines paid to the government.[2]

The other chapters in this book discuss both civil and criminal laws within the context of the topics covered. The international treaties and compacts addressed, such as the Convention on International Trade in Endangered Species and the International Whaling Commission, fit into a separate category of agreements, since they are entered into voluntarily by member states who join the coalitions of nations joined together for each agreement. But these agreements also are more in the nature of the civil law than criminal law. They are not civil law *per se,* although, as discussed in Chapter 6, they do carry significant weight in international dealings.

In the animal law context, the civil law provides the basis for lawsuits between individuals who have disputes that arise in connection with activities involving their animals—whether for damages caused to or by animals, or obligations related to the use of animals, or sales of animals or their products. The civil animal law also addresses the regulation by government of the use of animals—for whatever means. The regulatory side of the civil law can address aspects of animal welfare and proper forms of treatment and use of animals. In this area—welfare and care—there is an overlap, as these same areas may also be covered in part by the criminal law.

Criminal law, in contrast to the civil law, involves obligations to society as a whole, where the public is represented by the government. Both individuals and organizations are subject to criminal laws, although the vast majority of anticruelty cases involve individuals rather than organizations. Criminal laws carry a presumed societal sanction against the conduct involved, which is intended to act as a deterrent to commission of the crimes. In contrast to the civil laws, the remedies for violation of criminal laws are typically considered punitive in nature, though some criminal sanctions are aimed at rehabilitation or restitution.[3] Criminal laws generally carry potential fines or terms of incarceration, which vary depending on the severity of the crime and other factors.

One way of looking at criminal law is through the filter of social conscience. The different criminal statutes can be split into two general groups, based on societal views about the acts involved in committing the crime. Criminal laws address conduct that is classified as either *malum in se* or *malum prohibidum.* The first term, *malum in se*, refers to acts that are believed to be "naturally evil" or indisputably wrong as a matter of fundamental principles of human civilization. This is a reflection of the kind of sentiment behind the *jus cogens* doctrine, which assumes there are certain types of conduct (like murder, rape, and burglary) that are sanctioned by almost no society. While virtually all *malum in se* crimes are also codified in written statutes, they are generally uniform within a country. *Malum in se* crimes are understood to be part of the historical common law that has been a part of society for as long as there have been written or socially-understood laws.

Crimes that are *malum prohibidum* are those that involve actions that are generally seen as "wrong" only because they are prohibited. *Malum prohibidum* crimes are often based on a societal determination about the propriety of the conduct, rooted in contemporary morals which may vary from state to state or country to country. There is a wide spectrum of such laws, but by illustration, the laws against prostitution, gambling and illegal drug use fit soundly in that category. Because as a general matter social mores condemn activities related to these areas, laws are created to prohibit the conduct and enforce the moral sanction.

Malum prohibidum crimes are the codified result of majority decisions about certain conduct and the management of that conduct by a given society. *Malum prohibidum* crimes may also vary significantly between countries and even between jurisdictions within a country. For example, in the United States, drug laws vary from state to state, as do the laws that regulate gambling and prostitution. In an increasing trend, anticruelty laws are also receiving different treatment in different areas. But in which category (*malum in se* or *malum prohibidum*) do they fit?

The Anticruelty Laws—A Different Kind of Criminal Law

The anticruelty laws share many commonalities with the majority of criminal law in that they prohibit certain conduct. The anticruelty laws, like other criminal laws, mandate a penalty for violation of the law, and the penalties may include incarceration or a monetary fine or both. Conviction of animal cruelty may result in deprivation of the right to own animals (just as conviction of violent or gun-related crimes may result in the loss of ownership privileges). The laws set a legal and moral standard for humans' interactions with animals. Those similarities are clear and fairly universal.

One way of examining the anticruelty laws, in order to both appreciate their similarities and their differences with other criminal laws, may be to engage in an analysis of where they sit on the *malum in se/malum prohibidum* spectrum. Is there some level of animal cruelty that is naturally evil? Or do humans' multiple uses of animals result in a patchwork of principles that demonstrate that there is no type of animal abuse that is deemed inherently wrong? While the answers to these questions do not change the enforceability of the conduct, they may explain the limited attention these laws are given. Likewise, the status of animals as property may be a factor contributing to the relatively small number of animal cruelty prosecutions and the relatively light penalties and sentences given to convicted animal abusers. These factors may lead readers to a greater appreciation or more informed consideration of the identity of animal cruelty's victims.

Upon close analysis, certain forms of animal cruelty probably are *malum in se*, and others probably sit firmly on the *malum prohibidum* side. For example, it is a fairly universal principle that the torture of an animal, solely for sadistic pleasure, is always wrong and therefore *malum in se*. Other restrictions on conduct towards animals, or affirmative obligations placed on their owners and caregivers, may be closer to a *malum prohibidum* law. For example, Italy has laws governing the amount of exercise one must give a companion animal, and the European Union and select American states have established a series of minimum standards for the industries that turn farmed animals into meat and other products. These statutes are directed at providing a certain level of animal welfare, but certainly not one that is universal or even provided in a majority of countries.

There are other differences that make the anticruelty laws unique. Because of the nature of the crimes involved and the identity of the (animal) victims, the laws create a set of circumstances imbued with certain characteristics not seen when analyzing other crimes. Most notably, perhaps, the anticruelty laws make it a crime to destroy or injure a *specific type of property*. That is, because animals are considered personal property in every country, the anticruelty laws, in the abstract, single out a type of property—animals—for special coverage under the law. While most legal systems presumably protect against the nonconsensual destruction of one person's property by another person, it is uncommon to have a detailed statutory prohibition against causing *harm* to the property of another. And of course it is more than semantics that distinguishes the fact that only one type of property (animals) can suffer or experience pain. These are common terms used in anticruelty laws but not in laws concerning other types of property. That is, neither real or personal property—other than animals, because of their sentience—have sensations that we recognize as bearing some resemblance to the physical (and even mental and emotional) feelings that humans feel. And while one can "kill" vegetative property of another (such as plants or trees), there are virtually no laws expressly addressing that killing. The killing of one's vegetative property by another would be grouped with the wrongful destruction of other personal property. With limited exception, it is also an important distinction that one commits no crime if she destroys any of her *own* property (including plants)—unless that property is an animal she has wrongfully killed or caused to suffer. All of these differences set anticruelty laws apart from other criminal laws.

The nearly international concept of animal welfare demonstrates an important consideration in relation to the uniform status of animals as legal property. While animals remain property under the law, the presence of animal welfare and anticruelty laws represents a tacit rejection of animals' pure property status. These protections separate them from all other property. Thus, while the question of animal rights will continue to be debated, there can be no question that the animals-as-property paradigm is one that looks different than more traditional treatment of legal property.

Another major departure or discussion point in distinguishing anticruelty laws from other criminal laws concerns the targets and victims of animal cruelty. While we understand that the direct physical impact of animal cruelty falls on nonhumans, are they the only victims of animal cruelty? Is there more than one victim?

Many crimes, especially those that are *malum in se*, have an easily identifiable victim; consider acts of violence or theft. The *malum prohibidum* crimes may have a more ambiguous victim, *e.g.*, who are the direct victims of drug use or exceeding the speed limit? The anticruelty laws, as a separate category, have one easily identifiable victim (the animal), who is the subject of the criminal act, and who has no right to assert a claim (criminal or civil) for that injury. The direct victim is considered property under the law. There is no other parallel situation where a living being could suffer harm and yet at the same time be legally a piece of property. So this is a unique circumstance as compared to all other victims of crimes who are humans or organizations created by and represented by humans. If a person's companion animal is injured or killed by a third party, there is also arguably a human victim who suffers the loss of her property by the criminal act. We also understand that, when a companion animal is killed, there may be a more significant, emotional loss to that indirect victim, just as there may be such indirect victims in the wake of a crime of human violence to a loved one. Therefore, another notable circumstance of the anticruelty laws is that the potential victims of the crime include both a piece of property—who has no legal interests herself—and the human or humans most closely related to that property.[4] While the human owner/guardian may be able to make a report of the crime committed, she is still at the mercy of local law enforcement as to whether the offender will be prosecuted.

There is another complication with the animal abuse laws. If the owner of a cruelly-treated animal is also the perpetrator of the abuse, that person would not be a victim. In fact, there would be no specific human victim. Similarly, if an unowned animal is abused or beaten, there is no immediately-identifiable human victim. In those cases, the only representatives who might make a claim on behalf of the direct animal victim, other than government authorities, are animal welfare and advocacy groups. Nevertheless, there are other identifiable victims in any case of animal abuse. As with many crimes, the victims at least indirectly include all members of society, because of the impact of violence on society.

The most direct victims of animal cruelty also certainly include those members of society who are most concerned about animal welfare and the treatment of individual animals. When animals are mistreated, there is a direct impact on the interests of those individuals and groups that spend their time and resources fighting for and advocating better care and protection for animals. They are true stakeholders in the area of animal cruelty. Notably, since animals cannot register complaints with law enforcement and cannot be active litigants in court, these individuals and organizations also represent a crucial part of the judicial process. If these groups and individuals had the right to play an active role in the enforcement of the anticruelty laws, the direct (animal) victims would obtain a "voice" based on those groups' ability to report a crime and represent the animals.

Passive acts of animal cruelty—such as neglect—also present a challenge not routinely seen in most areas of the criminal law. In such cases, prosecutors, judges and juries must determine both criminal liability and the harm suffered by the animals because of the failure to properly care for them. While crimes of omission are present in other areas of the criminal law as well (*e.g.*, when parents neglect their children's health and welfare), the analysis becomes somewhat different when the direct victim is not human. Usually some level of intent to commit the abuse is required in order to obtain a conviction for animal cruelty. This standard is relatively easy to prove when a defendant has committed affirmative acts of aggression towards animals which cause physical injuries or death. In cases involving neglect, omission or abandonment of animals, the courts seem to focus more on the actual effect of the crime and less on the perpetrator's motives.

Animal cruelty cases are harder to prosecute because we are unable to adequately understand animal suffering. It is much harder for prosecutors to prove, and juries to appreciate, the pain and suffering of nonhuman animals, as compared to the experience of a neglected child. Expert opinion may be helpful to provide information and objective indicia of suffering in nonhumans; otherwise, the decision is left up to the often uninformed surmise of the judge or jury determining the facts. The nature of our relationship with and control of animals, with them dependent on us for sustenance, nutrition, and medical care, makes neglect a particularly problematic issue. If an animal is sick and not treated, or starving, the passive conduct of not taking them to a doctor, or not feeding them, creates the same harm to the animal as if they had been affirmatively beaten or starved. In some cases, however, the anticruelty laws allow the *effect* of the crime to override the normal intent requirement.

Who and what did the lawmakers have in mind when they enacted the anticruelty laws, and has that intention changed over the years since enactment, in line with changes in societal considerations about animals? There have been several bases for the creation and enforcement of anticruelty laws since their inception. Over the course of the last 200 years, the weight and importance of those justifications in society's eyes has probably varied, but some aspect of each remains to this day. Those reasons are:

1. The protection of property interests, given the economic importance of animals to many livelihoods. By attaching criminal sanctions to property damage, the law emphasizes the value of the property at issue and discourages destruction or damages to those assets.
2. A philosophical belief that it is immoral to perpetrate unnecessary and unjustifiable pain and suffering on animals.
3. A prohibition on cruelty in general, and to animals in particular, is supported by the social welfare and psychological doctrine that finds it is harmful to children and the social good to encourage or approve violence of any sort, especially against the innocent and those under our care.
4. The growing scientific understanding that nonhuman animals are sentient and experience pain and suffering in ways similar to humans.
5. There is increasing recognition that those who are violent towards animals are also likely to commit violence against humans, especially the submissive or weak, so that curbing animal-related abuse may diminish the likelihood of human-human crimes.[5]

Areas of Comparison and Contrast

The remainder of this chapter mirrors other chapters in the book and provides exemplar anticruelty laws in various jurisdictions around the world. As is the case throughout the book, these laws are illustrative and not exhaustive, and hopefully provide some context and food for thought about what the similarities and differences may be between countries. For purposes of readers' and students' approaches to the material, it is helpful to ask a series of questions in connection with any set of anticruelty laws; these questions should both stimulate discussion and lead to a more detailed analysis of the implications and coverage of each law. Not every question can be answered for each law discussed here, but those that can be addressed will hopefully generate a fuller picture of the strengths and weaknesses of the laws. One goal of this text is to provide answers to these questions and thereby provide a basis for comparison of different approaches to criminal prohibitions on animal cruelty, and to offer some basis to move forward towards a more global view of unacceptable conduct involving animals.

The threshold question in examining any law pertaining to animals, but especially the anticruelty laws, is—"who is covered"? This is actually two questions. First, what particular *animals* are given the protection of the law? Second, what *people* can violate the law?

The first question can often be answered by the specific statute at issue. The written law may define or limit the types of animals covered by the statute. If there is no definition in the statute, the term "animal" may be determined by a review of general statutes within the same set of laws, or some other reference utilized by the particular jurisdiction. There may be a separate statute that defines the word "animal" for purposes of the law. There may also be judicial or administrative opinions interpreting the term or limiting the scope of the statute's coverage. General anticruelty statutes will usually cover the broadest range of species and animals, with definitions such as "all mammals" or "all vertebrates except fish," or similar constructions, while more particular statutes may be limited to one or more species. Where there is a strict limitation (*e.g.*, a dogfighting statute), the animals covered are usually identified in the statutory language.

The second question that helps in evaluating which conduct constitutes illegal cruelty is whether there are exemptions or exceptions to the relevant anticruelty law so that certain actors are immune from prosecution based on the circumstances surrounding their conduct. Many jurisdictions provide exemptions for various commercial uses of animals, such as food and clothing production, exhibitions (zoos, circuses, racing, rodeos) and research (discussed in Chapter 4). Exemptions vary, but these are some of the most common, and they effectively remove not just the conduct but the actors from coverage of the laws. The implications of these exemptions are important. They signal a weighing of animal versus human interests which results in the decision on the nature and breadth of the exemption. The exemptions also say much about legislative intent and the power of industrial forces to influence the course of the law. Finally, the exemptions highlight a recurring theme in animal law: the dichotomy (usually based on either species type or the particular use of the animal) over what practices are acceptable and which are considered illegal and cruel. For example, much conduct that would be considered criminal cruelty if done to a companion animal is considered completely acceptable when done to a farmed animal or even a cat or a dog in a biomedical research laboratory.

A corollary third question is: what is the penalty for violating the law? The level of available punishment under the anticruelty laws provides an indication of the enacting legislature's evaluation of the seriousness of animal cruelty. While the question of enforcement and prevalence of sentencing under these laws is a harder set of data to evaluate, the possibility of more severe punishments may indicate a general sentiment about animal protection. Each animal cruelty law has its own particular set of potential sentences. When jurisdictions allow for longer terms of incarceration, this indicates a belief that either the prevention of violence, or the promotion of animal welfare, or some combination of the two, is of greater importance to the community.

The anticruelty laws in the United States and England have been considered in some detail by courts and commentators because those laws have been in existence for centuries, and many cruelty cases have been brought to the courts of those two countries. Because of this extensive dialogue, we begin with an analysis of the history and contemporary application of those countries' anticruelty laws, followed by a series of examples of anticruelty laws from other countries.

Historical Developments of the Anticruelty Laws—England and the United States

The origins of the criminal anticruelty laws, as mentioned above, were based on the protection of property. The moral considerations that now seem ascendant in this area were not a primary driver for the first iterations of these laws. This is demonstrated in part by the fact that initially, an owner of an animal was not liable for cruelty to his own animals, when the same conduct would be illegal if done to his neighbors' animals. The original laws were written in a context that mainly viewed animals as owned chattel and, the laws reasoned, one could not be cruel to one's own property/animals. Even if there was some early thought that unjustifiable infliction of pain on nonhumans was morally wrong, there was an implicit exception for animals one owned. This demonstrated that ownership excused and overrode any consideration of social values regarding humane treatment of animals.

The current system of anticruelty legislation is often said to date from the passage of England's Richard Martin's Act of 1822 (Martin's Law).[6] Laws in Ireland and the pre-constitutional United States, however, prohibited cruelty to animals almost two centuries before Martin's Law. Ireland's Thomas Wentworth's Act of 1635[7] stated, in pertinent part:

> Whereas in many places of this kingdome, there hath been a long time used a barbarous custome of ploughing, harrowing, drawing and working with horses, mares, geldings, garrens and colts, by the taile, whereby (besides the cruelty used to the beasts) the breed of horses is much impaired in this kingdome.[8]

The targeted practice in the above passage involved attaching plows to the tails of animals, who were then forced to drag the plows. This practice was prohibited by the Act, as was the practice of pulling wool off sheep, instead of shearing or clipping them.[9] The Irish law focused only on certain identified species. This early example of species-specific treatment demonstrates the duality that has been seen worldwide in the application of all anticruelty laws. The duality is that the same act may be considered a crime when done to one animal and be completely legal when done to another.

The previous discussion represents perhaps the single most consistent theme of humans' treatment of animals—selective decisions are made based on animals' appearance, utility and connection to humans. This theme is an international precept, and these early laws are simply the first examples of the evidence that human societies do not view the infliction of all pain and suffering as wrong. Rather, the notion of animal cruelty is a limited concept. In the application of the laws, the concept of cruelty is filtered by animal type and the particular circumstance surrounding their treatment. In the early laws, selective application identified the particular animals (horses, sheep, livestock) with whom humans at that point in time probably had the greatest involvement on a regular basis—and who were the most economically valuable to a significant part of the population. These laws also isolated and criminalized specifically objectionable practices, but left owners otherwise unlimited in their treatment of animals.

American (and most early) anticruelty laws were initially property-based and therefore applied only to economic interests. In general, the anticruelty statutes were applied to farmed animals and other animals of commercial value and the economic interest they represented as a person's personal property. Over time, virtually every U.S. state has switched to a set of anticruelty laws that criminalized acts against animals, regardless of ownership. With this type of law, animal cruelty is a crime whether the animal is owned by the perpetrator, another person, or even not owned at all (*e.g.*, stray or abandoned animals)—although most states limit the scope of the cruelty laws to either owned or abandoned animals, exempting (implicitly or expressly) all but captive wildlife from coverage under the cruelty laws.

In the U.S., the Massachusetts Body of Liberties of 1641 demonstrated a slight shift towards an era in which the law would begin to include a component of interest in the humane treatment of animals.[10] For the first time, the law registered a compromise between property rights and the importance of limiting animal cruelty by extending the provisions in the law to all citizens regardless of ownership. This impairment of the privileges of property ownership is significant in that it signals an unspoken but indisputable departure from the traditional notion that ownership provided the absolute right to destroy one's owned property. The logical basis for this limitation is a legislative recognition of animal sentience, although that notion is not expressly stated in early cases. The Massachusetts law also signaled the beginning of a type of statute now often seen, which includes generally-stated prohibitions of any kind of abuse. Facially, the 1641 law provided broad protection: "No man shall exercise any [tyranny or cruelty] towards any [brute] Creature which [is] usually kept for man's use."[11] Such sweeping limits, however, then become subject to judicial and community interpretation, so that, for example, if a particular form of animal abuse is routinely committed in a community, the courts might not interpret such action as illegal cruelty.

The Massachusetts law appears rather contemporary in some aspects. The law acknowledged animals could get fatigued when traveling long distances, and that rest should be allowed, even at the expense of others whose fields they might need to graze: "If any man shall have occasion to [lead] or drive [Cattle] from place to place that is far of[f], so that they be weary, or hungry, or fall sick, or [lame], It shall be lawful to rest or refresh them, for a competent time, in any open place that is not [corn], meadow, or [e]nclosed for some peculiar use."[12]

Laws like that in Massachusetts ushered in the next phase of anticruelty law history, during which legislatures and social commentators began to understand that animals had some inherent ability to suffer and therefore deserved legal protection from the worst abuses. After a series of attempts, Martin's Law was passed in 1822 in England. Like its international predecessors, it was limited in scope. Initially only livestock were covered. Its first iteration included language covering "improper Treatment of Horses, Mares, Geldings, Mules, Asses, Cows, Heifers, Steers, Oxen, Sheep, and other Cattle."[13] Amended several times, it was finally adopted as the Protection of Animals Act in 1911. Its current version is still the primary anticruelty statute in the United Kingdom.[14]

As originally drafted, complaints under Martin's Law had to be brought within ten days of the violation.[15] This requirement for quick action—even in an earlier time where access to the courts may not have been as difficult as it is now—could significantly limit the number of claims brought. The Law also included severe monetary penalties for frivolous complaints.[16] While a provision like this had the salutary benefit of limiting harassment by litigation, it also placed a definite chilling effect on those who might otherwise report animal cruelty and seek to have it punished.

As anticruelty laws included the possibility of abuse of animals by their owners, they impacted owners' property rights in those animals. But there has been an ironic tradeoff—as the laws expanded by increasing the potential defendants and number of animals included within the laws' purview, they significantly shrunk in terms of coverage of potential acts of cruelty. Exemptions have arisen in every country that eliminate the effect of the anticruelty laws for the large majority of animals. For example, roughly two-thirds of U.S. states have express exemptions from the anticruelty laws for most conduct that occurs in modern animal agricultural practices, entertainment activities, sporting events using animals, and scientific research. These exempted areas are where the largest number of animals are used and killed on a daily basis. The result is that a set of laws supposedly aimed at providing oversight and enforcing humane values—and preventing the worst cruelty—now does not cover the largest numbers of acts that cause the greatest amount of animal suffering.

The exemptions are tailored to protect humans' ability to decide how animals serving commercial purposes are treated—so that economics may become the driving force behind decisions regarding animal welfare. Exemptions are usually provided for standard industry practices, even if those practices would otherwise be considered criminal. Effectively, in this area the determination of the crime (cruelty) is made by the potential defendants (those using animals for profit and commercial gain). Those states that do not have specific exemptions may have judicially-created exemptions; courts may assume that because these practices have been continuing for some time, they are presumed to be legal. At the same time, a practical exemption may exist based on the fact that prosecutors are often unable or unwilling to take these cases, given their current caseloads or other factors.

On rare occasions, courts have found that standard exemptions do not apply to the most egregious acts of cruelty. In *Commonwealth v. Barnes*,[17] defendants severely neglected horses who were supposedly going to being sent to auction and slaughter. They attempted to invoke the "standard agricultural operation" exception when they claimed that it was "normal practice in the horse farming business to neglect horses that are no longer wanted and are going to be sent to 'killer pens' at the livestock auction and then sold for dog food."[18] The court held that defendants did not prove that the starvation of horses destined for slaughter was a "normal agricultural operation," nor that the term was so vague that defendants were not on notice of what the term meant.

In the United States, local jurisdictions can also enact laws that prohibit acts that local citizens consider animal cruelty. For example, the city of West Hollywood, California enacted an ordinance prohibiting nontherapeutic onchyectomy, commonly known as declawing, a surgical procedure in which the first segment of a cat's paws are amputated in order to remove their claws permanently. The procedure is often performed in order to prevent cats from scratching, and is equivalent to surgically removing the first segment of a human's fingers. The practice was outlawed based on the city council's determination that nontherapeutic onchyectomy (*i.e.*, where there was no valid medical reason for the procedure) constituted animal cruelty. The ordinance was met with strong opposition by a statewide group of veterinarians, the California Veterinary Medical Association (CVMA), which filed a lawsuit to strike the ordinance.[19] The CVMA argued that the ordinance improperly restricted the practice of veterinary medicine. CVMA's claim was rejected and the cruelty ordinance remains in effect.

Despite the fact that anticruelty laws exist in the large majority of nations the variations are surprisingly limited. Most jurisdictions have a general anticruelty law that covers all animal abuse generically; specific statutes that address common acts of cruelty that society wishes to curb (*e.g.*, animal fighting in many countries); and exemptions that allow most acts involving animals used in commerce to continue. Certainly some countries have much more extensive prohibitions and corresponding protections than others. Using the English and U.S. experience as a comparison, we next consider the laws adopted by the countries considered in the rest of the chapter. Some examples of the differences in treatment are set out below. As emphasized throughout the book, this list is illustrative and not exhaustive, to be used as a launching board for further discussion.

Global Comparisons

India

We begin with India, where the law is to some degree driven by the predominance of religions (such as Hinduism and Buddhism) with animistic and animal-friendly practices and beliefs.[20] Because of the presence of these religions, and the notion that legal doctrines follow cultural values, India is a logical starting point for our brief survey of anticruelty laws. With roots in its ancient religions, India's animal laws provide historical perspective and a view of early animal protection concepts, even though the country's older laws were at times at odds with those in most other countries. Accordingly, an examination of India's historical and religious-based animal laws are not so much illustrative of current international animal law, as much as they are reflective of how humans can adapt to and make concessions for the interests of animals in a legal structure—and have been doing so for years.

Ancient Laws of India

Emperor Ashoka of the Maurya Dynasty, who ruled from 273 to 232 B.C.E., issued a number of edicts protecting animals in the geographical environs of modern-day India and its neighbors. These precontemporary laws were recorded on large stone pillars and rocks, found throughout the region including India, Nepal, Pakistan, and Afghanistan.[21] Ashoka, a convert to Buddhism, spread the idea of vegetarianism and avoiding harm towards all life throughout his kingdom. Ashoka's directives provided more protection for animals than any current laws in any country, including India. While these laws have been lost over millennia, some of the ideas still remain in modern India, where a large segment of the population practices vegetarianism in connection with their religious tenets.[22]

By way of example, Ashoka declared that no animals could be slaughtered or sacrificed in his kingdom.[23] He also mandated medical treatment for all species—humans and nonhumans.[24] He declared entitlement to oversee and protect a wide variety of wild animals including birds, fish, tortoises, squirrels, deer, "all four-footed creatures that are neither useful nor edible," and even some insects.[25] Pregnant and nursing goats and pigs, as well as members of those species who were less than six months old, were separately protected. He prohibited the castration of roosters, and ordered that tree trunks "hiding living beings are not to be burnt and forests are not to be burnt either without reason or to kill creatures."[26] Finally, foreshadowing by many centuries a concern that arose in connection with the problems of "mad cow disease," which is caused in part by the ingestion by animals of members of their own species, Ashoka declared that "[o]ne animal is not to be fed to another."[27]

Modern Law

Ashoka's edicts never became formal Indian law. But as early as 1887, the British (then in control of India) enacted the Wild Birds Protection Act, which provided a basis to prohibit the keeping and selling of certain wild birds.[28] A 1912 law followed up on and strengthened the protections for wild birds, after the initial statute was proven largely ineffective.[29] This act made it a crime to kill or capture certain wildlife, although the targeted species were "food animals" as opposed to "trophy" animals. A 1935 law took another step forward, entitling the government to establish sanctuaries.[30]

India's current formal animal cruelty laws were enacted in 1960, and were accompanied by the establishment of the national Animal Welfare Board of India

(AWBI), one of the first of its kind internationally. The AWBI was created "[f]or the promotion of animal welfare generally [and] for the purpose of protecting animals from being subjected to unnecessary pain or suffering."[31] This oversight group, whatever actual effect and enforcement authority it asserts, was originally intended to provide a significant review of animal welfare issues in the country, and includes representatives of the government, industry, and animal welfare protection groups, including societies for the prevention of cruelty to animals.[32]

Surely owing to the multiple foreign influences that have been exerted on the country, some of the basic language of India's anticruelty codes looks similar to that seen in the individual states in the United States and England, but then extends the protections and prohibitions further. And in contrast with the United States, the anticruelty laws are of a federal nature; in the United States, each state enacts its own anticruelty law which applies only within that state's borders.

Chapter III of the Indian Prevention of Cruelty to Animals Act, "Cruelty to Animals Generally," begins with a general condemnation of beating, kicking, overdriving, torturing and inflicting unnecessary pain and suffering.[33] But it also includes bans not usually found in other anticruelty laws, and which are only slowly being enacted in the last five years in the United States. The Indian law criminalizes:

1. Transporting animals in a way that subjects them to "unreasonable pain or suffering"[34];
2. Confining animals in a way that denies them "a reasonable opportunity for movement"[35];
3. Tethering, including keeping animals for an "unreasonable time" on an "unreasonably short or unreasonably heavy chain or cord"[36]; and
4. Denial of exercise, abandonment, mutilation, animal fighting, and certain methods of killing.[37]

This sampling of the general animal cruelty laws of India also presents a key universal (and international) concept that pervades a majority of decisions regarding the law's determination of the line between legal treatment of animals and illegal cruelty. As discussed earlier in the chapter, that line is often difficult to draw and depends on many variables. Societal sensitivities to animal cruelty have increased over the past centuries and even the past several decades, making illegal animal cruelty a shifting concept. But as discussed in Chapter 1 and earlier in this chapter, the alterations in humans' feelings about animals are not uniformly shared or changing at the same rate everywhere—whether within a specific national or state's boundaries, or across those borders. It is an appreciation of that set of differences that we hope readers will use to move towards more universal concepts of animal protection.

A common legal mechanism to incorporate that indeterminate and shifting foundation of "cruelty" is the concept of reasonableness, as seen in the multiple references in the Indian law to "unreasonable" conduct. As a very broad doctrine, in most jurisdictions, reasonable treatment of animals is not cruel, and unreasonable treatment violates the anticruelty laws. But the Indian examples should make clear to readers the great difficulty in determining what is illegal, and the inability to describe with any certainty the cruelty concept. Certainly some cases are easy—brushing a cat to remove her fleas is not cruelty, but hitting her over the head with the brush until she is dead most likely would be illegal under any anticruelty code. But the majority of acts—and cases brought to any kind of public or judicial forum—are much closer to the middle. Looking at the Indian laws, the definition of an "unreasonable time" to be tethered, or an "unreasonably heavy" chain, or "unreasonable pain and suffering," is case-specific. The majority of anticruelty codes use this language in order to adapt to society's differential treatment of animals. The application of the reasonableness filter allows decisions to be made about situations in which conduct *looks* identical but where, because of the social value placed on the conduct, one will be permissible and reasonable (slaughter of animals for food or biomedical research protocols) while another will be unreasonable and illegal (performing the same acts on companion animals or outside of scientific institutions).

One aspect of the law that may be reflective of cultural influences in Indian society is a general ban on the use of animals for public entertainment. This is extremely rare in most anticruelty codes and especially in a federal declaration such as this. But Section 22 of the Indian law prohibits "exhibiting" or "training" any performing animal who is not registered with government authorities.[38] As discussed later, the Indian government has restricted the use of performing animals in a manner unique among anticruelty laws.

Like many anticruelty codes, the Indian law provides for several exemptions. As mentioned, in most jurisdictions exemptions cover standard agricultural practices used in the treatment and slaughtering of animals for food, and their use in entertainment and biomedical research protocols. The Indian exemptions are slightly more limited, permitting dehorning of cattle, as well as castration, "nose roping" and branding of any animal "in the prescribed manner," and killing animals "under the authority of any law."[39] There is also a general catch-all for agricultural practices related to food production, which again spreads the net wide for permissible activity, by exempting any conduct "in the course of destruction or the preparation for destruction of any animal as food for mankind unless such destruction or preparation was accompanied by the infliction of unnecessary pain or suffering."[40] There is also a very broad research exemption, covering "experiments ... on animals for the purpose of advancement by new discovery of physiological knowledge or of knowledge which will be useful for saving or for prolonging life or alleviating suffering or for combating any disease, whether of human beings, animals or plants."[41]

Indian anticruelty law also demonstrates that where particular practices in may be common, they may get singled out in laws regarding animal cruelty. The Indian laws single out "phooka or doom dev," two practices that supposedly increase the production of cows raised for milk, and which involve injecting substances (usually air) into the vaginas of milking cows.[42] Both a special section of the law and a special penalty apply. This provision is discussed in the context of other Indian laws in Chapter 2.

Canada

The Canadian province of Nova Scotia passed the first Canadian anticruelty law in 1822.[43] Passage of the law occurred before the current Canadian government structure was in place, and represented, for a long time, an anomaly in Canadian law—Canada's criminal prohibitions (notwithstanding the Nova Scotia law) have been largely federal in nature, adopted by the national government. Only in the past decade or two have Canadian provinces begun to adopt specific local laws addressing animal cruelty. (This is in contrast to the United States in which, as mentioned above, almost all anticruelty laws are based in state law.)

In 1869, shortly after the Dominion of Canada was formed, the first nationwide anticruelty law was passed.[44] Thus, in most of Canada for over a century (and still at the time of publication of this book, in some areas), the only mechanism to prevent animal abuse was based in the federal system. Centralized anticruelty legislation can be problematic in that it likely results in very little coverage of local problems and dilution of the already-limited attention paid to the problem of violence against animals. This type of arrangement is a problem because as a general rule, social obligations imposed to protect animals have traditionally been focused on community standards. Local sentiment and opinion motivate each smaller jurisdiction's conduct and laws with respect to the proper treatment of animals. The notion of what level of mistreatment constitutes animal cruelty varies widely, by geography and other identifiable demographics such as the type of industry that may be prevalent in a given area. Because of this range of opinion, without local laws, the possibility of a community addressing animal abuse is attenuated. And the federal restrictions of such laws will usually be only the lowest common denominator, leaving unchecked what many people might consider cruelty. In addition to the community values that usually determine cruelty, local law enforcement is typically responsible for policing most incidents of animal cruelty. National governments are unable and unequipped to engage in that level of oversight. The combination of the minimal protections and the unlikely intervention by federal authorities can leave animal cruelty unaddressed.

Canada also demonstrates another common aspect of anticruelty laws in those countries that have had such prohibitions for over a century—the coverage mainly of commercially valuable animals. The "current" laws are in the Canadian Criminal Code, sections 444 to 447,[45] and were first introduced in 1892, at a time when both language and social viewpoints were markedly different.[46] While current views of animal cruelty cover a broad range of activities, the Canadian statutes were initially written largely to protect working animals or those used in blood sports.[47] Since the enactment of the anticruelty laws in 1892, only minor revisions have been made.[48] While most laws are written in a flexible manner, responsive to change, in this area the language of the initial statutes often leaves judges, juries and advocates frustrated. In many situations the language utilized does not match up with contemporary ideas of what constitutes cruelty or with current practices impacting animals.

A detailed history of the anticruelty provisions was set out in a 2001 judicial opinion.[49] Under the 1892 law, a person commits animal cruelty if s/he:

(a) wantonly, cruelly or unnecessarily beats, binds, ill-treats, abuses, overdrives or tortures any cattle, poultry, dog, domestic animal or bird; or
(b) while driving any cattle or other animal is, by negligence or ill-usage in the driving thereof, the means whereby any mischief, damage or injury is done by any such cattle or other animal; or
(c) in any manner encourages, aids or assists at the fighting or baiting of any bull, bear, badger, dog, cock, or other kind of animal, whether of domestic or wild nature.

A cursory look at the statute reveals the ancient nature of the law. For example, cats are not covered at all, so that any act of cruelty (other than fighting or baiting) is not prohibited. To many in today's culture, dogs and cats are classified as "domestic animals"; at the time of the statute's enactment, however, "domestic animals" almost surely referred to animals kept on farms for commerce. Most courts interpreting the phrase "domestic animal" concur and sometimes exclude common companion animals like dogs and cats—especially when reviewing statutes written in a time when agrarian interests were more prevalent and even the term "companion animal" was uncommon. In the current version of sections 446 and 445.1, third parties as well as the owners of the animal are prohibited from inflicting unnecessary pain and suffering on animals.[50]

The inclusion of owners and third parties reflects a slight modernization of the law. Moving away from the strict property-based precepts, laws that prohibit owners as well as others from committing cruelty take a step in the direction of recognizing the interests of the animals as a separate consideration in the anticruelty laws. At the same time, such laws implicitly reject a pure personal property status for animals, by providing them with some protection.

Despite the early advent of a basic anticruelty law, the introduction of such laws in the provinces and territories that make up Canada's local jurisdictions was a very slow process. As late as the 1990s, Ontario and Quebec, the two most populous provinces, still did not have any criminal laws against animal cruelty. This meant that in those areas, animal abuse could only be punished by use of the federal Criminal Code provisions.[51]

Canada presents a good contrast between laws written in the first wave of anticruelty legislation, and those first drafted in the last thirty years. The latter incorporate notions of humane treatment and cruelty that were not previously considered. Ontario's Society for the Prevention of Cruelty to Animals (OSPCA) Act is also known as the "Provincial Animal Welfare Act" and provides an example of latter-day anticruelty laws.

On March 1, 2009, Bill 50 was enacted, apparently intending to modernize the Ontario law. Representing the first major revision of Ontario's animal anticruelty legislation in ninety years,[52] the new Act not only creates new provincial offenses, it also imposes stiffer penalties for those convicted of animal abuse. Some of the notable fundamental changes in the new Act are:

- An expansion of the coverage of the requisite minimum requirements and standards of care. While the requirements originally only applied to dogs and cats, the revision applied this part of the law to all animals[53];
- Adding to the types of offenses so that psychological suffering may be considered animal cruelty, in contrast to many laws which are interpreted to address only physical injuries and pain related to that harm[54];
- Increases in both the potential penalties and courts' discretion in deciding on penalties for cruelty. Offenders can now get jail time and fines up to $60,000;
- A notable contemporary change, and perhaps most importantly for animal welfare and safety, Ontario has recognized that one important way to prevent future abuse is to limit contact between abusers and animals. Thus, judges are now allowed to ban convicted abusers from owning animals, up to and including a lifetime ban on ownership[55];
- The OSPCA has been given broader powers of inspection on premises where animals are housed. Whether the animals are used for exhibition, entertainment, boarding, sale, or hire, the OSPCA is entitled to enter the premises to ensure the health and well-being of the animals[56];

- The OSPCA, in situations where merited, can apply for custody of abused animals pending disposition of the case against the defendant[57];
- Veterinarians are now required to report reasonable suspicions of animal abuse or neglect.[58] This is another provision that signifies a new approach to addressing the difficulties of animal abuse detection. Reporting requirements parallel similar laws that either require or allow doctors to report signs of child abuse. The importance of having such a law in place is that it encourages reporting and immunizes those doing the reporting (veterinarians, in this case) from liability for claims that might be brought by those who are reported;
- Animal fighting is specifically addressed in the new laws, so that both training an animal to fight with another, as well as possession or ownership of equipment related to animal fighting, is expressly prohibited.[59] This focus on specific types of animal cruelty represents a valuable form of animal protection legislation. While most anticruelty laws provide general proscriptions for animal abuse, using broad language which encompasses most types of inhumane treatment, the laws that single out particular activities make the intention of the legislative body as well as the public policy about that conduct clearer for courts as well as potential abusers.

The Ontario illustration provides a representation of the type of changes that are occurring, and can occur, in jurisdictions around the globe. These modifications or additions to traditional anticruelty statutes occur based on popular support. Increasingly, legislative bodies and the general populace are able to appreciate, as a unified principle, that existing laws are not sufficiently focused or strong enough to prevent a large amount of animal suffering and pain that most agree is unacceptable in modern society. Education, awareness, and a rising consciousness about the sentience of animals all contribute to these changes.

European Union (EU)

Each country in the European Union has its own set of anticruelty laws, much like the situation in Canada and the United States. But because of the formation of the EU, there is also a set of safeguards in place at the regional level. A series of Union-wide conventions and treaties have been enacted that provide additional guidelines, separate from those of the individual countries, which set a floor for further legislation. That is, the EU laws are the agreed-upon minimum standards with which all members of the EU must comply. Compliance is guaranteed through enactment of each country's laws. Each country may of course adopt stricter standards if it desires, and it is free to adopt animal-related measures that do not conflict with the specific EU rules. But the Union-wide rules guarantee a standard of care that should be met or surpassed throughout the EU.

There are several notable Union-wide laws mentioned throughout the book. We discuss a few here that are utilized by individual countries as the basis for their criminal anticruelty laws.

The title of the European Convention for the Protection of Pet Animals (PPA)[60] is somewhat self-explanatory, and its provisions generally prohibit individuals from subjecting companion animals to the same kind of conduct outlawed in most anticruelty laws—"unnecessary" or "unjustified" cruelty, pain and suffering. The PPA's focus on companion animals emphasizes the "special relationship" these species have with humans.[61] In many areas of animal law, this connection between humans and companion animals results in more legislative protections. The obvious basis for the special treatment is the beneficial aspects of the relationship to humans, and not the impact of specific conduct on the animals. That is, these laws, which target cruelty to animals, really determine cruelty based on a human-centric viewpoint. The suffering of the animal is only important, at least in the context of laws like the PPA, to the extent the animal is a member of a species typically connected with humans.

Thus, because of the societal distinction made between pets and other animals more commonly used for commercial purposes, and the heightened attention given to abuse of those animals designated as pets, the PPA and other laws like it have been adopted around the world. One of the PPA's loftier goals is to establish a "basic common standard of attitude and practice which results in responsible pet ownership."[62] One component of its protections, for example, specifically prohibits abandonment of companion animals.[63]

The PPA also gives attention to a controversial and ongoing international discussion regarding the propriety of the possession and purchase of wild animals, often known as "exotic animals," to be used as companion animals. The list of naturally wild animals kept as pets is extensive. Some of the most popular wild animals kept as pets are: ferrets, snakes, birds, nonhuman primates such as monkeys and chimpanzees, and large and small wild cats. Proponents of free ownership of such animals usually focus on humans' rights to capture and hold any species of animal, given animals' property status and humans' control over animals. Opponents cite the inherent dangers (for humans and animals) in housing wild animals and the potential problems if they escape; the suffering imposed on the animals by the necessary confinement associated with their cohabitation with humans; the effects on wild animals' own cultural and social lives; and the potentially negative impact on the number of stray and abandoned animals (mostly dogs and cats) adopted from local shelters and societies if other types of animals are available and seem more exciting or interesting to have.

The drafters of the EU PPA viewed this issue as enough of a concern to include it in the PPA, and the Act affirmatively discourages the harboring of wild animals as pets. The PPA Preamble states that "the keeping of specimens of wild fauna as pet animals should not be encouraged"[64] and that, if an animal does not "adapt to captivity," it cannot be kept as a pet.[65]

While the encouragement of the EU provisions does not mandate individual countries to enact criminal laws on these issues, they can serve as the foundational documents for such enactment, if a given country's legislature makes the decision that such laws are appropriate.

Some aspects of the Union-wide rules do require a conversion to bans in all EU countries. For example, the protections for companion animals seek to ensure general well-being and safe and painless euthanasia, but go significantly further than that as well.[66] Article 10 of the PPA prohibits nontherapeutic surgery on companion animals, including tail docking (excising the tail close to its connection to the body), ear cropping (amputating part of the ear), devocalization or "debarking" (severing or removing the vocal cords to prevent barking), declawing (onchyectomy, discussed above), and defanging (removing teeth).[67] If a veterinarian determines any of these procedures are needed for the health of the animal, she is permitted to perform the procedure, but she is prohibited from doing so for cosmetic reasons.

Outside of the companion animal area, the EU has enacted a series of Conventions covering individual specific care, maintenance, and treatment of animals used in commercial agriculture. Several of the Union-wide provisions that do apply to specific practices and species are discussed in some detail in Chapter 2. The laws range from species-specific declarations to more general laws that may provide significant oversight and restriction on the treatment of most farmed animals from birth to death. The most general law, and one that can be the basis for specific countries' criminal laws, is the European Convention for the Protection of Animals Kept for Farming Purposes.[68] The Convention focuses on the "keeping, care and housing of animals, and in particular ... animals in modern intensive stock-farming systems." As a template for overall treatment, the coverage is broad:

> "animals" shall mean animals bred or kept for the production of food, wool, skin or fur or for other farming purposes, and "modern intensive stock-farming systems" shall mean systems which predominantly employ technical installations operated principally by means of automatic processes.

Thus, factory farming practices (and virtually all animals affected by it) are directly targeted by this Convention, and were recognized by the drafters of the document as a threat to animal welfare in commercial operations. The language of the law, however, leaves significant room for commercial producers to interpret the Convention in a way that allows them to continue with typical intensive confinement practices and treatment. So, much like the criminal laws described earlier, the specific laws (criminal or otherwise) that may be enacted will have room to accommodate traditional practices. Article 3 of the Convention is illustrative:

> Animals shall be housed and provided with food, water and care in a manner which—having regard to their species and to their degree of development, adaptation and domestication—is appropriate to their physiological and ethological needs in accordance with established experience and scientific knowledge.[69]

The Article provides broad discretion to agricultural industry concerns that support the intensive confinement conditions of factory farming with "established experience and scientific knowledge." Thus, while the law pays some regard to the problems of factory farming, it still seems to leave the decision-making up to the same group that is subject to any restrictions on the practices. That is, the regulating is done by the regulated, which is often a problematic situation and leads to minimal restriction or enforcement of imposed prohibitions. There is no question that the agricultural industry supports factory farming practices and argues they are best for the animals as well as the industry. And that support—from professionals in the industry and their veterinarians—is probably enough to meet the requirements of the Convention. Likewise, Article 4 prohibits confinement that causes *unnecessary* suffering. If a commercial producer of animal products believes that a certain amount of suffering is necessary to maximize profit, there is nothing in this law that bars a practice involving suffering. In essence, then, the Convention simply recognizes the potential problems with intensive confinement situations, but does not require any greater enforcement of criminal laws preventing them.

France

France, as a member of the European Union, is bound by the Conventions discussed above but, like other Union member countries, can promulgate additional laws that govern and may raise specific animal cruelty prohibitions. The French model differs from the U.S. system of jurisprudence, where virtually all cruelty issues are covered by state laws. By contrast (and like Canada originally), France has enacted national anticruelty legislation. The French Penal Code Article 521-1, "Serious Mistreatment or Other Acts of Cruelty Towards Animals," prohibits

> unnecessary infliction, in public or otherwise, or serious mistreatment, including sexual maltreatment, towards or the commission of an act of cruelty on any domestic or tame animal, or any animal held in captivity.[70]

French courts, in sentencing offenders, can also impose restrictions on ownership or possession of animals. Court orders can range from a temporary ban on interacting with a particular animal, to a final and permanent prohibition on ownership. The facts of each case determine the courts' decisions in this area.

The French anticruelty law, like others discussed above, has exemptions that protect many practices that would otherwise come within the purview of the animal cruelty laws. For example, the French law is not applicable to bullfights or cockfights "where an uninterrupted local tradition can be shown."[71] As in other areas, if animal cruelty has been an accepted part of life in the jurisdiction, the French legislature has determined that longstanding practice should not be affected, and should be deemed to have not been included within the statutory prohibitions.

The French law shares an aspect in common with most anticruelty laws and is worth discussing for what it says about the scope of the anticruelty laws in most societies. Specifically, the law does not prohibit or regulate the treatment of animals in the wild, but only those who are either domesticated or in captivity. The reasons for this are probably both practical and ethical. On the practical side, the law incorporates the understanding that humans do not have control over wild animals and therefore that interactions between them are less able to be regulated by law—and that therefore the obligations placed on humans for animals in their control, such as the requirements to provide animals with adequate food, water and veterinary care, are not logically placed upon humans in connection with wild animals.

The exclusion of wildlife from legal protection is common. The ethical and policy considerations that omit wild animals from the anticruelty laws of France and most countries provide an interesting view of society's self-imposed obligations to the animal kingdom. It does make sense that humans would not be legally required to feed and care for all wild animals. What does not follow is that there should be no prohibition on affirmative acts of violence or cruelty against wild animals, yet that is also generally the state of the law. When looked at in the bigger picture, it draws a significant line of moral demarcation for humans in terms of the interests of certain animals over others. This bright line distinction between our treatment of captive and domesticated animals, on the one hand, and wild animals on the other, can be seen as a declaration of social policy that to the extent humans obtain possession and control over animals, they inherit a set of legal and moral obligations, but that the same obligations do not inhere to the relationship of humans to unpossessed, uncontrolled animals. If that distinction between wild and captive animals implies a policy, that policy may evidence less concern with eliminating cruelty to animals and more of a focus on a sense of duty towards those animals we reduce to property status.

The wild/captive and domestic distinction may create confusion and concern in some areas. For example, there has been an increase in focus on the large number of feral cats and even feral dogs living in and around human settlements. Based on the distinction seen in many anticruelty laws, feral animals would have no protections, and there may be no limits on the way humans treat them. This dilemma, with feral cats and other wild animals who live within urban and suburban societies, is of increasing interest. As wild habitats are destroyed and wild animal-human interactions increase, there is increasing attention to the question of humans' obligations to wild animals, and what coverage the animals deserve under the law.

The absence of anticruelty laws does not mean that wild animals are without any protection—only that the specific criminal laws focused on welfare and treatment do not apply to them. Laws discussed elsewhere in the book, such as the Convention on International Trade in Endangered Species (CITES), as well as national and local laws that provide coverage similar to CITES, protect certain species (usually those who are threatened with extinction) and exist worldwide. Additionally, even for species that are not threatened or endangered, most countries have limitations on the numbers and even methods by which many wild animals may be killed. In France, wild animals are regulated by French hunting laws under the Ministry of Environment. These laws are usually also criminal in nature, but have a different focus—management of wildlife and maintenance of biodiversity—than the anticruelty laws which are addressed here.[72]

Germany

The German Animal Welfare Act[73] is the primary piece of animal welfare legislation in that country. Its last significant amendment was at the end of the 1990s, after ratification of the European Convention covering pets.[74] The current version of the Act has been in effect since June 1, 1998. It provides broad coverage to many areas of societal interaction with animals, and "regulates the handling of animals in the private, agricultural and scientific spheres."[75]

As with many animal welfare laws, the stated purpose and intent is lofty and focused on a humane and humanitarian approach to the treatment of animals. The basis of the German law is the fundamental principle that animals should only experience harm, injuries or death if there is a "good reason."[76] In all cases, however, the determination of the threshold for that justification varies. Thus the German law is similar to other flexible standards discussed in this chapter. Regardless of the amount of suffering or harm the law allows, the standard usually remains the same, subject to interpretation of what level of conduct and injury to animals will be tolerated. The German law, and for the most part the international code, embodies an implicit responsibility of human beings for the care and protection of nonhumans, subject to our imposition of contemporary moral standards and current uses of animals.[77] By imposing an affirmative responsibility on citizens towards nonhumans, the anticruelty laws, at least facially, "enforce the idea that humans are stewards rather than dominators."[78]

Norway

Norway, like Germany, has chosen to include most animal-related interactions in a single comprehensive set of statutes, named (like its German equivalent) the Animal Welfare Act. Its coverage includes commercial uses of animals, the use of animals in research, and general welfare and cruelty prohibitions.

The law protects "live mammals, birds, toads, frogs, salamanders (newts), reptiles, fish, and crustaceans."[79] With different language than the German law, the Act provides a broad statement of purpose and aspirations for animal welfare in the country. Its intention is to ensure that "[a]nimals shall be treated well, and consideration shall be given to the instinctive behaviour and natural needs of animals, so that there is no risk of causing them unnecessary suffering."[80] The qualifying language, "unnecessary" suffering, again allows for a limit on animal injuries and harm, but provides that the determination of what is unnecessary is dependent on interpretations that may be left to industry, judicial, or community standards.

Despite those typical allowances for a flexible determination of what practices qualify as cruelty, there are certain absolutes under the Norwegian law that regulate more than most other jurisdictions. For example:

1. Under Norwegian law, individuals "*must help*[, …] as far as possible," any animal who is found "obviously sick, injured, or helpless."[81] If it is "impossible" to help the animal, the finder is required to locate the person responsible for the animal, or local authorities. This goes much further than most laws and creates what is often known as a "Good Samaritan statute" for animals. In comparison to the dis-

cussion above regarding a split between protections for domestic animals and wild animals, the Norwegian statute does not seem to make any distinction, and requires a passer-by, if possible, to help even an injured wild animal. The section makes provision for euthanasia of the found animal if a "complete recovery" is not possible.[82]

2. The law provides a specific list of prohibited acts are included in Section 8 of the Act. This contrasts with many anticruelty laws, which simply have a general prohibition on "cruelty" or "cruel killing" or "beating" without further clarification. While the general prohibition may be interpreted to include a larger list of acts, it is probably the specific bans that are easiest to enforce. The Norwegian law bars kicking and hitting animals; the use of a whip to urge horses on in races; the use of live animals as food or bait; force-feeding such as the manner in which *foie gras* is manufactured; the use of hot brands for livestock; and training that causes an animal to "suffer or be unnecessarily frightened."[83]

Penalties for violation of the Act are six months for the first offense, with increased penalties for repeat offenders. The Act also expressly grants the courts the ability to restrict ownership or interaction with animals (including limitations on hunting, fishing, or commercial uses) for a set period of time, or forever.[84] This is further evidence of the Norwegian legislature's modern-day approach to animal cruelty laws and punishments.

Switzerland

Switzerland has two pieces of federal legislation governing the treatment of animals in all areas, with some apparent overlap between the two sets of laws. The most comprehensive law is the Federal Act of Animal Protection (FAAP), which was adopted by the Federal Assembly of the Swiss Confederation in 1977. The broad scope of the FAAP is qualified by a general exemption in the language of Article 2, similar to that seen around the world, which allows for "justifiable" "pain, suffering, and physical injury."[85] Because justification may come in the form of business reasons for inflicting pain and suffering, the laws as written provide an implicit exemption where animals are used for commercial purposes. Additionally, as written the law covers only vertebrate animals, with an option for the Federal Council to include any invertebrates it deems appropriate for protection. On the civil/regulatory side, the Federal Council is also mandated to "issue regulations on the keeping of animals, covering such matters as the minimum dimensions, lay-out, lighting and ventilation" in their housing.[86]

Swiss law is more protective of companion animals than many other countries and local jurisdictions. The law forbids the declawing of cats, cropping of dogs' ears, and the debarking of dogs.[88] As discussed in this chapter, these practices are banned in jurisdictions with a more scientific approach to the concept of cruelty and suffering. The conduct is prohibited based on a social policy and belief that cosmetic procedures that result in painful mutilation, and are done primarily for human benefit, constitute cruelty.

Courts are given the ability to remove animals from their owners as part of a criminal penalty in the case of repeat offenders, those who commit extreme cruelty, or people who "are incapable of keeping an animal" because of some mental illness.[89] This is in contrast to American state laws which ordinarily do not allow courts to permanently remove animals from their owners, although temporary bans on ownership are usually tolerated for serious offenders.

The Swiss law is federal in nature, but carried out by local jurisdictions, like the original Canadian law discussed earlier. "Prosecution and passing of judgment on offenders" is the "responsibility of the cantons."[90]

Pursuant to the FAAP, the Federal Council is required to enact regulations that further set out the animal welfare laws of Switzerland.[91] This set of regulations, known as the Swiss Animal Protection Ordinance (APO), thus covers the same areas, with more detail.[92] The APO provides further guidance on permitted and prohibited practices. Many traditional practices of the agricultural and farming industry are permitted, including, all without anesthesia: the tail docking of young piglets and lambs; castration of young calves, sheep, goats, pigs and rabbits; and the debeaking and detoeing of birds.[93]

New Zealand

New Zealand's first anticruelty laws were incorporated into the country's legal framework in 1840.[94] But with those laws in place, New Zealand lacked any progressive animal welfare legislation for most of the 20th century.[95] Until 1960, like England and the United States in earlier centuries, there was no criminal liability for abuse of one's own animals, only for animals owned by another.[96] As already discussed in this chapter, the main intention behind this first tier of laws was not to prevent animal suffering but to punish those who caused financial damage that would occur if valuable (animal) property was damaged.

In the latter half of the last century, New Zealand began to develop a series of laws that at least facially exhibited very progressive notions of animal protection.[97] The New Zealand Animals Protection Act of 1960 signaled what appeared to be a shift, with a notable focus on animal cruelty and welfare. The Act became the first New Zealand law that demonstrated a recognition of the implications of animal cruelty as a social ill. The law made animal cruelty punishable supposedly because of its social implications as well as its impact on the animals. Like many modern-era anticruelty laws, this was a leap forward. As discussed in more detail in Chapter 2, concerns were raised with this and the subsequent legislation in New Zealand, that while "the APA attempted to curtail deliberate and malicious cruelty, … it failed to provide any impetus for the reform of agricultural practices."[98] The law did give lip service to animal welfare issues and concerns over animal cruelty, but it also provided standard exemptions for farmed animal practices. It therefore offered little protection for animals beyond that seen in other countries discussed above.

The next step in the process of animal welfare legislation in New Zealand was the passage of its Animal Welfare Act of 1999 (NZAWA).[99] The NZAWA came into effect on January 1, 2000, and replaced and updated the APA with more modern standards. The stated purpose of the law was the protection of the "physical, health and behavioural needs" of animals.[100] Domestic and wild animals are covered, and treatment is to be governed by "good practice" and "scientific knowledge."[101] As discussed in connection with other terms commonly used in animal welfare legislation, this leaves a broad range of interpretation possible, depending on the views of the particular professionals and laypersons determining the meaning of these terms.

The phrase "physical, health and behavioural needs" is defined in line with the international "five freedoms" of animal welfare,[102] which are generally accepted principles of minimal treatment that all animals should be given. Section 4 of the NZAWA incorporates the freedoms by defining them as including:

1. proper and sufficient food and water;
2. adequate shelter;
3. opportunity to display normal patterns of behavior;
4. physical handling in a manner which minimises the likelihood of unreasonable or unnecessary pain or distress; and
5. protection from, and rapid diagnosis of, any significant injury or disease.[103]

The application of these standards is most relevant in the companion animal area. In contrast, while the freedoms are incorporated into the law, the treatment of most animals used *commercially* in New Zealand is subject to "welfare codes" which modify and define the parameters of the NZAWA. As discussed in more detail in Chapter 2 (and similar to the "codes of practice" discussed in connection with Australia's anticruelty laws), in New Zealand it is a defense to animal cruelty if a "relevant code of welfare" exists that covers the challenged act (usually some regular practice of the agricultural industry), and if the requirements of that code of welfare are met.

The use of general terms such as those in the five freedoms can create areas of significant uncertainty, but in general the NZAWA may be considered ahead of the curve as compared to many other nations' animal welfare codes, at least to the extent the terms in the NZAWA provide for humane treatment and heightened deterrence. Thus, it is an advance over other laws both in terms of people's obligations to animals and the corresponding appropriateness of arrest and enforcement. However, many of the terms are very general and, as discussed elsewhere in this chapter, this causes a problem with criminal law especially, where citizens must be on notice of the nature of crimes. And in order for citizens to be on notice of what conduct constitutes a crime, they must generally be able to interpret the relevant language easily. The terms in the five freedoms and the NZAWA are ambiguous, and are open to varying interpretations by reasonable persons, and also by professionals like veterinarians. In terms of enforcement, this often means that prosecuting attorneys will limit their cases to the most egregious forms of cruelty which clearly fit within the statutory language and intent. Acts that so obviously fall out of the range of, for example, providing "sufficient" food and water, would only be seen in cases of extreme starvation and malnutrition. It is valuable to be able to bring such cases to the courts, but if a law limits its coverage to only those extreme acts, a large portion of conduct that constitutes animal abuse will go unpunished.

The New Zealand laws provide support for the notion that, on an international scale, sociocultural opinions of cruelty vary widely on a geographic basis. What may be completely unacceptable in one country may be a longstanding tradition in another. Consider bullfighting, which is a popular activity in some countries, and is completely banned in others; or dogfighting; or the eating of dogs and cats. Even within a country, more rural communities and indigenous cultures may engage in practices that city-dwellers and urban societies consider reprehensible. In countries with large immigrant populations, many cultures combine and overlap. Because there may be differences of opinion among these groups as to what is "proper" treatment of animals, phrases like those taken from the five freedoms allow courts to make determinations based on community values. By this measure, animal cruelty is a variable construct, not an absolute that applies universally. The history of animal law suggests that there is an acceptable definitional level of what is clearly cruel, and much argument and interpretation about conduct that falls into the gray area between illegal cruelty and legal use of animals.

An interesting aspect of the NZAWA, and one that varies from many other jurisdictions, is that many of the provisions do not require any actual criminal intent on the part of violators to trigger punishment. This relates to the proof required at trial, but where intent is a required element, it may be a significant limitation that defines the ability of prosecutors to bring animal abusers to justice. Normally the government is required to prove either "specific intent" or "general intent" in order to obtain a conviction for commission of a crime. "Specific intent" requires proof that the defendant wanted the actual outcome to occur, for example, that an animal die or suffer from an act of cruelty. "General intent" is a lower standard of proof but still a potential barrier to prosecution. General intent requires that the defendant intended to do the act which ultimately caused the death or suffering. Both requirements place a burden of proof on the prosecutor to prove the defendant's mental state while engaging in the criminal conduct. Defendants can often prevail in a case based on the prosecution's inability to prove the actual intent required. Thus, the need to prove intent can defeat a prosecution and may often prevent conviction or even the charging of someone who has otherwise caused injuries, suffering or death to animals. And the difficulty of proving intent may be an especially significant problem in animal cruelty cases because of the absence of witnesses or a victim who can testify about what happened.

The NZAWA has a procedural aspect that eliminates this often difficult "intent" problem for "animal welfare offenses" under Section 12, which states that a legal violation occurs when anyone

> (a) fails to comply, in relation to the animal, with section 10 [requiring that "physical, health and behavioral needs" of animals "[be] met in a manner in accordance with both ... good practice [and] scientific knowledge"]; or
> (b) fails, in the case of an animal that is ill or injured, to comply, in relation to the animal, with section 11 [requiring that persons in charge of "ill or injured" animals, "where practicable, ensure that the animal receives treatment that alleviates any unreasonable or unnecessary pain or distress being suffered by the animal"]; or
> (c) kills the animal in such a manner that the animal suffers unreasonable or unnecessary pain or distress.

Section 13 of the Act makes those acts of animal cruelty in New Zealand a "strict liability offense." Prosecutions for violation of Section 12 of the NZAWA, if brought, therefore do not require proof of intent (specific or general) to obtain a conviction, and one can commit animal cruelty unintentionally—whether negligently or even without knowing. Strict liability means that if the harm is caused, that is, if the animal is injured or killed and there is no defense to that harm or killing, the defendant is guilty of the crime. There are of course many potential defenses, such as the relevant welfare codes discussed above, but the elimination of the burden of proving intent is of significant value to prosecutors.[104] This is a notable difference from the proof required under most criminal laws. This relaxation of proof requirements may indicate an understanding of the difficulty of such proof in animal-related crimes.

As mentioned previously, multicultural issues may arise when criminal laws clash with traditional values and practices. One particular story in New Zealand highlights both the limits of the cruelty laws and the disparity in societal beliefs on an international basis.[105] Animal control authorities from the New Zealand Society for the Prevention of Cruelty to Animals arrived at the home of an Auckland man of Tongan descent who was barbecuing a dog for dinner. The dog had been humanely stunned before he was killed, in the same manner as pig or cow might be. The matter raises two notable issues.

First, there was no prosecution because the man's conduct was legal in the SPCA's view. The killing was not cruel, since the man followed a method of humane slaughter. And there is nothing illegal in New Zealand about eating the meat of animals, including dogs. Second, dog meat is a culinary delicacy in Tonga, and so to the individual, this was a perfectly normal activity. The head of the SPCA was quoted as saying that eating dog should be prohibited, but based solely on the cultural prerogative of modern New Zealand society: "'Clearly this culture is unacceptable in New Zealand, however, we must understand that to certain immigrants from the Pacific Islands the practice is considered normal.'"[106]

People's Republic of China (PRC)

The PRC is one of several notable countries that, throughout the twentieth century, had little or no general animal protection statutes. The anticruelty laws in other countries, like those discussed above, had no contemporary analog in the PRC at the time of publication of this text, though one was under consideration at the time. While there are a number of laws that have always provided some protection to animals, they have been typically motivated by economic or political/diplomatic reasons. They focus not on suffering or cruelty, but on resources, or on endangered or threatened species. For example, the Fisheries Laws address both economic and conservation issues, but do not include any consideration of the treatment of the individual animals.[107] The law was enacted in 1986, and primarily focuses on protection of the fish supply. Two Articles in the Fisheries laws address the conservation side, covering "rare aquatic mammals."[108]

In other words, like the first tier of anticruelty laws discussed above, these laws were enacted not because of any moral imperative regarding treatment of animals, but only because of the animals' value to humans—without consideration of animals' inherent sentience. But the actual progress of PRC animal protection must be put in context. The country was formally established in 1949 and its first official law was adopted in 1954.[109] Not until 1978 did China's legal system begin to work in earnest, so that the oldest Chinese laws are just three decades old.[110] Compared to the delay in establishing significant protections in other countries, China's move towards greater protection has not been out of step with other nations—it may even be progressing faster because of the era in which it has been developing.

News stories in 2009 indicated that there may be some reason for optimism that China may soon have anticruelty laws. According to the English Royal Society for the Prevention of Cruelty to Animals, in September 2009 the first "draft animal protection laws" were being introduced in the PRC.[111] Based on what the article suggests, this is truly just a first concept, and one that has not previously been considered by the Chinese government. Thus, while hopeful, there is no guarantee such a law will ever be passed or, even if it is eventually passed, how much effect it might have on current practices, or how long it might take for it to be enacted.

The PRC's nascent development provides a good opportunity to evaluate the effect of the growing social consciousness about animal suffering. Because China presents an area thus far untouched by modern anticruelty laws, the results will represent the contemporary compromises that this modern country is willing to entertain.

As mentioned at the outset of the chapter, most of the laws regulating the use, capture and killing of animals are criminal in nature. The reader should be mindful of that fact, and that the focus here has been on the anticruelty laws, since those embody notions of potential *animal* interests as well as human interests. Given the absence of any cruelty protection in the PRC, we briefly describe some other forms of criminal law that redound to the benefit of animals, even though there is little or no consideration of cruelty included in these laws.

Endangered species protection, in connection with environmental laws (which protect both fauna and flora), began in the PRC as early as 1978.[112] The PRC then signed the Convention on International Trade in Endangered Species (CITES, discussed in Chapter 6 and elsewhere) in 1981, joining the global support of conservation of endangered animals. In connection with that membership, the PRC enacted additional wildlife laws in 1989. The law creates a list of endangered species in China, and prohibits the trafficking in those, as well as species listed in CITES Appendices I and II.[113]

On the face of the laws and based on the potential penalties, China treats violations of these laws very seriously. In 1987, two individuals were given twelve and ten years sentences for smuggling a panda skin without a license. The court found that the violation had "damage[d] the social order."[114] And in 1992, a man convicted of hunting and killing a panda was given the death penalty. Three other defendants received sentences ranging from a thirteen-year imprisonment to short-term suspended sentences in connection with the same crime. Repercussions for smuggling Asian elephants, a wild buffalo, and trading in ivory tusks have been severe, and have included death sentences and life terms in prison. In general, the more extreme sentences are given to repeat offenders, or those with knowledge and intent of the illegality of their conduct.[115]

These sentences represent extremes unseen anywhere else. But punishment is not uniform or guaranteed. A Chinese law scholar noted that "some violators of China's endangered species legislation have escaped with fines of less than two dollars."[116]

The notion of having animals as pets or companions is also a relatively new development in Chinese society, and this may explain the delay in laws targeting greater protections for those animals.[117] Perhaps for this reason, there are no national laws in the PRC (to date)[118] addressing animal welfare as it relates to animal abuse or cruelty to animals. There is also very little case law regarding animal law in China,[119] and the law that does exist primarily concerns criminal prosecutions of illegal traffickers of "rare animals."[120]

Australia

Australia's first anticruelty laws appeared in 1837 in Van Dieman's Land, and spread through the country from that point.[121] Like the United States, Australia's cruelty laws are localized, with each state and territory enacting their own laws.[122] For various reasons, Australian courts have not significantly addressed animal cruelty cases, and so there is a dearth of case law to review, and there is a notable "imbalance between legislation and case law."[123] The laws are on the books, but the courts are not taking or being given the opportunity to provide their guidance and interpretations of the law. This delays development of the law.

While all the states and territories have laws with an anticruelty focus, there are variations (as in other countries) in some regards, including the basic definitions of both "animal" and "cruelty"—some states being more specific in their list of cruel acts, and others more general. Most Australian anticruelty laws include all vertebrates, with some laws including fish as well as consideration of crustaceans—but only if they are being used for human consumption.[124] For example, in the state of New South Wales, "animal" means any vertebrate species and "a crustacean but only when at a building or place (such as a restaurant) where food is prepared or offered for consumption by retail sale in the building or place."[125] South Australia's Animal Protection Act of 1985 excludes fish but includes all other vertebrates.[126] Several laws also have different requirements for the owners of animals, as opposed to conduct by nonowners—so that more severe penalties and greater legal requirements exist for owners.[127] This distinction makes sense because it places greater emphasis on the social responsibility imposed on those who voluntarily undertake to care for animals. The focus is on societal acceptance of, or disfavor with, the acts committed. The view and values imposed are always placed through the filter of social acceptance of treatment of animals.

In New South Wales, the general anticruelty provision is as simple as this: "A person shall not commit an act of cruelty upon an animal."[128] But there are more specific aspects of the statute, providing some detail for persons "in charge of an animal."[129] Cruelty is defined to include situations in which an animal is "unreasonably, unnecessarily or unjustifiably"

(a) beaten, kicked, killed, wounded, pinioned, mutilated, maimed, abused, tormented, tortured, terrified or infuriated,
(b) over-loaded, over-worked, over-driven, over-ridden or over-used,
(c) exposed to excessive heat or excessive cold, or
(d) inflicted with pain.[130]

The Australian anticruelty laws, as a general rule, cover the broad scope of conduct seen in other countries' laws, allowing ample room for interpretation, depending on the specific acts at issue. There are extensive exemptions for agricultural operations and animals used in research. In Australia, these exemptions are sometimes included in the anticruelty laws, and also in "codes of practice" (like in New Zealand, discussed above) usually written by government-appointed bodies with significant input from the regulated industries.[131] These codes describe "minimum acceptable animal welfare practices" in connection with the covered areas.[132] The codes have been codified as law in some Australian jurisdictions, but not in most. But even where they are not compulsory law, they may be used as defenses to cruelty and may be given much weight in determining whether certain acts are illegal.[133] Certainly the behavior described as acceptable by the codes may be considered in determining what is "reasonable" or "necessary," where those terms are applied to potential acts of cruelty.

Australia's anticruelty laws, as much by historical inheritance as any considered plan, are enforced by a joint group of authorities. In a majority of jurisdictions, the laws are primarily enforced not by local law enforcement or any governmental entity, but by a privately funded charity, the Royal Society for the Prevention of Cruelty to Animals (RSPCA).[134] The state or territorial government also shares jurisdiction in most situations, but the RSPCA is often the group doing most of the animal cruelty work. Because the RSPCA depends on donors and has a limited budget, animal cruelty enforcement may be limited by the amount of available funding. This is not much different than when local prosecutors in any state or country have difficulty covering all the cases that arise in their jurisdiction, but is of some greater concern because the effectiveness of the laws is delegated to a private entity.

Taiwan

Taiwan's history of criminal laws covering animal cruelty is most notable because of how much has been accomplished in such a short time. The country's first anticruelty laws were enacted in 1998.[135] These provided a good basic structure, and in the ensuing twelve years, significant advances were made in several areas.

Taiwanese anticruelty laws cover (1) animals that are kept by people for "pleasure and companionship"; (2) "economic animals" that are fed or kept for economic purposes, such as fur, meat, milk and labor; and (3) "experimental animals" who are used for "the application for the purposes of teaching, experiment, the manufacturing of biological products, experimental merchandise, drug, poison and organ transplant."[136] Perhaps most interesting, Taiwan animal protection law has a catch-all phrase, prohibiting "any act [against animals] that violates good social custom."[137] Indisputably vague and open-ended, the phrase in some way surrenders the determination of animal cruelty to each community, each situation, and each point in time. But as pointed out throughout this chapter, that is the nature of most anticruelty laws. The open-ended potential for a finding of cruelty has the advantage of enabling those trying to expand protections to argue for broader and more considerate evaluation of animal cruelty. It also represents a pronouncement that community standards and the specific facts of each case will very much control the determination of cruelty. But it has the clear disadvantage of providing no true guidance, and no standards by which law enforcement, courts, and private individuals can best determine what constitutes animal cruelty. And it allows courts to operate without limitation in making decisions about specific acts of animal cruelty.

As discussed previously, the consumption of dog meat is a longstanding practice in many countries, a prohibited one in others, and a controversial issue within and across international borders. Taiwanese law affords an excellent illustration of the way in which certain species, favored by the populace, may get special treatment within the coverage of the anti-cruelty laws. The Taiwan example demonstrates one way in which the law (and the lawmakers) address the dilemma that dogs are a popular companion but that their meat is also a food of choice for many.

Taiwan could have simply enacted a law that banned the sale or consumption of dog meat, or the slaughter of dogs for human consumption. Instead, Taiwan amended its anticruelty laws and made it illegal to commercially exploit or kill dogs, even if that dog was private property. This obtains the same result; if enforced and obeyed, the law is effectively a ban on the sale and consumption of dog meat. At the same time it avoids a direct conflict with the cultural phenomenon of eating dogs, focusing more on the treatment of those dogs destined for slaughter and sale. That is, it places the treatment of the animals in the context of a commercial practice within the anticruelty law, and focuses less on attacking the cultural practice itself. This may well make the law an easier one to accept, and to get passed. This is because, as established throughout this book, humans have a great capacity to mentally separate treatment of different species, even when the treatment looks similar. Thus, it is easier to describe the treatment of dogs prior to slaughter as a cruel practice, and therefore ban it under the cruelty umbrella, while still maintaining a belief that the similar treatment of other species that humans eat is not cruel. Because dogs are so highly respected by a large percentage of society, this approach attracts less objection when proposed. Unfortunately, it has been reported that dog meat is still easily available in Taiwanese restaurants.

In 2007, the Taiwanese Animal Protection Law was strengthened, by the addition of more severe penalties, with a focus on agricultural practices and food animals.[138] The amendments were intended to increase enforcement and oversight of slaughterhouse practices, and were enacted after video depiction of extreme cruelty in a slaughterhouse was made public, engendering significant responses to the relevant Taiwan agencies. Additional amendments in recent years have focused on other aspects of animal exploitation, including circuses and the use of animals in gambling schemes.[139]

Conclusion

This chapter's main purpose is to give readers insight into the means and methods the law uses to describe and proscribe the various forms of animal cruelty that are daily occurrences in our society. We have sought to demonstrate how the key terms of anticruelty statutes reflect different cultural values, such as which animals are covered, which acts are considered cruel, what influence commercial uses have, and how animals' property status affects the historical development of anticruelty laws.

Some of the laws that exist in states and nations, as written, are quite strong and are valuable deterrents to crimes against animals. But it is worth repeating the important reservation here. Even with strong laws on the books, the detection, investigation, conviction, and punishment of animal abusers cannot occur without the willingness of law enforcement authorities and courts to do their part in the process. Many anticruelty laws on the books are seldom enforced—and even less often do meaningful convictions and punishments result. The laws are the beginning, but there remains a definite need for increased societal recognition of the problem of animal cruelty and the need to address it through the criminal law.

Notes

1. The criminal laws cover most other animal-related issues. In virtually every country, hunting laws limit the number and type of animals that can be killed and the time periods in which they can be killed. Those laws are usually enforced by criminal sanctions. Ownership of wild or "exotic" animals is also similarly handled, and may be regulated by both criminal and civil law.

2. While the large majority of laws can be categorized as one type or the other, there are some civil laws that are considered "quasi-criminal" in that they have aspects which resemble punishment, whether in the way of fines or consequences for violation. There also may be penalties for the violation of civil laws. And monetary sanctions may be available for contempt of court in a civil action.

3. The civil law does provide one avenue for "punishment" through the award of "punitive" or "exemplary" damages. This type of monetary award to plaintiffs is obtained only in limited circumstances. Punitive/exemplary damages are given in addition to any compensatory payment for actual money lost, and are also in addition to any payments for emotional distress or other noneconomic damages. Punitive/exemplary awards are generally available only upon proof of reckless, malicious, or bad faith actions by an individual or organization, and are intended to punish the wrongdoer by affecting their net worth. The distinction between punitive damages and fines or penalties is that punitive damages are awarded to the individual party bringing the lawsuit, whereas fines or penalties in a criminal action are paid to the government.

4. It can also be argued that society as a whole is a victim and suffers when unjustifiable and unnecessary suffering is caused to animals. The theory is that societal limitations on violence and assertions of force are negatively affected by cruelty to animals, based on the recognized link between human-to-animal and human-to-human abuse.

5. Jared Squires, *The Link Between Animal Cruelty and Human Violence: Children Caught in the Middle*, 8 WTR KY. CHILD. RTS. J. 2 (2000).

6. United Kingdom Parliament [Richard Martin], An Act to Prevent the Cruel and Improper Treatment of Cattle, 1822, 3 Geo. 4, c. 71 §1 (Eng.).

7. Ireland Parliament [Thomas Wentworth], An Act Against Plowing by the Tayle, and Pulling the Wooll off Living Sheep, 1635 (hereinafter "Thomas Wentworth's Act") in THE STATUTES AT LARGE, PASSED IN THE PARLIAMENTS HELD IN IRELAND, 2d ed. (Dublin, 1786), 2: 168–169.

8. Thomas Wentworth's Act (1635).

9. *Id.*

10. Massachusetts Colony [Nathaniel Ward], "Off the Bruite Creatures," Liberty 92 and 93 in *The Body of Liberties of 1641,* (hereinafter "Massachusetts Body of Liberties of 1641"), reprinted in WILLIAM H. WHITMORE, A BIOGRAPHICAL SKETCH OF THE LAWS OF THE MASSACHUSETTS COLONY FROM 1630 TO 1686 (1890).

11. Massachusetts Body of Liberties of 1641, Liberty 92.

12. Massachusetts Body of Liberties of 1641, Liberty 93.

13. Martin's Law § 1.

14. Elaine L. Hughes & Christiane Meyer, *Animal Welfare Law in Canada and Europe,* 6 ANIMAL L. 23, 25–26 (2000).

15. "[N]o person shall suffer any Punishment for any Offense committed against this Act, unless the Prosecution for the same be commenced within Ten Days after the Offense shall be committed." Martin's Law § 2.

16. "[I]f on hearing any such Complaint as is herein-before mentioned, the Justice of the Peace or other Magistrate who shall hear the same shall be of opinion that such Complaint was frivolous or vexatious then and in every such Case it shall be lawful for such Justice of the Peace or other Magistrate to order, adjudge, and direct the Person or Persons making such Complaint, to pay the Party complained of, any Sum of Money not exceeding the Sum of Twenty Shillings, as Compensation for the Trouble and Expense to which such Party may have been put to by such Complaint." Martin's Act § 5.

17. 629 A.2d 123 (Pa. 1993).

18. *Id.* at 129.

19. *California Veterinary Medical Ass'n v. City of West Hollywood*, 152 Cal. App. 4th 536 (2007).

20. The tenets of these religions are not necessarily carried out in practice. *See*, *e.g.*, R. Huss, *Valuing Man's and Woman's Best Friend: The Moral and Legal Status of Companion Animals*, 86 Marquette L. R. 47 (Fall 2002) ("Notwithstanding the teachings of Hinduism, animal welfare in India is not well-developed, and many will eat meat so long as someone else kills the animal.") (citing LEWIS G. REGENSTEIN, REPLENISH THE EARTH; A HISTORY OF ORGANIZED RELIGIOUS TREATMENT OF ANIMALS AND NATURE—INCLUDING THE BIBLE'S MESSAGE OF CONSERVATION AND KINDNESS TOWARD ANIMALS 199, 227 (1991)).

21. *See* Ven S. Dhammika, THE EDICTS OF KING ASHOKA, THE WHEEL PUBLICATION No. 386/387 BUDDHIST PUBLICATION SOCIETY (1993), *available at* http://www.cs.colostate.edu/~malaiya/ashoka.html#INTRODUCTION.http://www.cs.colstate.edu/~malaiya/ashoka.html #INTRODUCTION.

22. Though exact figures are difficult to come by, see *Passage to India*, Country Profile, United States Department of Agriculture, Foreign Agricultural Service, Horticultural & Tropical Products Division, *available at* http://www.fas.usda.gov/htp/highlights/2001/india.pdf. "Many Indians are vegetarian by tradition; moreover, many can only afford a vegetarian diet. Meat may be regularly consumed by less than 30 percent of the Indian population, due to its higher cost and a predominance of vegetarianism and Hinduism. However, only 20 percent of the population is strictly vegetarian. Non-vegetarians typically consume meat only once or twice per week."

23. Dhammika, *supra* note 21.
24. *Id.*
25. *Id.*
26. *Id.*
27. *Id.*
28. Wild Birds Protection Act No. X of 1887.
29. Wildlife law: A Global Perspective 94 (Raj Panjwani ed., ABA 2008), discussing the Wild Birds and Animals Protection Act of 1912.
30. *Id.* at 94–95 (citing Wild Birds and Animals (Amendment) Act No. XXVII of 1935).
31. The Prevention of Cruelty to Animals Act, 1960 (59 of 1960), as amended by Central Act 26 of 1982, § 4.
32. *Id.* § 5.
33. *Id.* § 11.
34. *Id.* § 11(1)(d).
35. *Id.* § 11(1)(e).
36. *Id.* § 11(1)(f).
37. *Id.* § 11(1)(g)–(o).
38. *Id.* § 22. Under Section 21, "exhibit" meant to "exhibit or any entertainment to which the public are admitted through sale of tickets" and "train" meant to "train for the purpose of any such exhibition." These sections are discussed in other chapters in the book as well, especially Chapter 2.
39. *Id.* § 11(3)(a)–(d).
40. *Id.* § 11(3)(e).
41. *Id.* § 14.
42. *Id.* § 12.
43. Hughes & Meyer, *supra* note 14 (citing Charles D. Niven, History of the Humane Movement, at 108 (1967)).
44. *Id.* at 26 (citing Canadian Fed'n of Humane Societies, The Humane Movement in Canada 6 (n.d.); An Act Respecting Cruelty to Animals, S.C., ch. 27 (1869) (Can.), amended in 1870).

> *Original text of the 1869 statute was not found. However, Senator George J. Furey moved to amend the Criminal Code regarding cruelty to animals (Bill C-10B) with the following argument:*
>
> The twenty-eighth law that our young country passed on June 22, 1869 was entitled: "An Act respecting cruelty to Animals." This law was considered important enough that it was moved by Sir John A. Macdonald and seconded by George-Étienne Cartier.
>
> The act read:
>
> Whosoever wantonly, cruelly or unnecessarily beats, binds, ill-treats, abuses or tortures any Horse, Mare, Gelding, Bull, Ox, Cow Heifer, Steer, Mule, Ass, Sheep, Lamb, Pig or other cattle or any Poultry or Dog or Domestic Animal or Bird (is guilty of an offence).

Debates of the Senate (Hansard), 2nd Session, 37th Parliament, Volume 140, Issue 57, Tuesday, May 27, 2003, *available at* http://www.parl.gc.ca/37/2/parlbus/chambus/senate/deb-e/058db_2003-05-27-E.htm?Language=E&Parl=37&Ses=2.

45. *Id.*

46. Charles Hall, *Canadian Animal Anti-Cruelty Legislation,* Michigan State University College of Law, Animal Legal & Historical Center (2006), *available at* http://www.animallaw.info/nonus/articles/ddcananimalcrueltylegislation.htm#_ftnref8 (citing Robin MacKay, *Bill C-50: An Act to Amend the Criminal Code in Respect of Cruelty to Animals (LS-509E)*, Aug. 18, 2005 at 3, *available at* http://www.parl.gc.ca/38/1/parlbus/chambus/house/bills/summaries/c50-e.htm). For a link to the actual text of the first reading of the bill (available in English and French), *see* http://www.parl.gc.ca/38/1/parlbus/chambus/house/bills/government/c-50/c-50_1/c-50_cover-e.html.

47. Hall, *supra* note 46.

48. Simon Shields, Overview, Animals and the Criminal Law, *available at* http://www.isthatlegal.ca/index.php?name=start.animal_criminal_cruelty_law.

49. R. v. Clarke (Nfld. Prov. Ct. 2001).

50. Canada Criminal Code, 2008, c. 12, s. 1., R.S., 1985, c. C-46, s. 446.

51. Hughes & Meyer, *supra* note 14, at 29. Hughes and Meyer note that the exception is section 446, which was amended by S.C. 1974–75–76, §35 (Can.).

52. *Amended Ontario SPCA Act*, Ontario SPCA, *available at* http://www.ontariospca.ca/1-bill50.shtml; Ontario Ministry of Community Safety & Correctional Services, *available at* http://www.mcscs.jus.gov.on.ca/english/animal_welfare/paws.html.

53. R.S.O. 1990, c. O.36, s. 1–19, amended 2008, c. 16 §11.1, *available at* http://www.e-laws.gov.on.ca/html/statutes/english/elaws_statutes_90o36_e.htm.

54. *Id.* §11.2(1), (2).

55. *Id.* §18.1. Sociological research and law enforcement experts are consistently reaching the similar conclusion that humans who mistreat animals often continue cycles of abuse as soon as they are given access again. The best prevention, then, is this kind of ownership ban.

56. *Id.* §11.4.

57. *Id.* §14 (1.1)(b), (1.3), (1.4). This is a common type of provision in an increasing number of jurisdictions, intended to remove animals from harmful situations while legal action proceeds. Convicted defendants may be required to pay for the costs of care or forfeit their ownership in the animals as issue.

58. *Id.* §11.3.

59. *Id.* §11.2 (3), (4).

60. European Convention for the Protection of Pet Animals (ETS No. 125) (Strasbourg 1987); Paige Tomaselli, *Summary of International Comparative Animal Cruelty Laws*, Animal Legal & Historical Center (2003), *available at* http://www.animallaw.info/articles/qvusicacl.htm.

61. European Convention for the Protection of Pet Animals, *supra* note 60, at preamble.

62. *Id.*

63. *Id.* art. 3(2)).

64. *Id.* at preamble.

65. *Id.* art. 4, §3(b).

66. *Id.* art. 11.

67. *Id.* art. 10.

68. European Convention for the Protection of Animals Kept for Farming Purposes (ETS 87), *available at* http://ec.europa.eu/food/animal/welfare/references/farmspc/jour323_en.pdf.

69. *Id.* art. 3.

70. French Penal Code Art. 521-1, Serious Mistreatment or Other Acts of Cruelty Towards Animals, Act no. 2004-204 of 9 March 2004 art. 50 Official Journal of 10 March 2004, *available at* http://195.83.177.9/code/liste.phtml?lang=uk&c=33&r=3858.

71. *Id.*

72. The Act of July 10, 1976, Art. 36 establishes certain protected species and creates reserves and national parks, translation available here: http://translate.google.com/translate?hl=en&sl=fr&u=http://www.animallaw.info/nonus/articles/arfrintro.htm&ei=mrjVSbT1IaXcswP5veCoCg&sa=X&oi=translate&resnum=1&ct=result&prev=/search%3Fq%3Dhttp://www.animallaw.info/nonus/articles/arfrintro.htm%26hl%3Den%26client%3Dsafari%26rls%3Den-us.

73. German Animal Welfare Act, Federal Law Gazette I, p. 1094, ANIMAL LEGAL & HISTORICAL CENTER, *available at* http://www.animallaw.info/nonus/statutes/stdeawa1998.htm.

74. The European Convention for the Protection of Pet Animals (ETS 125) (May 1, 1992).

75. German Animal Welfare Act, *supra* note 73.

76. *Id.* §I, art. 1. "The aim of this Act is to protect the lives and well-being of animals, based on the responsibility of human beings for their fellow creatures. No one may cause an animal pain, suffering or harm without good reason." German Animal Welfare Act, *supra* note 73; Publication of the Revision of the Animal Welfare Act of 25 May 1998, *available at* http://www.nal.usda.gov/awic/legislat/awagertrn.htm.

77. *Id.*

78. Tomaselli, *supra,* note 60.

79. Norway Animal Welfare Act Code: 750.000, Ch. 1, Sec. 1, Issued: 16.06.95, *available at* http://www.animallaw.info/nonus/statutes/stnoapa1995.htm; unofficial translation of the Norwegian Animal Welfare Act, *available at* http://oslovet.veths.no/act.html.

80. *Id.* §2.

81. *Id.* §6.

82. *Id.*

83. *Id.* §8.

84. *Id.* §32.

85. Swiss Federal Act on Animal Protection, Swiss APA 1978, Sec. 1, art. 2(3), *available at* http://www.animallaw.info/nonus/statutes/stchapa1978.htm.

86. *Id.* §2, art. 3(3).

87. *Id.* §6, art. 13.

88. *Id.* §8, art. 22(2)(g).

89. *Id.* §10, art. 24.

90. *Id.* §11, art. 32(1). Switzerland is split into twenty-six cantons, each of which is a sovereign state within the federal state.

91. *See, e.g., id.* §12, art. 33(1) ("The Federal Council shall issue enforcement orders.").

92. *Swiss Animal Protection Ordinance*, ANIMAL LEGAL & HISTORICAL CENTER, *available at* http:/www.animallaw.info/nonus/statutes/stchapo1981.htm.

93. Swiss Animal Protection Act (1981), ch. 8, art. 65.

94. D. CAO, ANIMAL LAW IN AUSTRALIA AND NEW ZEALAND 107 (2010).

95. Peter Sankoff, *Five Years of the "New" Animal Welfare Regime: Lessons Learned from the New Zealand Experience with Farm Animals and Animal Welfare Legislation*, Proceedings from the 2004 International Animal Welfare Law Conference, p. 113. One new area of focus was the treatment of farmed animals, as discussed in Chapter 2.

96. *Id.*

97. Section 85 of New Zealand's Animal Welfare Act provides limited rights to non-human hominids who might otherwise be subject to research and scientific experimentation. Sankoff, *supra* note 95, at 111.

98. *Id.*

99. Animal Welfare Act 1999 No 142 (as of 01 October 2008), Public Act, *available at* http://www.legislation.govt.nz/act/public/1999/0142/latest/viewpdf.aspx?search=ts_act_animal+welfare+act_resel&p=1.

100. *Id.* §4.

101. *Id.* §10.

102. The Five Freedoms of Animal Welfare are ideal requirements from which animal welfare standards may be adapted. The concept originated with the Report of the Technical Committee to Enquire into the Welfare of Animals kept under Intensive Livestock Husbandry Systems, the Brambell Report, December 1965 (HMSO London, ISBN 0 10 850286 4). The Freedoms include freedom from (1) hunger and thirst; (2) discomfort; (3) pain, injury or disease; (4) circumstances which prevent the expression of normal behavior; and (5) fear and distress.

103. *Id.* §4.

104. *Id.* §13(1).

105. *SPCA Calls for Review of Animal Welfare Act*, STUFF.CO.NZ, Aug. 17, 2009, *available at* http://www.stuff.co.nz/national/2760551/SPCA-calls-for-review-of-animal-welfare-act.

106. *Id.*

107. *Fisheries Law of the People's Republic of China*, ANIMAL LEGAL & HISTORICAL CENTER, *available at* http://www.animallaw.info/nonus/statutes/stcnfish.htm. The law's purpose is, among other things, "enhancing the protection, increase, development and reasonable utilization of fishery resources, developing artificial cultivation, protecting fishery workers' lawful rights and interests and boosting fishery production, so as to meet the requirements of socialist construction and the needs of the people." *Id.* art. 1.

108. *Id.*

109. Wei Luo & Joan Liu, *Features—A Complete Research Guide to the Laws of the People's Republic of China*, LLRX.COM (Jan. 15, 2003), *available at* http://www.llrx.com/features/prc.htm.

110. John Copeland Nagle, *The Missing Chinese Environmental Law Statutory Interpretation Cases*, N.Y.U. ENVTL. L.J. 517 (1996), *available at* http://www3.law.nyu.edu/journals/envtllaw/issues/vol5/2/5nyuelj517.html.

111. *Royal Society for the Prevention of Cruelty to Animals: History in the Making as China Launches its First Ever Animal Cruelty Laws*, POLITICS.CO.UK (SEPT. 17, 2009), *available at* http://www.politics.co.uk/opinion-formers/press-releases/animal-welfare/royal-society-for-the-prevention-of-cruelty-to-animals-history-in-the-making-as-china-launches-its-first-ever-animal-cruelty-laws-$1327901$366366.htm.

112. John Copeland Nagle, *Why Chinese Wildlife Disappears as CITES Spreads*, 9 GEO. INT'L. ENVTL. L. REV. 435, 436 (1996–1997).

113. *Animal Law in China*, ANIMAL LEGAL & HISTORICAL CENTER, *available at* http://www.animallaw.info/policy/pocnindex.htm.

114. Charu Sharma, *Chinese Endangered Species at the Brink of Extinction: A Critical Look at the Current Law and Policy in China*, 11 ANIMAL L. 215, 239–40 (2005).

115. *Id.* at 239–43.

116. Nagle, *supra* note 112.

117. Although Chinese royal families have had pets for many centuries, ownership of animals as companions is still not common among the population. Song Wei, *The Attitude*

Towards and Application of Animals in Traditional Chinese Culture, A Global Perspective on Animals in the Legal System, International Animal Welfare Law Conference, California Western School of Law (2004).

118. Beginning in approximately 2000, there have been several initiatives in the National People's Congress (NPC) to address the possibility of animal cruelty legislation. China's Constitution, enacted in 1982, gives the Standing Committee of the NPC the power to promulgate legislation. Professor Song Wei of the University of Science and Technology of China has been working steadily to encourage animal welfare legislation; additionally, Legislator Li Gengping authored animal welfare draft legislation in 2004. *See Beijing Deliberates Draft Regulation on Animal Welfare,* CHINA ECONOMIC NET (Oct. 25, 2004).

119. It is difficult to research Chinese case law because of the newness of the legal system, the limited information technology devoted to legal sources, and the fact that government agencies, as opposed to the courts, determine many questions of statutory interpretation.

120. Sharma, *supra* note 114.

121. CAO, *supra* note 94, at 102.

122. Katrina Sharman, *Animal Law in Australia,* ANIMAL LEGAL & HISTORICAL CENTER (2004), *available at* http://www.animallaw.info/nonus/articles/art_detils/print.htm.

123. CAO, *supra* note 94, at 99.

124. *Id.* Katrina Sharman, *Animal Law in Australia,* ANIMAL LEGAL & HISTORICAL CENTER (2004), *available at* http://www.animallaw.info/nonus/articles/ovaustrailia.htm#_edn30.

125. Prevention of Cruelty to Animals Act 1979 (New South Wales), §4(1).

126. Animal Protection Act 1985 (South Australia), §3.

127. Animal Welfare Act 1985 (South Australia), §13(3)(b).

128. Prevention of Cruelty to Animals Act 1979 (New South Wales), §5(1).

129. *Id.*

130. *Id.* §4(a)(2)(a)—(d).

131. CAO, *supra* note 94, at 102–06.

132. *Id.* at 106.

133. *Id.*

134. *Id.* at 212–13.

135. H. Weng *et al.*, *Animal Protection Measures in Taiwan: Taiwanese Attitudes Toward the Animal Protection Law and Animal Shelters*, J. APPLIED ANIM. WELFARE SCI. 315 Vol. 9, No. 4 (2006).

136. Animal Protection Law (Taiwan) (1998), Ch. I, art. 3.

137. *Id.* at Ch. 10, art. 3.

138. *Animal Protection Breakthrough in Taiwan,* WORLD SOCIETY FOR THE PROTECTION OF ANIMALS (June 22, 2007), *available at* http://www.wspa-international.org/latest-news/2007/breakthrough_in_taiwan.aspx.

139. *See, e.g., Lucky Beasts! Taiwan's Animal Protection Law: No Racing, Betting, or Cockfighting,* TAIWAN PANORAMA, *available at* http://www.taiwan-panorama.com/en/show_issue.php?id=199958805076E.TXT&table=2&h1=Ecology%20and%20Environment&h2=Animal%20Protection (describing 2009 advances); *Lucky Beasts! Taiwan's Animal Protection Law,* TAIWAN PANORAMA, *available at* http://www.sinorama.com.tw/en/show_issue.php?id=199958805076E.TXT&table=2&cur_page=3&distype= (gambling issues).

CHAPTER 4

Animal Experimentation

Chapter Overview

The practice of using animals as experimental subjects in scientific research dates back to at least 450 B.C.E., when Alcmaeon of Croton, a Greek physician, removed the eyeball of a live animal to test his theories about sight and perception.[1] Today, between 50 million and 115 million vertebrate animals are used in experiments each year around the globe.[2] Over the last fifty years, governments have reacted to public concerns and passed a variety of laws and regulations concerning animal experimentation. In this chapter, we examine these laws and the domestic and international contexts that give rise to them.

First, we look at how domestic legislatures have regulated (and, in one case, banned) animal experimentation by attempting to balance the interests of animals against the perceived interests of humans. Different kinds of experimental uses of animals have solicited different kinds of regulations, so we discuss a variety of laws, including those that (1) prohibit experiments on specific species, (2) regulate the use of animals in medical and scientific research, (3) regulate the testing of the toxic effect of cosmetics and household products on animals, and (4) limit the use of animals in educational contexts.

After examining these domestic laws, we turn to the regional approach to animal experimentation adopted by the European Union. We look at the how the EU's provisions on animal research and cosmetics testing have developed and spurred controversies among member nations.

From the regional approach, we shift to the international context. In order to establish a background for comparison, we begin this section with a brief investigation of the state of treaties and customary international law limiting scientific experimentation on human subjects. Then we look at how various nongovernmental and intergovernmental organizations have attempted to establish nonbinding international standards for animal research. Finally, we look at some specific international controversies concerning animal experimentation, including the ways in which the demand for experimental animal subjects in certain countries has spawned a large international primate trade, with devastating effects on wild and captive primates.

Before getting into specific laws, it is important to understand the different contexts in which animals are used for experimental or scientific purposes. These uses may be broadly classified into three groups: research, testing, and education.[3]

Research refers to the countless ways in which animals are used to explore both specific and general biological functions and systems. Research may be either basic or applied. Basic research (also called fundamental research) is intended "to add to scientific understanding of basic biological functions, processes, and behavior," whereas applied research aims "to improve human or animal health by studying the natural history of disease, its pathophysiology and prevention, and by developing diagnostic and therapeutic methods."[4] Biomedical research may focus on any of the bodily systems, investigating for example how the brain, heart, or lungs work. Researchers may also seek to answer questions about how animals interact with and react to various stimuli in their environments; the protocols may include denying experimental subjects food, water, sleep, or maternal/familial/social contact to investigate how such deprivations affect development or function. Virtually every type of animal is used in research, including cats, dogs, mice, rats, primates, rabbits, flies, cows, pigs, guinea pigs, fish, and birds.

Testing refers to the use of animals to gauge the effectiveness and risks of specific chemicals and products, such as pharmaceuticals, cosmetics, industrial, and household items. Animal testing is designed to "assess the potency, effectiveness, or toxicity of substances that have established or potential usefulness for medical, scientific, or commercial purposes."[5] Given the ubiquity of chemicals in the products that hundreds of millions of people use every day, many governments require toxicity tests to determine whether new products endanger human health. Whether these toxicity tests require the use of animals has been a point of contention.

Education refers to the ways in which animals are used to teach students about biological systems, surgical practices, anatomy, physiology, pharmacology and other topics. The purpose of these educational uses is "to train the next generation of scientists."[6] Students in elementary and secondary schools may dissect worms, frogs, fetal pigs, and other animals in basic biology courses to learn anatomy. They may also use animals in science fair projects with little or no supervision.[7] At the college level, many professors use animals to teach students about physiology, zoology, biology, psychology, and other sciences. In medical and veterinary programs, students may use live animals to learn and refine surgical and medical skills related to the care of humans and animals.[8]

Domestic Laws on Animal Experimentation

In this section, we look at how different countries have approached animal experimentation through domestic legislation. We begin by looking at the lone country that categorically bans animal experiments. Then we turn to the increasing number of countries that are banning experiments on great apes (gorillas, chimpanzees, and orangutans. After looking at these proscriptive laws, we address the approach adopted by the majority of countries: regulating the use of animals in research, testing, and education.

Complete Prohibitions on Animal Experimentation

In 2007, San Marino, a small independent republic surrounded on all sides by Italy, became the only country in the world to categorically ban all animal experiments.[9] The passage of San Marino's legislation was the culmination of a grassroots campaign led by the Sammarinese Association for the Protection of Animals (APAS).[10] In February 2007, APAS, along with several other animal protection groups, introduced a citizens' initiative to the Grand and General Council (the Sammarinese parliament) proposing a ban on animal experimentation.[11] APAS collected a large number of signatures from citizens in support of the initiative and, after its submission to the Council, hosted a pair of conferences to inform residents about the proposed legislation and educate them about animal experimentation and its alternatives.[12] The Council established a committee to review the proposed experimentation ban, which recommended approval.[13] In September 2007, the full Council voted to ban all animal experiments.[14]

In passing the act, the Sammarinese Council made several remarkable findings. First, it endorsed the strong animal rights position that animal experiments are necessarily inhumane and thus should be abolished, not merely regulated: "All animal experimentation is in fact a condition of mistreatment, in that the animals are kept in conditions of imprisonment and constraint, are often submitted to procedures that cause them extreme suffering, and are in the end put to death."[15] Second, the Council acknowledged the often-cited view of animal experimentation as a potentially ineffective model that cannot reliably be extrapolated to the human context: "The scientific validity of animal experimentation is arguably controversial and there are scientists who oppose this practice and prefer the scientific method without animals for toxicity testing and for studies *in vitro*, and for clinical and epidemiological studies researching basic human diseases."[16] Finally, the Council recognized the unique symbolic impact of its new law: "We believe that the Republic of San Marino places itself as a nation in the vanguard of Europe and all over the world, declaring itself a nation 'without vivisection,' thanks to the present law that forbids every form of experimentation on animals."[17]

The Sammarinese law is indeed wide-ranging. It applies to not only vertebrate animals, but also invertebrate, larval, and fetal animals.[18] It prohibits every "use [of] animals for scientific or technological ends."[19] Among the acts prohibited by the law are the use of animals in biomedical research, surgical training techniques on animals, the collection of animal tissue for *in vitro* research, the use of animals in education, toxicity testing of cosmetics and household products on animals, the use of animals in the production of "war materials," and even "biological tests for the protection of the ecosystem in the interests of man, of animals, or of plants."[20] The law also prohibits breeding animals in San Marino for use in experiments elsewhere.[21] The law does not forbid "interventions in the interest of the animal himself, whether for diagnostic, therapeutic, epidemiological, or public hygiene purposes."[22] Notably, no animal experiments were being conducted in San Marino when the law passed.[23]

One other country, Liechtenstein, a small European principality and constitutional monarchy located between Switzerland and Austria, prohibited all animal experiments in 1936,[24] but relaxed its ban in 1989.[25] The current Liechtenstein law forbids "[a]ny animal experimentation that causes research animals to experience pain, or creates severe anxiety in them or significantly damages their general condition," but the law permits the government to grant exceptions from this prohibition "so long as such experiments are for the prevention, diagnosis or treatment of human or veterinary illnesses."[26] In this regard, the current law is no stronger than the regulatory schemes described in the rest of the chapter. Although the law does not unequivocally ban animal experiments, the government has very rarely granted exceptions, and typically only in cases where the research is aimed at benefiting the species that is the subject of the experiment.[27]

Liechtenstein is considering eliminating the prohibition altogether, to more generally allow some research on animals. As this book was going to press, Liechtenstein intended to introduce a new animal protection law to harmonize its law with Swiss law, which Liechtenstein mirrors in a variety of other contexts.[28]

National Prohibitions on Experiments on Certain Species

While San Marino is the only country to currently ban experiments on all animals, several other countries have isolated particular species that they believe deserve absolute protection from use in experiments: the nonhuman hominids, also known as "great apes." The great apes consist of chimpanzees, bonobos, gorillas, and orangutans. Where such bans exist, legislatures have expressly or implicitly recognized the scientific evidence that these animals possess important characteristics such as a level of higher consciousness and intentionality. Based on that recognition, the legislatures have determined that members of these species should be free from the conditions and consequences of treatment and confinement that are an integral part of animal-based research.

Scientists have used great apes as research subjects in a variety of contexts. For example, in behavioral research, great apes are the subjects of maternal deprivation studies in which infants are separated from their mothers to test the psychological and behavioral results of such isolation. In infectious disease research, scientists inject chimpanzees with diseases such as Human Immunodeficiency Virus or the various strains of hepatitis. In virtually all studies, the animals are kept in small, bare laboratory cages with virtually no mental, physical, or psychological stimulation. Great apes have also been sent into outer space as subjects in the American and Russian space programs, and subjected to research on the effects of that travel.

Chimpanzees and bonobos have been used in biomedical research since the 1920s, and they are the great apes most commonly used in research today.[29] The United States and the African nation of Gabon are the only countries that still use chimpanzees in invasive biomedical research, although Japan and several European countries maintained great ape laboratories until very recently.[30] In the United States, roughly 1,200 chimpanzees remain in labs; Gabon is estimated to have 75 chimpanzees.[31] The last decade has seen a significant global shift in public opinion and government policy with regard to the use of great apes in research, with the sentiment shifting away from their use.

In 1997, the United Kingdom became the first country to establish a policy against the use of great apes in scientific experimentation. The UK, however, did not explicitly ban such uses through legislation. Instead, it resolved not to grant licenses for experiments involving great apes. As discussed in more detail below, UK law requires all procedures involving animals to be approved through the Home Office, so the refusal to grant licenses effectively banned great ape research in the UK. Jack Straw, the Home Secretary, described the policy as "a matter of morality."[32] Straw explained that "[t]he cognitive and behavioural characteristics and qualities of [great apes] mean it is unethical to treat them as expendable for research."[33]

In 1999, New Zealand became the first country to legislatively prohibit experiments on great apes. The law came about as a result of pressure from the New Zealand chapter of the Great Ape Project, which asked its parliament to grant legal rights to great apes, including the right to life, the right to be free from torture, and the right to not to be used in experimentation.[34] Although the legislature rejected this invitation to establish positive rights for nonhuman hominids, it did provide them with protection against their use in experiments. Section 85 of the New Zealand Animal Welfare Act of 1999 prohibits "any research, testing, or teaching involving the use of a nonhuman hominid unless such use has first been approved by the Director-General" of the Ministry of Agriculture and Forestry.[35] The Director-General may approve such use of a hominid only under very limited conditions: the work= must benefit the individual hominid subject herself, or at least benefit her species, and it may only be performed if the harm to her does not outweigh the benefits to the species.[36] While the protections that New Zealand passed in 1999 exceeded every law for great apes then in existence, it is important to recognize that they were largely symbolic: at the time of the law's passage, there were only thirty-four nonhuman hominids living in New Zealand, and none of them were being used in research, testing, or teaching.[37] The law had value primarily as "a powerful precedent" for other countries to follow.[38]

The New Zealand law seems to have had the desired ripple effect. As of the time of this book's publication, six countries have followed New Zealand's lead by prohibiting great ape experiments or by granting legal rights to great apes: the Netherlands in 2002; Sweden in 2003; Austria and Japan in 2006; the Balearic Islands in 2007; and Belgium in 2008.[39] Each country has enacted new laws that recognize the special nature of great apes, to varying degrees. This trend may signal a separation between the treatment of nonhuman hominids and other animals that could extend into other areas as well.

In the United States, activists, advocacy groups, and members of Congress have pushed for an end to the use of great apes in invasive research. In April 2008, members of the House of Representatives introduced the Great Ape Protection Act.[40] The bill would have prohibited any person from "conduct[ing] invasive research on a great ape" and eliminated all federal funding for such research.[41] The Act included a ban on the transportation and breeding of great apes for use in invasive research and would have required the Secretary of Health and Human Services to permanently retire to a suitable sanctuary all of the great apes owned or controlled by the federal government who were being or had been subjected to invasive research.[42] The Act defined "invasive research" to cover "any experimental research that may cause death, bodily injury, pain, distress, fear, injury, or trauma to a great ape" but exempted post-mortem examinations and behavioral research that does not require removal from enclosures or sedation.[43] The Act defined "great ape" to include not just chimpanzees, gorillas, bonobos, and orangutans, but also gibbons, who are not taxonomically characterized as great apes.[44] Although the Act failed to pass out of the committee process in the 110th (2008) Congress, Representative Edolphus Towns (D-NY) reintroduced the bill in March 2009 in the 111th Congress, where it gained 146 cosponsors,[45] but did not successfully move forward to become law. At this time of publication, efforts were still under way to get the law passed.

National Regulation of the Use of Animals in Scientific and Biomedical Research

Although San Marino categorically prohibits animal experiments, and a few other countries prohibit experiments on certain species, most of the countries in which animal experiments occur have established regulatory, rather than prohibitory, laws. Regulatory laws accept the use of animals in scientific and biomedical research, but supposedly seek to minimize animals' suffering by regulating housing and hygiene, establishing oversight committees, minimizing redundant experiments, and promoting alternative methodologies.

These aspirations are reflected in the "Three R's," a set of principles that now predominate in nearly every discussion of laboratory animal welfare.[46] The Three R's are *reduce*, *refine*, and *replace*: reduce where possible the number of animals used in a given experiment; refine the experiment to keep animal pain to a minimum; and replace animals with non-animal models where possible.[47] The Three R's were first enumerated in 1959 by a pair of British scientists, William Russell and Rex Burch to provide a framework for making animal research progressively more humane.[48] While recognition of these principles constitutes the starting point for the majority of animal research regulations, all legislation is reached by compromise with those involved in the research industry. The resulting laws almost always fail to satisfy many animal advocates because they sacrifice animals' interests when they conflict with the asserted need for freedom in research protocols. In this section, we review some of these laws.[49]

Britain: Cruelty to Animals Act and British Animals (Scientific Procedures) Act

Biomedical research ascended as a discipline in Europe in the early 1800s and continued to grow throughout the century, much to the chagrin of the burgeoning antivivisection movement, whose members vociferously criticized the increase in animal experimentation.[50] In an attempt to placate these critics, the British scientific community established a voluntary code in 1871 to set general guidelines aimed at minimizing the suffering of animals used in research.[51] A few years later, the British parliament took action, passing the world's first law to regulate animal experimentation: Britain's 1876 Cruelty to Animals Act.[52] But the antivivisectionists saw the Act as too much of a compromise and refused to support it.[53] One prominent antivivisectionist, Frances P. Cobbe, sardonically referred to the law as the "Vivisector's Charter."[54]

The Cruelty to Animals Act laid the foundation for research regulations for decades to come. Many of its provisions, such as its licensing and inspection requirements, became standard components of animal research laws throughout the world. Like most research laws that followed, the Act was primarily concerned with the infliction of suffering, rather than the use of animals *per se*. It prohibited the performance of "any experiment calculated to give pain" to an animal unless the requirements of the law were followed.[55] The Act provided that "the animal must, during the whole of the experiment, be under the influence of some anaesthetic of sufficient power to prevent the animal feeling pain," and if the pain was likely to endure after the experiment, or if the animal had suffered "any serious injury," the researcher had to euthanize the animal before the anesthetic wore off.[56] The Act nevertheless permitted painful experiments without anesthetic if the Secretary of State certified that "insensibility [could not] be produced without necessarily frustrating the object of such experiments."[57] The same exception applied to the euthanasia requirement.[58]

The Act provided extra protections for dogs, cats, horses, asses, and mules. It prohibited experiments on unanesthetized dogs and cats unless these species were necessary for the purposes of the experiment and no other kind of animal was available.[59] Researchers could not experiment on equines, presumably even anesthetized ones, without the same showings: that the object of the experiment would be "necessarily frustrated" without their use and that no other animal was available.[60]

The Act arguably narrowed the scope of purposes for which animal research was justified; experiments calculated to cause pain had to "be performed with a view to the advancement by new discovery of physiological knowledge or of knowledge which will be useful for saving or prolonging life, or alleviating suffering."[61] The Act also required animal researchers to apply for and receive a license before they could perform experiments, and it provided for the registration of places where research would be conducted.[62] The Act established an inspection scheme, requiring appointed inspectors to periodically visit the registered laboratories where researchers conducted their experiments.[63]

The Cruelty to Animals Act remained in effect until 1986, when Parliament replaced it with the Animals (Scientific Procedures) Act (A(SP)A).[64] The A(SP)A, which remains the law today, governs all experiments and procedures that "may have the effect of causing [an] animal pain, suffering, distress or lasting harm."[65] Several million animals are used in research annually in Great Britain, and the number of procedures has increased steadily since 2000.[66] The A(SP)A's protections apply to all nonhuman vertebrates, as well as members of the species *Octopus*.[67] Under the law, no one may perform animal research in the UK without first obtaining the appropriate licenses from the Home Secretary.[68] The law requires two separate licenses: one for the researcher (a personal license) and one for the research project (a project license).

Before granting a personal license, the Secretary must be satisfied that the applicant "has appropriate education and training" for the proposed procedures and "is competent to apply those procedures ... and to handle and take care of laboratory animals."[69] Personal licenses must also include a condition requiring the licensee to "take precautions to prevent or reduce ... any pain, distress or discomfort to the animals," consistent with the purposes of the research, as well as a condition concerning the circumstances under which experimental animals must be euthanized.[70]

The Secretary may grant a project license only after considering the purposes of the research and weighing "the likely adverse effects on the animals concerned against the benefit likely to accrue as a result of the programme."[71] Project licenses must include a condition prohibiting the use of dogs or cats unless they come from a certified breeding establishment.[72] They must also include conditions prohibiting the use of endangered species and limiting the use of wild animals.[73] Finally, project licenses must provide conditions for either setting free or euthanizing the animals used.[74]

Before granting a project license, the Secretary must also be satisfied that the project's purpose "cannot be achieved satisfactorily by any other reasonably practicable method not entailing the use of protected animals," and that the project will include only those procedures that "use the minimum number of animals, involve animals with the lowest degree of neurophysiological sensitivity, cause the least pain, suffering, distress or lasting harm, and are most likely to produce satisfactory results."[75] The A(SP)A's project license requirement implicitly incorporates each of the Three R's: the Secretary must ensure that a proposed project "use[s] the minimum number of animals" (reduce); that the procedures "cause the least pain, suffering, distress or lasting harm" (refine); and that the goals of the project "cannot be achieved satisfactorily by any other practicable method not entailing the use of protected animals" (replace).[76]

Animal advocates have criticized the licensing system, arguing that it does not provide adequate and independent scrutiny of project proposals. For example, an undercover investigation of the Institute of Neurology by the UK's National Anti-Vivisection Society documented one instance in which the Home Office took just three days to grant a license for a complex, five-year set of experiments involving sixty-one monkeys, twenty-five rats, and four cats. One of these experiments involved "bolting a steel headpiece with tubes and electrodes permanently into the heads of macaque monkeys," then starving the monkeys so they would respond to proffered food.[77] The UK Home Office responded that it had already had discussions with the applicant before the application was filed, but no evidence of such conversations was produced.

Like the 1876 Cruelty to Animals Act, the A(SP)A provides certain species with extra protection. The Secretary may not issue a project license for research involving cats, dogs, primates, or equine animals unless no other species of animal is "suitable" or, if there is another suitable species, it is "not practicable to obtain."[78]

In addition to licensing researchers and projects, the A(SP)A requires that facilities where animal research is performed be certified by the Secretary.[79] To become certified, a scientific establishment must have someone on staff who is "responsible for the day to day care of the protected animals," as well as an employee who is "suitably qualified … to provide advice on [the animals'] health and welfare."[80] The Secretary must also include in the certificate conditions for staff training, euthanasia, record keeping, and animal identification.[81] Facilities must provide each animal with "the environment, housing, freedom of movement, food, water and care … appropriate for the animal's health and well-being," and "restrictions on the extent to which each … animal can satisfy [his or her] physiological and ethological needs [must be] kept to the absolute minimum."[82]

The A(SP)A establishes an inspectorate to ensure compliance with its terms. Inspectors are tasked with: advising the Secretary on applications for personal licenses, private licenses, and facility certificates, or on their variation and revocation; visiting and inspecting research facilities to determine whether researchers are complying with their project licenses and whether facilities are complying with the conditions of their certificates; and reporting violations of the A(SP)A or permit conditions to the Secretary.[83] Inspectors are authorized to require the immediate killing of any animal they determine to be "undergoing excessive suffering."[84]

The A(SP)A also created the Animal Procedures Committee (APC), which serves as an advisory body to the Secretary. The APC consists of a minimum of thirteen members, at least two-thirds of whom must be either registered medical practitioners or veterinary surgeons, or have "qualifications or experience in a biological subject approved by the Secretary."[85] In an evident attempt to avoid stacking the APC in favor of researchers, the A(SP)A requires that at least half of the members not presently hold, nor have held in the previous six years, a license under the Act.[86] In appointing members to the APC, the Secretary is instructed to "have regard to the desirability of ensuring that the interests of animal welfare are adequately represented."[87]

The APC advises the Secretary on a wide variety of issues concerning animal research. Although it is the Home Secretary's Animal Scientific Procedures Division that reviews most license applications, the APC provides input to the Secretary in particular cases, such as procedures involving wild primates and those that "raise serious societal concerns."[88] The APC publishes papers and reports on issues such as the severity of pain in laboratory animals and reporting requirements under the A(SP)A.[89] In all of its work, the APC must "have regard both to the legitimate requirements of science and industry and to the protection of animals against avoidable suffering and unnecessary use in scientific procedures."[90]

The A(SP)A also permits the Secretary to establish husbandry and welfare standards, according to *The Code of Practice for the Housing and Care of Animals Used in Scientific Procedures*.[91] This Code sets a series of minimum guidelines for the care of animals on issues such as space, light, and temperature. Animal advocates, however, have criticized the Code for having too many loopholes and leaving too many details to the discretion of researchers. The National Anti-Vivisection Society and Animal Defenders International have complained that "[i]nvestigations of the use of animals in laboratories in a dozen establishments over the past decade … have concluded that for most species the [Code] offers very little in terms of detailed requirements for animal comfort or environmental enrichment, and for those where there is some detail…, this is routinely ignored."[92]

United States: Animal Welfare Act

The organized antivivisection movement in the United States began in the 1860s after an increasing number of prestigious colleges, universities, and medical schools began using live animals in experiments and public demonstrations.[93] After Britain passed the 1876 Cruelty to Animals Act, U.S. lawmakers became inspired to pass a similar law. In 1880, the United States Congress considered a bill to regulate research on animals in the District of Columbia, but the bill failed to pass because of opposition by the American scientific community.[94] In 1883, the American Anti-Vivisection Society was founded, followed by a succession of other regional antivivisection societies, which solidified the issue of animal research in state and federal politics.[95] Between 1933 and 1934, for instance, thirty-two states were considering antivivisection bills.[96] Although strong state bills against animal research were consistently defeated throughout the first half of the twentieth century, the movement against animal research had its share of wins at the state level. These successes have included the passage of state bills to prohibit animal experiments in elementary and secondary schools and the defeat of several so-called "pound seizure" laws, which would have required animal shelters to surrender dogs and cats to research facilities.[97] Antivivisection organizations also convinced federal legislators to introduce a variety of pro-animal legislation, including seven bills to prohibit research on dogs. Not one of them was ever passed into law.[98]

It was not until 1966, ninety years after Britain passed the 1876 Cruelty to Animals Act, that the United States adopted legislation to protect animals in research. Many laws have their genesis in single individual events, which when disclosed to the public generate societal support. For the research community and animals subjected to research, such was the case. In 1965, a dealer who sold dogs to research laboratories stole a Dalmatian dog named Pepper from a farm in Slatington, Pennsylvania.[99] Pepper's guardians, the Lackavage family, embarked on a heart-rending expedition to recover her with the assistance of several animal welfare organizations and a member of Congress. Their story was played out in the mass media of the time and received national attention. But, in a series of events worthy of Hollywood, the dog dealers were always one step ahead as the Lackavages chased after them to recover Pepper. Finally, the family learned that a dealer had taken Pepper to a hospital in New York City, but after calling the hospital, they learned that they were too late: Pepper had been subjected to a surgical procedure to have an experimental pacemaker implanted. She died during the procedure and was cremated.[100]

The media coverage led to a public outcry against dog dealers and dog thieves who sold animals to research facilities. In February 1966, *LIFE Magazine* ran an eight-page photo spread of a raid on a dog dealer's property, entitled "Concentration Camps for Dogs."[101] The pictures and accompanying text "described puppies drenched in their own vomit, dogs forced to lie in their own feces, others gnawing at frozen entrails on the ground, and nearly every animal too weak to stand properly."[102] The photographs, and the public reaction they elicited, were the tipping point.[103] In August 1966, just a few months after the story ran, Congress passed the Laboratory Animal Welfare Act, which President Lyndon Johnson signed into law.[104]

The Act addressed concerns about both pet theft by animal dealers and the humane treatment of animals used in research. With regard to the first concern, it required all dog and cat dealers who sold animals for use in research to obtain licenses from the Secretary of Agriculture, and it forbade the sale, purchase, and transport of dogs and cats for use in research without such a license.[105] In order to give victims of pet theft an opportunity to recover their animals, the Act also required dealers to hold animals for five days before selling them to research facilities.[106] Research facilities were required to register with the Secretary, and they were forbidden from obtaining animals from unlicensed sources.[107] The Act established recordkeeping and animal identification requirements, both of which were likely inspired by Pepper's case.[108]

With regard to the second concern, the Act required the Secretary to create standards for the humane treatment of animals by dealers and research facilities,[109] though it limited the definition of "animals" to dogs, cats, monkeys, guinea pigs, hamsters, and rabbits.[110] These standards concerned "housing, feeding, watering, sanitation, ventilation, shelter from extremes of weather and temperature, separation by species, and adequate veterinary care."[111] Significantly, Congress specified that it did not intend to authorize the Secretary to create humane standards applicable "*during* actual research or experimentation."[112] In other words, the Act applied only to basic husbandry and conditions of confinement at the laboratory, but did not impact the type of research or the form it takes. The conduct of research and the development of research protocols remained firmly within the discretion of the researchers and the research facility.

Congress amended the Animal Welfare Act (AWA) in 1970, 1976, 1985, 1990, 2002, and 2007.[113] Today, it applies beyond the laboratory to some situations in which animals are sold as pets or exhibited (as in circuses and zoos), and it also prohibits animal fighting.[114] This section of the book focuses only on the provisions of the current AWA that apply to research. The strengths and weaknesses of these provisions are exceedingly important because the United States currently uses more animals in research than any other country in the world—approximately 17 million animals each year.[115]

As it has since 1966, the AWA requires the Secretary of Agriculture to "promulgate standards to govern the humane handling, care, treatment, and transportation of animals by dealers [and] research facilities," including "minimum requirements for handling, housing, feeding, watering, sanitation, ventilation, shelter from extremes of weather and temperatures, adequate veterinary care, and separation by species."[116] Pursuant to this directive, the Department of Agriculture (USDA) has established standards for the handling, care, treatment, and transportation of a variety of animals, including dogs, cats, guinea pigs, hamsters, rabbits, nonhuman primates, and marine mammals.[117] To give just a few examples: the regulations require dogs' and cats' primary enclosures to be "structurally sound" and "kept in good repair," and the enclosures must provide, among other things, "sufficient space to allow each dog and cat to turn about freely, to stand, sit, and lie in a comfortable, normal position, and to walk in a normal manner."[118] Guinea pigs and hamsters must receive food that is "free from contamination, wholesome, palatable and of sufficient quantity and nutritive value to meet the normal daily requirements for the[ir] condition and size."[119] Indoor primary enclosures for primates "must be sanitized at least once every 2 weeks and as often as necessary to prevent an excessive accumulation of dirt, debris, waste, food waste, excreta, or disease hazard."[120]

Under amendments passed in 1985, dogs and nonhuman primates receive extra protection. (Compare and contrast this with the British Animals (Scientific Procedures) Act, which provides special protections to dogs, primates, cats, and equines over and above those given to other animals.[121]) The AWA requires the Secretary to issue minimum requirements "for exercise for dogs ... and for a physical environment adequate to promote the psychological well-being of primates."[122] As discussed below, the regulations promulgated by the Secretary for these purposes have caused significant consternation for animal advocates.[123]

Under the implementing regulations, dogs who are housed in groups do not need additional exercise if their cages provide them with a space that is equal to the length of the dog plus six inches, squared.[124] In the case of a dog two feet in length, the research facility would need to provide him only 6.25 square feet (the equivalent of a square 2.5 feet by 2.5 feet) of space in order to avoid having to provide him with "additional" exercise. If the dog were housed individually, he would need a slightly larger area: 12.5 square feet (the rough equivalent of a square 3.5 feet by 3.5 feet).[125] Even for those dogs who do receive additional exercise, the details are left to the discretion of the research facility. Under the regulations, "[t]he frequency, method, and duration of the opportunity for exercise shall be determined by the attending veterinarian and, at research facilities, in consultation with and approval by the [Institutional Animal Care and Use] Committee."[126] Facilities are encouraged to "consider providing positive physical contact with humans that encourages exercise through play or other similar activities."[127] Dogs who have no contact with other dogs must receive "positive physical contact with humans" every day.[128] Research facilities may also forego the exercise requirement if the researcher "determines for scientific reasons set forth in the research proposal that it is inappropriate for certain dogs to exercise."[129]

The USDA has also promulgated regulations for the psychological well-being of primates, as required by the AWA.[130] These regulations require research facilities to "address the social needs of nonhuman primates of species" that live socially in the wild, and they suggest but do not require group housing.[131] Facilities must enrich primates' enclosures by taking steps to enable animals to express "noninjurious species-typical activities." Laboratories may do so by "providing perches, swings, mirrors, and other increased cage complexities; providing objects to manipulate; [providing] varied food items; using foraging or task-oriented feeding methods; and providing interaction with the care giver or other familiar and knowledgeable person consistent with personnel safety precautions."[132] As with the exercise requirement for dogs, the psychological well-being requirements may be disregarded by a researcher if he or she has "scientific reasons" for doing so.[133]

In 1991, the Animal Legal Defense Fund (ALDF) sued the USDA over the AWA regulations governing dogs and primates, contending that the Secretary acted arbitrarily and capriciously in violation of the Administrative Procedure Act by promulgating regulations that were at odds with the requirements and intent of the AWA.[134] A federal district court agreed, holding that both the dog regulations and the primate regulations failed to comply with the Congressional mandates in the AWA.

With regard to the dog exercise regulations, the court focused on the agency's delegation of all standards and details to on-site veterinarians and facility review committees, in effect making compliance with the AWA dependent on "good faith compliance by regulated entities."[135] Given this improper delegation and complete ambiguity about how often dogs should receive exercise, the court concluded that the regulations did "not fulfill even the minimal requirements set out by the plain language of the statute for the humane handling, care, and treatment of animals."[136] With a degree of candor unusual in written judicial opinions, the court opined that the USDA's regulations, and its concerns about inconveniencing research facilities, "may well be based more on the almighty dollar than the welfare of animals."[137] The court further admonished the USDA: "'A dog is man's best friend' is an old adage which the Defendants have either forgotten or decided to ignore."[138]

With regard to the primates' psychological well-being regulations, the court noted that nonhuman primates are "wonderful animals" and that many of them "have the distinctive qualities of human beings."[139] The court held that the regulations were inadequate because they failed to provide actual standards or requirements; rather, they referenced "generally accepted professional standards" for psychological well-being without explaining "[w]hat these standards are and how they are arrived at."[140] The court identified the regulations' failure to require group housing as inconsistent with the agency's previous factual findings that social isolation was a major cause of psychological problems in nonhuman primates.[141]

Having concluded that the existing regulations failed to properly implement the AWA, the court directed the USDA to promulgate new regulations.[142] The decision was vacated, however, by the appellate court (the United States Court of Appeals for the District of Columbia), not because it disagreed with the court's ruling on the regulations (it did not address that issue), but because the plaintiffs lacked "standing" to challenge the regulations.[143] Standing is a judicial doctrine in American federal courts that limits the class of people who can initiate lawsuits to those who have suffered a concrete and particularized injury that is fairly traceable to the defendant and that the court is capable of redressing.[144] Plaintiffs must also demonstrate that their injuries fall within the zone of interests that the operative statute seeks to protect.[145] In this case, the court held that none of the plaintiffs met these requirements.[146]

ALDF found new plaintiffs who it believed had standing, then filed another complaint challenging the propriety of the primate regulations. This time the plaintiffs complained specifically about the conditions at a roadside zoo, rather than a laboratory. The district court held that the new plaintiffs had standing. The court again ruled in favor of ALDF on the merits, reiterating the deficiencies of the regulations.[147] On appeal, the higher court again vacated the district court decision by holding that the plaintiffs lacked standing.[148] But a further "en banc" review was then set.[149] (En banc review involves a re-hearing of a case by all the judges on the higher court, who review a three-judge appellate panel's ruling.) The en banc court reversed the decision of the appellate panel and held that at least one of ALDF's plaintiffs had standing (which is all that is required to have the case move forward), because he had suffered an aesthetic injury when he witnessed primates suffering as a result of the lax regulations.[150] The en banc court sent the case back for another three-judge panel to determine on the merits whether the USDA had violated the law in promulgating the primate regulations. That panel ultimately upheld the regulations, concluding that the delegation of requirements to the regulated entities was consistent with the AWA.[151] After more than a decade of protracted litigation, the regulations were affirmed and still remain in place.

While dogs and primates receive slightly more consideration under the AWA, other animals receive no consideration whatsoever. The AWA defines "animal" to exclude birds, rats, and mice bred for use in research, animals who collectively comprise more than ninety percent of the animals used in experimentation.[152] The original version of the AWA passed in 1966 limited its coverage to dogs, cats, monkeys, guinea pigs, hamsters, and rabbits, but Congress expanded its coverage in 1970 to include "any ... warm-blooded animal, as the Secretary may determine is being used, or is intended for use, for research, testing, experimentation, or exhibition purposes, or as a pet."[153] Although birds, rats, and mice are undoubtedly warm-blooded animals who are used for research, the USDA published regulations to exclude them from coverage under the AWA on the same day that the expanded definition came into effect.[154]

ALDF sued the USDA over the regulations, arguing that the exclusion of birds, rats, and mice from the definition of "animal" was arbitrary and capricious, given that they were clearly warm-blooded animals used in research.[155] The district court agreed, holding that "the exclusion of rats, mice, and birds from the statute directly contravenes the statutory mandate of assuring humane treatment of laboratory animals."[156] It further recognized that "[t]he exclusion affirmatively communicates that regulated industries need not consider their treatment of these animals and will never be held in violation of the Animal Welfare Act regardless of whether these animals are denied food, water, appropriate housing or are subjected to excruciating and unrelieved pain."[157]

An appellate panel from the District of Columbia Court of Appeal vacated the opinion, holding that the plaintiffs lacked standing to challenge the regulations.[158] Several years later, the Alternatives Research and Development Foundation instituted a new lawsuit against the USDA over the exclusion of birds, rats, and mice.[159] The district court held that the plaintiffs had standing, but it deferred ruling on the merits until a later date.[160] Perhaps seeing the writing on the wall, the USDA agreed to settle the case and include birds, rats, and mice in its revised regulations.[161]

With the USDA poised to agree to cover birds, rats, and mice, Congress stepped in and used its appropriations power to preclude the agency from changing its definition of "animal."[162] Then, in 2002, Congress amended the AWA's definition of "animal" to explicitly exclude birds, rats, and mice. This legislative act officially and unequivocally removed birds, rats, and mice bred for research from the ambit of the AWA.[163]

Substantively, the AWA reflects Congress's general intent to avoid interfering with the conduct of researchers. The AWA states that the USDA may not "promulgate rules, regulations, or orders with regard to the *design, outlines, or guidelines* of actual research or experimentation by a research facility as determined by such research facility."[164] Neither may it "promulgate rules, regulations, or orders with regard to the *performance* of actual research or experimentation by a research facility as determined by such research facility."[165] Even during inspection, the USDA, unlike the British inspectorate, may not "interrupt the conduct of actual research or experimentation."[166]

But in 1985, Congress amended the AWA to require the Secretary to promulgate regulations for research facilities to minimize animals' pain and distress, including the provision of appropriate veterinary care and anesthetics, analgesics, and tranquilizers when appropriate.[167] If a proposed procedure causes "more than momentary or slight pain or distress to the animals," the researcher must use appropriate painkillers or sedatives. Despite these limits on painful research protocols, the pain-relief requirements can be avoided if "withholding such agents is justified for scientific reasons."[168] The AWA further requires the principal researcher to "consider[] alternatives to any procedure likely to produce pain to or distress in an experimental animal."[169] For procedures that cause animals pain, researchers must consult veterinarians.[170] Additionally, an animal may not be used more than once in a "major operative experiment from which [he or she] is allowed to recover" unless doing so is scientifically necessary or "special circumstances" exist.[171] As with the other humane standards mentioned above, researchers may avoid these restrictions "when specified by research protocol."[172]

Although the 1985 amendments for the first time touched on actual performance of research by requiring researchers to minimize pain where doing so was consistent with the goals of the research, it is still the case that the AWA does not govern the specific research protocols and provides great leeway for researchers to determine that pain connected with the research is necessary to achieve the desired research results. The AWA does not categorically prohibit any experiment, no matter how painful the procedure or trivial the knowledge gained. Unlike the British law, which requires the Home Secretary to weigh the harm to animals against the benefit to humans before granting a license, the AWA does not mandate any inquiry into the value of the research itself.[173]

Because the AWA does not regulate the substance of experiments and permits pain and distress where the researcher claims it is scientifically necessary, many experiments in which animals suffer are permissible in U.S. laboratories. For instance, studies that intentionally subject animals to painful diseases, addict them to drugs, or deprive them of social contact, sleep, food, or water, are ongoing, and do not on their own terms violate the AWA. If the experiment involves the deliberate induction of trauma or fear in the animal (as many experiments do), then the suffering is by definition "justified for scientific reasons."[174]

Review of such procedures is largely an internal affair: unlike the British Home Office, the U.S. government does not issue licenses for projects or personnel. The main oversight comes through "enforced self-regulation" by internal review committees.[175] Each research facility must establish and appoint a committee to oversee research involving animals.[176] These committees, known as Institutional Animal Care and Use Committees (IACUCs), are empowered to review protocols submitted by researchers to assess whether the proposed research project minimizes pain and distress, whether the researcher has considered alternatives, and whether the researcher has provided assurance that the project is not unnecessarily duplicative of existing research.[177] The AWA requires each IACUC to inspect its research facility semiannually and prepare inspection reports.[178]

Animal advocates have criticized the IACUC requirement for research facilities, arguing that in many cases oversight committees serve as little more than a "rubber stamp," simply agreeing with whatever research protocols are submitted to them.[179] The AWA requires that only one IACUC member represent "general community interests in the proper care and treatment of animals."[180] Given that this IACUC member is appointed by the CEO of the research facility, sincere animal welfare advocates are unlikely to ever be invited onto a committee. IACUC meetings are typically closed to the public and many institutions resist calls for transparency through public disclosure of discussion topics, documents and decisions. A 2005 audit by the USDA's Office of Inspector General (OIG) found that IACUCs are not adequately monitoring animal research facilities. The OIG's report found that "[m]ost [Veterinary Medical Officers] believe there are still problems with the search for alternative research, veterinary care, review of painful procedures, and the researchers' use of animals."[181] The report attributed these failures to a variety of factors, including poor training of IACUC members, infrequent committee inspections, and a high turnover rate among committee members.[182]

Although the government does not review or license research protocols, it does conduct annual inspections of research facilities.[183] The Animal and Plant Health Inspection Service (APHIS) is the agency within the USDA that undertakes the USDA's AWA responsibilities. APHIS's mission, however, goes beyond animal health and welfare,[184] and so the animal-related concerns are handled by the Animal Care (AC) program within APHIS.[185] AC conducts both pre-licensing inspections, to ensure that those facilities that are applying for licenses meet USDA regulations, and unannounced compliance inspections, to ensure that already-licensed facilities are continuing to comply with the regulations.[186] The AWA requires the USDA to inspect research facilities on an annual basis, and to conduct "follow-up inspections as may be necessary until all deficiencies or deviations ... are corrected."[187] When inspectors discover violations of animal welfare standards, they generally work with the facility to assist them in coming into compliance. If the violations go uncorrected, AC, along with APHIS's Investigative and Enforcement Services, may undertake an enforcement action that can result in "an official notice of warning or a stipulation offer."[188] In severe cases, more dramatic remedies may be available, including fines, suspension or revocation of licenses, civil penalties, and injunctions against violating welfare standards.[189]

Animal advocates have expressed serious concerns about the effectiveness of APHIS's inspection regime.[190] The aforementioned 2005 OIG audit concluded that the USDA "needs to improve its monitoring of research facilities."[191] It concluded that the deficiencies in APHIS inspections translated into "less assurance that protocols are properly completed, approved, and adhered to for the purpose of ensuring the health and safety of the animals."[192] The audit also found that fining AWA violators served little deterrent value, noting that "APHIS gives an automatic 75-percent discount to almost all violators ... as a means of amicably reaching an agreement on the amount of the fines and avoiding court."[193] In fact, "violators consider the monetary stipulation as a normal cost of conducting business rather than a deterrent for violating the law."[194] OIG concluded that these fines were "basically meaningless."[195] These failures are significant because the government has a monopoly on enforcement of the AWA. Unlike environmental statutes such as the Clean Water Act and the Endangered Species Act, which enable concerned citizens and organizations to sue violators in order to enforce the law, the AWA has no citizen-suit provision or private right of action.[196] When community members learn of clear violations of the AWA, they have virtually no ability to sue the offenders under the AWA to stop those violations.

Finally, it should be noted that other federal laws also regulate animal research. The Health Research Extension Act of 1985 directed the Secretary of Health and Human Services, through the Director of the National Institutes of Health (NIH), to establish regulations for the care and treatment of animals used in federally funded biomedical and behavioral research.[197] Any research project involving vertebrate animals that receives federal funds from the Public Health Service (PHS) must meet certain humane standards. These regulations include guidelines for the use of certain drugs, including anesthetics, analgesics, tranquilizers, and paralytics, as well as provisions governing euthanasia and veterinary care for animals used in surgical procedures.[198] The law makes clear, however, that "[s]uch guidelines shall not be construed to prescribe methods of research."[199] To implement the law, the NIH's Office of Laboratory Animal Welfare (OLAW) has issued a policy that covers all vertebrates, including rats, mice, and birds.[200] The policy requires federally-funded research projects to conform to the *Guide for the Care and Use of Laboratory Animals*, a set of "generalizations and broad recommendations" on laboratory practice.[201] The Guide includes recommended standards for animals excluded from the AWA, such as rats and mice.[202] Notably, the policy lacks the regular inspection requirements of the AWA, discussed above.[203] Accordingly, although OLAW oversees research facilities that receive federal funding, it is largely dependent on the research facilities themselves for "assurances" that humane standards are being met.[204]

Japan: Act on Welfare and Management of Animals

Depending on which figures one consults, Japan ranks either second or third in the world (after the United States, and possibly China) in the number of animals it uses in research. One study estimated that 11 million animals were used as research subjects in Japan in 2005.[205]

Originally passed in 1973 and revised in 1999 and 2005, the Act on Welfare and Management of Animals (AWMA) governs animal welfare in Japan.[206] The AWMA, also referred to as the Law for Humane Treatment and Management of Animals,[207] sets out general principles for humane treatment of animals "to engender a spirit for animal welfare among citizens and contribute to the development of a respect for life and sentiments of amity and peace."[208] The Act requires businesses that handle animals to register with their local prefectural governments, submit to inspections, and comply with regulations concerning animal health and welfare.[209] These provisions, however, exclude animals used in research and testing.[210]

Although the AWMA's general prohibitions on animal cruelty exempt animal research facilities, Article 41 of the Act does apply to animal experimentation. It requires researchers to give "consideration ... to the appropriate use of [laboratory] animals by such means as using alternative methods to that of the use of animals as much as possible and reducing the number of animals provided for such use as much as possible, within the extent that the purpose of the scientific use can be attained."[211] In other words, where researchers believe other methods can provide the same information as research on animals, they are encouraged to consider those alternatives and to reduce the number of animals they use. These two factors—the consideration of alternatives and the minimization of the number of animals used—reflect two of the Three R's: replace and reduce. The third R, refine, is also incorporated in Article 41: "In the case where an animal is provided for a scientific use, a method that minimizes the pain and distress to the animal as much as possible shall be used, within the limit necessary for such use."[212] Like the British A(SP)A and the American AWA, the Japanese AWMA requires researchers to euthanize animals who are irremediably injured, after the scientific research has concluded.[213]

The AWMA empowered the Minister of Environment to set more specific standards for these rather broad principles, which he did in June 2006.[214] These regulations, entitled *Standards Relating to the Care and Management of Laboratory Animals and Relief of Pain*, provide basic guidelines for animal husbandry and treatment.[215] Unlike the San Marino law, which provides a wholesale question of the scientific value of animal research, the Standards express a commitment to the use of animals as "necessary and indispensable for the advancement of biomedical science and the development of medical technology."[216] Japanese law, therefore, accepts the underlying use of animals, but suggests consideration of the Three R's.[217] In addition to the Standards, other Japanese ministries have created guidelines, as has the Science Council of Japan, an advisory organization under the jurisdiction of the Japanese prime minister.[218] The Science Council's guidelines very closely track the *Guide for the Care and Use of Laboratory Animals*, the manual by the Institute of Laboratory Animal Resources that governs federally-funded research in the United States, although the Science Council's guidelines place much less emphasis on veterinary care.[219] The Science Council's guidelines are voluntary, and thus evidently lack the force of law.[220]

With regard to oversight, Japanese law is much closer to the American AWA than to the British A(SP)A, in that it is premised on internal self-regulation by committees rather than external regulation by the government. Indeed, these committees even have the same name as their American counterparts: Institutional Animal Care and Use Committees.[221] As one Japanese official put it, "appropriate animal experimentation can be accomplished by self-control, not by stringent legislative restriction."[222] The AWMA does not require research facilities to register with the government and does not provide for regular inspections of research facilities.

China: Guiding Opinions on the Humane Treatment of Laboratory Animals

As with the United States, it is exceedingly difficult to find reliable data on the number of animals used in China. Estimates range from three million to nineteen million, the latter of which, if accurate, would make China the world's number one user of experimental animals.[223] According to officially-reported data in 2004, ten million animals were bred and seven million were used, which would make China third in number of animals used in experiments. Fifty percent of the animals used in 2004 were mice, twenty-four percent were hamsters, and thirteen percent were rats.[224] China also produces "transgenic and inbred miniature pigs, chickens, dogs, and monkeys for scientific use."[225]

Animal research in China dates back to 1918, but until very recently, China's regulation of animal experimentation was concerned almost exclusively with ensuring the quality and reliability of scientific data, rather than protecting animals.[226] In 1988, China's State Council approved regulations governing the breeding and use of laboratory animals.[227] The purpose of these regulations was to "guarantee[] the quality of experimental animals so as to meet the needs of scientific research, economic construction, and social development."[228]

The regulations reflect only the most basic concern for the welfare of animals used in experiments: animals must receive "wholesome" food, "hygienic" water, and "clean" bedding, although these are more attributable to the desire for scientific purity than animal welfare.[229] It also states that "[p]ersonnel dealing with experimental animals shall protect these animals and may not play with or maltreat them."[230] Aside from these minimal references, animal suffering is disregarded, with minimal limits on the practices to which animals can be subjected.

In 2006, China's Ministry of Science and Technology drastically improved legal protections for laboratory animals in China when it enacted the *Guiding Opinions on the Humane Treatment of Laboratory Animals*.[231] Under Chinese law, these guidelines are ministry regulations that have the effective force of law. The Ministry drafted the Guiding Opinions "to enhance the quality of laboratory animal management, protect animal welfare, promote harmony between humans and nature, and meet the needs of scientific research, economic development, and opening up to the outside world."[232]

The Guiding Opinions borrow from existing lab animal regulatory schemes in other countries and incorporate many of the provisions discussed above.[233] They define ethical treatment to require "effective measures ... to avoid unnecessary suffering, thirst, discomfort, fear, torture, illness, and pain."[234] The term "lab animals," unlike in the United States, includes rats and mice.[235] Animals must be able "to exercise their natural behaviors" and must "be properly cared for and managed."[236] The Guiding Opinions explicitly promote the Three R's.[237] Following the law in other countries, China requires research facilities to obtain licenses and establish internal ethical review boards.[238]

In the conduct of experiments, researchers must minimize pain and suffering.[239] Anesthesia is required during surgery, vivisection, and organ removal.[240] If an experiment involves restraining an animal, the Guiding Opinions require researchers to do so in a way that minimizes suffering and stress.[241] To avoid prolonged suffering, experiments must contain a "humane endpoint," which is the point at which an animal's suffering becomes sufficiently severe to necessitate a premature termination of the procedure.[242] Once an animal is no longer needed, she must be humanely euthanized, advisedly out of the sight of other animals.[243]

The Guiding Opinions provide special protections to primates, whose use is limited to only those experiments where it is necessary. Remarkably, after their use in experiments, primates must be kept and raised independently until their natural death. They may not be killed unless they are "suffering due to incurable sickness."[244]

In addition to the general prohibitions on unnecessary suffering, the Guiding Opinions enumerate acts defined as "torture":

1. To incite, irritate, batter, or electrocute animals, or feed animals with irritating food, poisons, or toxics, unrelated to research;
2. To willfully injure lab animals' organs, unrelated to research;
3. To cause the research animal facilities or environment to deteriorate; negligently and cause lab animals severe suffering, pain, or death;
4. During vivisection, surgery, or organ removal, to fail to provide anesthesia or other pain relief to animals according to the relevant regulations;
5. To cause death to lab animals without use of euthanasia;
6. During transport of animals, to act in contravention of the regulations of this Opinion and cause lab animals severe suffering or a large number of deaths;
7. Any other contravention of basic principles of ethical treatment of lab animals or any regulation in this opinion.[245]

In addition to regulating the practice of animal research, the Guiding Opinions cover the breeding and transportation of lab animals. Breeders must abide by basic husbandry requirements concerning cleanliness, cage size, handling methods, and nutrition. Breeding facilities must provide primates, dogs, and pigs with toys and a place where they can exercise.[246] Transporters must follow "principles of safety, comfort, and hygiene." Specifically, they must properly cage animals in a manner that lets them breathe freely, and, if the trip is "relatively long," transporters must provide animals with food and water.[247]

As mentioned elsewhere in this book, China recently began considering a broad new animal protection law, which would include animal research provisions.[248] Although early versions of the proposal included provisions that could have improved animal protection in Chinese labs, the most recent draft of the proposal has been heavily watered down, and offers little more protection than what is already included in the Guiding Opinions.[249]

To its credit, the proposed law would more clearly implement the Three R's. Specifically, the law would require researchers to choose "the experimental method which uses the smallest number of animals and which causes animals minimal pain, suffering, distress, or lasting harm, but which may still provide a valid result."[250] The proposed law states that researchers should, "as far as possible," avoid causing animals "unnecessary suffering" and should use anesthesia for surgery that will cause animals "intense pain."[251] It would require experimenters to use alternatives to animals whenever possible.[252] As a means of reducing the number of animals used in experiments, the law would promote national and international data-sharing.[253] In other words, open and transparent access to the results of others' tests may help avoid redundant and duplicative tests, thus sparing animal lives.

In addition to these national laws, some local governments have established their own animal research regulations. For example, Beijing, China's second largest municipality, established a set of animal research regulations several years before the Ministry of Science and Technology issued its Guiding Opinions.[254] The provinces of Yunnan and Heilongjiang also have regulations for the use of animals in laboratories.[255]

These national and provincial laws reflect the similarities between the philosophies underlying Western and Chinese uses of research animals: both ideologies reflect a willingness to cause pain and death to animals so long as their suffering is minimized, consistent with the demands of the research protocol. In fact, in China, "many institutions set up monuments to memorialize the lab animals that have given their lives to science."[256]

The growth of animal use in Chinese laboratories is likely to continue to grow. Officials from the animal research community have stated, "[w]e anticipate that lab animal research, education, and testing in China will ... continue to benefit from low costs, liberal regulations, and the absence of threats from animal rights activists, and that China will serve as a 'new provider' of animal-based science and technology for international clients."[257]

India: Prevention of Cruelty to Animals Act

In 1960, India passed the Prevention of Cruelty to Animals Act (PCAA) to replace the British colonial government's 1890 act of the same name.[258] The PCAA was amended in 1982 and remains in effect today, covering a wide variety of animal uses and abuses.

Chapter Four of the PCAA applies to animal experiments. India used almost one million animals in research in 2005.[259] Like other countries, the PCAA notably exempts animal experiments from its general prohibitions. Some control and oversight exists though, because the PCAA empowers India's Central Government to create a committee to regulate animal research.[260] It is the Committee's duty to "take all such measures as may be necessary to ensure that animals are not subject to unnecessary pain or suffering before, during or after the performance of experiments on them."[261]

As mentioned above, the question of what level of pain and suffering is "necessary" is a crucial issue in virtually every country's laws governing animal research. The question of necessity, though rarely litigated or defined in statutes, is generally gauged by a relatively insulated and subjective test. The final decision with regard to whether the suffering of the animals involved is "necessary" is often made by the researchers involved or the internal committees that review the researchers' work (committees that are usually comprised of the researcher's peers). As a general matter, if the research is aimed at some salutary benefit recognized by the scientific community, the methods will rarely be rejected, and any pain and suffering that is a consequence of the research will be considered necessary and justified, unless blatantly gratuitous.

The PCAA instructs the Committee to promulgate rules that ensure that researchers exhibit "due care and humanity," provide animals with anesthesia and pain relief "as far as possible" during operations, euthanize terminally injured animals, avoid animal experiments where possible, avoid research on "larger animals" where possible, provide animals with suitable care before and after experiments, and keep adequate records.[262] The PCAA empowers the Committee and its officers to conduct inspections of research facilities and prohibit future experiments if researchers have violated the Committee's rules.[263]

The Committee enacted such rules in 1968 and again in 1998.[264] The rules require all breeders and animal research establishments to register with the Committee.[265] Researchers must also obtain permission before experimenting on animals; the permission process is a hybrid of the British system, in which the government grants licenses, and the American system, in which an internal committee (the Institutional Animal Care and Use Committee) approves of projects.[266] Under the Indian rule, researchers may obtain permission from either the Committee (a governmental entity) or an internal review committee known as an Institutional Animals Ethics Committee (IAEC). An IAEC must include a biologist from outside of the facility, someone representing or nominated by the Committee, and "a non-scientific socially aware member."[267] In composition, then, an Indian IAEC is similar to an American IACUC, except that it includes a government representative.

The Indian rules establish guidelines for the conduct of experiments consistent with the requirements of the PCAA. In addition to requiring due care, proper husbandry, and anesthesia, the rules require researchers to terminate an experiment and painlessly kill any animal who "is suffering abnormal or severe pain at any stage of a continuing experiment."[268] The rules ban the debarking of dogs kept for experiments and prohibit the repetition of any "experiment the result of which is already conclusively known ... without previous justification."[269]

Despite these laws and regulations, undercover investigations have revealed significant animal suffering in Indian laboratories, including "[a]nimals living in filthy, unhygienic conditions; [e]xperiments being performed in similar unhygienic conditions; [s]ick and injured animals left unattended, and animals denied post-operative care ... includ[ing] animals which had been blinded [or] severely mutilated, or with open wounds; ... [r]ats and mice infected with disease, and infested with mites and tapeworms; [h]orses with their hooves infested with maggots; ... [and] [i]nadequate and often wholly unsuitable facilities."[270] This experience demonstrates a recurrent theme in societal treatment of animals: the laws are only as valuable as the enforcement authority makes them. Because animal experimentation is done behind closed doors, and because violations of the laws can only be discovered after expensive and long-term undercover operations, it is easy for individuals to carry on in daily breach of the protections set up for their nonhuman subjects.

Australia

In 2005, at least 5.3 million animals were used for research purposes in Australia.[271] As in other countries, it is probably difficult to determine the actual number of animals used. The legal requirements imposed on Australian animal research are directed by each state and territory, as opposed to the national government. Each jurisdiction adopts specific laws regarding research, but each of the eight Australian states and territories has also incorporated the same "Code of Practice for the Care and Use of Animals for Scientific Purposes" (Scientific Code) into its law.[272] Since this Code was adopted by the national government, there is to some degree a uniform written standards, although each state may have one or more slight variations written into its particular welfare or anticruelty laws.[273] While ostensibly following the three R's and providing an animal welfare component, commentators have noted that the Scientific Code seems to weigh heavily on "Refinement" of experimentation protocols, significantly less on "Reduction" of the number of animals being used, and almost not at all on "Replacement" of animal models.[274]

The Scientific Code has been revised seven times since its first promulgation in 1969; the current version at the time of this text's publication was the 2004 edition.[275] The Scientific Code covers all aspects of animal experiments and teaching using animals, including specific recommendations for researchers and the "animal ethics committees" that oversee institutional research, acquisition of animal subjects, and wildlife research.[276] Animal ethics committees (AEC) "apply a set of principles, outlined in the Scientific Code, that govern the ethical conduct of people whose work involves the use of animals for scientific purposes. The role of the AEC is to ensure that the use of animals is justified, provides for the welfare of those animals and incorporates the principles of the Three Rs."[277] Like the similar bodies discussed in connection with other countries laws regarding animal experimentation, though, it must be noted that these are committees established and run by the institutions actually doing the research on animals. While there may be input from the public and access to information regarding the process of the AECs, the majority of the decisionmaking is done behind closed doors by people invested in maintaining animal experimentation as an ongoing concern.

National Regulations for the Use of Animals in Testing Medicines, Cosmetics, and Household Products

Each year, millions of animals are subjected to a variety of tests to determine the properties, toxicity, and effectiveness of medicines, drugs, pharmaceutical products, cosmetics, pesticides, food additives, and many other products. This form of use is distinct from biomedical research on animals in which they are used as experimental models for researchers seeking to answer some question (usually related to a disease process or pathology) or assist in the development of a hypothesis. The tests discussed here are performed to determine the dangers or the efficacy of a variety of substances available on the open market. Animals are typically given increased doses of these substances in order to determine the quantities at which they might be dangerous to humans. Animals subjected to this type of testing may experience poisoning and related symptoms, vomiting, diarrhea, convulsions, seizures, insanity, multiple systems failure, intense, prolonged and inescapable pain, and, ultimately, death.

Many of the aforementioned domestic laws on animal research apply equally to animal testing. For example, the United States' Animal Welfare Act applies to any facility that uses covered species in "[q]uality-control studies—such as studies on the safety, effectiveness, durability, or other quality tests of commercial products."[278] Article 41 of the Japanese Act on Welfare and Management of Animals applies equally to testing as to research.[279] The Indian Prevention of Cruelty to Animals Act covers "testing activity" and explicitly forbids the application of chemicals to the eyes of animals if "calculated to only give pain."[280] The UK's Animals (Scientific Procedures) Act includes as one of the legitimate purposes for which a project license may be granted "the prevention (whether by the testing of any product or otherwise) or the diagnosis or treatment of disease, ill-health or abnormality, or their effects, in man, animals or plants."[281] Each year, the Home Office licenses approximately 400,000 toxicology procedures conducted to meet national or international requirements. This constitutes fifteen percent of the licenses granted under the A(SP)A.[282]

The British Home Office does not grant licenses for cosmetics testing. In 1997, it announced that the three companies that held licenses for testing finished cosmetics products on animals had voluntarily agreed to relinquish their licenses. Home Office Minister Lord Williams declared that the Home Office no longer intended to issue licenses for such testing, effectively accomplishing "a complete ban on the use of animals in cosmetic product testing."[283] One year later, the de facto ban was extended when the Home Office announced that it would no longer grant licenses for the testing of cosmetic *ingredients* (and not just finished products) on animals.[284] Today, the ban is codified in regulations issued by the Secretary of State to comply with the European Union's cosmetics testing ban, discussed below.[285] Austria, Belgium, The Netherlands, Germany, and Israel have also passed domestic laws banning cosmetics testing on animals.[286]

In the United States, California, New Jersey, and New York have enacted state laws limiting product testing on animals. Section 1834.9 of the California Civil Code, passed in 2000, prohibits the use of animal tests where there exists a non-animal alternative method that has been validated[287] by the Inter-Agency Coordinating Committee for the Validation of Alternative Methods (ICCVAM) and approved by the applicable federal agency.[288] The law exempts from its coverage tests that are required by federal and state law, and it does not apply to medical research.[289] Unlike the federal AWA, which does not cover birds, rats, and mice, the California law defines "animal" to include all non-human vertebrates.[290] In 2007, New Jersey followed California, adopting a virtually identical law.[291] In 2008, New York became the third state to require the use of validated non-animal alternatives for product testing.[292]

National Laws Concerning the Use of Animals in Education

From science fair projects to school biology classes to medical school, animals have long been used in biological sciences education.[293] Educational uses of animals raise several unique ethical issues.

First, unlike research or testing, the use of animals in education is not directly aimed at the alleviation of human suffering or the promotion of human health.[294] Experiments conducted in classrooms, such as the dissection of frogs, do not advance the general body of human knowledge (although they may advance the knowledge of individual students). Accordingly, these uses are more subject to charges of being unnecessary.

Second, the most common educational use of animals—dissection—differs from other forms of animal experimentation in that it involves the use of animals who are already dead. While the common concerns about animal husbandry and welfare apply at the facilities that breed animals for dissection, and while the requisite killing of animals for dissection raises ethical problems,[295] dissection avoids many of the concerns about pain and suffering that predominate in debates about the practice of animal research and animal testing.[296]

Third, the fact that educational uses of animals involve children raises important questions. Many animal advocates have argued that even if the dissection of dead animals causes them no pain, it conveys an implicit message that normalizes the use of animals in science and objectifies them in a way that dulls the sensibilities of young students and encourages them to accept the use of live animals should they choose a career in the life sciences.[297] It also implies that animals are instrumentalities to be used and disregarded, as opposed to cared for and protected.

This unique confluence of considerations has led several countries to regulate the ways in which students interact with animals in the classroom.

A few countries and local governments have prohibited the use of animals in education and training before the university level. Argentina, the Slovak Republic, Israel, Holland, Poland, and Switzerland have banned dissection at the elementary and secondary levels.[298] In 1991, the Indian state of Gujarat banned the dissection of frogs in secondary schools, observing that "the dissection of frogs by students is not considered right internationally."[299] In 1998, the Indian state of Rajasthan also banned dissection.[300]

No jurisdiction in the United States has banned dissection, but several states have prohibited or limited experiments on live animals at the elementary and secondary level, including California, Florida, Massachusetts, Maine, New York, New Hampshire, Illinois, and Pennsylvania.[301] Similarly, England, France, Germany, Holland, Poland, and Catalonia have banned experiments on live animals before the collegiate level.[302] India's Prevention of Cruelty to Animals Act states that animal experiments should be avoided "in medical schools, hospitals, colleges and the like, if other teaching devices such as books, models, films and the like may equally suffice" and "that, as far as possible, experiments [should not be] performed merely for the purpose of acquiring manual skill."[303]

Many governments, while not prohibiting the use of animals in education, give students the option of refraining from dissection or live animal experiments if they so choose. In 1993, Italy's parliament created a student choice policy that permits students to conscientiously object to participating in dissection.[304] In India, dissection and other animal experiments are optional for students.[305] In the United States, ten state legislatures have given students the statutory right to refuse to participate in classroom dissection.[306] Four other states (Maine,

Maryland, Massachusetts, and New Mexico) have given the same right to students via written policies from their departments of education.[307] Many colleges and universities have created their own internal student choice policies.[308]

Regional Regulation of Animal Experimentation

Thus far we have focused on national and domestic approaches to animal experiments, but one of the most significant regulatory regimes is regional: that of the European Union (EU). The countries that make up the European Union collectively use approximately 12 million animals in experiments each year; as a collective, then, the EU ranked second globally in animal use in 2005, behind only the United States and ahead of Japan and, depending on the statistics consulted, China.[309] In addition to existing domestic legislation, the EU has adopted regional approaches to the use of animals in research and cosmetics testing.[310] Globally, Europe is the only region to have adopted treaties and regional legislation concerning animal research.

The EU's most significant animal experimentation laws are (1) the European Convention for the Protection of Vertebrate Animals Used for Experimental and Other Scientific Purposes, a treaty among members of the Council of Europe; (2) the European Union's Directive 86/609/EEC, which lays out general policies concerning animal research; and (3) the EU's Directive 76/768/EEC, which establishes significant limitations on cosmetics testing on animals. These are discussed in turn below.

The European Convention for the Protection of Vertebrate Animals Used for Experimental and Other Scientific Purposes

The European Convention for the Protection of Vertebrate Animals Used for Experimental and Other Scientific Purposes is a treaty in force among signatory members of the Council of Europe.[311] The Convention was opened for ratification in March 1986 and remains in effect today, having been ratified by nineteen countries and the EU itself.[312]

Philosophically, the Convention reflects the signatories' belief that humans have "a moral obligation to respect all animals and to have due consideration for their capacity for suffering and memory."[313] Despite this moral obligation, the signatories "[a]ccept[] nevertheless that man in his quest for knowledge, health, and safety has a need to use animals where there is a reasonable expectation that the result will be to extend knowledge or be to the overall benefit of man or animal, just as he uses them for food, clothing and as beasts of burden."[314]

The Convention covers vertebrate animals used in "any experimental or scientific procedure ... that ... may cause pain, suffering, distress or lasting harm."[315] These animals must receive "at least a minimum degree of freedom of movement," as well as "food, water, and care appropriate to [their] health and well being."[316] During experimental procedures, however, these provisions may be waived if they are "incompatible" with the procedures' objectives.[317] The Convention requires researchers to limit "[a]ny restriction on the extent to which an animal can satisfy its physiological and ethological needs," but only "as far as practicable."[318] It also includes a detailed and lengthy appendix that sets out the recommended particulars for housing and care of research animals.[319]

The Convention implicitly adopts the Three R's approach discussed earlier. The replacement principle is embodied in Article 6, which requires researchers to use a "scientifically satisfactory" non-animal method, if such an alternative "is reasonably and practicably available."[320] The reduction principle is contained in Article 7, which dictates that researchers should choose procedures that use the least number of animals and that are "most likely to provide satisfactory results."[321] Article 7 also reflects the refinement principle by instructing researchers to choose the procedures that "cause the least pain, suffering, distress or lasting harm," again subject to the qualification that such procedures should also be those "most likely to provide satisfactory results."[322] The Convention also mandates the use of pain relief during procedures, except where providing such relief would impair the animals' welfare in excess of the pain induced by the procedure itself, or where such relief "is incompatible with the aim of the procedure."[323]

Directive 2010/63/EU

As a treaty, the Convention just discussed binds only those countries that agree to be bound by its terms by signing and ratifying the document. By contrast, Directives of the European Union bind all EU members, regardless of their consent.[324] Because of the importance to the European community of unifying animal research laws in Europe, the EU decided a binding directive on the issue was necessary.

In November 1986, the Council of European Communities adopted Directive 86/609/EEC (which borrowed heavily from the Convention).[325] The stated goal of Directive 86/609 was to harmonize regional regulations of animal experimentation so that disparate laws would not "affect[] the establishment and functioning of the common market."[326] In other words, the fact that different countries had varying requirements for the conduct of animal research undermined the ability of transnational and regional markets to function at their most efficient level. The Council also wished to reduce to a minimum the amount of animals used in experiments, promote adequate animal care, avoid unnecessary pain, suffering, and distress, and eliminate unnecessarily duplicative experiments.[327] Directive 86/609 governed animal research in the EU for almost twenty-five years.

In 2001, the European Commission announced it would substantially revise Directive 86/609 to update the then fifteen-year-old document.[328] A series of reports from various committees followed the announcement, each identifying areas in need of improvement.[329] The Commission also convened technical working groups, consulted with industry and public interest organizations, and solicited input from the public, which revealed widespread support for revising the Directive to increase animal welfare.[330]

In September 2010, after nearly a decade of preparation, debate, and negotiation, the European Parliament and the European Council adopted Directive 2010/63/EU on the protection of animals used for scientific purposes.[331] Directive 2010/63 affirms that "[a]nimals have an intrinsic value which must be respected" and that they "should always be treated as sentient creatures."[332] The Directive embraces the end goal of completely abolishing animal experiments "as soon as it is scientifically possible to do so," but states that such experiments "continue[] to be necessary to protect human and animal health and the environment," at least for the near future.[333] Accordingly, it adopts a regulationist approach, rooted in the Three R's discussed earlier in the chapter—replace, reduce, and refine.

The Directive structures the Three R's in "a strict hierarchy" so that in selecting experimental methods, researchers must first consider whether an alternative exists that could replace an animal experiment; if no such alternative is available, only then does the researcher consider reductions in the number of animals used and ways to refine the experiment to minimize animal suffering.[334] This is significant because a general implementation of the Three R's without prioritizing the search for alternatives may lead to a focus on refinement at the expense of replacement and reduction, which would contravene the Directive's stated goal of eventually eliminating animal experiments rather than simply refining them to be more humane.

To further promote the replacement of animal research methods, the Directive aims to avoid duplicative and redundant procedures by requiring member states to accept data and recognize the validity of experimental results from other member states.[335] It also requires each member state to promote research, development, and validation of alternatives to animal research at the national level.[336] Perhaps most significantly, the Directive establishes the Union Reference Laboratory, which it tasks with coordinating and promoting the validation, development, and implementation of non-animal alternative research methods.[337] This provision is significant because it is the first Europe-wide mechanism for eventually eliminating the use of animals in experiments by mandating the regular and ongoing development of alternatives. The Directive also requires the Commission to periodically and thematically review the Directive to address developments of non-animal test methods in order to continuously advance the goal of fully replacing animals.[338]

To reduce the numbers of animals in research and to refine research methods to decrease animal suffering, the Directive requires researchers to choose the experimental method that uses the fewest number of animals and causes the least amount of pain and distress, while still providing the highest likelihood of "satisfactory results."[339] In choosing which animals to use, the researchers should choose those "with the lowest capacity to experience pain, suffering, distress, or lasting harm."[340] During procedures, researchers must use general or local anesthesia unless doing so either will cause more trauma than the experiment itself or "is incompatible with the purpose of the procedure."[341] Where the experiment will cause "serious injuries" that will force the animal to endure "severe pain," anesthesia is required.[342] The Directive requires the use of particular methods of euthanasia that minimize pain and suffering, though these requirements can be waived "on the basis of scientific justification."[343]

To further address animal pain, the Directive introduced a "severity classification," also known as a "pain scale" or "animal-harm scale," which requires researchers to classify the severity of animal suffering involved in a given experiment after considering a variety of factors, including the duration, intensity, and frequency of the animal pain and distress, the ethological deprivations to which the animal is subjected, and whether anesthesia or analgesics are provided.[344] The severity categories consist of the following: "non-recovery," "mild," "moderate," and "severe."[345] The Directive prohibits procedures that subject an animal to "severe pain, suffering or distress that is likely to be long-lasting and cannot be ameliorated."[346] In passing the Directive, the EU recognized that "[f]rom an ethical standpoint, there should be an upper limit of pain, suffering and distress, above which animals should not be subjected in scientific procedures."[347] Nevertheless, the Directive permits the infliction of such severe, prolonged, and unameliorated suffering "for exceptional and scientifically justifiable reasons."[348] Such exceptions must be authorized by a committee established by the Directive.[349]

In addition to regulating the procedures used, the Directive also establishes standards for the care of animals in establishments where research is being performed. Animals must receive "accommodation, [and] an environment, food, water and care which are appropriate to their health and well-being."[350]

Detailed guidelines for husbandry are provided in Annex III to the Directive, which outlines requirements for physical facilities, cage size, lighting, noise, veterinary care, habitat enrichment, feeding, watering, and handling.[351] Significantly, however, such requirements may be waived for "scientific, animal-welfare, or animal-health reasons."[352]

Establishments that breed, supply, or use animals in scientific procedures must be authorized by and registered with the "competent authority"[353] in the nation in which they operate and are subject to requirements for personnel, record-keeping, animal welfare oversight by an internal body, and animal care.[354] Competent authorities must regularly inspect these facilities based on "a risk analysis" that considers the number and species of animals used, the number and types of projects conducted, the facility's history of violations of the Directive, and "any information that might indicate non-compliance."[355] At least some of these inspections must be unannounced.[356] The Directive requires that only one-third of facilities that use animals be inspected each year, although facilities that use non-human primates must be inspected annually.[357]

Under the Directive, competent authorities authorize not only facilities, but also scientific procedures before they are carried out.[358] Among the criteria weighed by the competent authority during project evaluation are ethical considerations such as whether "the project is justified from a scientific or educational point of view or required by law," whether "the purposes of the project justify the use of animals," and whether the procedures used are "carried out in the most humane and environmentally sensitive manner possible."[359] Before authorizing a procedure, the competent authority, in consultation with various experts, must engage in a harm-benefit analysis, considering the purposes and benefits of the research, the project's compliance with the Three R's, the severity of animal suffering, and "whether the harm to the animals in terms of suffering, pain and distress is justified by the expected outcome taking into account ethical considerations, and may ultimately benefit human beings, animals or the environment."[360] This method of project evaluation contrasts markedly with the American system, which requires neither prior approval of projects by an independent authority nor a balancing of the interests of animals against those of humans.[361]

Another significant component of the Directive is the differential treatment it gives to various kinds of animals. Much broader than the American Animal Welfare Act, which excludes mice, rats, birds, cold-blooded animals, and invertebrates from its scope, the Directive covers all "live non-human vertebrate animals, including [] independently feeding larval forms [] and foetal forms of mammals ... from the last third of their normal development," as well as cephalopods, a class of invertebrates that includes octopuses and squid.[362] The

Directive provides special protections to endangered species, wild-caught animals, stray and feral animals (especially dogs and cats), and non-human primates (especially great apes). Endangered species may not be used in procedures unless for a limited purpose that cannot be achieved by using a non-endangered species.[363] Similarly, animals taken from the wild may not be used unless the purpose of the experiment cannot be achieved with animals who were purposely bred in captivity for research, and stray and feral animals may not be used unless the procedure's purpose can only be met by using such animals and "there is an essential need for studies concerning the health and welfare of the animals or serious threats to the environment or to human or animal health."[364]

The level of protection afforded to the 10,000 nonhuman primates used in European laboratories was one of the most controversial issues in the drafting of the new Directive. Many members of the public and of the animal welfare community argued for extra protections for these animals based on their belief that primates possess a higher level of cognition and a more acute set of feelings than other research subjects. In fact, in 2007, the European Parliament declared that stopping scientific experiments on wild-caught apes and primates is "an urgent priority," and that the European community should establish timetables for the replacement of all primates in research, including those bred in captivity.[365] According to the declaration, "almost all primate species share more than 90% of their DNA with humans and ... it is acknowledged that primate species have a capacity to suffer greatly in captivity."[366]

The theory behind affording extra protection to primates is that these species, especially the great apes, feel responses to painful research activities in ways that are more similar to humans and less like those of other species. This theory may of course be a total fallacy that highlights the scientific inability to discern how other species experience negative stimuli. The distinction between the experience of a rat and that of a chimpanzee may be quite minimal, but many humans may be more likely to protect those species that look or act more like them.[367] Thus, because of humans' membership in the great ape family, and the fact that studies have documented an overlap in basic genetic material among the great apes, that group has received special attention. Based on this, many animal advocates urged the Commission to follow up on the European Parliament's declaration by proposing a ban on all research on nonhuman primates.[368]

The Directive does not go that far, however. It holds that research on nonhuman primates is "still necessary," even though it "raises specific ethical and practical problems in terms of meeting their behavioural, environmental and social needs in a laboratory environment."[369] The Directive limits research on non-human primates to basic research, procedures aimed at preserving the subject species, and experiments "undertaken with a view to the avoidance, prevention, diagnosis or treatment of debilitating or potentially life-threatening clinical conditions in human beings."[370] There must also be no other species of animal that would suffice for the project's purpose.[371] The Directive defines "debilitating clinical condition" to mean "a reduction in a person's normal physical or psychological ability to function."[372] Given the breadth of this definition and the ability to still conduct "basic research," many animal advocates have expressed disappointment at the Directive's failure to meaningfully limit research on non-human primates.[373]

The Directive gives great apes its highest protection, because they are "the closest species to human beings with the most advanced social and behavioural skills."[374] Great apes can be used in research only in cases where the experiment is "essential" to preserve the species or "relat[es] to an unexpected outbreak of a life-threatening or debilitating clinical condition in human beings" and no other species or method will achieve the experimental purpose.[375] As with experiments that cause severe, prolonged, and unameliorated pain, any plan for research on great apes must be authorized by the committee established under the Directive.[376]

The Directive, although already adopted by the EU, must still be transposed into domestic law in each of the member countries. Such implementing legislation must be adopted by November 2012 and come into force by January 1, 2013.

Directive 76/768/EEC

In 1976, the EU passed a comprehensive law governing cosmetics to ensure public safety and remove disparities in regulations that imposed direct and indirect restrictions on trade.[377] At the time the law was passed, it did not address animal testing. But in 1993, the Council amended the Cosmetics Directive to set a timeline for the elimination of cosmetics testing on animals. The 1993 Amendment prohibited the marketing of "ingredients or combinations of ingredients tested on animals after" January 1, 1998, giving the cosmetics industry and the scientific community five years to develop and validate non-animal alternatives "offering an equivalent level of protection for the consumer."[378] The Council recognized, however, that the discovery of adequate alternatives might not happen that quickly, so it reserved the right to postpone the deadline. It did in fact extend the deadline twice. The first time, the date was changed to June 2000, then a second postponement pushed the date back to June 2002.[379] In 2000, the Commission offered another amendment to the

Cosmetics Directive, proposing to weaken the law by replacing the *marketing* ban with a *testing* ban, which would have allowed cosmetics companies to test their products and ingredients outside of the EU, then sell them inside the EU.[380] After a series of exchanges in the legislative process, the marketing ban was returned to the amendment, which was ultimately passed in 2003.[381]

The 2003 Amendment reflects the Council's belief that "it is essential that the aim of abolishing animal experiments for testing cosmetic products be pursued."[382] To that end, it promotes the replacement of animal tests where there exists a valid method that does not involve the use of animals and that had been established for the particular type of testing. The new Article 4a in the Cosmetics Directive prohibits the marketing of cosmetics that have been tested on animals. The scope of the prohibition covers products that have been tested in their final formulation, as well as those that contain ingredients that have been tested on animals, if a validated non-animal alternative testing method exists.[383] This means that no cosmetic product can be sold in Europe if it or any of its constituent ingredients were tested on animals anywhere else in the world, at least after such time as a non-animal alternative method has been validated.[384] Article 4a also prohibits testing finished cosmetics or their component ingredients on animals within the European Union.[385] The prohibition on testing finished cosmetics took effect in September 2004, while the remaining prohibitions (on testing ingredients and marketing both finished products and ingredients) took effect in March 2009.[386]

As with any rule, there are exceptions. At the time of the Directive's adoption, there were no validated alternative testing methods for repeated-dose toxicity tests, which examine the cumulative and acute effects of multiple exposures to the same chemicals. Similarly, no validated alternatives existed for testing of the reproductive toxicity of most chemicals and products. Finally, the field of toxicokinetics, the study of what happens to substances as they move through the body, still lacked validated alternatives. Thus, these three categories of animal tests remain permissible until at least 2013.[387] The Directive also permits the Commission to grant other exceptions from the prohibitions for ingredients that are "in wide use and cannot be replaced by another ingredient able to perform a similar function."[388]

France, Europe's largest manufacturer of cosmetics, opposed the 2003 Amendments to the Cosmetics Directive and, after they passed, challenged their legality in the European Court of Justice (ECJ) by instituting an annulment proceeding.[389] France contended that Article 4a violated general principles of the European Union, in that it failed to provide legal certainty about the purposes for which testing could remain permissible, interfered with the professional freedoms of cosmetics manufacturers and animal researchers, were disproportionate in that they protected few animals at the purported expense of humans, violated the precautionary principle by exposing cosmetics consumers to unacceptable risks, and discriminated against those cosmetics manufacturers that did not also conduct tests on pharmaceuticals, as those who did could potentially continue to test dual-use ingredients on animals.[390] The ECJ ultimately did not reach these challenges, holding instead that Article 4a was not severable from the rest of the Cosmetics Directive. Under EU law, the ECJ cannot annul or sever a provision if doing so would change the substance of the underlying legislation. In this case, the "annulment of the contested provision ... would objectively alter the very substance of the provisions adopted by the Community legislature in regard to testing on animals for the purpose of developing cosmetic products, as those provisions, moreover, constitute one of the principal axes of that directive."[391] The ECJ therefore dismissed the challenge.

Notably, the Directive applies only to cosmetic products. Household products of all kinds, as well as pesticides, pharmaceuticals, and industrial chemicals—and their constituent ingredients—may still be tested on animals in the EU. In fact, due to a European Community regulation known as REACH (Registration, Evaluation, Authorisation and Restriction of Chemical Substances), and despite the Directive, animal toxicity testing is actually on the rise in Europe. REACH, which came into force in June 2007, requires companies to document the composition and ensure the safety of a variety of chemicals.[392] Scientists and animal protection groups have expressed concern that as many as 54 million animals could be killed in safety tests associated with REACH.[393] But the European Chemicals Agency, the registry and oversight body for REACH, recently announced that it would not require preliminary tests for chemicals already set for more comprehensive testing, an announcement that animal protection organizations estimated would save 4.5 million animals.[394] The British agency in charge of implementing REACH in the UK has also issued a guidance document advising companies on how to minimize animal testing while complying with REACH.[395]

International Regulations of Animal Research

There are currently no binding international laws governing research on nonhuman animals. There is, however, a fairly developed body of international law governing research on humans that could, at least in theory, serve as a model for limiting scientific experiments on some animals.

Humans have a right not to be used in scientific experiments without their informed consent. This international human right derives from both treaties and customary international law and has its genesis in the post-war reaction to the horrific experiments conducted by Nazis on human subjects. The Nuremberg Tribunal found that the Nazis had subjected prisoners to a battery of ghastly experiments, such as placing them in tanks of freezing water for hours at a time, infecting them with diseases such as malaria and typhoid, and poisoning them with chemical weapons.[396] The Tribunal's written opinion in the prosecution of the Nazi doctors included a set of standards for future human experimentation, including an insistence that "[t]he voluntary consent of the human subject is absolutely essential."[397] These standards have come to be known as the Nuremberg Code, which forms the basis for the international prohibition of nonconsensual human experimentation.[398] Although the Nuremberg Code has been extremely influential in debates about how to govern human experimentation, it is not itself binding international law. Several non-governmental bodies have attempted to more fully develop and refine (and in some cases weaken) the principle of informed consent in several documents, including the World Medical Association's Declaration of Helsinki and the guidelines of the Council for International Organizations of Medical Sciences Guidelines (CIOMS). These documents, like the Nuremberg Code, lack the binding force of law.[399]

The prohibition against nonconsensual human experimentation finds its legal footing in several treaties, as well as in customary international law.[400] Article 7 of the International Covenant on Civil and Political Rights (ICCPR) guarantees that "no one shall be subjected without his [or her] free consent to medical or scientific experimentation."[401] The Council of Europe's Convention on Human Rights and Biomedicine (CHRB) provides that "[a]n intervention in the health field may only be carried out after the person concerned has given free and informed consent to it."[402] These treaties require their signatories to implement the requirement of informed consent for all human experimentation. Even non-signatories may be bound by the requirement: in January 2009, the United States Court of Appeals for the Second Circuit held that the prohibition against experiments on unconsenting humans had risen to the level of "a norm of customary international law to which States universally subscribe."[403]

One could make the case for extending these international legal rights to at least some animals. Tom Regan has argued that nonconsensual experiments on animals violate their moral rights, and others have argued that "the study of great apes should follow ethical principles generally similar to those currently used on human subjects who cannot give informed consent."[404] Animals could be assigned human guardians *ad litem*, who would defend the animals' interests and, where appropriate, grant consent on their behalf, as is done now with young children or others who are incapable of giving informed consent.[405]

This is all just suggestion, and we remain a long way away from binding international protections for animals in research. Nevertheless, several organizations have established broad, nonbinding guidelines seeking to standardize and regulate animal research internationally. These groups include the Council for International Organizations of Medical Sciences, the World Organization for Animal Health, and the International Organization for Standardization.[406]

Council for International Organizations of Medical Sciences

In 1985, the Council for International Organizations of Medical Sciences (CIOMS), a non-governmental organization that represents the biomedical research community, released a document entitled *International Guiding Principles for Biomedical Research Involving Animals* (IGP), which sought to "provide useful criteria to which academic, governmental and industrial bodies may refer in framing their own codes of practice or legislation regarding the use of laboratory animals for scientific purposes."[407] CIOMS's motivation to draft international guidelines was to launch a preemptive strike at animal protection groups that sought to stop the use of animals in research. The CIOMS document expressed concern that "in several countries political action was being taken to stop or severely limit animal experimentation," research that CIOMS views as "fundamental to the biomedical sciences" and "indispensible."[408] CIOMS hoped that the IGP would "provide a conceptual and ethical framework, acceptable both to the international biomedical community and to moderate animal welfare groups" that would form the basis for national and international regulations of animal research.[409]

The IGP outlines a set of "basic principles," the first of which reiterates CIOMS's belief that biological and medical progress "require recourse to experimentation on intact live animals of a wide variety of species."[410] The IGP also covers the use of alternatives when appropriate, consideration of the purposes of experiments, proper selection of subject species, minimization of the number of animals used, treatment of animals as sentient beings deserving of proper care, acknowledgement of animal pain, use of anesthesia or analgesia unless waived by a review body, euthanasia, provision of good living conditions and veterinary care, and training and qualification of personnel.[411] The IGP also includes "special provisions" addressing acquisition, transportation, housing, environmental conditions, nutrition, veterinary care, and record-keeping.[412] All the IGP provisions are very broad and vague, using general and undefined terms that are open to wide interpretation, such as "humane," "hygienic," "appropriate," "adequate," and "proper." CIOMS does encourage those adopting the IGP to establish quantifiable norms for their implementation where possible.[413] The IGP also promotes independent monitoring of animal use, although it accepts "voluntary self-regulation" as one option of doing so.[414] Finally, the IGP gives a minimal endorsement to non-animal alternatives, though it sees them as "complementary to the use of intact animals."[415]

World Organization for Animal Health

Another organization that has begun to establish international standards for the treatment of animal test subjects is the World Organization for Animal Health (OIE), an inter-governmental organization concerned with the control of epizootic illnesses—the outbreak of diseases in the animal kingdom, such as foot and mouth disease, avian influenza, and swine fever.[416] The OIE, which consists of 174 member countries and territories, works closely with the United Nations to control these problems but, since 2001, its mission has also included the promotion of animal welfare.[417]

The OIE publishes the *Terrestrial Animal Health Code*, which serves as "an international benchmark for OIE Members" and establishes standards that help govern trade regulations under the World Trade Organization.[418] Section 7 of the Code addresses animal welfare, but it is almost exclusively concerned with animals raised for human consumption, providing standards for the transportation and slaughter of such animals.[419] Only the "guiding principles" portion of Section 7 references laboratory animals: it endorses the Three R's, but lacks the specificity necessary to turn this vague commitment into meaningful limits on the use of animals in experiments.[420]

However, the OIE's Animal Welfare Working Group is taking steps to remedy the lack of any significant animal welfare recommendations for research animals in OIE standards. It has created an ad hoc Group on Laboratory Animal Welfare, which drafted a report on how the OIE might involve itself in the field of international animal research standards.[421] The ad hoc group began by engaging stakeholders in the planning and evaluation process.[422] Among these stakeholders are organizations such as the International Council of Laboratory Animal Science (ICLAS) and the International Association of Colleges of Laboratory Animal Medicine (IACLAM), groups that promote the use of animals in research.[423] The group has consulted with animal welfare groups as well, including the World Society for the Protection of Animals (WSPA).[424]

As of early 2010, the OIE Animal Welfare Working Group had prepared, then revised, a set of draft standards for the scientific use of animals in research, testing, and education.[425] As this book went to press, however, the standards had not yet been approved by the OIE members or added to the *Terrestrial Animal Health Code.*

The draft standards include the basic components of most animal research laws: program oversight, training and credentials for researchers and technicians, veterinary care, animal sourcing, standards for physical facilities and environmental conditions, and animal husbandry.

Under the draft standards, program oversight may be provided by review committees at either the governmental or institutional level. These review committees should include at least one scientist, one veterinarian, and one representative of "general community interests." Oversight should include review of project proposals before their initiation, annual inspection of facilities, and regular review of animal care and use programs.[426] The draft veterinary care standards include monitoring zoonotic diseases in experimental animals and advising researchers on surgical methods, the use of pain relief, and the establishment of humane endpoints for experiments.[427] The sourcing standards promote the use of animals specifically bred for research, and encourage "humane" techniques for capturing wild animals. Furthermore, "[t]he use of wild caught nonhuman primates is generally discouraged."[428] The draft standards for physical conditions at research facilities include general recommendations on ventilation, temperature and humidity, lighting, and noise.[429] The husbandry standards offer advice on housing animals in suitable cages and pens; the provision of adequate food, water, bedding, and psychological enrichment; the maintenance of hygienic conditions; the transportation of lab animals; the acclimatization of new animals; and the identification and marking of animals for adequate recordkeeping.[430] As with most animal welfare regulations, the OIE standards may be set aside when the limitations they impose interfere with the aims of the research.[431]

The Working Group members hope these standards, though non-binding, could "become a useful tool ... for less developed countries where there is little support for introducing welfare standards."[432] The draft preamble "recommends that Members address all the essential elements identified in these standards in formulating a regulatory framework that is appropriate to their local conditions."[433]

International Organization for Standardization

The International Organization for Standardization (ISO) has also addressed the issue of laboratory animals. ISO is a non-governmental organization consisting of members of the national standards institutes of 162 countries, as well as those from the private sector or industry associations.[434] The ISO has no legal power but it issues standards that "define and set authoritative, publicly available, common, objective, agreed and mutually recognised standards for which there is an international need for a common technical specification."[435] These standards are non-binding and voluntary, but some national legislation may incorporate the standards by reference, thus giving them regulatory force in those countries.[436]

In 1992, ISO issued the 10993 series of standards, which dealt with the biocompatibility of medical devices.[437] This series included the ISO's first set of standards pertaining to the welfare of animals used in experiments. While these animal welfare standards technically apply only to biocompatibility tests, they serve as "a normative reference within the much wider range of ISO standards making reference to the use of animals for scientific purposes."[438] The generality and vagueness of the initial standards, however, have meant that they have had "little impact."[439] In 2006, ISO revised the standards to try to remedy this failure. Substantively, the standards incorporate the Three R's, as well as general guidelines that should be familiar by now to readers: "the minimization of pain, suffering, distress or lasting harm, high standards of accommodation and care, [and] competence of personnel."[440]

Perhaps what is most interesting about the ISO animal welfare standards is the discourse that surrounds them. The welfare standards are motivated not primarily by ethical concerns about animal suffering, but by ISO's interest in "ensuring and safeguarding scientific validity."[441] The standards are also cast as the work of "technical experts" who have "set aside their personal and national interests."[442] The working group that drafted the standards is purported to have "appl[ied] its talents purely to the technical considerations free of ideological or political considerations."[443] In doing so, it is said to have "properly balance[d] the legitimate needs of science and industry ... against the protection of animals from unnecessary use and suffering."[444] This assumes that the "legitimate need" for animal experimentation is not itself an "ideological or political" judgment but rather a "technical" one. Most vivisection critics strongly disagree with that assumption and argue that the threshold premise supporting animal research is a fallacious one. Questions of the legitimacy of controversial practices generally involve difficult questions of morality. Perhaps the issue of animal protection is not a technical question of expertise, but a fundamentally ideological question of ethics and politics. For now, however, the debate and the changes in law focus mainly on welfare within the laboratories, and not on the question of whether the laboratories should function at all.

Transnational Networks of Animal Research

In this final section, we address a few specific controversies that demonstrate the inter- and transnational aspects of animal research.

Perhaps the clearest example of the globalization of animal experimentation is the immense international trade in laboratory animals, primates in particular. The primate trade in Southeast Asia has increased significantly in recent years, raising concerns among animal advocates. Countries throughout the region have burgeoning captive-breeding industries that supply long-tailed macaques (also known as crab-eating macaques) to laboratories in the United States, Europe, Japan, and China. Many of these operations capture macaques from the wild, then intensively confine them in factory-like conditions in order to breed them and sell their offspring to laboratories.[445] The rise in trading of captive-bred macaques also provides cover for the trade of wild-captured animals, who are often reported as captive-bred to avoid stricter regulations. The Cambodian primate trade in particular is threatening the viability of long-tailed macaques in the wild, as wild monkeys are taken from their homes, often through methods that destroy their natural habitats.[446] From 2004 to 2007, Cambodia exported approximately 40,000 long-tailed macaques to China.[447] Cambodia's Southeast Asian neighbors, Laos, Vietnam, Indonesia, and the Philippines also send tens of thousands of macaques each year to China, Europe, and the United States for use in experiments. The facilities in which these animals are bred and held before exportation provide them with only the most basic level of animal welfare.[448] One facility in Vietnam has the capacity to hold 30,000 monkeys, and another in Laos houses 10,000.[449]

The United States is one of the world's largest importers of monkeys. In 2009, the U.S. imported more than 22,000 monkeys, almost all of them long-tailed macaques.[450] China was the export leader by far, sending more than 13,000 primates to the United States. The African island nation of Mauritius was second, exporting about 3,200 primates; Vietnam was third, with about 3,100 primates. Of the 22,000 primates imported into the United States, almost 1,000 were wild-caught and about 5,300 were "captive-born," meaning their parents were wild-caught. The vast majority of these animals were imported by two American corporations: Covance Research Projects and Charles River Laboratories, which together imported almost 16,000 primates.[451]

In addition to importing animals from other countries, biotechnology companies are outsourcing controversial animal research to regions with fewer animal protection laws and/or less influential animal protection movements. China has quickly become the country that corporations look to when outsourcing animal tests. In the words of one pharmaceutical CEO, "big pharma is looking to move to China in a big way."[452] Like other industries, the animal research industry looks to decrease costs wherever possible, and research is simply cheaper to conduct in China, where animals (especially primates and beagles) and labor are much less expensive. China and its municipalities have also offered perks such as tax breaks to encourage biotechnology companies to relocate. And, as discussed above, until very recently China lacked regulations to address the welfare of lab animals. Because the existing Chinese research regulations are significantly weaker than those in the United States and the EU, many companies see China as a less restrictive place to conduct research. Additionally, due to because of state repression, the fledgling animal protection movement in China lacks the confrontational and protest-oriented aspects of its American and European counterparts. In short, biotechnology companies see China as a place "where scientists are cheap and plentiful and animal-rights activists are muffled by an authoritarian state."[453]

The animal research industry has looked to other areas as well. In 2009, Puerto Rico found itself at the center of a heated international debate over the construction of a primate breeding facility in Guayama, a city on the island's southern coast. Bioculture, a primate breeding and supply company based in Mauritius, sought permission to build the facility to supply researchers in the United States with long-tailed macaques. When news of the proposed facility was leaked, the issue garnered international attention from a broad coalition of animal protection groups, celebrities and scientists. The Puerto Rican Senate Environmental Committee issued a report condemning Bioculture for failing to fully examine the environmental effects of the project. Local residents sued to stop the construction of the facility, alleging that it lacked the necessary environmental permits.[454] The trial court ruled in favor of the residents, holding that the project was not "agricultural" and therefore inconsistent with zoning laws.[455] On appeal, however, a higher court blocked the trial court's order without explanation, allowing the construction to move forward while the appeal was pending.[456] The opposition continued, however, and the construction was eventually halted. First, Guyama's ruling body unanimously enacted an ordinance banning any import, export, breeding, or use of monkeys in experiments within its borders. This stopped Bioculture's efforts there. This was followed by a resolution by the Puerto Rican Senate that "[e]xpress[ed] the most forceful objection" to Bioculture's plans.[457]

Similar outcries arose over reports of a French company's plans to construct a primate testing facility in Johor, Malaysia and an Indian company's plans to construct a testing facility for dogs, primates, and rats in Malacca, Malaysia.[458] When activists in the United Kingdom learned about the French project from Malaysian animal welfare groups, they protested at the Malaysian High Commissioner's office in London, and a coalition of organizations urged the Malaysian government to reject the French proposal.[459] Similarly, in the case of the Indian project, animal advocates staged protests in front of the Indian High Commissioner's Malaysian office, and a coalition of animal protection organizations urged the Malaysian government to rescind approval of the facility.[460] The fate of these testing facilities was still uncertain when this book went to press.[461] Advocates have also reported cases of animal cruelty at a British-run testing facility in Penang, Malaysia.[462]

The projects in Puerto Rico and Malaysia are just a few examples of a growing trend to build animal research and breeding facilities in regions with limited animal protection laws. In choosing these locations, the research industry hopes to avoid both the growing legal regulations and the vocal animal advocates that purportedly impede animal research in Europe and the United States. The head of the Malaysian Society for the Prevention of Cruelty to Animals, for example, accused the French firm of "relocating misery" to a country with no laws governing animal research.[463] Other groups echoed this sentiment, expressing the "concern[] that European research companies, in an effort to avoid growing public criticism of animal experimentation, may be looking to set up primate testing facilities in countries where regulations are more lax."[464] And although Puerto Rico, as a U.S. territory, is bound by the American Animal Welfare Act, Bioculture was likely expecting to encounter little local resistance because of the perceived absence of an animal protection movement in Puerto Rico, but the local resistance to the Guayama project refutes that perception. The transnational dialogues between the local animal protection groups in Malaysia and Puerto Rico and the larger organizations in Europe and the United States prove that as the animal research industry has globalized, so too has the animal protection movement.

Notes

1. Andreas-Holger Maehle & Ulrich Trohler, *Animal Experimentation from Antiquity to the End of the Eighteenth Century: Attitudes and Arguments*, in VIVISECTION IN HISTORICAL PERSPECTIVE 14, 15 (Nicolaas A. Rupke ed., 1990). Animal experiments occurred in antiquity, especially through the influence of the physician Galen in the second century, and they increased significantly during the Renaissance, but they did not become institutionalized and widespread until the nineteenth century. *Id.* at 3–4; C. Ray Greek & Jean Swingle Greek, SACRED COWS AND GOLDEN GEESE: THE HUMAN COST OF EXPERIMENTS ON ANIMALS 23 (2000) (referring to Galen as "the father of vivisection").

2. Katy Taylor *et al.*, *Estimates for Worldwide Laboratory Animal Use in 2005*, 36 ALTERNATIVES TO LABORATORY ANIMALS 327 (2008) (115 million); Paula Gerber, *Scientific Experimentation on Animals: Are Australia and New Zealand Implementing the 3Rs?*, in ANIMAL LAW IN AUSTRALASIA 212, 217 (Peter Sankoff & Steven White eds., 2009) (hereinafter "ANIMAL LAW IN AUSTRALASIA") (75 to 100 million); F. Barbara Orlans, *Ethical Themes of National Regulations Governing Animal Experiments: An International Perspective*, in APPLIED ETHICS IN ANIMAL RESEARCH: PHILOSOPHY, REGULATION, AND LABORATORY APPLICATIONS 131, 135 (John P. Gluck, Tony DiPasquale, & F. Barbara Orlans eds., 2002) (50 to 100 million).

It has been estimated conservatively that 58.3 million animals were used in animal experiments in 2005 in the 179 countries that have a human population greater than 200,000. Taylor *et al.*, *supra* note 2, at 336. This estimate increased to 115.3 million if one includes "animals killed only for tissue supply (21.1%); animals used to maintain genetically-modified strains (17.2%); and animals bred for laboratory use but considered as surplus ... (59.3%)." *Id.* The 58.3 million figure relies on the European Union's definitions of the terms "animal" and "use." *Id.* at 337.

According to this analysis, the top ten users of animals in 2005, rounded to the nearest tenth of a million, were as follows:

1. United States (17.3 million)
2. Japan (11.2 million)
3. China (3.0 million)
4. Australia (2.4 million)
5. France (2.3 million)
6. Canada (2.3 million)
7. Great Britain (1.9 million)
8. Germany (1.8 million)
9. Taiwan (1.2 million)
10. Brazil (1.2 million)

Id. But, as discussed below, this analysis may drastically underestimate the number of animals used in experiments in China.

3. *See, e.g.*, F. Barbara Orlans, In the Name of Science: Issues in Responsible Animal Experimentation 39 (1993) at 39 ("There are three major reasons for animal experiments: (1) research to obtain original knowledge, (2) testing of products for safety or efficacy, and (3) pedagogic purposes as in veterinary or biology education."). *See also* Tom Regan, The Case for Animal Rights 363 (1983) ("(1) biological and medical education; (2) toxicology testing, where the potential harmful effects for human beings of new products and drugs are first tested on animals; and (3) original and applied research, including not only research into the causes and treatment of various diseases but also into the basic biochemical nature and behavior of living organisms"). In this chapter, we use the term "experimentation" to refer to all of these uses collectively.

One could also add to these lists *production* and *breeding*, that is, the creation of biological material, such as plasma, tissues, organs, and infectious agents used to produce antibodies, and the intentional propagation of animals to create or maintain genetically modified lines. Some production methods cause high levels of suffering. For example, rabbits may be given open wounds to produce monoclonal antibodies, and the United Kingdom has banned the ascites method of antibody production in mice because of the high level of suffering. The UK used an estimated 30–50,000 mice per year before the ban. E-mail from Tim Phillips, Vice President, Animal Defenders International, to Matthew Liebman (Apr. 27, 2010) (on file with author).

As explained, we use the term "experimentation" to refer to all of these uses collectively, but because the majority of domestic laws covering experimentation focus on the use of animals in research, testing, and education, we focus on those uses.

4. Orlans, *supra* note 3, at 39.

5. *Id.* at 39–40.

6. *Id.* at 40. *See also id.* at 191–208.

7. *Id.* at 202.

8. *Id.* at 193.

9. Demographic information on San Marino is available at United States Department of State, *Background Note: San Marino*, *available at* http://www.state.gov/r/pa/ei/bgn/5387.htm.

10. *La Repubblica di San Marino ha ditto no alla vivisezione!*, APAS Informa (Associazione Sammarinese Protezioni Animali, San Marino), Oct. 2007.

11. *Antivivisezione a San Marino*, APAS Informa (Associazione Sammarinese Protezioni Animali, San Marino), April 2007.

12. *San Marino Bans Vivisection,* Of Human and Nonhuman Animals Blog (Oct. 12, 2007), *available at* http://globalphilosophy.blogspot.com/2007/10/san-marino-bans-vivisection.html; APAS Informa, *supra* note 10.

13. Vivisezione: Aprovate in Commissione Consiliare la Proposta di Legge per Viertarla a San Marino, Informa (Associazione Sammarinese Protezioni Animali, San Marino), Aug. 2007.

14. Disposizioni Sul Divieto di Sperimentazione Animale Nella Repubblica di San Marino [Dispositions on the Prohibition of Animal Experimentation in the Republic of San Marino], Legge No. 108 (2007) (San Marino), *available at* http://faolex.fao.org/docs/pdf/smr74542.pdf.

15. *Id.* preamble.

16. *Id.*

17. *Id.*

18. *Id.* art. 1(1).

19. *Id.* art. 2(1).

20. *Id.* art. 1(2).

21. *Id.* art. 2(2).

22. *Id.* art. 1(3).

23. *Id.* preamble.

24. Liechtensteiner Tierschutzgesetz [Animal Welfare Act], Jan. 22, 1936, LGBL. 1936 No. 4, art. 3 (Liech.) (cited in Mary T. Phillips & Jeri A. Sechzer, Animal Research and Ethical Conflict : An Analysis of the Scientific Literature, 1966–1986 13, 114 (1989)).

25. Some have incorrectly assumed that Liechtenstein's absolute ban remains in effect. *See, e.g.*, Orlans, *supra* note 2, at 133 (stating, in 2002, that "[o]nly one country officially bans all animal experiments—the small European principality of Liechtenstein"); James Randerson, *Vivisection: Study Finds 115 Million Animals Used in Tests Worldwide*, Guardian, Aug. 13, 2008, *available at* http://www.guardian.co.uk/science/2008/aug/13/controversies inscience.ethicsofscience (stating, in 2008, that "Liechtenstein and San Marino are the only countries to have banned research involving animals altogether").

26. Liechtensteiner Tierschutzgesetz [Animal Welfare Act], Jan. 25, 1989, LGBL. 1989 No. 3, art. 12, ¶ 1 (Liech.).

27. E-mail from Dr. Peter Malin, Office of Food Quality Control and Veterinary Science (ALKVW), Regional Administration of Liechtenstein, to Vince Field (Aug. 7, 2009) (on file with author).

28. E-mail from Dr. Peter Malin, Office of Food Quality Control and Veterinary Science, (ALKVW), Regional Administration of Liechtenstein, to Vince Field (Aug. 10, 2009) (on file with author).

29. Kathleen M. Conlee, *Chimpanzees in Research and Testing Worldwide: Overview, Oversight and Applicable Laws*, 14 Alternatives to Animal Testing & Experimentation

(Papers & Proc.) 111, 111 (2008), *available at* http://www.asas.or.jp/jsaae/zasshi/WC6_PC/paper111.pdf.

30. It is important to distinguish between the type of research described here and less physically invasive, "cognitive" behavioral research. The latter type of research is performed in many countries that otherwise ban invasive biomedical research.

31. Conlee, *supra* note 29, at 112, 115.

32. Jack Straw, *quoted in International Bans*, New England Anti-Vivisection Society's Project R&R: Release & Restitution for Chimpanzees in U.S. Laboratories, *available at* http://www.releasechimps.org/mission/end-chimpanzee-research/country-bans.

33. *Id.*

34. Rowan Taylor, *A Step at a Time: New Zealand's Progress Toward Hominid Rights*, 7 Animal L. 35, 37 (2001). *See also* Animal Law in Australasia, *supra* note 2, at 221–23; Paula Brosnahan, *New Zealand's Animal Welfare Act: What Is Its Value Regarding Non-human Hominids?*, 6 Animal L. 185 (2000).

35. Animal Welfare Act 1999, §85(1) (NZ).

36. *Id.* §85(5)(a)–(b).

37. Peter Sankoff, *Five Years of the "New" Animal Welfare Regime: Lessons Learned from New Zealand's Decision to Modernize Its Animal Welfare Legislation*, 11 Animal L. 7, 8–9 (2005).

38. Gerber, *supra* note 2, at 223. Several countries subsequently did so, including The Netherlands, Sweden, Japan and Austria. Animal Law in Australasia, *supra* note 2, at 223, n. 55.

39. Conlee, *supra* note 29, at 115; New England Anti-Vivisection Society's Project R&R: Release & Restitution for Chimpanzees in U.S. Laboratories, *International Bans*, *available at* http://www.releasechimps.org/mission/end-chimpanzee-research/country-bans.

40. H.R. 5852, 110th Cong. (2008).

41. *Id.* §3(a)–(b).

42. *Id.* §§3(b)–(d), 4(a), 5(c), 5(e).

43. *Id.* §5(b).

44. *Id.* §5(a). Gibbons are not considered great apes by most scientists.

45. H.R. 1326, 111th Cong. (2009). The new bill slightly modifies H.R. 5852, but the material provisions remain substantially the same.

46. *See* Darian M. Ibrahim, *Reduce, Refine, Replace: The Failure of the Three R's and the Future of Animal Experimentation*, 2006 U. Chi. Legal F. 195, 201–04 (2006) (identifying purported endorsement of the Three R's by animal protection organizations, animal research organizations, and corporations that use and breed animals for research).

47. *Id.* at 197–201.

48. W.M.S. Russell & R.L. Birch, The Principles of Humane Experimental Technique (1959).

49. Our focus in this section is primarily on European countries and the United States because they are where the majority of animal experimentation takes place, and are consequently the countries with the most developed set of laws regulating research. *See* Orlans, *supra* note 2, at 133 ("Currently, no legislation on humane use of laboratory [animals] exists in South American, African, or many Asian countries."). Japan, China, and India, discussed below, are noteworthy exceptions. Nevertheless, the International Network for Humane Education (InterNICHE) has organized groundbreaking conferences on non-animal research and testing methods in Africa and the Middle East. The First Pan-African Seminar on Alternatives to Animal Experiments took place in September 2009 in Nairobi,

Kenya, and the First Middle East Seminar on Alternatives to Animal Experiments took place in February 2010 in Cairo, Egypt.

50. Orlans, *supra* note 3, at 4–5. *See generally* Vivisection in Historical Perspective, *supra* note 1.

51. Orlans, *supra* note 3, at 18.

52. Cruelty to Animals Act, 1876, 39 & 40 Vict., c. 77 (U.K.).

53. Orlans, *supra* note 3, at 19.

54. Diane L. Beers, For the Prevention of Cruelty: The History and Legacy of Animal Rights Activism in the United States 23 (2006).

55. Cruelty to Animals Act, 1876, § 2.

56. *Id.* § 3(3)–(4).

57. *Id.* § 3(2).

58. *Id.* § 3(3).

59. *Id.* § 5.

60. *Id.*

61. *Id.* § 3(1).

62. *Id.* §§ 3(2), 7, 8.

63. *Id.* § 10.

64. Animals (Scientific Procedures) Act, 1986, c. 14 (U.K.). For a detailed discussion of the politics surrounding the passage of the A(SP)A, *see* Robert Garner, Political Animals: Animal Protection Politics in Britain and the United States 176–201 (1998).

65. Animals (Scientific Procedures) Act, 1986, § 2(1).

66. Taylor *et al.*, *supra* note 2, at 333 tbl.1 (estimating that Great Britain used 1.9 million animals in research in 2005); *but see* Home Office, Statistics of Scientific Procedures on Living Animals 19 tbl.1a (2009), *available at* http://www.homeoffice.gov.uk/rds/pdfs09/spanimals08.pdf (listing number of animals used in 2008 as 3.6 million). Part of the large gap between the Taylor 2005 statistics and the Home Office 2008 statistics is attributable to definitional differences: the Taylor study used the European Union's definitions of "animal" and "experiment," which are narrower than the British definitions. Nevertheless, the statistics do demonstrate that the number of animals in use in Great Britain is rising sharply. *See* Ian Sample, *Drug Safety Testing Drives Steep Rise in Animal Experiments in UK*, Guardian, July 21, 2009, *available at* http://www.guardian.co.uk/science/ 2009/jul/21/science-animal-medical-experiments (discussing fourteen percent rise in the number of licensed procedures from 2007 to 2008); *id.* at 6 (stating that animal research has steadily increased since 2000).

67. Animals (Scientific Procedures) Act, 1986, § 1(1). The Act empowers the Home Secretary to extend protection to any other invertebrate animals. *Id.* § 1(3)(a).

68. *Id.* § 3.

69. *Id.* § 4(4A).

70. *Id.* § 10(2).

71. *Id.* § 5(3)–(4). Acceptable purposes are limited to the following:

> (a) the prevention (whether by the testing of any product or otherwise) or the diagnosis or treatment of disease, ill-health or abnormality, or their effects, in man, animals or plants;
>
> (b) the assessment, detection, regulation or modification of physiological conditions in man, animals or plants;
>
> (c) the protection of the natural environment in the interests of the health or welfare of man or animals;

(d) the advancement of knowledge in biological or behavioural sciences;
(e) education or training otherwise than in primary or secondary schools;
(f) forensic enquiries;
(g) the breeding of animals for experimental or other scientific use.

Id. §5(3).

72. *Id.* §10(3)(a).

73. *Id.* §10(3)(c)–(d).

74. *Id.* §10(3B)–(3D).

75. *Id.* §5(5).

76. *Id.*

77. A full copy of the National Anti-Vivisection Society's report, ACCESS DENIED (1996), is *available at Institute of Neurology: NAVS undercover investigation 1995*, NATIONAL ANTI-VIVISECTION SOCIETY, *available at* http://www.navs.org.uk/about_vivisection/27/42/337/.

78. *Id.* §5(6).

79. *Id.* §6(1).

80. *Id.* §6(5). The Act establishes similar requirements for facilities that breed animals for use in research. *Id.* §7.

81. *Id.* §10(5)–(6A).

82. *Id.* §10(6B)(a)–(b).

83. *Id.* §18(2).

84. *Id.* §18(3).

85. *Id.* §19(2)–(4).

86. *Id.* §19(3)(b).

87. *Id.*

88. *The Work of the Committee*, ANIMAL PROCEDURES COMMITTEE, *available at* http://www.apc.gov.uk/aboutapc/ourwork.htm.

89. *See, e.g.*, Animal Procedures Committee, Report of the Suffering and Severity Working Group on the Strengths and Weaknesses of the Current System of Severity Limits as a Way of Prospectively Assessing Suffering and Severity (2009), *available at* http://www.apc.gov.uk/reference/Suffering%20and%20Severity%20paper.pdf.

90. Animals (Scientific Procedures) Act, 1986, §20(2).

91. *Id.* §21.

92. ANIMAL DEFENDERS INTERNATIONAL, ANIMAL EXPERIMENTS AT INVERESK 18 (2005), *available at* http://www.navs.org.uk/downloads/invereskreport.pdf.

93. BEERS, *supra* note 54, at 122–23.

94. CHRISTINE STEVENS, *Laboratory Animal Welfare*, in ANIMALS AND THEIR LEGAL RIGHTS 66, 66 (Animal Welfare Inst. ed., 4th ed. 1990).

95. BEERS, *supra* note 54, at 123, 137, 141.

96. *Id.* at 144.

97. *Id.* at 138–39, 143–44. Many pound seizure laws, however, did pass. *See id.* at 170; Stevens, *supra* note 94, at 67. Some of these laws were later repealed, while others remain in effect. *Id.* at 70.

98. BEERS, *supra* note 54, at 144.

99. For a thorough discussion of the Pepper saga and its aftermath, see Daniel Engber's excellent five-part series at Slate: Daniel Engber, *Where's Pepper?*, SLATE (June 1, 2009), *available at* http://www.slate.com/id/2219224/; Daniel Engber, *Man Cuts Dog*, SLATE (June 2, 2009), *available at* http://www.slate.com/id/2219225/; Daniel Engber, *Pepper Goes to Washington*, SLATE

(June 3, 2009), *available at* http://www.slate.com/id/2219226; Daniel Engber, *Brown Dogs and Red Herrings*, SLATE (June 4, 2009), *available at* http://www.slate.com/ id/2219227; Daniel Engber, *Me and My Monkey*, SLATE (June 5, 2009), *available at* http://www.slate.com/id/2219228/.

100. *Id.*; *see also* Beers, *supra* note 54, at 175.

101. Bernard Unti, "*Concentration Camps for Lost and Stolen Pets*": *Stan Wayman's LIFE Photo Essay and the Animal Welfare Act*, *available at* http://www.hsus.org/about_us/accomplishments/history/concentration_camp_for_pets.html.

102. BEERS, *supra* note 54, at 177.

103. UNTI, *supra* note 101.

104. Pub. L. No. 89-544, 80 Stat. 350 (1966).

105. *Id.* §§3, 4.

106. *Id.* §5.

107. *Id.* §§6, 7.

108. *Id.* §§10, 11.

109. *Id.* §13.

110. *Id.* §2(h).

111. *Id.* §13.

112. *Id.* §18 (emphasis added).

113. For a discussion of these amendments, *see* Henry Cohen, *The Animal Welfare Act*, 2 J. ANIMAL L. 13, 15–22 (2006); Benjamin Adams & Jean Larson, Animal Welfare Info. Ctr., U.S. Dep't of Agric., AWIC Resource Series No. 41, Legislative History of the Animal Welfare Act, *available at* http://www.nal.usda.gov/awic/pubs/AWA2007/intro.shtml (2007).

114. 7 U.S.C. §2156.

115. *See, e.g.*, Taylor *et al.*, *supra* note 2, at 333 tbl.1 (estimating 17.3 million animals used in the U.S. in 2005); *cf.* Orlans, *supra* note 2, at 136 tbl.1 (estimating 12.1 million animals used in the U.S. in 1998).

116. 7 U.S.C. §2143(a)(1)–(2). The regulations are at 9 C.F.R. ch. 1.

117. 9 C.F.R. §§3.1–3.142. These standards are specifically made applicable to research facilities by 9 C.F.R. §2.38(k). Research facilities, however, may make exceptions to these standards "when such exceptions are specified and justified in the proposal to conduct the activity and are approved by the [Institutional Animal Care and Use Committee]." *Id.*; *see also* 7 U.S.C. §2143(a)(3)(E). IACUCs are discussed in more detail below.

118. 9 C.F.R. §3.6(a)(1).

119. 9 C.F.R. §3.29(a).

120. 9 C.F.R. §3.84(b)(2).

121. Animals (Scientific Procedures) Act, 1986, §5(6).

122. 7 U.S.C. §2143(a)(2)(B).

123. *See, e.g.*, Valerie Stanley, *The Animal Welfare Act and USDA: Time for an Overhaul*, 16 PACE ENVTL. L. REV. 103 (1998); Collette L. Adkins Giese, *Twenty Years Wasted: Inadequate USDA Regulations Fail to Protect Primate Well-Being*, 1 J. ANIMAL L. & ETHICS 221 (2006).

124. 9 C.F.R. §§3.8(b), 3.6(c)(1)(i).

125. *Id.* §3.8(a).

126. *Id.* §3.8(c)(1). IACUCs are discussed below.

127. *Id.* §3.8(c)(2).

128. *Id.*

129. *Id.* §3.8(d)(2).

130. *Id.* §3.81.

131. *Id.* §3.81(a).
132. *Id.* §3.81(b).
133. *Id.* §3.81(e)(2).
134. *Animal Legal Def. Fund v. U.S. Sec'y of Agric.*, 813 F. Supp. 882 (D.D.C. 1993), *vacated by Animal Legal Defense Fund v. Espy*, 29 F.3d 720 (D.C. Cir. 1994). ALDF had already sued USDA over the agency's years-long delay in promulgating the regulations. *Animal Legal Def. Fund v. Yeutter*, No. 88-3640 (D.D.C. 1988).
135. *Animal Legal Def. Fund v. U.S. Sec'y of Agric., supra* note 134, 813 F. Supp. at 887.
136. *Id.* at 887–88.
137. *Id.* at 887.
138. *Id.* at 888.
139. *Id.* at 888, 889.
140. *Id.* at 888.
141. *Id.* at 889.
142. *Id.* at 893.
143. *Animal Legal Def. Fund v. Espy, supra* note 134, 29 F.3d at 723.
144. *See Lujan v. Defenders of Wildlife*, 504 U.S. 555, 560–61 (1992).
145. *Animal Legal Def. Fund v. Espy, supra* note 134, 29 F.3d at 723.
146. *Id.*
147. *Animal Legal Def. Fund v. Glickman*, 943 F. Supp. 44 (D.D.C. 1996).
148. *Animal Legal Def. Fund v. Glickman*, 130 F.3d 464 (D.C. Cir. 1997).
149. *Animal Legal Def. Fund v. Nat'l Assoc. for Biomedical Research*, 136 F.3d 829 (D.C. Cir. 1998).
150. *Animal Legal Def. Fund v. Glickman*, 154 F.3d 426 (D.C. Cir. 1998) (en banc).
151. *Animal Legal Def. Fund v. Nat'l Assoc. for Biomedical Research*, 204 F.3d 229 (D.C. Cir. 2000).
152. 7 U.S.C. §2132(g); *see* WAGMAN, WAISMAN & FRASCH, ANIMAL LAW: CASES AND MATERIALS 506–07 (4th ed. 2010) (stating that twenty to twenty-five million birds, rats, and mice are used in research, which is ninety percent of total research animals); Cohen, *supra* note 113, at 13 (stating that the AWA excludes ninety to ninety-five percent of animals used in research).
153. Pub. L. No. 91-579, §3(3), 84 Stat. 1560 (1970).
154. Cohen, *supra* note 113, at 19 n.66; 36 Fed. Reg. 24,919 (Dec. 24, 1971).
155. *Animal Legal Def. Fund v. Madigan*, 781 F. Supp. 797 (D.D.C. 1992).
156. *Id.* at 802.
157. *Id.*
158. *Animal Legal Def. Fund v. Espy*, 23 F.3d 496, 498 (D.C. Cir. 1994).
159. *Alternatives Research & Dev. Found. v. Glickman*, 101 F. Supp. 2d 7 (D.D.C. 2000).
160. *Id.* at 9.
161. Cohen, *supra* note 113, at 20.
162. *Id.* at 20–21.
163. Pub. L. No. 107-171, §10301, 116 Stat. 491 (2002). This is the AWA's current definition of "animal":

> The term "animal" means any live or dead dog, cat, monkey (nonhuman primate mammal), guinea pig, hamster, rabbit, or such other warm-blooded animal, as the Secretary may determine is being used, or is intended for use, for research, testing, experimentation, or exhibition purposes, or as a pet; but such term excludes

> (1) birds, rats of the genus Rattus, and mice of the genus Mus, bred for use in research, (2) horses not used for research purposes, and (3) other farm animals, such as, but not limited to livestock or poultry, used or intended for use as food or fiber, or livestock or poultry used or intended for use for improving animal nutrition, breeding, management, or production efficiency, or for improving the quality of food or fiber. With respect to a dog, the term means all dogs including those used for hunting, security, or breeding purposes.

7 U.S.C. §2132(g).

164. 7 U.S.C. §2143(a)(6)(A)(i) (emphasis added).

165. *Id.* §2143(a)(6)(A)(ii) (emphasis added).

166. *Id.* §2143(a)(6)(A)(iii).

167. Pub. L. No. 99-198, 99 Stat. 1645–1650 (1985); 7 U.S.C. §2143(a)(3)(A).

168. 9 C.F.R. §2.31(d)(1)(iv)(A).

169. 7 U.S.C. §2143(a)(3)(B).

170. *Id.* §2143(a)(3)(C)(i).

171. *Id.* §2143(a)(3)(D).

172. *Id.* §2143(a)(3)(E).

173. Orlans, *supra* note 2, at 144 ("In general, existing laws do not address the fundamental ethical question, 'Should this particular animal experiment be done at all?' The usual presumption of the law is that animal experimentation is justified and that proposed projects should be approved so long as the individual investigator believes that useful scientific knowledge might be gained.").

174. 9 C.F.R. §2.31(d)(1)(iv)(A).

175. Office of Laboratory Animal Welfare, Institutional Animal Care and Use Committee Guidebook 12 (2nd ed. 2002), *available at* http://grants.nih.gov/grants/olaw/GuideBook.pdf .

176. 7 U.S.C. §2143(b).

177. 9 C.F.R. §2.31(d)(1).

178. 7 U.S.C. §2143(b)(3)–(5).

179. *See, e.g.,* Katharine M. Swanson, Note, *Carte Blanche for Cruelty: The Non-Enforcement of the Animal Welfare Act*, 35 U. Mich. J.L. Reform 937, 958–62 (2002).

180. 7 U.S.C. §2143(b)(1)(B)(iii).

181. Office of Inspector General, Audit Report: APHIS Animal Care Program Inspection and Enforcement Activities iii, 19–23 (2005), *available at* http://www.usda.gov/oig/webdocs/33002-03-SF.pdf [hereinafter OIG Report].

182. *Id.* at 19.

183. 7 U.S.C. §2146(a).

184. APHIS's mission is "to protect the health and value of U.S. agricultural, natural and other resources." Animal and Plant Health Inspection Service, U.S. Dep't of Agric., Strategic Plan (2007–2012) 1 (2007).

185. *See generally* Animal and Plant Health Inspection Service, U.S. Dep't of Agric., Animal Care Annual Report of Activities: Fiscal Year 2007 (2007), *available at* http://www.aphis.usda.gov/publications/animal_welfare/content/printable_version/2007_AC_Report.pdf [hereinafter AC Report 2007]. APHIS also has a Veterinary Services program, but that program does not undertake any duties with respect to the AWA.

186. *Id.* at 8.

187. 7 U.S.C. §2146(a).

188. AC Report 2007, *supra* note 185, at 14.
189. *Id.*; 7 U.S.C. §§2149, 2159.
190. *See, e.g.*, Swanson, *supra* note 179, at 955–57.
191. OIG Report, *supra* note 181, at 13.
192. *Id.*
193. *Id.* at 10.
194. *Id.* at ii.
195. *Id.* at 10.
196. *But see* Joshua E. Gardner, Note, *At the Intersection of Constitutional Standing, Congressional Citizen-Suits, and the Humane Treatment of Animals: Proposals to Strengthen the Animal Welfare Act*, 68 Geo. Wash. L. Rev. 330 (2000) (proposing citizen-suit amendment to AWA).
197. Pub. L. No. 99-158, 99 Stat. 875 (1985); 42 U.S.C. §289d(a).
198. *Id.* §289d(a)(2).
199. *Id.*
200. Office of Lab. Animal Welfare, Nat'l Instit. of Health, Public Health Service Policy on Humane Care and Use of Laboratory Animals 8 (2002), *available at* http://grants.nih.gov/grants/olaw/references/PHSPolicyLabAnimals.pdf. The Policy is made binding by reference in the Code of Federal Regulations. *See* 42 C.F.R. §52.8.
201. The Guide's introduction states, "The Guide is deliberately written in general terms so that its recommendations can be applied in the diverse institutions and settings that produce or use animals for research, teaching, and testing; generalizations and broad recommendations are imperative in such a document." Institute of Laboratory Animal Resources, National Research Council, Guide for the Care and Use of Laboratory Animals (1996) [hereinafter Guide for the Care and Use of Laboratory Animals], *available at* http://www.nap.edu/readingroom/books/labrats/introduction.html.

Significantly, the Guide also serves as the basis for accreditation by the Association for Assessment and Accreditation of Laboratory Animal Care (AAALAC), a private, international, non-governmental organization that accredits animal research facilities on a voluntary basis. AAALAC International has accredited facilities in thirty-two different countries. *See also About AAALAC*, AAALAC Int'l, *available at* http://www.aaalac.org/about/index.cfm (last visited Mar. 1, 2010); *see also Accredited Organizations*, AAALAC Int'l, *available at* http://www.aaalac.org/accreditedorgs/index.cfm (last visited Mar. 1, 2010).

202. *See, e.g.*, Guide for the Care and Use of Laboratory Animals, *supra* note 201, at 27 tbl.2.1 (providing space "recommendations" for mice and rats).
203. Cohen, *supra* note 113, at 14 n.9. Section 289d provides for the creation of internal animal care committees to oversee research, just as the AWA does. 42 U.S.C. §289d(b).
204. *Id.* (mentioning absence of inspection requirement); 42 U.S.C. §289d(c) (requiring "assurances"). *See also* Memorandum from Patricia A. Brown, Director, Office of Laboratory Animal Welfare, to Record (Aug. 8, 2007), *available at* http://grants.nih.gov/grants/olaw/ComplianceOversightProc.pdf ("OLAW holds accountable and depends upon institutional officials, Institutional Animal Care and Use Committees, research investigators, and other agents of the institution to assure conformance with the institution's Assurance and thus with the PHS Policy and other federal statutes and regulations relating to animals.").
205. Taylor *et al.*, *supra* note 2, at 333 tbl.1.
206. Act on Welfare and Management of Animals, Law No. 105 of 1973, *revised by* Law No.68 of 2005, *translated at* http://www.cas.go.jp/jp/seisaku/hourei/data/AWMA_2.pdf.

207. *See, e.g.*, Katsuhiko Shoji, *Japanese Concept and Government Policy on Animal Welfare and Animal Experiments*, 14 Alternatives to Animal Testing & Experimentation (Papers & Proc.) 179, 179 (2008), *available at* http://www.asas.or.jp/jsaae/zasshi/WC6_PC/ paper179.pdf.

208. Act on Welfare and Management of Animals, Law No. 105 of 1973, art. 1.

209. *Id.* art. 10–24.

210. *Id.* art. 10(1).

211. *Id.* art. 41(1).

212. *Id.* art. 41(2); *see also* Tsutomu Miki Kurosawa, *Japanese Regulation of Laboratory Animal Care with 3Rs*, 14 Alternatives to Animal Testing & Experimentation (Papers & Proc.) 317 (2008), *available at* http://www.asas.or.jp/jsaae/zasshi/WC6_PC/ paper317.pdf.

213. Act on Welfare and Management of Animals, Law No. 105 of 1973, art. 41(3).

214. *Id.* art. 41(4); Makoto Suzuki, *Education and Training System in Japanese Research Laboratories in a Global Pharmaceutical Company*, 14 Alternatives to Animal Testing & Experimentation (Papers & Proc.) 253, 254 (2008), *available at* http://www.asas.or.jp/jsaae/ zasshi/WC6_PC/paper253.pdf.

215. *Id.*

216. Kurosawa, *supra* note 212, at 318.

217. *Id.*

218. Suzuki, *supra* note 214, at 254; Science Council of Japan, Guidelines for Proper Conduct of Animal Experiments (2006), *available at* http://www.scj.go.jp/ja/info/ kohyo/pdf/kohyo-20-k16-2e.pdf; *About Us*, Science Council of Japan, http://www.scj.go.jp/ en/scj/index.html.

219. Guide for the Care and Use of Laboratory Animals, *supra* note 201; Kurosawa, *supra* note 212, at 319.

220. Science Council of Japan, *supra* note 218, at 3 ("Each institution should formulate voluntary in-house regulations for proper scientific conduct of animal experiments based on these Guidelines.").

221. *Id.* at 5.

222. Shoji, *supra* note 207, at 179. *See also id.* ("According to these guidelines, control and monitoring of animal experiment [procedures are] performed by scientists themselves.").

223. *Compare* Taylor *et al.*, *supra* note 2, at 333 tbl.1 (estimating three million) *with* Zhang Qian, *Lab Rats, Mice, Dogs, Rabbits, Monkeys—Do They Have Rights?*, Shanghai Daily, Nov. 3, 2009, *available at* http://www.shanghaidaily.org/article/print.asp?id=418252 (citing David Gao, president of the Shanghai Laboratory Animal Science Association, estimating eighteen to nineteen million); *see also* Qi Kong & Chuan Qin, *Analysis of Current Laboratory Animal Science Policies and Administration in China*, 51 Inst. for Laboratory Animal Res. E-J. E1, E1 (2010), *available at* http://dels.nas.edu/ilar_n/ilarjournal/51_1/PDFs/v51%28e1% 29Kong.pdf (estimating sixteen million).

224. E-mail from Dr. He Zhengming, Dir., Dep't of Standardization of Lab. Animals, Nat'l Inst. for the Control of Pharm. & Biological Prods., China, to Agnes Tam (Jan. 14, 2010) (on file with author).

225. Kong & Qin, *supra* note 223, at E1.

226. *Id.*

227. Shi Yan Dong Wu Guan Li Tiao Li [Regulations for the Administration of Affairs Concerning Experimental Animals] (promulgated by the State Sci. & Tech. Comm'n, Nov. 14, 1988, effective Nov. 14, 1988) (P.R.C.).

228. *Id.* art. 1.

229. *Id.* arts. 13–15.

230. *Id.* art. 29.

231. Guan Yu Shan Dai Shi Yan Dong Wu De Zhi Dao Xing Yi Jian [Guidelines on the Humane Treatment of Laboratory Animals] (promulgated by the Ministry of Sci. & Tech., Sept. 30, 2006) (P.R.C.) [hereinafter *Guidelines*].

232. *Id.* art. 1.

233. *See* Kong & Qin, *supra* note 223, at E9 (noting that the Chinese Ministry of Science and Technology "has funded projects to study and translate animal welfare laws and guidelines from the United States, Europe, Japan, and Australia").

234. *Guidelines, supra* note 231, at art. 2.

235. *Id.* art. 28(1).

236. *Id.*

237. *Id.* arts. 6, 28(2).

238. *Id.* arts. 5, 24.

239. *Id.* art. 14.

240. *Id.* art. 15.

241. *Id.* art. 16.

242. *Id.* arts. 18, 28(5).

243. *Id.* art. 17.

244. *Id.* art. 19.

245. *Id.* art. 27.

246. *Id.* ch. 2.

247. *Id.* art. 21.

248. Prevention of Cruelty to Animals Law of the PRC (Experts' Draft Proposal), *available at* http://www.aldf.org/downloads/ChinaCrueltytoAnimalsProposal3-10.pdf (translated by Paul Littlefair, Royal Society for the Prevention of Cruelty to Animals, and Chang Jiwen, Chinese Academy of Social Sciences Institute of Law, Mar. 2010) [hereinafter China Draft Proposal].

249. *Compare id.* with Animal Protection Law of the People's Republic of China (Draft), *available at* http://www.actasia.org/index/uploads/file/legislation%20forum/China%20draft%20law%20Eng%20RSPCA%20Dec09.doc (translated by Paul Littlefair, Royal Society for the Prevention of Cruelty to Animals, Dec. 2009). For instance, the original draft proposed establishing a nation-wide animal ethics committee "to supervise and manage the scientific use of laboratory animals," and each province would have been required to set up a similar committee. *Id.* art. 90. These committees would each have included at least one representative from an animal protection organization. The committee oversight was removed from the revised draft proposal, replaced with a call for "[d]etailed regulations ... stipulated by the science and technology administrative department under the State Council." China Draft Proposal arts. 30–33.

250. *Id.* art. 30.

251. *Id.* arts. 30, 32, 33.

252. *Id.* art. 30.

253. *Id.*

254. Beijing Shi Shi Yan Dong Wu Guan Li Tiao Li (2004 Xiu Ding) [Regulations of Beijing Municipality for the Administration of Affairs Concerning Laboratory Animals (2004 Revision)] (promulgated by the People's Congress of Beijing Municipality, Dec. 2, 2004, effective Jan. 1, 2005) (P.R.C.).

255. Yunnan Sheng Shi Yan Dong Wu Guan Li Tiao Li [Regulations of Yunnan Province for Administration of Laboratory Animals] (promulgated by the People's Congress of Yunnan Province, July 27, 20007, effective Oct. 1, 2007) (P.R.C.); Heilongjiang Sheng Shi Yan Dong Wu Guan Li Tiao Li [Regulations of Heilongjiang Province for Administration of Laboratory Animals] (promulgated by the People's Congress of Heilongjiang, Oct. 17, 2008, effective Jan. 1, 2009) (P.R.C.).

256. Kong & Qin, *supra* note 223.

257. *Id.*

258. Prevention of Cruelty to Animals Act, 59 of 1960 (India) (*replacing* Prevention of Cruelty to Animals Act, 11 of 1890 (British Raj); *amended by* Prevention of Cruelty to Animals (Amendment) Act, 26 of 1982 (India)). It is worth noting that India regulated animal research six years before the United States passed the Animal Welfare Act.

259. Taylor *et al.*, *supra* note 2, at 333 tbl.1.

260. Prevention of Cruelty to Animals Act, 59 of 1960, §§14, 15.

261. *Id.* §17(1).

262. *Id.* §17(2).

263. *Id.* §§18, 19.

264. The Experiments on Animals (Control and Supervision) Rules, 1968, reprinted in MANEKA GANDHI, OZAIR HUSAIN, & RAJ PANJWANI, ANIMAL LAWS OF INDIA 99 (3rd ed. 2006) [hereinafter GANDHI ET AL.]; The Breeding of and Experiments on Animals (Control and Supervision) Rules, 1998, *reprinted in id.*, at 102.

265. *Id.* §§3, 4.

266. *Id.* §8.

267. *Id.* §13.

268. *Id.* §9(f).

269. *Id.* §9(m), (k).

270. ANIMAL DEFENDERS INTERNATIONAL, ANIMAL EXPERIMENTATION IN INDIA 5 (2003), *available at* http://www.navs.org.uk/downloads/animalexperimentsinindia.pdf.

271. ANIMAL LAW IN AUSTRALASIA, *supra* note 2, at 223.

272. *Id.*; DEBORAH CAO, ANIMAL LAW IN AUSTRALIA AND NEW ZEALAND 260 [9.20] (2010).

273. *Id.* at 266 [9.80]–271 [9.160]; *see also* ANIMAL LAW IN AUSTRALASIA, *supra* note 2, at 223.

274. *Id.*

275. CAO, *supra* note 272, at 260 [9.30].

276. *See id.* at 262 [9.40]–266 [9.70].

277. *Id.* at 266 [9.70].

278. U.S. Dep't of Agric., *Licensing and Registration Under the Animal Welfare Act: Guidelines for Dealers, Exhibitors, Transporters, and Researchers*, *available at* http://www.aphis.usda.gov animal_welfare/downloads/aw/awlicreg.pdf. Many product testing facilities use only mice and rats and are therefore exempted from the AWA. Few private commercial labs get federal funding and so the PHS guidelines for mice and rats are also inapplicable.

279. Act on Welfare and Management of Animals, Law No. 105 of 1973, *revised by* Law No.68 of 2005, art. 41(1) (Japan).

280. The Breeding of and Experiments on Animals (Control and Supervision) Rules, 1998, §§2(e), 9(l) (India).

281. Animals (Scientific Procedures) Act, 1986, § 5(3)(a) (U.K.). British law contains a separate provision for the testing of "medicinal products" on animals. Medicines Act, 1968, c. 67, §§ 32–39 (U.K.).

282. ANIMALS SCIENTIFIC PROCEDURES INSPECTORATE & DIVISION, HOME OFFICE, ANNUAL REPORT 2008, at 32 (2009), *available at* http://scienceandresearch.homeoffice.gov.uk/animal-research/publications-and-reference/publications/reports-and-reviews/ASPI_Annual_Report_2008.pdf?view=Binary.

283. Press Release, Animal Procedures Committee, *Cosmetic Product Testing On Animals Ends Today*—Lord Williams (Nov. 6, 1997), *available at* http://www.apc.gov.uk/press_releases/971106.htm; *see also Cosmetic Testing on Animals to Cease*, BBC NEWS, Nov. 6, 1997, *available at* http://news.bbc.co.uk/2/hi/uk_news/24295.stm.

284. Press Release, Animal Procedures Committee, *Government Announces End to Cosmetic Testing on Animals* (Nov. 16, 1998), *available at* http://www.apc.gov.uk/press_releases/981126b.htm.

285. Cosmetic Products (Safety) Regulations, 2008, S.I. 2008/1284, art. 10 (U.K.).

286. AMERICAN ANTI-VIVISECTION SOCIETY, *Laws, Animals, & Research: Laws on Product Testing, available at* http://www.aavs.org/lawsProducts.html. The EU ban is discussed in more detail below.

287. "Validation" is a term of art in the scientific research community and is not synonymous with the general definition "valid." The process of validation involves multiple steps of examination of the type of test, along with data collection and analysis, in order to determine whether the test can be validated.

288. CAL. CIV. CODE § 1834.9(a). ICCVAM is "a federal committee comprised of representatives from 14 federal regulatory or research agencies, including the Food and Drug Administration, Environmental Protection Agency, and Consumer Products Safety Commission, that reviews the validity of alternative test methods. The committee is the federal mechanism for recommending appropriate, valid test methods to relevant federal agencies." *Id.* § 1834.9(f)(4).

289. *Id.* § 1834.9(c), (e).

290. *Id.* § 1834.9(f)(1).

291. N.J. STAT. ANN. §§ 4:22–58, 4:22–59.

292. N.Y. PUB. HEALTH LAW § 505.

293. JONATHAN BALCOMBE, THE USE OF ANIMALS IN HIGHER EDUCATION: PROBLEMS, ALTERNATIVES, & RECOMMENDATIONS 2–3 (2000).

294. It is not our contention that animal research and testing actually do alleviate suffering or promote health. We acknowledge the existence of a contentious debate on this question. *See, e.g.*, Greek & Greek, *supra* note 1. In any case, much research and testing is at least aimed at those ends, regardless of whether they actually *achieve* them.

295. *See* BALCOMBE, *supra* note 293, at 26–32 (describing suffering of animals in their procurement for dissection).

296. This discussion does not address the use of live animals who are used in education. *See id.* at 51–68.

297. *See, e.g.*, Thales A. Tréz, *The Hidden Values: Ethics and the Use of Animals in Education* (2001) (unpublished M.A. thesis, Katholieke Universiteit Leuven), *available at* http://www.vet.uu.nl/nca/userfiles/other/The_hidden_Values_thesis_thalez_trez.pdf; BALCOMBE, *supra* note 293, at 9–22; Nick Jukes & Siri Martinsen, *Three's a Crowd: The 1R of Replacement for Education and Training*, 14 ALTERNATIVES TO ANIMAL TESTING & EXPERIMENTA-

TION (Papers & Proc.) 291, 292 (2008), *available at* http://www.asas.or.jp/jsaae/zasshi/WC6_PC/paper291.pdf; Marcia Goodman Kramer, *Humane Education, Dissection, and the Law*, 13 ANIMAL L. 281, 282 (2007).

298. BALCOMBE, *supra* note 293, at 75–76; Jonathan Balcombe, *A Global Overview of Law And Policy Concerning Animal Use in Education*, *in* PROGRESS IN THE REDUCTION, REFINEMENT, AND REPLACEMENT OF ANIMAL EXPERIMENTS: PROCEEDINGS OF THE 3RD WORLD CONGRESS ON ALTERNATIVES AND ANIMAL USE IN THE LIFE SCIENCES 1343 (Michael Balls *et al.* eds., 2000) ("*Global Overview*"), *available at* http://www.humanelearning.info/assets/resources/Legislation%20Balcombe%201999.doc.

299. Government of Gujarat, Education Dep't, T K UMS/1190/692/G 1 (Apr. 16, 1991), *reprinted in* Maneka Gandhi, Ozair Husain & Raj Panjwani, ANIMAL LAWS OF INDIA 733–34 (3d ed. 2006).

300. *Global Overview*, *supra* note 298.

301. CAL. EDUC. CODE § 51540; FLA. STAT. ANN. § 1003.47; MASS. GEN. LAWS ANN. Ch. 272, § 80G; ME. REV. STAT. ANN. tit. 7, § 3971(1); N.Y. EDUC. LAW § 809(5); N.H. REV. STAT. ANN. § 644:8-c; 105 ILL. COMP. STAT. 5/27-14; 24 PA. STAT. ANN. § 15-1514.

302. *Global Overview*, *supra* note 298.

303. Prevention of Cruelty to Animals Act, No. 59 of 1960, § 17(2)(d), (f) (India); *see also* Breeding of and Experiments on Animals (Control and Supervision) Rules, 1998, § 9(g)–(i) (prohibiting animal experiments whose purpose is solely for illustration or public demonstration and stating that experiments aimed at "attaining or retaining manual skill" may only take place "in schools, colleges and programmes duly scrutinized and permitted in registered establishments by the Committee").

304. *Global Overview*, *supra* note 298.

305. The Experiments on Animals (Control and Supervision) Rules, 1968, § 4(n).

306. These states are Florida, California, Pennsylvania, New York, Rhode Island, Illinois, Virginia, Oregon, New Jersey, and Vermont. *See* FLA. STAT. ANN. § 1003.47; CAL. EDUC. CODE § 32255; 24 PA. STAT. ANN. § 15-1523; N.Y. EDUC. LAW § 809(4); R.I. GEN. LAWS § 16-22-20; 105 ILL. COMP. STAT. 112/1 to 112/99; VA. CODE ANN. § 22.1-200.01; OR. REV. STAT. § 337.300; N.J. STAT. ANN. § 18A:35-4.25; VT. STAT. ANN. tit. 16, § 912. For a more detailed discussion of student choice laws, including litigation aimed at establishing a constitutional right to refuse participation in dissection, see Kramer, *supra* note 297.

307. *See Questions and Answers About Dissection*, HSUS, *available at* http://www.humanesociety.org/issues/dissection/qa/questions_answers.html#What_states_have_dissection_laws_resolut.

308. Laura Ducceschi, Lynette A. Hart, & Nicole Green, *Guidelines for the Development of Student Choice Policies Regarding Dissection in Colleges and Universities: An Ethnographic Analysis of Faculty and Student Concerns*, 14 ALTERNATIVES TO ANIMAL TESTING & EXPERIMENTATION (Papers & Proc.) 273 (2008), *available at* http://www.asas.or.jp/jsaae/zasshi WC6_PC/paper273.pdf.

309. Taylor *et al.*, *supra* note 2, at 327, 333 tbl.1; *but see BUAV International Work*, BRITISH UNION FOR THE ABOLITION OF VIVISECTION (BUAV), *available at* http://www.buav.org/ euandinternationalwork (estimating that Europe uses 27 million animals in research each year).

310. *See* Paul Craig & Gráinne de Búrca, EU LAW: TEXT, CASES AND MATERIALS (4th ed. 2007).

311. European Convention for the Protection of Vertebrate Animals Used for Experimental and Other Scientific Purposes, Mar. 18, 1986, Europ. T.S. 123.

312. Council of Europe, Signatories of the European Convention for the Protection of Vertebrate Animals Used for Experimental and Other Scientific Purposes, *available at* http://conventions.coe.int/Treaty/Commun/ChercheSig.asp?NT=123&CM=8&DF=24/08/2009&CL=ENG (last visited Aug. 23, 2009).

313. *Id.* at preamble.

314. *Id.*

315. *Id.* art. 1(1).

316. *Id.* art. 5.

317. *Id.* art. 10.

318. *Id.* art. 5.

319. *Id.* appendix A.

320. *Id.* art. 6.

321. *Id.* art. 7.

322. *Id.*

323. *Id.* art. 8.

324. Member states are permitted to implement directives domestically through methods of their own choosing. Treaty Establishing the European Community, art. 249, Nov. 10, 1997, 1997 O.J. (C 340) [hereinafter EC Treaty].

325. Council Directive 86/609/EEC of 24 November 1986, On the Protection of Animals Used for Experimental and Other Scientific Purposes, 1986 O.J. (L 358) [hereinafter Directive 86/609].

326. *Id.* art.1, preamble.

327. *Id.* preamble.

328. Animals Scientific Procedures Inspectorate & Division, *supra* note 282, at 23.

329. *Id.* at 23–25.

330. Commission Proposal for a Directive of the European Parliament and of the Council on the Protection of Animals Used for Scientific Purposes, at 6, COM (2008) 543 final (Nov. 5, 2008). A poll solicited by the European Coalition to End Animal Experiments found a large majority of respondents favored eliminating experiments that cause pain and suffering to primates, dogs, and cats; that cause severe pain and suffering to any animal; and that are not related to serious or life-threatening conditions. European Coalition to End Animal Experiments, Public Opinion, *available at* http://www.eceae.org/a1_poll.php.

331. Council Directive 2010/63/EU of 22 September 2010 On the Protection of Animals Used for Scientific Purposes, 2010 O.J. (L 276) [hereinafter Directive 2010/63].

332. *Id.* recital 12.

333. *Id.* recital 10.

334. *Id.* recital 11; *id.* arts. 4, 13.

335. *Id.* art. 46.

336. *Id.* art. 47.

337. *Id.* art. 48, annex VII.

338. *Id.* art. 58.

339. *Id.* art. 13(2).

340. *Id.* art. 13(2)(b). Such a determination can only be made on the current state of scientific knowledge. The "capacity" described is arguably not a quantifiable or scientifically ascertainable fact, and is undoubtedly subject to constant change, reinterpretation, and differences of opinion.

341. *Id.* art. 14(2).

342. *Id.* art. 14(1).

343. *Id.* art. 6, annex IV.

344. *Id.* art. 15, annex VIII; *see also* ORLANS, *supra* note 3, at 118–27 (discussing the use of pain scales in domestic legislation in various countries); Orlans, *supra* note 2, at 145 (referring to harm scales as "the cutting edge of new reforms"). The Commission convened a working group to more fully develop the severity classifications. *See* EXPERT WORKING GROUP ON SEVERITY CLASSIFICATION OF SCIENTIFIC PROCEDURES PERFORMED ON ANIMALS, FINAL REPORT (2009), *available at* http://ec.europa.eu/environment/chemicals/lab_animals/pdf/report_ewg.pdf.

345. Directive 2010/63, *supra* note 331, annex VIII, sec. 1. "Non-recovery" procedures are those that "are performed entirely under general anaesthesia from which the animal shall not recover consciousness." *Id.* "Mild" procedures are those that cause "short-term mild pain, suffering or distress, as well as procedures with no significant impairment of the well-being or general condition of the animals." *Id.* "Moderate" procedures are those that cause "short-term moderate pain, suffering or distress, or long-lasting mild pain, suffering or distress as well as procedures that are likely to cause moderate impairment of the well-being or general condition of the animals." *Id.* "Severe" procedures are those that cause "severe pain, suffering or distress, or long-lasting moderate pain, suffering or distress as well as procedures that are likely to cause severe impairment of the well-being or general condition of the animals." *Id.*

346. *Id.* art. 15(2).

347. *Id.* recital 23.

348. *Id.* art. 55(3).

349. *Id.* arts. 55(4), 56.

350. *Id.* art. 33(1)(a).

351. *Id.* art. 33(2), annex III. This represents a significant change over the 1986 Directive, which included "guidelines" to which states were merely required to "pay regard." Directive 86/609, *supra* note 325, art. 5. The 2010 Directive replaced these non-binding guidelines with minimum standards that states are required to meet. Directive 2010/63, *supra* note 331, art. 33(2).

352. *Id.* art. 33(3).

353. The Directive defines "competent authority" as "an authority or authorities or bodies designated by a Member State to carry out the obligations arising from this Directive." *Id.* art. 3(7). In other words, a country's competent authority is responsible for implementing and administering the Directive within the country. Competent authorities need not be government agencies or public authorities, so long as the entity "has the expertise and infrastructure required to carry out the tasks [] and [] is free of any conflict of interests as regards the performance of the tasks." *Id.* art. 59.

354. *Id.* arts. 20–33.

355. *Id.* art. 34.

356. *Id.* art. 34(4).

357. *Id.* art. 34(3).

358. *Id.* art. 36.

359. *Id.* art. 38(1).

360. *Id.* art. 38.

361. *See* Ibrahim, *supra* note 46, at 211–12 ("[T]he AWA explicitly deprives IACUCs of the ability to challenge experimental purpose.... IACUCs cannot ask whether an experiment is trivial, unnecessary, or likely to cause animal suffering that outweighs human benefits."). Ibrahim contends that the Three R's are deficient because they "were not designed to allow

for challenges to the *purpose* of experiments that will use animals," but rather "are designed to accept that purpose, whatever it may be." *Id.* at 210. While this statement may be true with regard to the Three R's in isolation, it is at least possible to supplement the Three R's with a more searching inquiry into the purpose of experiments, as the Directive requires.

362. Directive 2010/63, *supra* note 331, art. 1(3).

363. *Id.* art. 7.

364. *Id.* arts. 9, 11.

365. Declaration of the European Parliament on the use of primates in scientific experiments, P6_TA(2007)0407.

366. *Id.*

367. *But see* Taimie L. Bryant, *Similarity or Difference as a Basis for Justice: Must Animals Be Like Humans to Be Legally Protected from Humans?*, 70 Law & Contemp. Probs. 207 (2007).

368. *See, e.g.*, *Primate Ban Campaign*, Save the Primates, *available at* http://www.savetheprimates.org/primateban/.

369. Directive 2010/63, *supra* note 331, recital 17.

370. *Id.* art. 8(1)(a).

371. *Id.* art. 8(1)(b).

372. *Id.* art. 8(1).

373. *See, e.g.*, European Coalition to End Animal Experiments, A Missed Opportunity, *available at* http://www.eceae.org/en/what-we-do/campaigns/12-million-reasons/a-missed-opportunity.

374. Directive 2010/63, *supra* note 331, recital 18.

375. *Id.* arts. 8(3), 55(2).

376. *Id.* arts. 55(4), 56.

377. Council Directive 76/768/EEC of 27 July 1076, On the Approximation of the Laws of the Member States Relating to Cosmetic Products, 1976 O.J. (L 262) [hereinafter Cosmetics Directive]. A cosmetic product is defined as "any substance or mixture intended to be placed in contact with the various external parts of the human body (epidermis, hair system, nails, lips and external genital organs) or with the teeth and the mucous membranes of the oral cavity with a view exclusively or mainly to cleaning them, perfuming them, changing their appearance and/or correcting body odours and/or protecting them or keeping them in good condition." *Id.* art. 1(1).

378. Council Directive 93/35/EEC of 14 June 1993, art. 1(3), 1993 O.J. (L 151) (amending Cosmetics Directive, art. 4(1)).

379. *Id.*; *see also* Laura Donnellan, *Animal Testing in Cosmetics: Recent Developments in the European Union and the United States*, 13 Animal L. 251, 256 (2007).

380. Azalea P. Rosholt, *The Seventh Amendment Directive—An Unnecessary Measure to a Necessary End*, 60 Food & Drug L.J. 421, 426 (2005).

381. Donnellan, *supra* note 379, at 256–57. For a criticism of the 2003 Amendment, *see generally*, Rosholt, *supra* note 380.

382. Council Directive 2003/15 of 27 February 2003, 2003 O.J. (L 66) (EC) (amending Council Directive 76/768/EEC).

383. *Id.*

384. The Amendment does not apply retroactively, so products that were tested on animals before the effective date of the Amendment can remain on the market. *See* Donnellan, *supra* note 379, at 267.

385. Council Directive 2003/15, *supra* note 382.

386. *Id.*; *see also* Donnellan, *supra* note 379, at 258.

387. Council Directive 2003/15, *supra* note 382; Donnellan, *supra* note 379, at 258–59.

388. Council Directive 2003/15, *supra* note 382. The Commission may also grant a derogation if a "specific human health problem is substantiated and the need to conduct animal tests is justified and is supported by a detailed research Protocol." *Id.*

389. Case C-244/03, *French Republic v. European Parliament and the Council of the European Union*, 2003 O.J. (C 171) 20–21. The case is discussed in Donnellan, *supra* note 379, at 260–67.

390. *Id.* at 260–61.

391. Case C-244/03, *French Republic v. European Parliament and the Council of the European Union*, 2005 E.C.R. I-04021.

392. Commission Regulation 1907/2006, Registration, Evaluation, Authorisation and Restriction of Chemicals (REACH), 2007 O.J. (L 396) 1.

393. Ben Hirschler & John Stonestreet, *EU Chemicals Law "Spells Surge in Animal Testing,"* REUTERS, Aug. 26, 2009, *available at* http://www.reuters.com/article/GCA-BusinessofGreen/idUSTRE57P41620090826.

394. Press Release, European Chemicals Agency, *Clarification Will Avoid Unnecessary Animal Tests* (Sept. 15, 2009), *available at* http://echa.europa.eu/doc/press/pr_09_13_animal_testing_carification_20090915.pdf.

395. Health & Safety Executive, UK REACH Competent Auth. Info. Leaflet No. 18, Minimisation of Animal Testing (2010), *available at* http://www.hse.gov.uk/reach/resources/18animaltesting.pdf.

396. *See* Benjamin Mason Meier, *International Protection of Persons Undergoing Medical Experimentation: Protecting the Right of Informed Consent*, 20 BERKELEY J. INT'L L. 513, 521 (2002).

397. Nuremberg Code, *reprinted at* Office of Human Subjects Research, National Institutes of Health, Nuremberg Code, *available at* http://ohsr.od.nih.gov/guidelines/nuremberg.html.

398. *See generally* George J. Annas & Michael A. Grodin, *Medical Ethics and Human Rights: Legacies of Nuremberg*, 3 HOFSTRA L. & POL'Y SYMP. 111 (1999); THE NAZI DOCTORS AND THE NUREMBERG CODE (George J. Annas & Michael A. Grodin eds., 1992).

399. Meier, *supra* note 396, at 525–27.

400. "Customary international law results from a general and consistent practice of states followed by them from a sense of legal obligation." RESTATEMENT (THIRD) OF FOREIGN RELATIONS LAW OF THE UNITED STATES § 102(2) (1987).

401. International Covenant on Civil and Political Rights, art. 7, Dec. 16, 1966, S. Exec. Doc. E, 95-2, 999 U.N.T.S. 171, 6 I.L.M. 368.

402. Convention for the Protection of Human Rights and Dignity of the Human Being with Regard to the Application of Biology and Medicine: Convention on Human Rights and Biomedicine, art. 5, 15–16, *opened for signature* Apr. 4, 1997, E.T.S. No. 164, *available at* http://conventions.coe.int/Treaty/en/Treaties/html/164.htm.

403. *Abdullahi v. Pfizer, Inc.*, 562 F.3d 163, 177 (2d Cir. 2009). The case involves allegations that Pfizer, the world's largest pharmaceutical corporation, tested an experimental meningitis drug on unconsenting Nigerian children. For a full discussion of the prohibition on nonconsensual experimentation and its status as a norm of customary international law, see *id.* at 174–88. One judge dissented. *Id.* at 191–213 (Wesley, J., dissenting).

404. Regan, *supra* note 3, at 379, 381–82; Steven M. Wise, *The Entitlement of Chimpanzees to the Common Law Writs of Habeas Corpus and De Homine Replegiando*, 37 Golden Gate U.L. Rev. 219, 239 (2007) (quoting Pascal Gigneux *et al.*, *The Ethics of Research on Great Apes*, 437 Nature 27, 28 (Sept. 1, 2005)).

405. Arthur Birmingham LaFrance, *Animal Experimentation: Lessons from Human Experimentation*, 14 Animal L. 29, 49 (2007).

406. As discussed above, the Association for Assessment and Accreditation of Laboratory Animal Care also provides international accreditation for animal research laboratories, using as its basis the Guide for the Care and Use of Laboratory Animals. Guide for the Care and Use of Laboratory Animals, *supra* note 201.

407. Council for International Organizations of Medical Sciences, International Guiding Principles for Biomedical Research Involving Animals (1985), *reprinted in* Institute for Laboratory Animal Research, The Development of Science-Based Guidelines for Laboratory Animal Care app. D, at 240, 242 (2004), *available at* http://books.nap.edu/openbook.php?record_id=11138&page=240.

408. *Id.* at 240–41; *see also id.* at 243 ("Past progress has depended, and further progress in the foreseeable future will depend, largely on animal experimentation which, in the broad field of human medicine, is the prelude to experimental trials on human beings of, for example, new therapeutic, prophylactic, or diagnostic substances, devices, or procedures.").

409. *Id.* at 241, 244; *see also id.* ("The Principles strongly emphasize that there should not be such restrictions as would unduly hamper the advance of biomedical science or the performance of necessary biological tests, but that, at the same time, biomedical scientists should not lose sight of their moral obligation to have a humane regard for their animal subjects, to prevent as far as possible pain and discomfort, and to be constantly alert to any possibility of achieving the same result without resort to living animals.").

410. *Id.* at 244, § 1(I).

411. *Id.* at 244–45, § 1(II)–(XI).

412. *Id.* at 245–46, §§ 2.1–2.7.

413. *Id.* at 245.

414. *Id.* at 247, § 3.

415. *Id.* at 247–48, § 4.

416. Sarah Kahn, *The Role of the World Organisation for Animal Health (OIE) in the Development of International Standards for Laboratory Animal Welfare*, 14 Alternatives to Animal Testing & Experimentation (Papers & Proc.) 727 (2008), *available at* http://www.asas.or.jp/jsaae/zasshi/WC6_PC/paper727.pdf.

417. *Id.* at 727–28; *About OIE*, World Organization for Animal Health, *available at* http://www.oie.int/eng/OIE/en_about.htm.

418. Kahn, *supra* note 416, at 728 ("As the normative publication on standards for international trade in animals and their products, the Terrestrial Code has legal force for World Trade Organisation (WTO) Member countries."); World Organisation for Animal Health, Terrestrial Animal Health Code, foreword (2009), *available at* http://www.oie.int/eng/normes/mcode/en_preface.htm ("The World Trade Organization (WTO) Agreement on the Application of Sanitary and Phytosanitary Measures (SPS Agreement) formally recognises the responsibility of the OIE to specify standards and recommendations as the international references for animal health and zoonotic diseases.... The Terrestrial Code is thus an integral part of the WTO legal framework for international trade.").

419. *Id.* §7, *available at* http://www.oie.int/eng/normes/mcode/en_titre_1.7.htm. Section 7 also contains a chapter on killing animals for disease control and one on controlling stray dog populations. *Id.* §§7.6, 7.7.

420. *Id.* §7.1(3). The principle in its entirety reads: "the internationally recognised 'three Rs' (reduction in numbers of animals, refinement of experimental methods and replacement of animals with non-animal techniques) provide valuable guidance for the use of animals in science."

421. OIE Working Group on Animal Welfare, Report of the Sixth Meeting of the OIE Working Group on Animal Welfare 173 app. J (*Discussion Paper: Issues and Options Regarding a Future International Role for the OIE in Laboratory Animal Welfare*) (Sept. 2007), *available at* http://www.oie.int/eng/bien_etre/ENG_WG_September%202007_final%20report.pdf.

422. *Id.* at 173–75.

423. The ad hoc group seems as if it may have an industry bias, as its report praised these groups for, among other things, "countering the misinformation promulgated by 'antivivisection' groups." *Id.* at 174.

424. Kahn, *supra* note 416, at 729; Agreement Between the World Organisation for Animal Health (OIE) and the World Society for the Protection of Animals (WSPA), May 15, 2007, *available at* http://www.oie.int/eng/oie/accords/en_accord_wspa.htm.

425. The original draft standards are available at OIE Terrestrial Animal Health Standards Commission, Meeting of the OIE Terrestrial Animal Health Standards Commission 463–476 (*Draft Standards for Use of Animals in Research, Testing or Teaching*) (March 2009), *available at* http://www.oie.int/downld/SC/2009/A_TAHSC_March2009_PartB.pdf. The revised draft standards are available at OIE Terrestrial Animal Health Standards Commission, Meeting of the OIE Terrestrial Animal Health Standards Commission 351–364 (*Draft Standards for Use of Animals in Research and Education*) (September 2009), *available at* http://www.oie.int/downld/SC/2009/A_TAHSC_Sept%202009_Part%20A%28b%29.pdf [hereinafter Draft OIE Standards].

426. *Id.* at 354–56.

427. *Id.* at 358–59.

428. *Id.* at 359.

429. *Id.* at 361.

430. *Id.* at 362–64.

431. For example, the draft standards recommend that researchers provide social animals with group housing rather than isolation, "provided that such housing is not contraindicated by the protocol in question," and that psychological enrichment be provided unless doing so would "significantly interfere with the scientific goals." *Id.* at 363.

432. OIE Working Group on Animal Welfare, Report of the Seventh Meeting of the OIE Working Group on Animal Welfare 5 (June 2008), *available at* http://www.oie.int/eng/bien_etre/A_WG_AW_June%202008.pdf.

433. Draft OIE Standards, *supra* note 425, at 351.

434. *About ISO*, International Organization for Standardization, *available at* http://www.iso.org/iso/about.htm.

435. Jon Richmond, *Animal Welfare and the ISO—the International Organisation for Standardization*, 14 Alternatives to Animal Testing & Experimentation (Papers & Proc.) 723, 724 (2008), *available at* http://www.asas.or.jp/jsaae/zasshi/WC6_PC/paper723.pdf.

436. *Id.*

437. Biocompatibility refers to the ability of a material, such as a prosthetic device, to integrate into a living system without causing adverse effects.

438. Richmond, *supra* note 435, at 725.

439. *Id.*

440. *Id.* at 726 tbl.3.

441. *Id.* at 726.

442. *Id.*

443. *Id.*

444. *Id.*

445. *Torn from the Wild*, British Union for the Abolition of Vivisection, May 22, 2009, *available at* http://www.buav.org/buavtv/tornfromthewild (video); David Fox, *Animal Rights Group Slams Cambodia Monkey Trade*, Reuters, Nov. 23, 2008, *available at* http://www.reuters.com/article/idUSTRE4AM0TC20081123.

446. Ardith A. Eudey, *The Crab-eating Macaque* (Macaca fascicularis): *Widespread and Rapidly Declining*, 23 Primate Conservation 129, 130 (2008).

447. *Id.* at 131.

448. *Monkey Misery in Laos*, British Union for the Abolition of Vivisection, Feb. 22, 2010, *available at* http://www.buav.org/buavtv/monkeymiseryinlaos (video) (Laos); British Union for the Abolition of Vivisection, *Monkey Business*, Apr. 26, 2009, *available at* http://www.buav.org/buavtv/monkeybusiness (video) (Vietnam); British Union for the Abolition of Vivisection, *Chain of Suffering*, May 24, 2009, *available at* http://www.buav.org/buavtv/chainofsuffering (video) (Indonesia).

449. *Monkey Business*, British Union for the Abolition of Vivisection, *available at* http://www.buav.org/investigations/monkeybusiness; *Monkey Misery in Laos: The Investigation*, British Union for the Abolition of Vivisection, *available at* http://www.buav.org/investigations/monkeymisery/theinvestigation.

450. Posting of Shirley McGreal, Executive Director, International Primate Protection League, to AR-News@googlegroups.com (Jan. 30, 2010) (on file with author). These figures are based on IPPL's analysis of data supplied by the United States federal government.

451. These statistics are consistent with previous years. The United States imported 28,091 primates in 2008, and 25,899 primates in 2007. Helen Thirlway, *U.S. and UK Primate Imports*, IPPL News (Int'l Primate Prot. League, Summerville, S.C.), May 2009, at 14.

452. Jehangir S. Pocha, *Outsourcing Animal Testing: US Firm Setting Up Drug-Trial Facilities in China, Where Scientists are Plentiful but Activists Aren't*, Boston Globe, Nov. 25, 2006, *available at* http://www.boston.com/business/healthcare/articles/2006/11/25/outsourcing_animal_testing (quoting Glenn Rice, chief executive officer, Bridge Pharmaceuticals, Inc.); *see also* Jayne Mackta, *Perspectives on Pre-Clinical Outsourcing in China*, ALN Mag., July–Aug. 2008, *available at* http://www.alnmag.com/article/perspectives-pre-clinical-outsourcing-china.

453. Pocha, *supra* note 452.

454. This is not to say that all Guayama residents opposed the facility. Many supported the construction as a way to improve the local economy. Jill Laster, *Plan to Breed Lab Monkeys Splits Puerto Rican Town*, U.S. News & World Report, Nov. 30, 2009, *available at* http://www.usnews.com/science/articles/2009/11/30/plan-to-breed-lab-monkeys-splits-puerto-rican-town.html.

455. *Judge Bars Construction of Controversial Monkey-Breeding Facility in Puerto Rico*, L.A. TIMES, Dec. 31, 2009, *available at* http://latimesblogs.latimes.com/unleashed/2009/12/judge-bars-construction-of-controversial-monkeybreeding-facility-in-puerto-rico.html.

456. Jose Alvarado Vega, *Appeals Court Overturns Ruling Halting Bioculture Monkey-Breeding Facility*, P.R. DAILY SUN, Jan. 30, 2010, *available at* http://www.prdailysun.com/index.php?page=news.article&id=1264822157.

457. Raul Colon, *Senate votes to bar monkey breeders*, PUERTO RICO DAILY SUN, Oct. 12, 2010, *available at* http://www.prdailysun.com/index.php?page=news.article&id=1286855671; *Puerto Rico senate says monkey-breeding facility not wanted*, CARIBBEAN NEWS NOW, Oct. 13, 2010, *available at* http://www.caribbeannewsnow.com/headline-Puerto-Rico-senate-says-monkey-breeding-facility-not-wanted-2590.html.

458. Darshini Kandasamy, *Monkey Lab: French Proposal for Johor Lab Draws UK Protest*, MALAY MAIL, July 6, 2009, *available at* http://www.mmail.com.my/content/8247-monkey-lab-proposal-still-under-study [hereinafter *Monkey Lab*]; Darshini Kandasamy, *Animal Groups in Protest Over Planned Animal Test Lab*, MALAY MAIL, Apr. 27, 2010, *available at* http://www.mmail.com.my/content/34684-animal-groups-protest-over-planned-animal-test-lab [hereinafter *Animal Groups*].

459. *Monkey Lab*, *supra* note 458.

460. *Animal Rights Groups Protest Against Indian Company's Plan*, PEOPLE'S DAILY ONLINE, June 9, 2010, *available at* http://english.peopledaily.com.cn/90001/90777/90851/7019645.html; *Animal Groups*, *supra* note 458.

461. Darshini Kandasamy, *Monkey Lab Proposal Still Under Study*, MALAY MAIL, July 16, 2009, *available at* http://www.mmail.com.my/content/8247-monkey-lab-proposal-still-under-study; Darshini Kandasamy, *Malacca Still Mulling Over Animal Test Lab Plan*, MALAY MAIL, Apr. 26, 2010, *available at* http://www.mmail.com.my/content/34578-malacca-still-mulling-over-animal-test-lab-plan.

462. *Malaysia Probes British-Funded Animal Testing Lab*, AGENCE FRANCE-PRESSE, June 13, 2010, *available at* http://www.google.com/hostednews/afp/article/ALeqM5izAOCwlwbJpPXBWqvrU45RMour5Q; Derrick Vinesh, *Dept to Inspect Animal Testing Lab*, STAR ONLINE, June 13, 2010, *available at* http://thestar.com.my/news/story.asp?file=/2010/6/13/starprobe/6462421.

463. *Monkey Lab*, supra note 458 (quoting Christine Chin, Chair, Malaysian Society for the Prevention of Cruelty to Animals).

464. *Id.* (quoting Sarah Kite, BUAV Special Projects Director).

CHAPTER 5

CONSTITUTIONAL LAW

This chapter focuses on laws that are placed in a specific area of the written law, the constitution of a nation, or national subdivision. Most of this book's other chapters evaluate particular types of laws from the viewpoint of their effect, intent, or subject area. In contrast, this chapter examines the laws discussed first from a strictly legal and procedural perspective—its placement in the document known as the constitution. That is, it is the nature of the process—and its significance—that is the focal point. The organizing theme is the importance and value of placing laws in the federal or state constitutions of the country at issue. This is so regardless of whether the constitutional provisions discussed are (1) intended for animal protection, (2) written to legislate specific conduct related to animals, or (3) for neither of these purposes but ultimately have a significant impact on human behavior involving animals.

Constitutional laws carry with them different political and procedural considerations, depending on the structure of the particular government involved. Constitutional laws, because of their special placement in the hierarchy of legal systems, obtain exceptional meaning within the context of the law. We will first explain the significance of inclusion in a constitution, which varies depending on the country and the nature of its government. The remainder of the chapter will focus on an examination of illustrative constitutional provisions that directly or indirectly affect animals in their text or application.

Constitutional provisions, because they are often subject to broad construction and interpretation by courts, may also ultimately exert unanticipated but clear influence on individuals who use animals for certain things (whether pleasure, prayer, or profit), or on those who seek to protect animals. These impacts obviously can cause change in the lives of animals. Examples of these kinds of laws are included in the chapter.

One interesting consideration is the list of factors underlying the decision to place a law in a constitution, as opposed to simply in the statutes or codes of a nation or state. More generalized legal texts can provide a detailed examination of political science and lawmaking that plays into the decision. We can also identify certain relevant issues that factor into the location of a particular law. The examination of that determination—to place a law within the text of a constitution—clearly implicates some of the themes that are evident throughout the book and that are discussed in detail in Chapter 1, involving the position of animals in our society and the broader considerations we give to them, our ability to use them, and concerns for their welfare.

In virtually every case, legal rules and doctrines that end up in constitutions are placed there because their supporters and drafters made a concerted effort to put them there for identifiable reasons of strategy and intent. There are particular requirements for placement in a constitution, and these vary from one nation/state to another. In order to give readers unfamiliar with the nature of constitutions and with the varied importance and treatment of constitutions worldwide a fuller appreciation of the laws discussed here, we will first provide a brief explanation of constitutions in general.

The actual text and purpose of the constitutional laws we discuss are equally interesting. While the significance of placing a law in a constitution varies to some degree, depending on the weight the constitution carries and the particular government's requirements for amending constitutional laws, there is always something special—and likely some definite political reason—for placing a law in a constitution. Given the centrality of constitutions in legal systems, the creation of constitutional animal protection principles reflects the seriousness with which some jurisdictions are confronting animal issues.

Constitutions—The Basics

The verb "constitute" indicates the act of composing, forming or establishing something; a constitution is the establishing document for a particular government. As initially conceived, it represents one of the most fundamental elements of governmental structure. A governmental entity's constitution provides, in essence, the rules of running the business of the government. The document almost always includes a description and determination of the inner procedural workings of the government, defining leaders' positions, their roles, and the rules governing those roles. Governance provisions like these are important structural components and serve to limit and define the scope of a government's powers over its citizenry. A constitution also usually sets down basic parameters for the ordering of the daily lives of a governing body's citizens: a sort of template for common behaviors. Constitutions are responsible for addressing and defining basic civil rights that can be used as guidelines in many aspects of society and in determining the propriety of many human interactions with government and with other members of society.

In contrast to constitutions, most laws that exist in national or state codes or local rules and ordinances deal with specific issues, practices or industries; they are focused on specific acts and grouped with other laws that deal with related issues.[1] For example, most countries have numerous laws dealing with criminal acts, or with taxation, or with the operation and incorporation of businesses. Although constitutional provisions can and do sometimes address specific acts, as a general rule, a constitution provides the overriding rules and principles that direct the governance of a nation/state.

Not all nations have, or have always had, constitutions. The United States, although a relatively young country, began its history with a constitutional government and is one model for constitutions based on a government of republicanism. In the United States and other governments modeled after it, the written federal constitution is considered the principal governing document for the country. In the U.S. form of constitutional governance, the central national document has a parallel constitution in each American state. The state constitutions operate as the commanding documents for each state in the same way that the federal constitution controls the conduct of federal leaders and the nation's citizens. These documents, along with the myriad other laws not included in the constitutions, complement each other and make up the universe of laws applicable to the country's populace. In circumstances where there is a conflict between the law of a state and the federal constitution and any other law, the doctrine of "preemption" may apply to bar the provisions of the competing law and give the federal constitution precedence and authority.[2]

In most countries with constitutions, the constitution is the central document and governs the basics of a country's government. In a minority of countries, the document may have less force and control, depending on the degree to which the country's central government relies upon, or is bound by, the constitutional mandates. In some countries the constitution is "unwritten." That is, while there is no actual governing document, the various legislative enactments of the country are considered, as a whole, to comprise the equivalent of a written constitution.

Some countries are more traditional monarchies, in which the leader has relatively unrestricted authority. But in many countries with unwritten constitutions, as with the United Kingdom, the same basic principles of law and procedure apply that are described above and found in a written document in countries like the United States. That is, much of the "constitutional" text in these societies is actually written down, but it is not in a single document, in contrast to the U.S. model. Instead, the laws of the unwritten constitution countries are generally gleaned from two sources. First, the nation's written laws that do exist are used as the basis and subtext for the overriding principles that would otherwise be found in a constitution. Second, fundamental rules and guiding principles in such societies come from the traditions and doctrines known as "natural law" and "common law." Both may be just as important, controlling, and valuable as traditional constitutional provisions. Courts and governments will rely on the policies, rights, and basic fundamental values that are found in these other sources, and that provide the basics of operation and law for these countries.

The United Kingdom, comprised of England, Scotland, Wales, Northern Ireland, and other British territories, is a prime example of a government with an unwritten constitution. It is a constitutional monarchy, where the country's leaders are bound by a set of documents, although there is no central controlling constitutional document.[3] The documents that could be called the "British constitution" include the Magna Carta (written in 1215), the Bill of Rights (1689), and the European Communities Act (1972).[4] In addition to those key writings, United Kingdom society is governed by the principles of common law, basic fundamental beliefs, and historical traditions that have woven themselves into the fabric of law over the centuries.[5]

Constitutions may separately be characterized as "flexible" or "rigid."[6] The terms refer to the relative strength of rules established within the constitution. A flexible constitution does not have any specific rules—or very few—that restrict the ability to amend the document. Flexible constitutions operate like traditional laws, which can be amended any time the relevant legislative body decides to change the law. Usually only a majority vote is required. Like the general law, flexible constitutions are more likely to be subject to change that tracks both the social and political climate of a country.

But flexible constitutions, again like most laws, do not simply change at the whim of individual citizens or legislators. The process of making new law or amending existing laws takes considerable effort and procedure on the part of lobbyists, supporters, and legislators. In countries with flexible constitutions and majority rule, this also means that fundamental values and rights found in flexible constitutions are subject to shifting influences and ideologies as social and societal change moves through the body politic.

Unwritten constitutions are relatively flexible. Even the most fundamental constitutional principles can be altered by the legislative process, although concepts of natural law are rarely affected. Nevertheless, the British Parliament, through the normal legislative process, can adjust the process of governmental functions and the triggers for government action; if desired, it can even change civil rights granted to the populace.

The United States Constitution and others modeled after it are rigid constitutions, and are more difficult to change. These documents cannot be altered by the normal legislative process of lawmaking, and so the underlying concepts are entrenched in large part because of the procedures required to amend or supplement the documents. Because of their coverage and presumed longevity, this type of constitution sets forth a certain and uniform set of principles and priorities for a nation. To elaborate on the discussion above, these constitutions control (1) the government's lawmaking processes, (2) the procedures behind elections and voting rights of individual citizens, (3) the rules governing those who hold public service positions, especially the leaders and legislators, and (4) the basic rights granted to the citizenry. Rigid constitutions can be altered, but they generally take a larger percentage of citizens or legislators who agree on the changes, voting together, to make those changes. For example, in order to amend the United States Constitution, the proposed amendment must be approved by a two-thirds majority of both houses of Congress, and then be ratified by three-fourths of the states. In contrast, a simple majority (just over one-half of the votes) of state representatives is all that is required to change other laws.

While textual constitutional amendments usually require some significant "supermajority" in countries with rigid constitutions, the practical effect of constitutional provisions may change significantly without any actual amendment. This is especially true where judicial branches of government are tasked with interpreting the meaning of constitutional provisions through a series of decisions. For this reason, and despite the high burden for amendment, constitutions are generally seen as "living documents" that are subject to changing and new interpretations as new applications and arguments are presented to the courts. For example, American courts have interpreted their constitution in a fluid and flexible way, finding in its text answers to ever-evolving and new questions that arise with respect to the meaning of its language, much of which is over 200 years old. Thus, without an actual amendment or any textual change, the courts'—and in turn, the populace's—understanding of a constitution changes to some degree with each new judicial interpretation on issues that have not been previously considered.

The general principle regarding judicial interpretations of constitutional provisions applies to any constitution, and courts routinely refine, reinterpret, and redefine the parameters of the basic rights and freedoms granted. Because the words and principles are often broad and subject to interpretation, the constitutional protections inherent in those words are developed over time, through judicial analysis and usage. The United States Constitution, one of the oldest and shortest written constitutions, has generated thousands of pages of judicial opinions, examining the scope and limits of those provisions.

It bears mention that constitutions are also partially defined by the political climate in which they are initially created. In the context of human rights, a significant difference may be seen in a constitution that was drafted while a colonial government ruled and before the advent of modern civil rights movements came to the fore, as opposed to one written in the midst of substantive human rights activity.[7] This may be an obvious caveat, but it is one that is valuable in subsequent considerations of the constitution and the potential for change.

Constitutional Provisions Including Animals

Regardless of the type of constitution, it can generally be stated that if a law is found in a constitution, it carries especial force and authority and indicates social values and policy. Constitutional provisions are given heightened respect and therefore there is significant value in getting a law affecting animals into a constitution. Thus, incorporating animals into constitutions brings them into the very structure of the body politic. The intent behind the law does not change the fact that placement in the constitution gives it added authority. If a constitutional provision works to increase animal welfare, provides greater protection for animals in the wild, or limits their use in institutional settings, it represents a strong statement in their interest. If a new constitutional section sets industry standards for the treatment of animals, establishes industry oversight of its own practices, or raises barriers to further animal welfare efforts by private interest groups, it will work to diminish the likelihood of positive change for animals. A constitutional provision that allows those in agribusiness to set standards of care for the animals they use would be equally important as one that sets welfare standards proposed by animal protection groups. In recent years both types of provisions have been adopted, as discussed later in the chapter.

New constitutional law also results from judicial opinions in countries with judicial branches that publish interpretations of the constitution that are binding on the government and the populace. Courts interpret constitutional provisions, and those interpretations are effectively incorporated into law as part of the constitutional authority. Courts often presume a general policy that is implied by constitutional language, and apply those policies in creating new law separate from the constitutions themselves. Laws that have not previously been considered relevant to animals may be applied to situations involving animals, therefore expanding the field.

The inclusion of animal interests and issues in a constitution—a relatively new development in a limited number of jurisdictions—provides strong evidence of the increasing global spotlight on animals and their treatment under the law. The contrary is not true: there is likely no significance to be attached to the *absence* of any animal-friendly provisions in a constitution. Given the very recent development in this area, no real conclusion can be reached if animals are not mentioned. Nevertheless, a lack of constitutional provisions will not stop a shift in other laws on animal issues.

There are aspects of the constitutional protections for animals that vary in interesting ways from the general nature of most constitutional amendments. These differences provide another example of the law adapting and adjusting to the social desire to incorporate animal interests while working within a structure that has typically addressed human rights and interests only. First, most constitutional provisions that focus on rights actually *grant* permission for citizens to engage in a general practice, or else the laws support a general public and social policy. Many of the provisions with respect to animals actually *remove* a right from the human populace. Constitutional provisions that directly limit citizens' rights are not completely unprecedented—prior U.S. constitutional amendments have taken away Americans' rights to drink alcoholic beverages (subsequently repealed) and keep other humans as slaves.[8] Still, it is the exception rather than the rule.

There is an even more interesting side to these constitutional amendments, in that they become aspects of the constitutions that arguably *give rights to nonhumans*. A number of commentators have extensively addressed the issue of "animal rights," and it is not in the purview of this book to enter that dialogue. Yet the ban on certain conduct seems to grant the affected animals the "right" to be free of such conduct. Because of animals' status as property in every jurisdiction, those rights are naturally limited; but even the implication that constitutional rights are being conferred on animals is a break from tradition. And it seems hard to dispute that the inclusion of animal protection language (or the prohibition on animal exploitation) in a constitution is at least facially a most affirmative official act of granting rights to nonhumans. For while these sections admittedly remove the extent to which humans can use animals, they also clearly extend a formal protection to the affected animals. A parallel exists in laws prohibiting cruelty to animals—but these are of course not constitutional sections.

With that introduction, the remainder of the chapter addresses specific constitutional provisions pertinent to this area.

India

The Indian constitution was established after the country gained independence in 1947.[9] It is the "most extensive and detailed constitution in the world" with 395 articles, and it had been amended 93 times as of 2008.[10] The Indian constitution is the supreme law of the land, and the central government has the authority to govern in many substantive areas related to individual rights and obligations.[11]

Also quoted in Chapter 1 is the Indian constitution, which provides significant protections for animals. Article 51A(g) of the constitution states: "It shall be the fundamental duty of every citizen of India—to protect and improve the natural environment including forests, lakes, rivers, and wildlife, and to have compassion for living creatures." On its face, this provision restricts the conduct of Indian citizens and their ability to disturb the non-animal "natural environment" (since "protection" limits use and abuse) and, even more importantly, arguably places an affirmative duty on them to "improve" that same part of the biosphere.[12] It also makes the rather vague requirement of "compassion" for animals an obligation of every citizen. While subject to broad and disparate interpretations, the provision facially still places greater emphasis on animal welfare than virtually any other law. Undefined, the term "compassion" has potentially broad-ranging interpretations, and litigants have used this section of the constitution to challenge claimed harms to both the environment and animals.[13]

The strength of the constitutional provisions was tested in *People for Animals v. State of Goa*.[14] The petitioner in that case was an animal protection group that claimed that the traditional entertainment practice of bullfighting was a violation of the constitution's mandate to the state to prevent animal cruelty. Petitioner sued the state for its refusal to prohibit and shut down bullfighting operations.

In the Indian bullfighting challenge, the court examined the language of the constitution and found that the law effectively prohibited bullfighting. The court quoted the mandate to each Indian citizen, citing the very broad "duty" of "compassion for living creatures."[15] Considering the government's obligations, the court further found that police officers were required to prevent animal cruelty crimes when possible, based on the mandate of the general laws in the Indian Code of Criminal Procedure.[16] The case was thus a victory for animal protectionists on two different fronts, substantively and in terms of enforcement, and it established valuable precedent for future concerns.

As a major shift in Indian law and a declaration of Indian social policy, the court's ruling broke new ground with respect to bullfighting. The opinion represents a judicial determination that bullfighting is *per se* cruel, and that it violates Article 51A, the constitutional provision requiring compassion for animals in daily conduct. This opinion could be relied upon to hold that bullfighting also violates the Indian anti-cruelty statute. In short, if given its full effect, this opinion could signal an end to bullfighting as a practice in India, without the requirement of any other legislative enactment. In this way, the judicial opinion and interpretation of a constitutional provision amended the general cruelty law and affected a significant change of social practice.

The opinion includes a second important aspect for animal cruelty cases. That is, the court's ruling placed a strict limit on the discretion usually accorded law enforcement when faced with animal cruelty issues. The court clarified the role of law enforcement when faced with a clear violation of the constitutional prohibitions on cruelty. It found the state had an affirmative "responsibilit[y] to prevent the cruelty to the animals"[17] and that this responsibility involved an almost mandatory duty to investigate and prosecute that conduct.

The court's ruling is notable because law enforcement is usually given significant discretion in deciding whether or not to prosecute criminal activity. In this case, the court seemed to be saying that because of the constitutional recognition of the animal cruelty prohibition as one of overriding social importance and social policy, that typical leeway is effectively eliminated in this area. The court stated its firm belief in the force and intent of the Indian constitution:

> It cannot be disputed that all animals are born with an equal claim for life without any cruelty to them. Perhaps if this right was given proper recognition by the human beings, there would be no necessity to bring on the statute books the [Prevention of Cruelty to Animals] Act.[18]

The potential reach of the court's holding is expansive because it suggests that the provision applies to any and all animals, regardless of species. (Many animal protection statutes in other countries exclude certain animals, and certain practices, from their coverage.) Despite that plain language interpretation, the scope of that rule would likely not apply to all uses of animals, and would surely be restricted by the accepted uses of animals in Indian society. The limited reach is fairly clear, given the pervasive use of animals throughout the country and the language of Article 48 of the constitution, discussed below.

Another form of entertainment using animals—ox racing—was examined under the same constitutional provisions. Ox racing involves a public exhibition in which oxen are loaded down with boulders weighing 1800 kilograms (approximately 3960 pounds) and forced to race other similarly-situated animals. In *Peela Ramakrishna v. Govt. of Andhra Pradesh*, petitioners alleged, as with bullfighting, that this public exhibition violated both the constitution and the anti-cruelty law.[19] The facts of the practice were undisputed. The court's task was simply to determine whether this common event, previously carried out legally in India, was a violation of the general public policy under the constitution, and the specific terms of the general cruelty law. The court, noting that the allegations were not denied, found that ox racing violated both laws. The request for a writ was granted and the law that previously provided permission for ox racing was overturned.[20]

Article 48 of the Indian constitution also addresses animal interests, while implicitly recognizing that animals will be used for commercial purposes. It thus provides a legal counterbalance to the otherwise broad and seemingly expansive stretch of Article 51. The section, entitled "Organisation of Agriculture and Animal Husbandry," reads: "The State shall endeavor to organise agriculture and animal husbandry on modern and scientific lines and shall, in particular, take steps for preserving and improving the breeds, and prohibiting the slaughter of cows and calves and other ... cattle." Article 48 is unique among constitutional provisions internationally, as it directly incorporates and recognizes the special relationship between a society and animals (here Indians and cows)—and the interest in protecting them above and separate from other species.

This provision promotes the industrial production of animals and their use for commercial purposes, but may also have an indirect welfare component. It is different from Article 51A, because while that section is directed at both the citizenry and the government, Article 48 primarily invokes an affirmative requirement for the government with respect to animals in industry. Under Article 48, the government has the duty and obligation to carry out the constitutional directive. This directive to the state is in contrast to many constitutional provisions—like Article 51 discussed above—which direct conduct of individuals, or those which provide specific protections to individuals, as opposed to those which direct government conduct. This requirement for the state can lead to enactment of additional laws supporting the same policy. At the same time, the direct application of the constitutional provision will result in increased laws that cover Indian animals, when the government acts in line with the social policy established by Article 48.

Article 48 presumably includes a requirement that the government enact laws that will ensure breed viability and that it enforce industrial operations and oversee industry practices regarding animals. The constitutional provision therefore serves to continue the functions of agribusiness at an agreed-upon level. It represents an affirmative protection of the use of animals for humans, as opposed to Article 51's protection of animals from abuse by humans.

The central government applied Articles 48, and 51 and banned the training and exhibition of lions, bears, monkeys, tigers, and panthers in circuses.[21] The High Court of Delhi found the constitutional provisions embodied a policy of protection of animals and upheld the ban.[22] The court found that the ban was in the public interest because of the "pernicious nature" of allowing such treatment of animals for "mere entertainment."[23] This opinion demonstrates the value of a constitutional provision that may be interpreted by a court as a broader grant of authority than a more specific law prohibiting animal cruelty with general language.

In a similar case in the High Court of Kerala,[24] the court adopted a broad approach to protection for animals. It extended the constitutional policy to animals not previously covered and ruled in favor of animal welfare even though the animals were engaged and being used in typical and traditional circus activities. The court examined the standard treatment of animals in circus exhibits and determined the constitutional provisions intended to stop that conduct for all animals in public exhibition across India. As a factual matter the court found that "[c]ircus animals [were] being forced to perform unnatural tricks, ... housed in cramped cages, subjected to fear, hunger, pain, not to mention the undignified way of life they have to live, with no respite."[25] The court held that the animal protection laws that were being challenged (and that had been adopted pursuant to the constitutional provisions) were held to be proper because they "prevent[ed] the infliction of unnecessary pain or suffering on animals."[26]

The ruling is significant on many levels. It soundly established the strong public policy written into the constitution to prevent all manner of cruelty to animals. It upheld the ban of activities that had previously been both commonplace, considered normal, and completely legal. And, if followed, the ruling promised a significant improvement in the lives of many animals.

Mohd. Habib v. State of Uttar Pradesh[27] further demonstrates the degree to which the constitutional provision may tread on traditional commercial practices that are completely protected from challenge in most countries. This case addressed the use of animals for food production and, specifically, the slaughter and butchering of animals for meat—among the most common and historically accepted uses of animals. The Court was petitioned by butchers who "contend[ed] that their vocation and profession is their fundamental right ... to slaughter buffaloes and make a business from the meat which they sell."[28] Once again the court was petitioned by industry interests concerned about the application of the constitutional provision to the core of their members' livelihoods. A group of butchers claimed a "fundamental right" to kill animals based on their longstanding professional activities and the acceptance of that work by the general public. The butchers sought a judicial declaration of their right to continue to carry on this practice, unfettered by the constitutional provisions. The petitioners claimed that "from their ancestors they have taken to the family profession to slaughter buffaloes and sell the meat."[29] Therefore, they argued, given the economic and traditional interests involved, and the widespread use and express and implied endorsement of their work, the constitutional policy established for the protection of animals should either be directly rejected or else significantly restricted. In essence, the petitioners wanted a ruling that the proscription against animal cruelty had to be construed to exempt this standard practice that was in place when the law was passed.

Surprisingly, the court refused the butchers' request and did not issue a declaration. Finding that it would be a "negation of the tenets of our Constitution," the court found that "the Constitution of India does not permit any citizen to claim that it is his fundamental right to take life and kill animals."[30] While the court did not expressly outlaw the slaughter of animals for food, or the butchers' practices, it did reject the effort to directly strike down the constitutional provisions. The court held to a tenuous middle ground in which it upheld the constitutional policy but did not condemn the practice. The court was likely creating a compromise ruling while cautiously considering the conflicting interests involved and avoiding the dilemma posed by the breadth of the constitutional language.

Germany

The German constitution, the Grundgesetz, is known as the "Basic Law" of the country, and establishes a democratic government. The terms of the Grundgesetz, adopted after Germany was reunified in 1990, confer many fundamental rights and "appl[y] to the entire German people."[31] A very notable constitutional amendment came about in 2002 when the German legislature amended Article 20A of the constitution and provided special protection for animals.[32] While the constitution previously had vague language protecting "the natural bases of life," the amendment confirmed that animals must be considered and covered by the central government in future acts:

> Mindful also of its responsibility toward future generations, the state shall protect the natural bases of life and the animals by legislation and, in accordance with law and justice, by executive and judicial action, all within the framework of the constitutional order.[33]

The "and the animals" phrase was added in 2002. Because the German constitution is of the rigid type, constitutional procedure required that the amendment be approved by a two-thirds majority of the federal legislative body (the

Bundestag). This made Germany the first country in Europe (and one of the first worldwide) to codify animal protection in its constitution.[34] The potential impact on animals in Germany is obvious, and this modification is a significant step at least in language. It remains to be seen what the ultimate effect of the provision will be on Germany's animals.

Article 20A, on its face, is a mandate to the national government to enact laws protecting animals. It acts, like some provisions discussed previously, to bind the government in an obligation to protect animals. It thus codifies a widespread, nationwide public policy supporting the protection of animals in all government.

The scope of Article 20A is worth emphasizing. First, as mentioned above, the significance of its placement in the constitution cannot be underestimated. Of equal note is that, unlike other laws that might target only certain species (endangered, companion animals, or some other discrete category), this is a general requirement for the entire nation to provide for protection of animals. In 2011, it is still too soon to tell what actual effect the amendment to Article 20A will have on German animals, and how far the provision's reach will be extended if challenges are made to standard practices involving animals. As mentioned earlier and seen in the Indian example, this amendment could result in judicial decisions affecting previously approved treatment of animals. It could also lead to an influence on new laws being adopted, amendments to existing laws, or increased enforcement of current statutes that protect against animal cruelty and other forms of mistreatment.

It is also possible that there will be no change at all, despite the constitutional amendment. If the addition of the phrase "and the animals" is seen as simply a clarification, no change would be warranted. Additionally, the provision does not create any mechanism for enforcement of the law. Therefore, it may be that it has very little effect on the lives of German animals. Governments are given a significant amount of discretion in carrying out their duties, so that without any supplemental legislation or successful courtroom challenges, the *status quo* may prevail. Without further action by legislatures and animal advocates, the amendment may be just a statement of policy without force.

The possibility that the new broad language will be limited in effect by traditional and overriding societal beliefs and established practices is hinted at even in the constitution itself. Because the constitution provides for both the protection of animals and, indirectly, the interests of people who use animals for commercial purposes, there is an internal conflict that could set the stage for a clash of policies.

There is no provision in the German constitution that expressly protects the commercial use of animals, or their exploitation in artistic or public displays, but some provisions in the German constitution protect freedom of expression[35] and the right to one's chosen occupation.[36] There is thus an inherent clash between broad protection of animals and occupational rights, where those occupations involve the pain, suffering, and death of animals. And a reasonable interpretation of the constitutional amendment could be that the legislature was well aware of the many animal-related professions when it made the 2002 amendment, and that it did not intend to change the longstanding practices of both those using animals commercially and those who relied on their products. Thus, while occupations involving food production, biomedical research, and entertainment are not directly mentioned in the constitution, its protection of both freedom of expression and the right to engage in one's chosen livelihood may act as implied exemptions that protect most traditional commercial uses. Researchers in other countries have made the argument that involvement in research is a form of expression that should be protected; and they are of course longstanding recognized professions.[37] There will need to be an examination of the conflict between these competing public policies—those supporting one's livelihood and expressive interests and those prohibiting mistreatment of animals. It is most likely that courts will try to harmonize the potentially conflicting provisions, which could lead to a restriction of the breadth of animal protection under the 2002 law.

Notably, biomedical research is already directly regulated in the *Tierschutzgesetz*, the general German animal welfare law. The inclusion of research suggests a belief by the German legislature that research can accommodate animal welfare issues. Despite the constitutional amendment, the most likely reconciliation of the issues will be that biomedical research will continue as it did before the constitutional amendment. The constitution would be read in conjunction with the general anticruelty law, which says that "'[r]esearch on vertebrate animals may only be undertaken when the expected pain, suffering, or injury to the animal are ethically acceptable.'"[38] A flexible definition of acceptability will then become a question for the courts to decide on a case-by-case basis:

> [P]ermits for proposed experiments are rarely denied. Additionally, permission is not required for experiments which are mandatory under other legislation (*e.g.*, consumer safety) or if the experiment would not cause damage, pain or suffering to the animals involved. Despite the language in the *Tierschutzgesetz*, restricting an animal research activity on ethical grounds is nearly impossible and is left almost entirely to the discretion of the researcher and his or her institution.[39]

Nevertheless, given the focus on animal welfare, the amendment should at least place a more direct focus on animal interests in devising and examining research protocols. And while the "right to research" some find in the constitution may be used as a deterrent to a broader enforcement of the general animal welfare law's prohibitions, the presence of the constitutional provision may also lead to a shift in practices to some degree. Any kind of change—towards a focus on ethics and welfare—will be subject to community standards and a balancing test. On the one side will be the perceived value of common practices and their acceptance, and on the other will be a consideration of the potential pain inflicted on animals while those practices are carried out.

If a court is asked to interpret the conflict between commercial use of animals and the constitutional protection, principles of statutory construction may dictate a result that retains only the protections for animals that existed before the amendment. But an equally reasonable construction would be that by adding "and the animals," the legislature and populace were intentionally changing the animal protection landscape. Because the legislature can be imputed with the knowledge of the laws at the time of the amendment, the change arguably elevates the doctrine of animal protection and alters its status in German society. Under that construction, animal welfare would trump freedom of expression and occupational practices that result in harm to animals, requiring a change in those practices.

The foregoing makes clear that there has been a significant development in the law of animal welfare in Germany, and the law will undoubtedly continue to be tested on various specific points after the publication of this text. The German experience demonstrates one of the major themes of this chapter—that adding an animal welfare provision to a constitution may trigger renewed consideration of animal interests while not immediately changing traditional practices. Rulings since the amendment have confirmed that animal welfare must be weighed against other community interests, such as religious freedom and ritual slaughter, and that, as suggested above, longstanding practices will be allowed to continue:

> the introduction of animal protection as an objective of the state does not prohibit granting exemptions from the stunning [rendering individuals destined to be eaten unconscious prior to slaughter] requirement. The fundamental rights concerned have to be weighed against the objective of the state, as the intended goal of the constitutional amendment was not to award one-sided preference to animal protection.[40]

United States of America

General Constitutional Provisions that Indirectly Affect Animals

There are no provisions in the United States federal constitution directly addressing animals. Nevertheless, judicial opinions have demonstrated that other more general clauses can influence animal-related legal issues. This is undoubtedly the case around the world, and the American examples are provided as illustrations of the ways in which seemingly unrelated constitutional provisions can have significant effect on the treatment of animals.

The "Bill of Rights" is a series of amendments that have been incorporated into the United States Constitution, although they are not part of the original document. But they were ratified with the Constitution by the First U.S. Congress in the late 1700s, and establish fundamental liberties for most citizens. Two of those rights, both found in the First Amendment to the Constitution (part of the Bill of Rights), are the rights to (1) freedom of expression, and (2) free exercise of one's religion. These are considered valuable and strong interests, held by all free citizens, and courts and legislatures alike give great deference to those rights. However, the protections are not absolute.

Constitutional privileges may not always trump valid interests in protecting animals from cruelty—although they may tip the balance a bit more in favor of the constitutional rights granted. Nor does the absence of a constitutional animal protection provision eliminate the possibility of a challenge to forms of animal cruelty that are arguably protected by law. The case of *Church of the Lukumi Babalu Aye, Inc. v. City of Hialeah*[41] highlights the potential conflicts.

In the *Lukumi Babalu Aye* case, the city of Hialeah, in the state of Florida, enacted a series of local ordinances directed at preventing local practitioners of the Santeria religion from engaging in ritual animal sacrifice and related practices that were central to their religion. The local Santeria church sued the city, claiming the ordinances impermissibly restricted their religious freedom rights under the First Amendment. One of the reasons the city gave for the ordinances was its policy against animal cruelty, which was also embodied in the state anti-cruelty statutes and local regulations. These laws prohibited, among other things, "unjustified" acts of animal cruelty.

The case went to America's highest court, but the United States Supreme Court did not rule directly on the clash between the importance of preventing animal cruelty and the right to religious freedom. The Supreme Court instead found that the city had violated the Constitution when it directly and selectively targeted the Santerians' rights and discriminated against them because of their religion. Because of this direct attack on their rights to the free exercise of their religion, the conflict with the cruelty laws was not of central importance in the case. The analysis might have been different if two different express constitutional rights were at issue, or even if there had not been a blatant violation of the Santerians' interests.

This possibility was raised by one of the concurring justices, who suggested that if the facts of the case had presented a simple conflict between the general animal cruelty statutes and the First Amendment, that might have led to a different opinion.[42] That is, if the City of Hialeah had not enacted any special ordinances targeting the Santeria religion, but only argued that the Santeria practices violated the anticruelty laws, the church's challenge might have failed. Because that was not the factual setting before the Court, this question remains unresolved.

The *Lukumi Babalu Aye* case presents one example of a clash between general constitutional rights and anticruelty laws, and many other possibilities certainly exist. For example, most constitutions provide citizens with a right to own and use property—including a grant of privilege to exploit that property for profit, and to dispose of the property as the owner sees fit. This right could easily impact both constitutional and statutory protections given to animals, if the two were in conflict.

The property right is one of the oldest and most important in a market system, and so it would (and does) usually trump the interests of animals, even in a society with a public policy towards humane treatment of animals. But there are exceptions. In any country where cruelty to animals is prohibited, owners' property rights may be somewhat limited with respect to *some* animals, because the owners' rights to use/abuse their property are limited by such laws. These restrictions on animal property owners' rights, however, are usually limited to significant mistreatment, while still allowing owners relative freedom in how they treat their property.[43] One example is the relatively unfettered right to have one's animal killed, as long as certain parameters are followed. The act of killing avoids the "cruelty" label based on the method used. And when it comes to farmed animals used for food or clothing, or research animals used in cosmetics and biomedical research, most countries and states exempt practices that would otherwise be cruel from coverage under the anticruelty statutes.[44]

Individual States—Florida

As mentioned above, each U.S. state has its own constitution, which is the governing document for the state, subject and subordinate to federal laws and the federal Constitution. And in recent years, some American states have enacted constitutional provisions directly addressing the use of animals by humans. In 2002, Florida voters approved a constitutional amendment that "limit[s] the cruel and inhumane confinement of pigs during pregnancy" by prohibiting intensive and extreme confinement of pregnant sows.[45] The law was mainly directed at eliminating the use of "gestation crates" or "sow stalls"—a common industry practice used by commercial enterprises manufacturing pigs for meat.[46]

The Florida amendment makes it illegal "to confine a pig during pregnancy in an enclosure, or to tether a pig during pregnancy, on a farm in such a way that she is prevented from turning around freely."[47] The restriction on human behavior or, conversely, the "right" granted to animals, is very limited. Still, the Florida amendment is a rare type of constitutional provision in that it focuses on a very specific practice. This kind of constitutional declaration is seldom seen with respect to conduct related to humans, and is especially notable given that it does focus on treatment of animals. The restriction even goes so far as to limit its scope to a particular species, even though extreme confinement techniques are utilized with many other species in industrial farming practices, especially cows and chickens.

The Florida amendment also reads more like a criminal law than a constitutional amendment in that it provides for a specific penalty for its violation. Both the potential fine and time of incarceration are set out in the text—virtually unheard of in other American constitutional contexts. In contrast, constitutional violations not involving animals are usually enforced by civil actions in which an injured person (typically the person whose rights are violated) sues the person or governmental entity that has violated the complainant's rights. Here again the atypical circumstance of a constitutional prohibition/protection involving animals required some creative drafting of the amendment by those involved, in order to ensure it was not an ineffective and unenforceable law. Because there may not be a particular individual whose rights would be impaired or who would be legally injured by a violation of the provision, some other consideration needed to be made. To meet this dilemma, the gestation crate amendment provides its remedies in the constitution itself, with state authorities as the intended enforcers. Given the nature of the penalty, the injury for violation can be seen as one suffered by all citizens, or the collective State—an interesting concept with respect to a restriction on what is a common industry practice across the United States and the world.

A final oddity of the Florida amendment—as far as constitutional provisions go—is its "phase-in period" for compliance. The legal prohibition did not actually take effect until its compliance date, which was six years after the time of adoption of the amendment in 2002. That is, while the Florida voters approved the change in the constitution in November 2002, and while the assumption on that day was that gestation crates and other tethering were illegal and constitutionally impermissible, the law was created with a six-year delay. The obvious reason for the delay was to allow time for a change in practices for farmers using illegal confinement and tethering methods at the time of the amendment's adoption.[48] The Florida "phase-out period" illustrates a mechanism seen in legislation directed at ending an existing and long-term practice. The agreement to delay the application of a new prohibition provides a valuable compromise position for those advocating for the law. But the idea of giving some time until a practice is finally banned is a concept at odds with most constitutional protections, which are deemed effective upon adoption.[49] The use of phase-out periods in this type of legislation another good demonstration of (1) the variations necessary with laws involving animals and (2) the recognition by animal protection groups that advance this type of legislation, that consideration and cooperation is an important part of the process of change.

Other State Provisions

A number of other American states now have constitutional provisions that protect certain uses of animals, including hunting. The enactments are intended to prevent challenges to these practices by animal welfare groups. For these laws there is generally no phase-in period because they are simply preserving the *status quo*. By way of example, in Alabama, the "Sportsperson's Bill of Rights" guarantees all citizens the "right to hunt and fish."[50] In Oklahoma, "[a]ll citizens ... have a right to hunt, fish, trap, and harvest game and fish, subject only to reasonable regulation...."[51] California and Rhode Island grant their citizens the constitutional right to *fish*, but not hunt.[52]

As discussed in the introductory section, these provisions cloak this form of animal use with an approval by the state that will make it much harder for its opponents to challenge. A related effort by special interest groups is the establishment of a constitutional minimum percentage of the legislature (or populace) required to change laws on animal-related issues such as recreational or commercial activities. Such provisions are known as "supermajority" requirements because they set the required voting "majority" at something greater than a simple majority, which is strictly more than fifty percent. If adopted, this type of law limits the potential for change in the area it covers.

One example of such a provision was passed in Utah in 1998. Article VI, Section 1(2)(a)(ii) of the Utah Constitution states, in pertinent part, that "legislation initiated to allow, limit, or prohibit the taking of wildlife or the season for or method of taking wildlife shall be adopted upon approval of two-thirds of those voting."[53] In short, it requires a supermajority for any law that might impact hunting interests. A legal challenge to this provision, based on its effect on a specific type of speech (that of those opposed to hunting), was rejected.[54] The motivation for the law, as well as the potential effect on the ability to change animal-related practices, is clear. In an area that is already controversial and in which moneyed interests often oppose nonprofit groups, the likelihood of legislative change will be correspondingly reduced.

Constitutional authority is being recognized by both sides in the animal welfare wars as a powerful means of protecting one's interests. A rather unique example of the use of that power was seen in the state of Ohio in 2009.[55] Farming interests lobbied for and got legislative support for an amendment to the Ohio constitution which established the Ohio Livestock Standards Board as a constitutional body.[56] "Issue 2"—the law establishing the Board—was approved by both houses of the Ohio legislature and the governor over a short period in June and July, and put to a vote for the public in November 2009. It passed with over sixty-three percent of the vote.[57] The Board established by Issue 2 was given the task of establishing standards for animals involved in food production around the state. The Board is mandated to consider "agricultural best management practices for care and well-being, biosecurity, disease prevention, animal morbidity and mortality data, food safety practices, and the protection of local, affordable food supplies for consumers."[58] It was made up of thirteen individuals, with the majority having direct connections with the commercial use of animals for food production.[59] At least one commentator suggested that Issue 2 was the farming industry's response to planned activity by animal protection groups that intended to advocate for a limitation on intensive confinement practices.[60] The agricultural industry's interest in the Board is likely based on the Boards's ability to give a seal of approval to common industry practices currently under attack.

The polarized positions of Issue 2's sponsors and the immediate response from its opponents provides a good epilogue and summary for the ideas expressed in this chapter. Issue 2's supporters, largely from the farming industry, claimed that the creation of the Board would allow an expert body to opine on important issues of animal care and welfare. The Issue's opponents criticized it as an attempt by the agriculture industry to establish a stronghold in Ohio government and to block attempts by animal protection groups to increase animal welfare. An important central point was that by making the Board a matter of Ohio constitutional law, it took on increased significance and power. Clearly the presence of the Board as an established entity within the constitution was a significant matter, highlighting the point made throughout this chapter about the value of constitutional inclusion of animal issues. In virtually every other similar situation, such boards would be formalized within some governmental department or agency, and be run within that agency.

In the wake of Issue 2's passage, the Humane Society of the United States and other animal protection groups mounted a campaign to have their own constitutional amendment to Issue 2.[61] The publicly-supported ballot initiative would have been placed on the Ohio ballot for 2010, and would have mandated the Board established by Issue 2 to enact rules that made several standard farming practices crimes (misdemeanors) under state law. In June 2010, faced with the threat of an expensive campaign that would expose the nature of many of these practices, the state of Ohio and farm interests agreed to a compromise which would ultimately require significant changes in practice for farmers.[62] The Ohio experience was certainly the first major constitutional battle over animal welfare, and may indicate a process that could be repeated in the United States and around the world, using the different political strategies and procedures available in other countries.

Notes

1. Each level of government also has rules regarding the operation of its "business," guidelines for its officials, and governing principles.

2. *See, e.g.*, U.S. Const., art. VI, cl. 2; *Cipollone v. Liggett Group, Inc.*, 505 U.S. 504, 516 (1992).

3. *See, e.g.*, G. Brinton Lucas, *Structural Exceptionalism and Comparative Constitutional Law*, 96 Va. L. Rev. 1965, 1988–89 (Dec. 2010) ("The unwritten constitution with which American colonists were most familiar was the English Constitution, a combination of ancient custom, revered documents, and common law.").

4. Ernest A. Young, *The Constitution Outside the Constitution*, 117 Yale L. J. 408, 410 (Dec. 2007).

5. *Id.*

6. *See, e.g.*, Joel Colón-Ríos, *The Legitimacy of the Juridical: Constituent Power, Democracy, and the Limits of Constitutional Reform*, 48 Osgoode Hall L.J. 199, 234–35 (Summer 2010) (discussing rigid and flexible constitutions).

7. *See, e.g.*, Vijayashri Sripati, *Constitutionalism in India and South Africa: A Comparative Study from a Human Rights Perspective*, 16 Tul. J. Int'l & Comp. L. 49 (2007) ("While the Indian Constitution was conceived and drafted before the adoption in 1948 of the Universal Declaration of Human Rights (UDHR), the South African Constitution was adopted in 1996, at the peak of the modern international human rights movement. The Indian Constitution was forged by an elitist process whereas the South African constitution was the product of a sharply participatory process.").

8. U.S. Const. amend. XVIII (repealed 1933); U.S. Const. amend. XIII.

9. Paul Enriquez, *Deconstructing Transnationalism: Conceptualizing Metanationalism as a Putative Model of Evolving Jurisprudence*, 43 Vand. J. Transnat'l L. 1265, 1312 (Nov. 2010).

10. *Id.* at 1312–13.

11. *Id.*

12. *See also* Article 48A, "Protection and improvement of environment and safeguarding of forests and wildlife," which reads: "The State shall endeavor to protect and improve the environment and to safeguard the forests and wildlife of the country." This directive is almost a parallel mandate to the government, similar to that of Article 51A, which is directed at individuals.

13. *See generally* Maneka Gandhi, Ozair Husain & Raj Panjwani, Animal Laws of India 253 (3rd ed. 2006).

14. Writ Petition No. 347 of 1996. High Court of Judicature at Bombay, Panaji Bench.

15. *See* footnote 21 of the opinion for the court's description of the activities involved in bull fights. Based on that description the court concluded: "Considering these facts, we wonder, how anybody can say that there is no cruelty involved in conducting bull fights."

16. *Id.*

17. *Id.*

18. *Id.*

19. Andhra Pradesh High Court, Hon'ble Mr. Ramanujulu Naidu, J. Writ Petition No. 4414 of 1987 (Decided May 12, 1989).

20. *Id.*

21. Wildlife Law: A Global Perspective (Raj Panjwani ed., 2008). *See also* Gandhi *et al.*, *supra* note 13, at 115. Article 48A mandates the protection of wild life.

22. *Id.* at 116, citing *Nair v. Union of India*, (Kerala H.C. June 6, 2000) No. 155/1999.), 2000 Kerala 340, 351–52.

23. *Id.*

24. *Balakrishnan v. Union of India* (2000), *available at* http://www.elaw.org/ node/1831.

25. *Id.*

26. *Id.*

27. *Mohd. Habib v. State of Uttar Pradesh*, Civil Misc. Writ Petition No. 38469 of 1994 (Decided on 1st Aug. 1997), in Gandhi *et al.*, *supra* note 13.

28. *Id.*

29. *Id.*

30. *Id.*

31. Grundgesetz fur die Bundersrepublik Deutschland (Basic Law) preamble, *available at* http://www.iuscomp.org/gla/statutes/GG.htm#Preamble.

32. *See generally*, Claudia Haupt, "Assessing the German Constitution's Animal Protection Clause" (May 29, 2008) (paper presented at the annual meeting of the Law and Society Association, Hilton Bonaventure, Montreal, Quebec, Canada), *available at* http://www.allacademic.com/meta/p230025_index.html.

33. Grundgesetz art. 20A.

34. Claudia Haupt, *Free Exercise of Religion and Animal Protection: A Comparative Perspective on Ritual Slaughter*, 39 Geo. Wash. Int'l L. Rev 839 (2007).

35. Grundgesetz art. 5 (freedom of speech and expression).

36. Grundgesetz art. 12 (right to choose one's occupation).

37. Consider this situation described on one website, referencing an Austrian well-known for his depictions of crucifixions and scenes of violence:

In July 1998, Austrian artist Hermann Nitsch stage-managed a macabre public slaughter and disemboweling in the name of art. This offensive event was held in a castle in southern Austria, and involved naked participants gyrating in animal entrails and drinking their blood. As freedom of artistic expression is included in the Austrian constitution, the authorities would not consider any interference with this constitutional right.

See Animal Protection and Constitutions, World Animal Net, *available at* http://www.worldanimal.net/component/content/article/14-constitution-project/53-animal-protection-and-constitutions.

38. Kate Nattrass, "*... und die Tiere.*" *Constitutional Protection for Germany's Animals*, 10 Animal L. 301 (2004).

39. *Id.*

40. Claudia Haupt, *supra* note 34, at 871.

41. 508 U.S. 520 (1993).

42. 508 U.S. at 597 (Blackmun, J., concurring) ("A harder case would be presented if petitioners were requesting an exemption from a generally applicable anticruelty law. The result in the case before the Court today, and the fact that every Member of the Court concurs in that result, does not necessarily reflect this Court's views of the strength of a State's interest in prohibiting cruelty to animals. This case does not present, and I therefore decline to reach, the question whether the Free Exercise Clause would require a religious exemption from a law that sincerely pursued the goal of protecting animals from cruel treatment.... [T]hat it is not a concern to be treated lightly.").

43. As discussed elsewhere in this text, in many jurisdictions statutory exemptions to cruelty laws mean that standard practices are exempt from coverage under those laws, converting factually cruel conduct into legal treatment. These practices often include virtually any agricultural practice in industrial farming operations involving tens of thousands of animals, as well as biomedical research protocols and experiments.

44. Bruce Wagman, Sonja Waisman & Pamela Frasch, Animal Law: Cases and Materials 92–93, 421–23 (4th ed. 2010).

45. Fla. Const., art. X, § 21.

46. *Id. See* Chapter 2 for further discussion of gestation crates and laws affecting them.

47. *Id.*

48. *Id.*

49. Some constitutional enactments are even applied retroactively to past practices or pending actions involving conduct affected by the amendment.

50. Ala. Const., art. 1, § 36.02.

51. Okla. Const., art. 2, § 36. *See also* Va. Const., art. 11, § 4; Wis. Const., art. 1, § 26; Vt. Const., Chapter 2, part 67, 1777.

52. Cal. Const., art. 1, § 25, 1910; R.I. Const., art. 1, § 17, 1844.

53. Utah Const., art. VI, § 1(2)(a)(ii).

54. *Initiative and Referendum Inst. v. Walker*, 450 F.3d 1082 (10th Cir. 2006) (en banc). One commentator suggests that supermajority requirements may still be subject to challenges under the Equal Protection Clause of the United States Constitution. *See* E. Maher, Comment, *When a Majority Does Not Rule: How Supermajority Requirements On Voter Initiatives Distort Elections and Deny Equal Protection*, 15 Geo. Mason L. Rev. 1081 (2008).

55. E. Springsteen, *A Proposal to Regulate Farm Animal Confinement in the United States and an Overview of Current and Proposed Laws on the Subject*, 14 Drake J. Agric. L. 437, 455–57 (Fall 2009).

56. Ohio Const., art. XIV, § 1(A).

57. Springsteen, *supra* note 55, at 456 n.164.

58. Ohio Const., art. XIV, § 1(B).

59. Springsteen, *supra* note 55, 456 n.165.

60. *Id.* at 455 n.162.

61. *Seeking Common Sense Farm Measure in Ohio,* Humane Society of the United States (May 25, 2010), *available at* http://www.humanesociety.org/news/news/2010/03/ohio_farm_ballot_032510.html.

62. *Landmark Ohio Animal Welfare Agreement Reached Among HSUS, Ohioans for Humane Farms, Gov. Strickland, and Leading Livestock Organizations* (June 30, 2010), HSUS, *available at* http://www.humanesociety.org/news/press_releases/2010/06/landmark_ohio_agreement_063010.html.

CHAPTER 6

INTERNATIONAL LAW

Introduction

This chapter focuses on international agreements entered into between two or more countries, where those agreements either intentionally or indirectly affect animal welfare. This chapter focuses on truly "international animal *law*," because it addresses mutual concerns and binding legal agreements among multiple nations. The issues raised in the chapter are simultaneously broader and narrower than many of those addressed elsewhere in the text. The chapter's scope is broader because, whereas other chapters focus on the domestic laws of individual nations that mainly impact only the citizens of those countries, this chapter looks globally at transnational and transcultural considerations that arise in multinational agreements and how the needs of animals are either balanced or ignored, in contrast with the needs (or perceived needs) of governments and people. At the same time, the focus is narrower in that these agreements are generally limited to species of particular concern whose very existence is at risk. That is, concerns about extirpation and extinction inform and permeate the majority of these agreements. The focus is on endangered animals in the debates of the delegates who draft these international compacts and the minds of those who address the controversies and questions that these agreements raise. Animal welfare and issues of humane treatment often may not come into play, as you will see, but largely the focus is on animals who could disappear from the planet if human exploitation or use of their habitats is not controlled.

Treaties designed to protect animals have existed for more than a century. Although even the earliest animal treaties made explicit reference to animal welfare, they were primarily concerned with facilitating human use of animals, not with protecting animals for their own sake.[1] The historical tension between protection and economic exploitation continues to this day. The controversies that arise over the treaties discussed in this chapter have both a market analysis component and an animal welfare consideration. While these issues are not necessarily mutually exclusive, the main tensions come between those interested in providing outright protection to animals and those more concerned with the value of animals to the marketplace and the effects that protection of a species may have on the economy in their countries.

Because countries often hold extremely disparate, even diametrically opposed, views with respect to any given species, analyzing these treaties and agreements is an excellent tool to contrast and compare competing views of the role and value of animals in human societies. Such analysis also exposes how scientific views may vary; and how sentiments about certain species may be different from country to country. This difference is a central theme of this book and the construction of a worldview of animal law. These disparities also create interesting challenges for the decision makers and member states who vote on the issues.

At their cores, both the open discussions and the unspoken assumptions that lead to the development of these pacts map the contours of a global approach to animals and the law. They demonstrate the important values at stake and expose the political and social underpinnings that come into play when advocates raise questions beyond purely economic or anthropocentric concerns. The international discussion that takes place in the formation and revision of these agreements pointedly and constantly challenges the world's commitment, or lack thereof, to factoring the interests of animals into its considerations of policy.

The documents, pacts, and agreements discussed here were developed over long processes, involving extended meetings and reviews, and usually refined over many years. They were ultimately created through negotiations between non-governmental organizations and representatives of multiple nations, each with its own unique set of circumstances and its own particular relationship with the animals at issue. The agreements—with varying degrees of success—control and determine behavior both within a given country and internationally. While the agreements do not always carry the absolute force of law to the citizens of participating countries, there exist various mechanisms of ensuring compliance. International agreements may directly or indirectly affect legislative change in the participant countries because member nations follow up treaty adoption by implementing domestic legislation to carry out the terms of the agreement. These agreements also provide a certain amount of oversight and awareness from the global community on domestic conduct that would otherwise not be available at all.

As with each of our chapters, we seek here to highlight some of the most valuable, controversial, and challenging agreements, to provide readers with food for thought and ideas for continuing the progression towards an international consensus on the treatment of animals. The treaties vary in style, effect, intent, and of course coverage. It is not our intention to cover the entire field. Our focus is to provide illustrations of the variety of protections accorded, in order to develop an understanding of the possibilities for animals around the world. The representative sample we have chosen also demonstrates many of the difficulties that animal protectionists may encounter in trying to use treaties to help animals.

The chapter presents three major treaties, with three different foci. First, we discuss perhaps the most well-known, and one that covers a multitude of species—the Convention on International Trade in Endangered Species of Wild Fauna and Flora (CITES), which protects a multitude of species from the negative impacts of the wildlife trade. It is anthropocentric and resource-oriented. It specifically and intentionally impacts the animals within its range, and is flexible with respect to which species it governs. Next, because many trade agreements have significant impacts on animals across international boundaries, we discuss the World Trade Organization (WTO) and its agreements. This section is also presented as a contrast, since the WTO does not directly address animals, but affects them greatly. It is offered to demonstrate some basic concerns about the potential negative impact of international trade regulation on animal welfare. Finally, we discuss the International Convention for the Regulation of Whaling (ICRW), as an example of a treaty that is focused on a particular species or group of animals.

International Law[2]

One must distinguish initially between national (also called "domestic") law and international law. National law is the body of laws adopted by a country to govern its own citizens. Disputes over national law may be settled definitively by the courts of that nation, or changed by its legislature, and the state may compel compliance with the law through prisons, fines, and other coercive mechanisms.

International law, on the other hand, is much less precise—harder to enforce and wider in scope. There exists no effective international adjudicator with universal jurisdiction to settle every dispute over the meaning of international law.[3] Nevertheless, most participants in international law agreements also concede the governance of a central body that is entitled to control the actions of an agreement's member countries and, indirectly, that of individual citizens within those countries. Additionally, the spirit of much international law is carried out by the force of domestic laws enacted in connection with international treaties, as well as the power of economic incentives for trade.

International law generally derives from multiple sources, including agreements and legal customs, and opinions of individual countries' courts.[4] One important source is a set of principles known as *jus cogens*, or "peremptory norms." These doctrines, though they are not codified or formally expressed, have a strong effect on law, society, policy, and politics. The Latin term *jus cogens* means "compelling law" and consists of those notions that are "accepted and recognized by the international community of States as a whole as norm[s] from which no derogation is permitted."[5] In other words, these are proscriptive rules against conduct that few, if any, societies currently condone, and that all or most roundly condemn. For example, the use of torture (of humans) is generally disapproved in modern society.[6] The deliberate infliction of severe pain on a member of the community of equals, either wantonly or for an alleged benefit to others, is regarded as torture and is universally condemned, at least publicly. Other examples of conduct that are generally considered inherently wrong include (human) slavery, genocide, and apartheid. There is a public condemnation of these practices in contemporary law even though such acts may have once been permitted, and despite the fact that they may continue to occur behind closed doors.[7] Once discovered, such conduct is criticized by international society. Under international human rights law, these prohibitions are *jus cogens* principles. No country may derogate the bar set by *jus cogens* principles, and no international agreement can validly preempt it. A nation is bound by *jus cogens* standards (by the international community at least) even if it does not consent to their application.

There have been no universal historical or customary legal protections for animals, and there are likewise no *jus cogens* principles or customary norms that protect animals.[8] Any international protection or attention that animal welfare receives derives from the other sources of domestic or international law, such as those listed above or discussed throughout the text.

We begin, then, with a discussion of how international agreements designed to protect animals can bind member nations. Unlike domestic laws, treaties are not drafted and debated in the first instance by the national legislators who (at least ostensibly) represent the people of their country; rather, they are negotiated by appointed delegates from each country. These representatives do of course represent their citizens, but at a more distant regard than elected officials. Once an agreement is adopted by the international representatives, each country's legislature must ratify the treaty if it is to have any effect on the particular nation's law and citizenry.

Whether a treaty becomes domestic law immediately upon ratification depends on the specific government in each country. In "dualist" jurisdictions, such as the United Kingdom, the nation's legislative body must enact implementing legislation to make the treaty part of its domestic law. The system is dualist because national law is viewed as wholly separate from and independent of international law. By contrast, in countries such as the United States, once a treaty is ratified, it takes precedence over national laws. Such systems are termed "monist," because they see the law as singular and permit no conflict between domestic laws and those international laws to which the nation has assented.[9]

It is helpful to appreciate, with respect to each treaty and agreement, how and why international laws obtain their authority within a country.[10] Even though the procedural mechanisms of law may be the same, the reasons and interests served in each case may be different. For example, a country's willingness to enter into international trade pacts is likely related to its self-interest and how the issues at hand may affect its economy, as well as whatever political benefits it may gain from concession, compromise, and cooperation on issues that matter to other nations. The consequences of not being involved must also be considered: noncooperation may subject a nation to trade embargoes and boycotts, the impact of which can be of great significance domestically and in the world community.

International agreements need to have a common goal or incentive—some might say a mutually shared threat—to make parties adhere to (and enforce) their proscriptions. Similarly, countries may be more likely to comply with agreements in which they feel vested and that they regard as legitimate, as opposed to ones that they perceive as external and coerced.

One cannot overestimate the possible benefits—and harms—to animals from the adoption of these agreements, even those that do not directly address animals. The remainder of this chapter analyzes these benefits and harms in the context of three international agreements: CITES, the WTO, and the ICRW.

The Convention on International Trade in Endangered Species of Wild Fauna and Flora[11]

CITES (pronounced \sī-tēz\) is an international compact focused on the protection of plant and animal species that are in danger of depredation or extinction. It works by mutual agreement of its 175 member nations,[12] who submit to regulation and/or prohibition of international trade in the identified species. CITES protects more than 33,000 species of plants and animals.[13] Its coverage of threatened species has domestic parallels in many countries, such as the Endangered Species Act (ESA)[14] in the United States and the Environment Protection and Biodiversity Conservation Act (EPBC Act) in Australia. These laws all encourage and establish protection of threatened and endangered species through various means, including trade regulation and habitat protection.

Historical and Legal Background

CITES was adopted in the early 1970s. At that time national governments were just beginning to realize what environmentalists had been arguing for decades: that the for-profit trade of certain animals and plants posed major threats to conservation and had brought or were bringing many species to the brink of extinction. Prior to the creation of CITES in 1973, international regulation of the wildlife trade had not focused on the conservation of endangered species, but instead on basic economic issues such as tariffs on trade.

CITES originated as a concept of the International Union for the Conservation of Nature and Natural Resources (IUCN), which was founded in 1948 as an international organization dedicated to conserving natural resources.[15] At the 1963 IUCN General Assembly in Nairobi, Kenya, the IUCN's members expressed concern about the damage to plant and animal species resulting from exploitative international trade. The IUCN decided that an international convention dealing with the trade of rare and endangered wildlife species was needed.[16] IUCN's legal team then prepared and presented drafts of the convention (agreement) to governments and nongovernmental agencies.[17] This early work eventually formed the basis for CITES, which was adopted in Washington, D.C. in March 1973.[18]

The document that came out of the Washington meeting reflects a significant shift in international animal and environmental law. For the first time, international leaders acted as a cohesive group in this area. And for the first time international law recognized extinction as a problem that needed to be addressed, and as a threat to the global commons. CITES' preamble signals this shift in global consciousness by stating that "wild fauna and flora in their many beautiful and varied forms are an irreplaceable part of the natural systems of the earth."[19] The "fundamental principles" of CITES outline its signatory countries' intention to regulate or prohibit trade in "all species threatened with extinction which are or may be affected by trade."[20]

CITES was founded on the notion "that international co-operation is essential for the protection of certain species of wild fauna and flora against overexploitation through international trade."[21] One of the greatest threats to wild animals around the world the international wildlife trade, which is worth billions of dollars. Combined with habitat loss and other external factors, the business of capturing and killing animals and transporting them internationally is a major contributor to the endangerment and extinction of species. Recognizing that it might be possible to slow these processes, the apparent view of CITES' founders was that only through international collaboration does the global community stand a chance of staving off the loss of far more species than would otherwise disappear naturally.

Against this backdrop of concern about human-caused extinction, the drafters of CITES established a framework to abolish the trade of certain endangered species and to limit the negative effects of trade in other species that are not yet in grave threat of extinction, but that are close to that point, according to population scientists.[22] To ensure the protection of these species, CITES lists wildlife in three separate appendices. Each succeeding level signifies a greater level of protection, and the appendix a given species enters is based on how serious the threats are to the species' survival. These appendices are thus tiered to reflect the varying strictness of controls on trade in the species: the more threatened a species is, the greater the controls on its use in international trade. Typically, an entire species will be listed, although in some cases only a single sub-species or geographical distribution of a larger species is listed for protection.

Appendix I species, such as the chimpanzee, the giant panda, and the tiger, are given the highest level of protection because they are the closest to extinction, based on current scientific data. Trade in Appendix I species is "subject to particularly strict regulation in order not to endanger further their survival and must only be authorized in exceptional circumstances."[23] Appendix II species, such as the hippopotamus, the American crocodile, and the green conure (a type of parrot), are those species that might be threatened with extirpation without "strict regulation in order to avoid utilization incompatible with their survival."[24] Species placed in Appendix III, such as the Dorcas gazelle, the walrus, and the king vulture, are those species that are not necessarily threatened in a population dynamics sense, but that a member nation already regulates domestically, and that the country believes can only be protected if other CITES countries also provide some protection in order to prevent detrimental trade practices.[25] Appendix III regulation, to the extent it is effective and enforced, demonstrates the collaborative nature of international agreements, even in the absence of a compelling scientific warning.

As of 2009, there were 892 species, 39 subspecies, and 22 geographically-isolated populations (within a given species) listed in Appendix I, including plants and animals.[26] The animal groups number 597 species, 36 subspecies and 22 populations.[27] Trade in wild-caught "specimens" of Appendix I species is strictly prohibited except in limited circumstances which require licensing and certification. CITES establishes permit requirements for both the country from which an animal is exported as well as the country into which s/he is imported. A country may issue an export permit only if it finds that the export

> will not be detrimental to the survival of that species; ... that the specimen was not obtained in contravention of the laws of that State for the protection of fauna and flora; ... that any living specimen will be

> so prepared and shipped as to minimize the risk of injury, damage to health[,] or cruel treatment; and ... that an import permit has been granted.[28]

On the receiving side, the importing country may not permit the importation unless it finds "that the import will be for purposes [that] are not detrimental to the survival of the species involved; ... that the proposed recipient of a living specimen is suitably equipped to house and care for [him or her]; and ... that the specimen is not to be used for primarily commercial purposes."[29]

If any one of these conditions is not met, the international transport is prohibited as a matter of international and domestic law. For example, in one American case, a zoo obtained a CITES import permit from the federal government for two giant pandas from China. A wildlife conservation organization challenged the permit, contending that the zoo was profiting from the pandas by charging an extra admission fee for the exhibit. An U.S. court agreed, holding that the permit was improperly granted because the added fee demonstrated that the importation was "for primarily commercial purposes."[30]

As this case makes clear, when CITES is followed, it provides strict limitations on the international transfer of Appendix I species, and the laws of the participating nations will govern and compel the activities of their citizens to ensure compliance. By prohibiting commercial transfers, CITES bans the legal for-profit wildlife trade for those species that are at the highest risk of extinction. Wild-born specimens of Appendix I species may not, under any circumstances, be imported to be sold in pet stores, ridden at carnivals, or hunted at game preserves. These protections do not apply, however, to those animals who have been bred in captivity: trade in captive-bred members of Appendix I species is governed by the rules applicable to Appendix II species.[31]

Appendix II covers those captive-bred animals just mentioned, as well as species that are not currently threatened with extinction, but that still need protection to prevent them from getting to that endangered status.[32] Appendix II also contains some species that, although not threatened, may have a similar appearance to threatened and endangered species. These "lucky" species are therefore protected in order to prevent accidental killing of the protected species. As of 2009, 33,033 species, as well as 26 subspecies and 19 specific populations, have been listed in Appendix II; 4,359 of these species are animals. The vast majority of species that CITES protects are Appendix II species.

As with Appendix I species, CITES establishes a permitting requirement for international transfers of Appendix II species, albeit a less stringent one. International trade in Appendix II species is allowed with an export permit, but no import permit is required. The country from which the animal is being exported must, prior to granting an export permit, make the same findings required for an Appendix I species, except for the finding that an import permit has been granted. In other words, Appendix II species may be transferred only if the exporting country finds (1) the import will not negatively impact species survival; (2) the animal was obtained legally; and (3) the risk of harm during transport has been minimized.[33] Because no import permit is required, there is no inquiry into whether the importation is for primarily commercial purposes. The most significant difference, then, between Appendix I and Appendix II species is that the latter may be traded for profit, whereas the former may not be. As a consequence, animals listed as Appendix II species are still traded in international commerce on a regular basis.

Appendix III includes non-threatened species that still can benefit from restrictions on trade. It covers all species identified "as being subject to regulation within [a Party's] jurisdiction for the purpose of preventing or restricting exploitation, and as needing the co-operation of other Parties in the control of trade."[34] In 2010, there were 152 animal species and 8 animal subspecies listed in Appendix III.[35] An Appendix III listing can be made unilaterally after one member country asserts that it needs the cooperation of other CITES parties in controlling trade in a species about which the initiating party has concern. Appendix III species are not usually threatened with extinction globally, but the member countries have the right to designate these species based on their enrollment in CITES.[36]

For species listed in Appendix III, trade is permitted only with an export permit from the listing country and a certificate of origin. The findings required for an export permit overlap with those required for Appendix I and Appendix II species: the specimen cannot have been obtained illegally and the shipment must minimize injury and cruel treatment.[37] There is no required showing that the export will not negatively impact species survival; the CITES presumption is that the exporting country is sufficiently concerned, given its listing, to allow it to monitor this issue. And the export/import of these species may be done for profit and commercial purposes at the determination of the exporting country.

Various countries have utilized the Appendix III listing option. For example, Costa Rica listed Hoffmann's Two-toed Sloth and Deppe's Squirrel, while Guatemala identified the Northern Tamandua Anteater and the Double-striped Thick-knee (a species of bird in the Wader family). India has listed several marmot species and six species of mongoose. In 2006, the United States obtained a listing for the alligator snapping turtle. The turtle exists only in the waters of the southern United States. Since the Appendix III listing limits exportation from the United States, and the U.S. gets to regulate all export in this species, the Appendix III designation provides the turtle significant protection.

CITES requires some consideration of animal welfare issues. CITES members must "ensure ... that all living specimens, during any period of transit, holding or shipment, are properly cared for so as to minimize the risk of injury, damage to health or cruel treatment."[38] In other words, all animals, regardless of which Appendix they are listed in, must be treated and transported in a humane fashion if CITES is followed. This is a significant aspect of CITES—if followed—as it acknowledges the sentence of the subjects of the law.

All members are invited to discuss changes to or issues regarding these appendix listings and other CITES business at the Convention of the Parties, which is the CITES regular meeting that occurs every two to three years.[39] Two–thirds of the Parties must approve the additions of any species to one of the Appendices, or the removal from any of the protected lists, or transfers between Appendices.[40] Each Party has one vote. At the meetings, the Parties also propose, debate, and vote on new procedures, resolutions, and decisions—both procedural and substantive, related to governance as well as specific rules of practice under the agreement.

CITES' governing body also issues periodic reports, sanctions, and restrictions. For example, as part of the CITES contract, the Parties are required to submit documentation on ongoing projects and evaluations of animals listed in the Appendices.[41] The governing body will collect this information for its publications, and make determinations on party status and conduct. If a Party does not comply with deadlines established by the governing body, it may be sanctioned by the CITES Secretariat, which is empowered to issue recommendations to suspend trade with noncompliant parties.[42] These notifications, along with notice of other programs of interest, are posted to the CITES website regularly. Matters of significance unrelated to listings require a two-thirds majority, while less significant decisions require only a simple majority.[43]

Nongovernmental organizations (NGOs) often attend the Convention, but they have no votes and can only participate as observers and informal lobbyists. The NGOs are an important check on the activities of CITES representatives, as they are able to report back to the populace and often present factual and scientific data to the Parties that may not otherwise be made available. They operate in a watchdog/oversight and lobbying capacity, and often are a vital information source for the world regarding how individual Parties voted, and the Convention's decision-making process. (Sometimes votes are not public, in which case the NGOs are unable to ascertain this news.) The right to observe provides NGOs with valuable access to key facts and, in the best circumstances, permits them to serve as influential moral watchdogs for Parties voting on issues of public concern.

CITES in Practice

Many practical and political questions are raised by the work the Convention does. Obviously, the identification and determination of which species get listed in which Appendix generates significant controversy. The decision of which animals are listed, and in which Appendix, is of vital importance to ultimate species survival as well as the treatment of individual animals. Even after listing, individual animals are subject to case-by-case determinations on the issuance of export and import permits. The listing process generates great controversy, with conflicting interests battling over the ultimate decisions. A government's decision on permits may also eventually affect species survival. Some examples of the issues that arise are addressed here.

One vital issue, determinative of CITES' effectiveness, is CITES membership. The countries that decide to become members obviously define CITES' scope and its ability to protect endangered species. Without membership there is no control; the threat of injury even to the species the Convention seeks to protect is naturally limited if its members do not include countries in which those species have significant populations.

As of 2010, 175 countries were parties to CITES. The large nations of the world play a major role in CITES governance, but participation by the entire international community is necessary in order to provide the best web of protection for species in danger. Some countries may be especially important to CITES' success because of the high number of threatened species within their borders and the correspondingly high involvement of their citizens in illegal trade.

By one estimate, Southeast Asian countries are responsible for as much as twenty-five percent of the world's total illegal sales of animals.[44] The Southeast Asian illegal trade in wildlife is in part a product of the rising levels of affluence in China. This has resulted in an increased demand for new and different sources for animals used for food and fur. New types and larger numbers of pets and other animals used for entertainment are also being sought, including endangered animals. Finally, traditional medicine often relies on the body parts or bodily fluids of exotic animals (most famously rhinoceros and bears), and as these species' numbers are diminished, threats to their survival are heightened. Given the market demand for these animals, there is a regular supply of illegally captured and killed animals and animal parts. The animals come mainly from Southeast Asia and some African nations, where poverty and corruption combine with immense biodiversity to feed an opportunistic market. Therefore, membership in CITES and adherence to CITES policies are especially important in this area of the world.[45] In October 2004, the Association of Southeast Asian Nations (ASEAN) announced an initiative to neutralize the region's illegal wildlife trade, an essential step toward addressing this problem.[46] In 2005 the ASEAN-WEN (Wildlife Enforcement Network) was formed.[47] ASEAN's efforts are an admirable attempt to implement the objectives of CITES in the area of the world where probably the greatest threat to endangered species is occurring.

Many of the so-called "developing" or "newly industrialized" countries encounter significant problems with respect to active and substantive involvement in CITES, for multiple reasons. Meaningful participation in CITES requires a substantial dedication of time, resources, and expertise, and implementation of CITES' rules may be extremely difficult within a given country. CITES restrictions may have a significant impact on ongoing activities in a given country, and so there are conflicting interests at play when making the decision. Mexico, for example, was extremely hesitant to join CITES because of the extensive bans on trade in wildlife species which are present and have historically been actively hunted within its borders.[48] The concern was at least partially due to Mexico's anticipated costs of controlling the killing of endangered species within its borders, if it became a CITES member. Nevertheless, the international community pressure apparently prevailed. Although Mexico asserted it did not have the resources or ability to control illegal wildlife trade, it joined CITES in 1991, at the same time that it was actively seeking international approval for its membership in the North American Free Trade Agreement (NAFTA).

The dilemma Mexico faced is not unique, nor is the interplay between a country's desire to enter into economically favorable contracts within the international community and the burden of entering into agreements like CITES. Many countries have policies that conflict with CITES' goals or have an active legal or illegal wildlife trade that is not actively controlled by government authorities and agencies. Countries considering CITES membership, like Mexico, recognize that in order to comply with CITES requirements, significant resources would need to be devoted to areas that may have traditionally been ignored. Still they may ultimately join CITES because doing so is a condition (express or implied) of entering into unrelated but highly desirable trade agreements with other nations that are CITES members and that want to see CITES policies in effect on a broader scale.

At each Convention of the Parties, certain species attract special attention and extensive discussion. These animals are usually highlighted because of competing desires between commercial exploitation and species protection. Conflicts arise over whether to list or delist a species, or to move a species from one appendix to another. For example, at the 2007 Convention of the Parties, China pushed for removing restrictions on the trade in tiger products, which has been banned since CITES listed the tiger in Appendix I in 1993.[49] Tiger body parts are an integral ingredient in some traditional Chinese medicines, and therefore are in great demand. In China, thousands of tigers are bred and confined on "farms," which often double as tourist attractions and circuses.[50] Chinese traditional medicine is a global industry, and Chinese tiger farm owners could make a significant profit if trade in tiger parts were opened up to the international community.[51] With the current ban, tiger parts can only *legally* be sold within the country, and any exportation is a violation of CITES. Nevertheless, China has allowed tiger farms to flourish.[52] While the tiger parts cannot legally be sold, the farmers are stockpiling the parts in hopes that the ban will be lifted, and according to reports, the illegal trade in tiger parts flourishes.[53] Additionally, tourists come to these farms to watch tigers attack live prey (such as cows) and pose with declawed and defanged tigers.[54]

At the 2007 Convention, China sought to have the ban on sale of tiger parts lifted with respect to products derived from captive-bred tigers. One of China's arguments for the expansion of sales was actually based on conservation. Tiger populations in India—the largest habitat range for tigers—have dropped to dangerously low levels, and China argued that sale of the parts of Chinese captive bred tigers (who are listed in Appendix II, while India's wild population is in Appendix I) would benefit the Indian tiger populations, which were at greatest risk. The reasoning is that by increasing the available products on the market (through the sale of captive bred tiger parts) the global response would be a decrease in demand for illegally-poached Indian animals. China also argued that the captive-bred population can be monitored and controlled much easier than a wild population. Those in support of the commercial farming of tigers argued that the guaranteed supply of captive-bred body parts and fluids would decrease the incentive for illegal poaching and indirectly protect the Indian tigers.[55] Other CITES members roundly criticized this argument, because if trade in captive tiger parts were allowed, there would be no way to distinguish wild from captive tiger parts. Legalizing *some* tiger products would only legitimize the industry and increase demand, allowing both captive *and* wild parts to flow much more freely. As one advocate put it, the legalization of trade in captive-bred tiger parts would "provide smugglers with a convenient cover for laundering wild tigers."[56] The debate was hotly contested, and ended with the decision to reject China's request to open up trade in tigers and an agreement to slowly phase out the raising of captive tigers on farms.[57]

The tiger controversy highlights the complex relationship between CITES listings and the black market. CITES listings are arguably designed to provide species with more protections than they might have if each country was legislating in these areas separately. This principle has the potential to cause greater problems, since the depletion of legal products raises the demand for illicit ones. In the case of endangered animals, this may actually increase the threats faced by a species in danger. For example, when CITES listed the South African white rhinoceros in Appendix I, the species gained added protections, yet simultaneously the black market price for their coveted horns increased and so did poaching attempts. The adverse effect on the rhinoceros presumably occurred because the Appendix I listing affirmed the rareness of the species and increased the likelihood that supply of the horn would drop (or even disappear), thus raising its value on the black market. The problem of an increased illegal market for listed species is further compounded by the fact that CITES has no enforcement power or component. There are numerous species that remain seriously endangered because of poaching and their circulation in the black market trade despite their protection by CITES. These include elephants, rhinoceros, tigers, and several species of parrots and sharks.[58]

Potential Problems

The sometimes counterintuitive relationship between CITES and the black market is just one indicator that more needs to be done if the Convention is to fully realize its goals of protecting endangered species. Although most commentators and experts agree that CITES remains the most important international protection for selected species across international borders, some have expressed doubt over CITES' effectiveness. The criticisms range from the particular—with respect to specific provisions and practices—to the general, challenging CITES' limited scope and its effective exclusion of less affluent countries.[59] Members of the international community have sought ways to provide broader coverage, urging the Convention to address vital issues that it does not cover at all and that directly impact the animals it is trying to save. These areas include: habitat loss, socioeconomic motivations for species exploitation, and species identified by special interest groups that have not been listed by the Convention but which some groups feel should obtain protected status. With respect to the last concern, the process of listing requires a scientific inquiry and review, and also entails a significant amount of diplomacy, politics, and debate each time a new species is considered for a change in status. Commercial interests certainly can apply some influence on the process in the framework of supplying scientific data.

CITES has also been criticized for not adequately enforcing its provisions. Its detractors claim that this lack of meaningful enforcement undermines its effectiveness and simultaneously provides a false sense of security regarding how well the interests of the international animal community are being safeguarded. Another weakness in CITES is that its regulation is limited to international trade and exploitation—the passage of products across international boundaries. CITES does not specifically regulate domestic or internal use, trade, and exploitation of animals within a country, although it does require countries to enact parallel legislation with respect to its protections. Thus, CITES does not directly reach local practices that may threaten the existence of a species; a species, protected under CITES, could nevertheless be wiped out where the local laws are either not sufficiently protective of that group, or where domestic enforcement is ineffective. In many countries, this leads to a gaping hole in the protection of species whose geographical range may be limited to a given territory within its borders. For instance, as discussed in Chapter 1, although the moon bears used for bile farming in China are a protected species under Appendix II of CITES, almost all of the exploitation of the bears and the use of their products occurs within China, so CITES is not directly implicated. If Chinese wildlife laws are not followed or enforced, the requirement for a corollary set of domestic laws is ineffective.

As with any compromise agreement, there are ongoing concerns regarding species protection that reflect the different interests at issue. For example, some feel CITES does not go far enough in promoting conservation efforts, for the reasons discussed above, and because it does not address other greater global problems that may directly or indirectly impact endangered populations. Proponents of a revamped, heightened protection effort argue that the international community should be promoting more conservative uses of sustainable populations in the immediate future.[60]

Conservation economists often attack CITES for giving what they perceive as too much consideration to animal protection/welfare concerns, and not enough consideration to market factors and demands. And the animal protection community argues that while CITES encourages limitation and prohibitions on wildlife exploitation, it provides little support for enforcement. These may be fair criticisms, but much of the difficulty comes from the fact that CITES compliance is a definite drain on resources. The unfortunate fact is that the countries most severely affected by CITES are typically less affluent, and may not be willing or able to share the disproportionate burden of protecting listed species. Another concern is that because CITES compels protection of the listed species, member countries are forced to spend a greater percentage of their precious resources on protecting those species at the expense of other, unlisted species that may be just as significant from a cultural or ecological perspective.[61] Because unlisted species are not protected today, they could more easily become the endangered species of tomorrow.

Finally, critics have raised concerns that the criteria for listing species are not as objective as they should be and are slanted towards the commercial and market value of a given species, erring on the side of use and away from the more conservative approach that takes fewer chances with the potential for extinction.[62] There is a view that the Convention has been more reluctant to list economically valuable species, such as sharks and certain timbers. There is also a significant concern that wealthy and powerful countries have priority in the listing process, while countries containing species in equal or greater need of protection are neglected.[63] Thus, the decisions made and priorities given to species protection may not be related to need, but to other unrelated factors.[64]

One animal whose listing has been very controversial and politically charged is the African elephant, which is currently subject to what is known as a "split listing." This species—very different than Asian elephants—are listed in both Appendix I and Appendix II, depending on the animals' home location. Elephants residing in Botswana, Namibia, South Africa and Zimbabwe are listed in Appendix II, with the others in Appendix I. The differential listing is supposed to be based on clear scientific data, and until 1990, CITES listed all populations of the African elephant in Appendix II. Products from species listed in Appendix II can be commercially traded internationally, although they are subject to extensive restrictions. Concerns were heightened that the Appendix II listing did little to protect the elephant, based on reports that "from 1979 to 1989, more than half of Africa's elephants were killed by poachers."[65]

In 1990, international public awareness of the plight of the African elephant led CITES to list *all* African elephants in Appendix I.[66] By that time, the United States had already passed the American Elephant Conservation Act of 1988 and had joined Great Britain, France, West Germany, and Kenya in support of an international ban on commercial ivory.[67] Immediately after the Appendix I listing, elephant populations began to recover.[68] Population recovery was actually so rapid that, by 1997, the CITES Panel of Experts found that the elephant populations in several African countries were larger than the maximum numbers that would allow them to be listed.[69] Some countries also wished to sell their stockpiles of ivory that had accumulated over the years during the ivory ban.[70] The argument on behalf of African citizens and nations was that if the elephant populations had reached the point where they were self-sustaining, the ban was no longer justified, and the countries should not be required to dedicate the amount of resources that protecting them under CITES required. Because the elephants had recovered and therefore proven the ability to maintain their population without further protection, the nations urged a lifting of the ivory ban. The eventual result was the current split-listing of the African elephant—a compromise where the countries with the healthiest populations were entitled to issue permits for their elephants to be killed.

An illustration of the type of concessions that can be made in the context of CITES negotiations is demonstrated by the corresponding decision to sell the stockpiled ivory from a number of African countries (Zimbabwe, Namibia, and Botswana) to Japan in a one-time deal.[71] The demand for ivory in Japan, coupled with the Appendix II listing of the elephants in these countries, set the framework for this deal. Some have argued for a permanent lifting of the ivory ban, contending that limited trade in African elephant ivory may be beneficial to the elephants' home countries' economies, as well as sustainable for the near-future.[72] However, resuming ivory sales clearly runs the risk of an unregulated assault on elephant populations, coupled with an inability to monitor populations until it is potentially too late. The other problem—as discussed above in the context of Chinese tiger farming for traditional Chinese medicine—is that a free and legal trade market can provide cover for poachers selling illegally-obtained ivory. It is theoretically possible, in a world without criminal elements, to support elephant populations even if there is a limited trade in African elephant ivory. It may even be a positive move in terms of forging alliances between adverse parties—although it is clearly not positive in any way for the individual elephants affected. But that theoretical paradigm is a virtual impossibility in a world where poaching and illegal uses of elephant parts are prevalent. Suppliers (those killing the elephants and those selling their parts) and purchasers (who buy their parts around the world) would be incentivized far too much by the existence of any market in these products. The controls on the supply side in Africa and the international purchasing side cannot be satisfactorily controlled and so any free trade in their parts will likely lead to the complete decimation of African elephants. The ivory concession, made as a means to cater to the longstanding ivory import trade in Japan and elsewhere, may have been seen as a temporary measure, but in reality it probably only continues to forestall the recognition that the industry will have to be seriously curtailed (if not completely discontinued) if elephants are to survive on our planet.

Domestic Implementation

The preceding discussion has focused on the requirements, effects, and enforcement of CITES itself. As mentioned earlier, listed species are often provided with significant protections in the member states by domestic legislation. CITES explicitly permits parties to enact "stricter domestic measures regarding the conditions for trade, taking possession or transport of specimens of species includes in [the] Appendices."[73] By way of example, consider the legal protections provided to a highly endangered animal, the manatee, with three different manatee species in different countries. The manatee is a marine mammal also known as the "sea cow," usually measuring about nine or ten feet long and weighing roughly 500 kilograms (1100 pounds). The three species are the Amazon Basin manatee, the West Indian manatee (of which the American Florida manatee is a sub-population), and the West African manatee. CITES protects manatees from international trade, as the West Indian and Amazonian manatees are listed in Appendix I and the West African manatee is listed in Appendix II.

In the United States, the manatee population lives almost exclusively in the waters off the state of Florida. Both federal and state laws have been passed to protect manatees. Federal laws prohibit hunting, capturing, killing, or harassing these animals. Both the Marine Mammal Protection Act of 1972 and the Endangered Species Act grant the manatees protection and provide for significant penalties for breaking these laws.[74] In addition, the state of Florida protects the manatee separately, and the Florida Manatee Sanctuary Act of 1978 provides for the establishment of manatee sanctuaries in Florida.[75]

In addition to CITES, the West African manatees are protected by a separate international treaty. Manatees are classified as a highly protected Class A animal under the African Convention of Nature and Natural Resources, adopted in 1969, with 38 members.[76] Class A provides the highest protection to African animals, similar to that of Appendix I CITES animals. The African Convention is an example of an international group like CITES, but it specifically pertains to the protection of the natural components of Africa—soil, water, flora and fauna.[77] Similarly, the Amazon Basin Manatee is protected by various South American nations by the same laws as the Florida Manatee, separate from CITES. Amazonian manatee hunting has likewise been prohibited in Brazil and other countries since 1973.[78]

These examples demonstrate how one set of related species can receive protection domestically, regionally, and internationally. The international community, through CITES and its domestic implementation component, has demonstrated its concern about the risk of extinction of certain species. While CITES covers only the species its experts have identified as threatened or endangered (and those listed in Appendix III) by member countries, a much larger number of animals is impacted by the more general provisions of the most powerful international economic agreements, as discussed in the following section.

The World Trade Organization (WTO) and General Agreement on Tariffs and Trade (GATT)

The WTO and GATT are controversial agreements that cover broad areas of trade policy; the focus here is exclusively on the impact that the agreements have on animals. As we explain below, the globalization of capital markets and the formation of international networks of economic exchange have enormous implications for many species. The institutional framework governing international trade, which developed in earnest after World War II, is sprawling and complex and not a topic for this text. In this chapter, we examine only the impact that international trade institutions and agreements have on animals and their habitats. We begin with a very cursory primer on the essential aspects of the WTO and GATT simply to set the stage for understanding the implications of these influential agreements for species around the world.

The WTO is "the only international organization dealing with the global rules of trade between nations."[79] The WTO's history begins with the GATT. In January of 1948, the GATT was adopted by twenty-three original contracting parties with the purpose of encouraging trade liberalization and international economic cooperation in the area of making trade fair, profitable, and subject to consistent rules.[80] This was the start of what is now recognized as the omnipresent global economy; and "[d]espite its provisional nature, the GATT remained the only multilateral instrument governing international trade from 1948 until the establishment of the WTO" in 1995.[81] Since animals are treated as legal property by every country, international trade involving live animals or animal products was governed by GATT's provisions. The trade agreement simply considers them as a commodity to be transferred and sold on the market.

The WTO was established on January 1, 1995 as a direct successor to GATT. Roughly 150 countries are members, and the WTO claims to cover 97 percent of international trade.[82] WTO rules have a significant controlling effect on member countries' trade conduct, as described here. The WTO's main activities include

> negotiating the reduction or elimination of obstacles to trade (import tariffs, other barriers to trade) and agreeing on rules governing the conduct of international trade (*e.g.*, antidumping, subsidies, product standards, etc.); administering and monitoring the application of the WTO's agreed rules for trade in goods, trade in services, and trade-related intellectual property rights; monitoring and reviewing the trade policies of [WTO] members, as well as ensuring transparency of re-

> gional and bilateral trade agreements; settling disputes among [WTO] members regarding interpretation and application of the agreements; building capacity of developing country government officials in international trade matters; assisting the process of accession of some 30 countries who are not yet members of the organization; conducting economic research and collecting and disseminating trade data in support of the WTO's other main activities; explaining to and educating the public about the WTO, its mission and its activities.[83]

Both GATT and the WTO are based on three core principles that provide the foundation for trade obligations and rights, as well as the basis for challenges by member countries of the trade actions of other member countries. First, the Most Favored Nation Obligation[84] prohibits discrimination between "like" products from different countries. In simplified terms, this means that countries cannot give any kind of trade advantage (financial, practical or procedural) to one country's product without immediately and unconditionally extending the identical benefit to all other countries importing the same products. Conversely, all similar products from all countries must be given an equal opportunity to enter a country's marketplace.

The determination of what constitutes a "like product" is an area of some focus for animal protectionists. In general, like products are defined as those goods that are physically and scientifically (biologically) similar. This has been somewhat of an issue for the animal welfare community, and the debate continues. Chicken eggs can provide a reasonable illustration of the issues that arise in the "like product" analysis, where animal products are concerned. All chicken eggs look essentially the same (other than variations in color and size) and function the same, and all are made up of the same basic components—a shell, a yolk, and a viscous "egg white." Therefore, open questions remain under the "like product" rules of the WTO, whether countries can distinguish between eggs based on their origin nor the way the chickens who produced the eggs were treated. In other words, can a no trade restriction or discrimination be undertaken based on the level of cruelty that occurs during egg production? If Country A is importing eggs, can it restrict the import of eggs that come from chickens who were treated cruelly? Some believw that until new rules are established under the WTO, Country A must allow the importation of eggs that, if produced in Country A, would be the product of illegal activity because of the treatment of the hens. In short, some say an egg is an egg, and despite what might be a national policy against mistreatment of chickens, Country A can not currently make a differentiation that resulted in discrimination in trade based on its opinion that chickens from Country B were being cruelly treated in order to produce eggs. As discussed later in the chapter, there is ongoing debate over the application of this principle, and room for change.

A second overriding doctrine of the WTO prevents a rule that parallels the Most Favored Nation Obligation. The "National Treatment Obligation"[85] prohibits a country from favoring its own domestic products over imported like goods. A country cannot engage in conduct that in any way differentiates or discriminates domestic from foreign products, or makes the purchase of domestic goods more favorable (less expensive) than that of imports. No local or national protections for domestic goods are allowed, and likewise no taxation can be unfairly or unreasonably placed on foreign goods.

The third foundational rule for the WTO is the Prohibition on Quantitative Restrictions.[86] This is a general prohibition against bans, quotas, and licenses on exported and imported products. In line with the overriding purpose of the WTO—the efficient and fair passage of goods across international borders—the purpose of this rule is to provide the general sense of fairness and uniformity that is at the core of the WTO.

The WTO is distinguishable from most international agreements and institutions for several reasons. The most notable factor is the extent of its power; it is more broad-ranging and includes more countries as signatories than any other economic treaty. It is also recognized for its relatively effective enforcement mechanisms and conflict settlement processes, which lead to authoritative determinations in a manner similar to that familiar to most lawyers.

The WTO provides for formal challenges and a generally accepted form of dispute resolution by nations impacted by countries that fail to comply with the WTO rules.[87] Enforcement is sometimes difficult in the international arena, but the WTO is structured so that the central organization has developed procedures for sanctions and trade-based remedies that can have a persuasive effect on member countries. This is intended to avoid unilateral retaliation by any one country and to promote "security, predictability and mutually acceptable solutions to trade disputes."[88]

These mechanical and procedural aspects have allowed the WTO to effectively pursue its self-stated overriding objective of "help[ing] trade flow smoothly, freely, fairly and predictably."[89] The WTO promotes economic and geopolitical stability and protects global wealth. WTO also has a stated goal to protect natural resources and the environment.[90] Despite this claim, the rules discussed above may counteract that intention. That is, the WTO may negatively impact the ability of nations to protect their domestic environments, and their animals, by the operation of the same rules that promote and safeguard trade.[91]

There are many examples of this paradox. Broadly and simply stated, WTO members are limited in their ability to protect animals because they are limited in their rights to restrict imports. Because all like products must be allowed into a country equally, a country cannot control how the animals (or animal parts and products) entering its borders have been treated in the country of origin. For example, there is an active trade in greyhounds from Australia to certain Asian countries—for both racing and food. Australia, South Korea, and China are all WTO members and, as such, have agreed to abide by its international trade obligations. Even if it wanted to, Australia probably could not ban greyhound exports to China only (where there have been heightened concerns expressed about the treatment of dogs), because it would arguably violate the WTO rules against impermissible restrictions on exports. Therefore, even if treatment of the dogs in China violates animal welfare standards in Australia (which it does in many identified circumstances), a prohibition on the dog trade to an identified country like China would run afoul of the general WTO rules. Thus, an attempt by the Australian government to protect the dogs by restraining the trade is not possible. Other examples are discussed later in this section.

That impact is demonstrated by a number of cases that have been brought before the WTO tribunal. In most of these cases, a member country's desire to protect threatened or endangered species has been deemed a violation of the WTO prohibitions on restriction of free trade. An examination of the cases provides for clearer explanation of the processes and functions of the WTO, and the dilemma faced by countries trying to both provide for animal welfare and protection and avoid creating problems in the international trade community.[92]

Tuna-Dolphin I Case[93]

Fishers taking yellowfin tuna in the Eastern Tropical Pacific long ago discovered that bottlenose dolphins swim along with large groups of these commercially valuable fish. Although the tuna were difficult to locate from fishing boats and the surface of the water, dolphins, who must surface for air, became good indicators of the presence of the fish below. Based on this connection, a new method of fishing was adopted, using large "purse-seine" nets. The nets were set up to encircle the dolphins, relying on the fact that the fish would be below. Large hauls of tuna resulted from this process, once the nets were pulled up. At the same time, many dolphins were caught in the nets. The dolphins died from suffocation and other causes, resulting in a very significant mortality rate. Because of the much smaller number of dolphins as compared to tuna, and the significantly slower reproduction rate of dolphins as compared to fish, this practice had a significant effect on the dolphins' survival. Additionally, because dolphins are biologically mammals (like humans), they are often considered to be worthy of greater protections by a large portion of society. Nor are dolphins typically sold for food; their deaths were in most cases simply the incidental consequences of the tuna industry, and the dolphins were discarded.

In 1972 the United States passed the Marine Mammal Protection Act (MMPA),[94] which imposed a moratorium on harming, killing, capturing, harassing or importing marine mammals or marine mammal products. The Act was "founded on a concern that certain species of marine mammals were in danger of extinction or depletion as a result of man's activities."[95] The United States Congress stated that these "species should not be permitted to diminish beyond their optimum sustainable population [the number of animals which will result in the maximum productivity of the population of the species]."[96]

Under the MMPA, the described method of purse-seine fishing for tuna was (and still is) illegal, because of its effect on the dolphins. Thus, this practice was severely limited in American waters.[97] But it is the quickest and most profitable way to gather large groups of tuna. As a result, United States fishers were in a competitive bind and found that the expense of harvesting tuna was much higher for them than for their international colleagues. Foreign fishing companies were not bound by the MMPA and so they were able to gain a significant market advantage over those fishing in American waters.[98] Latin American countries actually could move in to waters usually utilized by American companies and harvest tuna in much greater numbers. The United States quickly reduced its participation in the tuna market, but dolphin mortality continued to increase, since there was no international agreement to limit the purse-seine practice.

Certain foreign and extraterritorial activities that adversely affect marine mammals were also addressed by the Act.[99] Under pressure from the domestic fishing industry, the United States Congress amended the MMPA to prohibit importation of tuna from countries that did not have similar protections with respect to dolphins. The Congress also amended the definition of "dolphin-safe" to prohibit using purse-seine nets on dolphins. These amendments mandated nations exporting tuna to the United States to certify that they were not using purse-seine nets, so that dolphin mortality from fishing would be comparable to U.S. dolphin mortality rates.

In 1990, Mexico challenged the amendments to the MMPA before a GATT dispute settlement panel, arguing that the American legislation violated Article XI of GATT which proscribed quantitative restrictions on exportation. The panel found for Mexico, ruling that countries could not "export" their domestic laws with regard to the method of production of tuna or the way in which they were caught.[100] Therefore the MMPA discriminated between *like* products and was an impermissible restriction on free trade. Dolphin-safe tuna was physically indistinguishable from purse-seined tuna. In sum, "[h]ow the tuna got into the can is irrelevant to GATT jurisprudence."[101]

The GATT panel emphasized the rule of "extra-territoriality": the international trade agreements do not provide a member country with the authority to protect plant or animal life outside the territory of the nation imposing the restriction.[102] "A country can effectively control the production or consumption of an exhaustible natural resource only to the extent that the production or consumption is under its jurisdiction."[103] Thus the panel ruled that the trade rules prohibit discrimination between products both on the basis of where and *how* they are produced.

Without the ability to prevent the introduction of products that a country deems to be dangerous to the continued existence of a species, the country's power to provide protection decreases. Of course, if a country completely bans a product—whether for sale within or export into the country—the ban actually does solve the problem of allowing the imports. That is, if it is illegal to import a product or sell it within the country, the product is absolutely blocked from entering the country legally and there is no prohibition on restricting imports. In the case of tuna, however, because the United States still wishes to catch, sell, and eat tuna, that is clearly not an option it is likely to entertain.

Tuna-Dolphin II Case[104]

Another challenge to the MMPA's ban on dolphin-unsafe tuna came from across the Atlantic. The European Economic Community (EEC) and the Netherlands imported tuna from Latin America, processed it in the EEC, and then exported it to the United States. When the United States, pursuant to the MMPA, refused to accept tuna caught with purse-seine methods from these nations, the EEC brought a complaint, similar in nature to that brought by Mexico, to the WTO panel.[105]

The Article XX General Exceptions of GATT lay out a number of specific instances in which WTO member countries may be exempted from GATT rules. These include identified circumstances in which action is required for environmental and species protection purposes. As long as rules are not applied as a means of "arbitrary or unjustifiable discrimination between countries where the same conditions prevail," and are not "a disguised restriction on international trade," a WTO member country may enact laws that would otherwise be contrary to WTO rules.[106] These exceptions to the restrictions apply where laws or sanctions are "necessary to protect human, animal or plant life or health" or relate to "the conservation of exhaustible natural resources if such measures are made effective in conjunction with restrictions on domestic production or consumption ..."[107] If a country can make that proof, then sanctions that would otherwise be violations of WTO rules would be permissible.

The United States maintained that the embargo on the intermediary importing nations was justified under Article XX(g) as a measure relating to the conservation of dolphins—an exhaustible natural resource—and under Article XX(b) as a measure necessary to protect animal life and health.[108] The EEC and the Netherlands argued that Article XX(g) and (b) could not be invoked to protect dolphins outside U.S. jurisdiction. Although the United States lost the case, the panel concluded that when invoking the provisions of Article XX(g), a country could consider conservation effects outside of its own borders. Thus, the American effort to protect dolphins in the eastern tropical Pacific Ocean was covered by Article XX(g).

Shrimp-Turtle Case I[109] *and* Shrimp Turtle Case II[110]

The Shrimp-Turtle cases were triggered by another collateral and fatal consequence of the fishing industry and the American response to the problem. Much of the shrimp industry utilizes nets to catch shrimp. These nets carry the potential for, and do, trap thousands of air-breathing sea turtles every year some of which are threatened or endangered. The turtles, like the dolphins in the tuna nets, drown or are suffocated in the shrimp nets. In response to concern over the number and nature of these deaths, the United States began requiring domestic shrimpers to use a protective technology called Turtle Excluder Devices (TEDs). The TEDs provide turtles with a method of escape from shrimp nets and were designed to reduce the number of deaths. In 1989, the U.S. Congress passed section 609 of the federal Endangered Species Act which, along with its implementing regulations, prohibited importation of shrimp into the United States unless the shrimpers had used comparably effective TEDs.

The regulation was challenged before the WTO on the grounds that it presented a limitation on trade that was improper under the WTO and therefore could not be enforced against other WTO signatories. The WTO Court made an important distinction and clarification in deciding this case:

> Notwithstanding the decisions of the cases already cited, ... the [WTO's] Appellate Body has acknowledged ... the validity of unilateral trade measures aimed at protecting the environment. While the [Appellate Body] did not declare a *per se* rule against the environmental trade measures employed, they went to some lengths in clarifying the standards required for these measures to be suitable

> for an Article XX exception. Thus, the Appellate Body recognized the validity of unilateral trade measures aimed at protecting the environment, but was also sensitive to their potential for abuse. It is this type of nuanced balancing act in which the WTO must engage, deciding whether a measure is a disguised restriction on free trade or a legitimate exercise of self-governance.[111]

The Appellate Body, despite recognizing the intent and potential validity of such measures, found that section 609 violated the GATT. The Appellate Body found that section 609 did not avoid the bar of the Article XX "chapeau," which is the general provision that prohibits unjustifiable or arbitrary discrimination between countries.[112] Thus, section 609 was deemed to violate America's obligations under the GATT.

Leghold-Trap Restrictions and Cosmetics Testing Ban

Steel-jawed leghold traps are used to capture animals in the wild typically for use in clothing. When triggered by an animal, the trap snaps shut and clamps sharp-toothed jaws onto an animal's limb or other body part in a vise-like grip. In trying to extricate themselves from the traps, animals may tear muscles and ligaments, or attempt to chew off the trapped limb in order to escape. Those who cannot escape may starve or bleed to death. During the period of time between the trapping and discovery by a trapper, the animals are in an undisputed state of extreme pain and suffering. Concerned with the level of inherent cruelty in the use of these traps (which are common and legal in America and Canada, among other countries), the European Community (EC) acted to halt the practice.

The European Leghold Trap Restriction provide another illustration of how WTO trade policies affect animal welfare standards internationally. In 1991 the EC banned the use of leghold traps and simultaneously banned imports of fur and fur products of certain species from countries that allowed the use of leghold traps.[113] The banned species had been imported to Europe mainly from the United States and Canada, where leghold traps were legal and commonly used. Since more than half of the two countries' fur exports were to Europe, the Leghold Trap Restriction was a serious impairment of the North American fur industry's ability to maintain its production and sales. The United States and Canada claimed that the European Restriction was a violation of WTO rules, while the EC defended the import ban as a way of protecting animals in other countries. No final decision was issued by the WTO, because the parties resolved the matter between them. EC awareness that it could lose the case in

WTO court may have contributed to the establishment of an agreement on International Humane Trapping Standards.[114] The import ban was relaxed as part of the agreement, which provides far less protection to animals than the complete ban enacted by the EC, but did constitute a compromise.[115] Despite a growing public sentiment that such traps should be outlawed, the WTO ultimately worked against the EC's efforts in that direction. Thus, even though the import ban was a natural partner to its internal prohibition of the targeted practice, the WTO pressure led to the EC's reversal of the ban.[116]

Another practice (discussed in Chapter 4) that has gained public scrutiny and objection is the use of animals for "toxicity testing" of cosmetics. This common use of animals generally involves the application or ingestion of new (and existing) cosmetic products on animals. The tests are intended to determine the amount of cosmetic exposure that will cause sickness or death in the captive animals. Once that answer is obtained, researchers attempt to extrapolate the effect on humans. Toxicity testing has been heavily criticized by animal welfare advocates. They argue the tests are inapplicable to humans; there are alternatives to testing on animals; and the suffering inflicted is unjustifiable and unnecessary.

In line with the animal welfare concerns, the European Community banned cosmetics testing and products upon which such testing had been done. It also prohibited the import of tested products. But again the WTO and international trade issues prevailed. While the cosmetics testing ban still exists in the EC, import and marketing bans on companies that continue to do this testing have been limited. Due to a concern over the WTO rules' conflict with the import ban, the EC has been prevented from realizing its public policy against this conduct.[117]

Effect of WTO on Animals

There are other examples, but the foregoing demonstrates that the WTO affects animals by limiting member countries' abilities to control how animals (or their parts or products) entering their borders have been treated. Because a nation cannot discriminate against another nation for using a certain method of producing an animal product, commerce and WTO compliance may promote the inhumane treatment of animals in other countries, or at least delay a change in practices.

In the area affecting the largest number of animals, factory farming, the EU has also adopted legislation ending some common practices. But the current trade regime may prevent the EU from prohibiting the import of agricultural products from countries where these same prohibited practices are still used.[118] For example, international concern has been raised over egg production in which laying hens are confined in "battery cages."[119] A WTO member country concerned with the welfare of chickens could not preferentially import "cage-free" or "humane" eggs from one country over battery cage eggs from another country because the products—the eggs—are essentially the same, therefore meeting the requirement for like products. And if, as industry leaders often claim, the cruel restricted confinement methods on factory farms are more cost-effective, there is an economic incentive to treat animals cruelly. With the WTO's restrictions, a country enforcing more humane standards is compromising the financial interests of its own citizens because their "like products" will be less profitable and/or higher priced.

The tension between care and cash is clear, and the global community is thus hindered in its ability to move towards more humane practices by the strict limitations of the international trade rules. The purpose of the WTO is, very generally, to unify trade and eliminate open conflict in policy that may lead to discrimination. This ignores the increasingly strong public sentiment in support of humane treatment laws—which exhibit a societal desire to prevent the cruelty and suffering occurring in many industries, especially industrial farming. That discord between international economics and national animal protection displays the conflicts and concerns that economic legislation may cause for animals on a local and global scale. In sum, while public policy behind humane treatment laws exhibits a social desire to prevent the cruelty occurring in many industries, the tension between WTO's goals and these social values presents an issue that may never be resolved.

Because of the detrimental impact that WTO rules may have on animal welfare and improvements in animal protection in member countries, much thought has gone into ways to continue the support the WTO provides while preventing a detrimental effect on animals or a deterrence to efforts towards more humane practices. The most obvious solution would be a reformation or reinterpretation of the WTO so that its rules do not or cannot interfere with animal welfare efforts. Or it could be restructured so there is at least a process of weighing and decision-making between commercial interests and animal protection concerns. While these are the most direct and effective methods for change, it may be difficult to get consensus on this kind of alteration from the member countries and their representatives. There would likely be extensive debates on the dividing lines between acceptable and unacceptable practices. And tellingly for the theme of this book, there would be a wide disparity among the many nations as to which practices needed to be barred, and which ones are perfectly acceptable. It is hard to imagine, at this point in our history, that a very meaningful consensus would be reached. Members could also raise concerns that any ambiguity in terms of permissible practices could lead to increased disputes. Indeed, if abused, the fear that generated the current rules—that humane practices rationale could be used as a pretext for trade discrimination—could be realized.

Perhaps the biggest barrier to such a change is the fact that the WTO has never had even a secondary focus on animal issues. It is primarily a market economy organization, and its rules are focused almost exclusively on maximizing the function of the global market. Neither general nor specific animal welfare issues have ever been a topic of consideration for the WTO. This counsels against a sea change in its documentation but does not eliminate the possibility for change. With that in mind, another more practical possibility for change would be simply to advocate for a new interpretation of the current rules, one that could incorporate these concepts without changing focus.

As discussed above, there are provisions of the WTO that allow for some ongoing concerns over imports to be addressed. And those concepts have been around since the GATT was the operative program. The doctrines and principles have been established by the cases mentioned above, and the global community is indisputably more concerned with and aware of the potential for abusive practices that affect animals. Likewise the pathway to changing these practices is more and more in the minds of decision makers, politicians, and the public. Rather than viewing the WTO as a static document that cannot change unless its language is radically altered, the approach should be to treat it like a living document (like a constitution or international declaration) that can adapt and respond to contemporary values. The WTO can be treated more like a constitution of the world economy. It could be reinterpreted to allow for greater consideration of animal welfare, simply as part of the processes already established. And the decisions of its adjudicators could reflect that change in interpretation and sentiment. This effort may be met with less opposition and result in the same (or greater) benefit to animal welfare, as compared with an attempt to add new and broader provisions to the WTO's established set of rules.

The WTO can be read more broadly on issues of animal welfare and concern such as those raised above. The governing body and members could safely acknowledge that implied within the WTO constraints and decisions there is (and always has been) a general, or specific, animal welfare component, and one that should now be more expressly recognized. Despite its focus on the economic bottom line, the WTO was never intended to have a *deleterious* effect on animals' welfare and well-being—which it now is in some quarters. Therefore, as a matter of basic international ethics, there is no reason the WTO should be used—unintentionally or otherwise—to support animal abuse or to delay progressive animal welfare. The principle of humane treatment to animals should be controlling and incorporated into all decisions involving the WTO rules.

Such an effort may be met with backlash as well as resistance, but it is the only way to include universal notions of humane treatment to animals into international politics and practice. As the cases above demonstrate, without some formal reinterpretation or successful challenge, any significant animal welfare advances in the global community could be directly cut back in order to prevent potential WTO sanctions. At the same time, if countries around the world are slowly moving towards more humane standards of treatment of animals, there will hopefully be a shift in thinking as well for the basic tenets of the WTO. Any attempt to reinterpret the WTO's underlying considerations will surely be aided by a global shift that includes member countries.

There is one other possibility that may lead to positive change for the animals. As background, the WTO already allows countries to require different treatment based on what are known as "process and production methods." These "PPM distinctions" already exist as a matter of WTO rules. They set up a process for permissible disparity in treatment depending on how products are prepared or manufactured.[120] The PPM doctrine means that countries can make determinations about what products to import, and still be in compliance with WTO rules. The differentiation of products, and the reasons for the distinctions, are open to an interpretation that may favor an animal welfare viewpoint.

By way of example, a country could apply the PPM distinctions and claim that there is a difference in the "process" and "production" of humanely-raised animals, kept in uncrowded conditions, and animals who raised in intensive confinement and subjected to cruel actions in factory farms. If a PPM distinction could be made between these types of animals, a distinction could also be made between the products of these animals. Countries that have adopted more humane practices as national policy could then ban imports of animal products from animals who were treated in a manner that would be illegal in the country, without violating WTO principles. This interpretation is not currently supported by prior WTO decisions—thus far, PPM distinctions have only been recognized where the different treatment is somehow "incorporated" into the final product in some physical way.[121]

Because an egg looks (and possibly tastes) the same whether it comes from a hen who lived uncaged or one who was kept in intensive confinement and subjected to cruelty, the current understanding of PPM distinctions does not include a consideration of that treatment. But while an animal welfare component is not currently part of the PPM doctrine, this may be an area ripe for change, at least with respect to the most egregious forms of agricultural food production. Because the difference in products must be *incorporated* into the product, science needs to be developed that demonstrates a substantive distinction between animals raised in intensive confinement situations and those raised more "naturally." One argument could be that there is a chemical difference in the products of animals farmed in high-volume, intensive confinement situations. They are often given nontherapeutic, prophylactic levels of antibiotics and other medications; a biochemical analysis of their tissues and organs could result in a substantive difference that is indeed "incorporated" into their tissues. A slightly more principled distinction can be made by demonstrating the levels of stress hormones present in factory-farmed animals, which are not as prevalent in animals raised under other systems.

If countries desire to incorporate humane standards into trade decisions, it is possible that a shift can be made to reorient the WTO in that direction. The process will take some time, with challenges towards the current view of PPM distinctions, and new decisions that develop the concept. If the failure to treat animals humanely becomes a valid basis for refusing imports, there will be some resistance based on the general WTO prohibition on discrimination in trade. The difficulty of enforcement, evaluation, and discovery of proper humane standards must also be taken into consideration. As it stands today, the PPM distinction mainly allows a prohibition or differentiation on import details if it can be shown that the products are actually biologically or chemically different, or that local health will suffer from the consumption of the products in question. Regardless, the definitional criteria for what constitutes "like products" will need to be changed to pave the way for a broader protection of animals by those countries willing to enforce bans on confinement and other cruelty situations for animals being exploited for use in agriculture, research or entertainment.

The summary conclusion for the WTO is that, while there are some relatively limited possibilities for countries to protect commercially valuable species, there remain many barriers forced upon WTO members which compromise and limit those efforts. There is much work that can be done to urge changes at this level and that could take a bigger view of trade restrictions that impact humane treatment of animals, or the preservation of species.

The International Whaling Commission (IWC)

The World of Whales

For reasons both cultural and biological, whales have captured the interest of the lay public and scientists for centuries. From the Old Testament story of

Jonah to Herman Melville's literary classic *Moby-Dick* to the films *Free Willy* and *Whale Rider*, whales and other cetaceans (the biological group to which they belong) have occupied a significant place in the popular imagination. For generations, indigenous peoples along the Pacific coast of the United States and Canada, the M_ori people of New Zealand, fishers in Vietnam, and others throughout the world have attributed significant totemic, divine, and cultural value to a wide variety of whale species. Whales' unique biological (mammalian) and social characteristics have gained them a level of human interest and appreciation similar to that given to other visible and accessible marine mammals such as seals, sea lions, porpoises, and dolphins. Nevertheless, their use by industry has nearly decimated many whale species from the planet. Despite a global moratorium on commercial whaling that has been in effect since 1986 (discussed in more detail below), whales continue to face serious threats to their existence from ongoing hunting (despite the ban), collisions with large ships, and entanglements in fishing gear that result in tragic and long-suffering deaths.[122]

We have chosen whale issues to close this chapter because they present a good illustration for a more detailed examination of the value and limitations of international law, and for a greater appreciation of international legal principles and issues. Like other animals covered by international agreements (most notably many species of birds), they are in great need of protection specifically because of their migratory nature. Their regular movement across borders and in the open sea means that many countries have at least transitory control over the species, enough to effect their existence and future. Outside of coastal waters, the sea has no borders, making the adoption of voluntary agreements between countries essential to the survival of cetacean species. The attention to the whales' situation has been international in scope for the better part of the last 100 years, and many countries have made efforts to protect them. This section explores the IWC and other bodies that regulates whaling.

Whales demonstrate the intertwined layers of protection and threat to which some species are subject, especially those who share the characteristics of being (1) commercially valuable, (2) threatened by habitat destruction and/or hunting, and (3) transient and migratory. Whales exemplify species that are protected by many countries in domestic laws and also by the international community in multiparty treaties. Nevertheless they may be the group that is most in danger because of the continued and inevitable harmful human encroachment and interaction, and the economic value of their bodies or products of their bodies.

Whales also demonstrate how the potential (and actual) disparity in scientific opinion about the viability of any given population can affect species' futures. When legislative bodies (domestic or international) make decisions about species that are threatened, and any laws or treaties involving them, the rule makers usually look to scientific opinion. This is a crucial consideration in deciding the amount of protection animals are given. Conservation biologists' determinations of a species' viability incorporate a wide range of factors into their analysis. These factors, rarely an exact science, include: (1) reproductive potential of the current breeding population; (2) the minimum amount of animals required to keep the genetic pool of the species healthy; (3) the potential for disease transmission among the population or from other populations (including humans in some cases); (4) any anticipated destruction or limitation of habitat; (5) projected food supply for the species; (6) the likelihood of fatal interactions with humans; and (7) other factors relevant to the particular population.

With any wild population, there are always multiple unknowns. Because whales live beneath the surface of the sea, the calculations become even harder still, due to the inherently difficult process of estimating their health, population size, and demographics. This means that with this broad range of factors and unknowns, none of which are mathematical certainties, reasonable scientific minds often come up with disparate determinations of the numbers of animals necessary for healthy species survival. Personal and professional agendas also may play a part in determining which tests to apply and which factors to give significant weight. The tension between protection of the remaining whales in the world and the diminished but still extant desire to continue whaling has provided additional and different considerations in the international community.[123] As discussed below, exceptions to the moratorium allow several countries to continue the practice, killing large numbers of whales each year, further complicating the efforts to predict viability of a species.[124] The complex considerations indisputably affect the ultimate conclusions, regardless of the care with which the calculations are made.

Despite a broad disapproval of the continued depredation of whale species, the WTO antidiscrimination rules discussed above allow countries that oppose whaling to prohibit the sale or import of whale products. But they prohibit anti-whaling countries from imposing any other kind of sanction or limitation (unrelated to whale products) on those still whaling and selling whale products. The American dilemma—its desire to be publicly seen as a country working to restrict commercial whaling, versus its duty to satisfy its WTO obligations—is representative of the complexities caused by international trade compacts like WTO, even in light of the existence of the IWC. While the U.S. has laws that authorize trade sanctions,[125] they are limited in use because of the WTO.

The IWC—Beginnings

The early twentieth century saw a gradual realization of the finitude of natural "resources," including whales. The IWC, which came into being in 1946, has its roots in a series of earlier attempts to regulate international whaling that date back to 1918.[126] The initial efforts were undertaken in response to a dramatic decrease in whale populations—so drastic that whalers feared that it would soon become impossible to maintain their livelihoods and profitably continue whaling. The clear purpose of these original regulations was to increase whale populations so that commercial exploitation by the whaling industry could continue. Sustainability and preservation of the whaling industry was the primary focus; conservation of whales was a necessary component. This example serves as a good demonstration that the motivation for treaties and agreements that protect a species may not be related to individual animal welfare in any way, but to commercial interests that rely on a viable and self-perpetuating population.

The first significant and relatively comprehensive regulation in the area was the 1931 Convention for the Regulation of Whaling (CRW). The CRW was very much a population management effort, with the goal being to maintain the whale populations so that they could continue to be killed for profit. The CRW prohibited whalers from killing calves and their mothers. It also identified certain whale species that seemed to be in danger of extirpation and banned any whaling on those animals.[127] The CRW did not effectively stop the depletion of the populations, and the continued crisis necessitated another, more comprehensive agreement.

The International Agreement for the Regulation of Whaling (IARW) was adopted in 1937.[128] The IARW expanded coverage to provide greater protection for some species; it banned the hunting of gray whales and established whaling seasons, with the hopes that the off-season periods would allow for some recovery of the depleted populations. Like its predecessor, however, the IARW failed. It did not create a sustainable population for whaling, despite several amendments and protocols that increased protections for some of the most threatened species.

As a result of these unsuccessful attempts and the continuing decline of whale populations, whaling nations convened another conference in 1946. The International Convention for the Regulation of Whaling (ICRW) was the result. The ICRW was established in 1948 and is still in effect as the authoritative body today.[129] As with the prior efforts, its initial focus was sustainable whaling—not the protection of whales because of their inherent qualities, or as a matter of animal welfare. The group began in earnest with the goal being a maintained, stable, or growing whale population that could continue to be harvested by commercial interests, and an effort to keep whaling profitable. The ICRW saw conservation as a mere means to the end of "mak[ing] possible the orderly development of the whaling industry."[130] The parties wanted to ensure "increases in the size of whale stocks [that] will permit increases in the number of whales [that] may be captured...."[131]

Legal Structure of the IWC

The ICRW established the IWC as a means of implementing the regulations and policies of the Convention. The ICRW empowers the IWC to undertake a variety of activities to effectuate its mandates and rules. The IWC elicits and conducts studies concerning whales, collects and evaluates statistical data on whale populations and how whaling affects these populations, and reviews and disseminates information about how to sustain whale stocks. The IWC also publishes and releases reports on its activities and other topics concerning whales and whaling.[132]

One of the ICRW's most vital tasks is its delegation of authority to the IWC, to enact and enforce regulations of whaling. All members must follow the established regulations set up or be subject to sanctions. There are important exceptions/exemptions to the requirements, as discussed below. Among other things, the IWC is empowered to set limits on the (1) species of whales that may be hunted, (2) number of whales that may be killed within each species, (3) methods by which whales are killed, (4) times during which whaling may occur with respect to different regions and species, and (5) areas in which whaling is permitted. The ICRW and ICW are subject to certain requirements so that the regulations must "be based on scientific findings," and they must "take into consideration the interests of the consumers of whale products and the whaling industry."[133] Thus, the commercial aspect of whale use is still an important part of the decision making process. The ICRW also empowers member nations to kill whales for scientific research, a controversial issue discussed in more detail below.[134]

The IWC in Practice

From 1948, when the ICRW came into effect, until 1982, the IWC set quotas designed to facilitate ongoing commercial whaling while permitting whale stocks to recover. These measures, as all those before, still failed to stop the decline of populations, for two main reasons. First, the IWC could not accurately predict population numbers despite the science available. Its inability to perform a census demonstrates the potential problems with relying on scientific analysis when evaluating the future population of any species. Even when experts provide numbers based on scientific data, factors that were not or cannot be considered may influence the ultimate numbers of a species in a population. These unknowns include the possibility of violations of imposed restrictions on whaling, as well as unexpected acts of nature that may impact a population, and the inherent difficulty in evaluating a population that is not amenable to standard means of terrestrial population calculations. The obvious and irresolvable problem with species like the whales is that they are in danger of extinction if not sufficiently protected; thus, if scientific predictions are not realized or wrong, the result could mean a permanent end to the species' presence on earth. But the IWC, under pressure from whaling nations to ensure a commercially viable industry, set quotas that were, in hindsight, too high for whale populations to actually recover.

A second reason that the IWC's quotas did not adequately protect whale populations was the IWC's (and the international community's) inability to ensure compliance. That is, even when quotas were set at levels that might allow for population rebound and growth, the IWC lacked adequate enforcement or policing powers. Whaling occurs on the open seas without the means for sufficient oversight if whalers do not honor the rules. This allowed dishonest whalers, for example, to drastically under-report the number of whales they had caught, further skewing and damaging the wild population, which is exactly what happened during the IWC's quota approach to whaling.

A shift in concern about the whales began as early as 1958. This was a major change in the approach previously taken: for the first time, the whales were being considered as sentient beings, as opposed to simply populations whose numbers needed to be managed. In line with that notion, the humaneness of some whaling methods was put into issue at the IWC's annual meetings, demonstrating concern about animal suffering. This was a new consideration for the IWC, supplementing its primary concern with conserving whales solely as a population and at the species level.[135] For animal protectionists, this marked an important turning point. The incorporation of humane interests indicted that the IWC appreciated that the whales could suffer. On a larger scale, whenever a governing body introduces humane standards into legislation or treaties governing the use of animals, it represents a statement that animal cruelty in commercial enterprises is occurring and should be avoided. Concern about whale welfare also arose in the 1958 Geneva Convention on Fishing and Conservation of the Living Resources of the High Seas,[136] which urged nations "to prescribe, by all means available to them, those methods for the capture and killing of marine life, especially of whales and seals, which will spare them suffering to the greatest extent possible."[137] The emphasis on whales and seals is notable and in line with the recurring theme, throughout the world and the text, that humans view certain animals as more worthy of protection than others. The distinction here is being made between mammalian and nonmammalian marine life, and humans' general feeling that mammals have some characteristics which make them deserving of greater safeguards.

The added welfare concerns reflected changing sentiments arising in the 1950s and 1960s in many of the member countries. These societal changes translated into more serious consideration of humane issues which were being brought forward to the IWC. This formative alteration continued to gain force and the perception of the IWC changed significantly in the 1970s. Thus, although the IWC's original member nations created the ICRW to promote and improve the profitability and size of the whaling industry, the repeated failure of that effort, combined with a new public interest in whales, resulted in this development. The new voices in some member nations and the entry of new member countries into the IWC moved the organization's course from resource management towards species protection, without officially altering its general principles and purposes.[138]

By 1972, the international community was discussing the possibility of a moratorium on whaling, and by 1979, the case was being made based on the possibility of extinction and, partially, on ethical grounds related to the nature of whales and the methods of killing. For example, Australia premised its opposition to whaling on "the potentially high intelligence of whales, a growing community conviction of the immorality of whaling, the imminent availability of substitutes for whale products, the inhumane way that whales are killed, and the risks to the maintenance—and even survival—of some species."[139] At the IWC's 1980 meeting, three different moratorium proposals were introduced, making it clear that "moratorium was destined to be the IWC's topic of the decade."[140] The proposals failed, but new moratoria were introduced in 1981, and by the following year, enough anti-whaling nations had joined the IWC to secure passage of a phased-in moratorium on commercial whaling at the 1982 meeting.[141]

The 1982 moratorium gave members three years to phase out commercial whaling, with the ban taking effect in 1986. It prohibits whaling of any large whale species by setting a zero-catch quota.[142] Although the moratorium was not expected to be permanent, it was still in effect in 2011. The 2010 meeting of the IWC saw a renewed effort to end the moratorium, but after extensive discussions the issue was tabled for another year.[143] The moratorium continues even though the IWC's Scientific Committee has repeatedly determined that a variety of whale species have recovered to the point that they could be commercially hunted while still maintaining a sustainable population level.[144]

Despite the moratorium, whaling still occurs across the globe—both legally and illegally. There are several reasons for this. First, nations that are not parties to the IWC are not subject to the moratorium and may whale with impunity. This highlights the ultimate weakness of international treaties. Canada left the IWC in 1982 and its whaling is unregulated by the IWC. Canadian indigenous Inuit hunters still kill bowhead whales.[145] Additionally, exemptions and loopholes in the IWC provide some countries with the authority (often disputed) to continue to whale. The two largest whaling nations, Norway and Japan, are members of the IWC, but they continue to support whaling based on different justifications under the Convention's rules. As explained in further detail below, Norway claims that it has stated a valid "objection" to the moratorium which, according to IWC procedure, gives a member permission to continue whaling. Japan performs all its whaling under the coverage of the scientific research exemption to the IWC, which authorizes hunting if it is done for research reasons.

Norway filed a formal objection, pursuant to IWC rules, in 1982 when the IWC voted to establish the moratorium. Article V of the ICRW explicitly permits such objections.[146] The objection procedure allows any member country to refuse to be bound by an amendment to the IWC schedule, and the whaling ban was just such an amendment. The legal issues with Norway are interesting, however, because in spite of its objection, it voluntarily ceased whaling in 1987. In 1993, it resumed commercial hunting of whales.[147] As of 2009, Norway allowed hunting of Minke whales. In 2006, it raised its quota by thirty percent to allow for the slaughter of 1,052 minke whales each year, though its actual catch has fallen short of the quota for several years.[148] In 2009 it lowered its catch quota to 885.[149] Because of its initial formal objection to the moratorium, Norway maintains that its current whaling practices are legal, despite its membership in the IWC and despite its initial concession to the moratorium.

Iceland is the only other country in the world that openly practices commercial whaling. It justifies its commercial whaling by claiming an objection to the moratorium, as Norway has done. Iceland's objection raises other controversial issues. The legality of Iceland's whaling is disputed because of its past history with the IWC.[150] As one of the world's most prominent whaling nations, Iceland was an original signatory of the ICRW in 1946. Although Iceland voted against the moratorium in 1982, it did *not* lodge a formal objection, as Norway did.[151] Iceland instead chose to continue to hunt endangered Fin and Sei whales every year under a "scientific permit."[152] Where valid, scientific permits do allow for continued whaling, and the scientific permit/research exception to the moratorium is discussed in more detail below. After receiving criticism for these hunts, Iceland ceased all whaling in 1989, choosing instead to ask the

IWC if it could engage in sustainable commercial whaling.[153] After the IWC refused to grant the allowance, Iceland made a decision that demonstrates the limits of authority for international conventions and agreements. That is, most likely because it was unhappy with the decision of the IWC, Iceland simply quit the ICRW in 1992, and continued whaling.[154]

Ten years later, Iceland *rejoined* IWC. Because it was "just" joining, Iceland claimed its right to object to the IWC rules. It registered a formal objection to the commercial whaling moratorium, as Norway had done upon the adoption of the moratorium.[155] The legality of this objection under the ICRW rules is hotly contested. Anti-whaling activists claim Iceland cannot lodge such an objection to the moratorium after initially accepting it when it was implemented.[156] Over heavy objections, Iceland resumed limited commercial whaling in 2006.[157] After Iceland's economy collapsed in late 2008, it increased its whaling quota to 100 minke whale and 150 fin whales for 2009 in the hopes of creating jobs and stimulating economic growth.[158]

While Norway and Iceland continue commercial whaling under objections to the moratorium, Japan has taken a different approach that has placed it in the middle of another current and hotly argued debate over whaling and the IWC. Although Japan voted against the moratorium and initially filed an objection, it withdrew its objection after the United States threatened to revoke Japanese access to fishing in U.S. waters.[159] Japan ended all whaling that was solely for commercial purposes, and instead has used the IWC rules, and a specific exception, to continue to allow whaling.

Japan and its whaling industry now hunt and kill whales by claiming the whaling is subject to an exception to the moratorium that permits any member nation to grant permits to its nationals "to kill, take and treat whales for purposes of scientific research."[160] Lethal whale research is allowed by the IWC under Article VIII of the ICRW. Japan characterizes the scientific research provision as a "fundamental right" of every member state.[161] Thus, despite the global ban on commercial whaling, Japan hunts between 700 and 1200 whales a year. All Japanese whalers are operating under the presumption and claim that they are engaging in this scientific research.[162]

Iceland and Japan, the only two nations that engage in lethal scientific research, argue that the primary goal of such research is the sustainable use of all marine resources. Therefore, they argue, their whaling is valuable to both the industries and the animals themselves. From 1987 to 2005, Japan's research focused on random catches of whales in order to identify and characterize the sustainable populations, and to evaluate "the role of whales in the Antarctic marine ecosystem and the effect of environmental changes on cetaceans."[163] Once slaughtered, the whales are tested for parasites, pollutants, diet, and the nature of their sex hormones. These tests are designed to increase scientists' knowledge of whale populations and are directly connected to studies intended to determine the best way to engage in sustainable harvesting of whales. Indeed, not only are lethal methods permitted under the IWC's Convention, they are required for scientific accuracy in predicting and evaluating human impact on current populations.[164]

Japanese whalers' research subjects are, in the end, treated like any other commercially-killed animal. That is, the meat of these research whales ends up being sold in fish markets and to restaurants as a delicacy. This provides a powerful economic incentive for continued whaling under the protective "scientific research" umbrella. It is important to note, however, that Article VIII of the ICRW *does* allow the country to do what they wish with the whales' bodies after they have used them for research: "Any whales taken under these special permits shall so far as practicable be processed and the proceeds shall be dealt with in accordance with directions issued by the Government by which the permit was granted."[165]

While not out of technical compliance with IWC requirements, the practice of selling whale meat is not ideologically in line with the IWC's current intent and may increase consumer demand for whale meat in spite of the commercial moratorium. Furthermore, although Japan is allowed to kill only certain "sustainable" species of whales, DNA testing conducted on whale meat in fish markets has reportedly shown that many endangered species are killed and sold for food as well.[166] It is also recognized that because no one can tell the difference between whale meat from a legally killed "research whale" and an illegally hunted one, the presence of legitimate whale meat in stores certainly encourages those willing to break the international moratorium. And one final controversy over the Japanese research was that whales were being taken from the IWC's Southern Ocean Whale Sanctuary. This is an area where other research was ongoing to study whales who were *not* being hunted.[167] Thus, the two types of research could clash and affect some results that could be crucial for determinations regarding the whales' future.

Based on the ongoing controversy over Japan's continued significant whaling activity, the IWC has passed numerous resolutions criticizing Japan's scientific whaling and related practices.[168] Despite the resolutions, Japan continues its efforts.

In its defense, Japan claims its actions are not illegal, and that it must engage in its lethal research protocols to perform the important scientific inquiry it is undertaking. Japan claims there is no alternative to the lethal tests, and that the research is actually helping answer questions about maintaining sustainable populations of whales.[169] Countries opposing the research say that it is either unnecessary or that the same results can be obtained through non-lethal methods.[170] Some discussion has focused on the potential for trade sanctions against Japan for its alleged violation of international whaling regulations; if undertaken, the sanctions could cause a significant disruption in global trade.[171] Japan has cited other international law agreements as a peremptory defense and response to the threat of sanctions for its whaling activities. As might be expected from a review of the preceding section of this chapter, Japan maintains that trade sanctions or other trade-related restrictions would violate the WTO.[172] As of 2011, the controversy over Japanese whaling is ongoing, and is one that is likely to continue into the foreseeable future.

In addition to Norway and Iceland's commercial whaling and Japan's scientific research whaling, there is a third category of whaling currently in practice and approved under the IWC rules. This final exception to the moratorium is based on the IWC's allowance for indigenous peoples to hunt whales for subsistence or cultural purposes. This practice is also controversial,[173] but it is of less significance because of the limited numbers of whales killed, and because it involves different sociocultural and political dynamics. The affected groups are not powerful industries, corporations, and nation-states, but rather indigenous groups who have historically been politically voiceless, often marginalized, and who have relied on whaling for their survival.[174] The IWC has always considered aboriginal subsistence whaling as fundamentally different from commercial whaling for these reasons.

The IWC's policies, though they may have shifted to some consideration of whales' sentiency, still focus largely on species survival and not the fate of the individual animals killed. Since indigenous whalers have never killed large numbers of whales (as compared to commercial interests), there is less concern that aboriginal whaling will work against the primary (species preservation) purpose of the IWC and actually extinguish whale species. Additionally, where culture and not commerce is the driving force for whaling, public opposition to whaling is not as strong. A social calculation seems to be made that if harm to animals comes as a result of a traditional practice, it is less egregious than if it is the result of profit-driven enterprises. While the impact on the animals is the same, the harm is usually done to smaller numbers of their population. And cultural and traditional values are generally given greater respect than an interest in financial gain by many in the international community. Based on all of these considerations, the IWC has permitted indigenous subsistence whaling to provide for indigenous groups' "cultural and nutritional requirements," with the condition that such whaling must not "seriously increase" the risk of extinction.[175] In the U.S., the allowance for aboriginal whaling is greatly circumscribed by restrictions on the methods of whaling and the use of the whales after slaughter—all takes,[176] even those by a tribe, must occur only within the confines of the MMPA.[177]

Although it does not spur the same outrage that scientific whaling does, indigenous whaling has proven highly political at times.[178] In 2002, the IWC delegates for the U.S. and United Kingdom accused the Japanese delegates of engaging in political retaliation directed at indigenous whaling. Japan had refused to allow indigenous groups to utilize their subsistence whaling rights in Alaska and Russia. This denial by Japan followed the IWC's denial of Japan's request for permission to allow coastal whaling off its shores.[179] The U.S. had also promised whaling rights to the Makah in its initial treaty with the tribe, which predated and was unrelated to the IWC.[180] In that treaty between the U.S. and the Makah and based on a settlement of those two parties' interests, the U.S. promised the Makah the right to continue their whaling tradition.[181]

The debates continue. At the 2010 IWC meeting, indigenous people of Greenland bargained for and obtained the right to kill additional whales over the number previously set in their quota.[182] It is often stated that indigenous whaling rights "continue to be used as a bargaining chip by both pro- and anti-whaling governments seeking something in return."[183]

Controversies within the IWC about each kind of whaling—commercial, scientific, and aboriginal—have highlighted how international disputes about "resource" exploitation may be a function of many considerations, including economics, culture, history, animal welfare and sentience, and emotion. They also demonstrate that international law is ultimately only "voluntarily binding" on those who choose to be bound by it. This means willful participation is crucial—and that unhappy players in the international community can simply step out of the pack and adopt laws that are either more or less restrictive than those approved by the international community.

Unhappy stakeholders may even form their own new "competitor" groups. The disputes within the IWC have generated a parallel track for those nations that wish to continue whaling but remain in some bloc of countries regulating the practice. In 1992, four whaling countries, Iceland, Greenland, Norway, and the Faroe Islands (an autonomous province of Denmark), founded the North Atlantic Marine Mammal Commission (NAMMCO) as an alternative to the IWC.[184] NAMMCO allows those nations interested in continuing commercial whaling to justify their practices and avoid welfare-oriented arguments in support of protecting whales. While the IWC is now largely seen as a program to defend and care for whales and discontinue most whaling, NAMMCO allows for a continuation of ostensibly sustainable hunting in the North Atlantic. NAMMCO has not replaced the IWC, although it was viewed as an alternative to the IWC at its inception. NAMMCO is much smaller, covers only the North Atlantic ocean, and has yet to develop a regulatory scheme made up of quotas and management tools, such as that created by the IWC. Although NAMMCO may create the incentive and structure for other whaling nations to leave the IWC and create similar organizations, NAMMCO itself is unlikely to challenge IWC authority globally. However, as Iceland and Norway have stated their objection to the moratorium and continue to whale, and as Japan threatens to leave the IWC, the IWC's coverage and power is certainly vulnerable. Like every other international agreement, the IWC's authority is dependent on adherence by member countries, especially those that are still interested in whaling.

The politics surrounding the moratorium have reshaped the modern membership of the IWC in a very interesting way. As of 2011, there were eighty-eight members of the IWC.[185] Many member countries have *no* history of whaling, but have joined amidst pressure from either Japan (which may be urging these nations to join the IWC to support its opposition to the moratorium and other measures) or the United States, Australia, and the United Kingdom (which may seek new member nations that will support their positions). Thus, nations that have no real interest in the fight are joining the IWC solely as a political move to ensure continued relationships with the key players.

The whaling issue also further demonstrates the way in which international agreements can be bolstered by domestic laws. As a supplement to the protections created by the IWC, many countries have enacted heightened protection for whales. For example, in the United States, the Marine Mammal Protection Act (MMPA) prohibits the "taking"[186] of all marine mammals in United States waters and by United States citizens on the high seas, as well as the importation of marine mammals and marine mammal products into the United States. The MMPA reflects the U.S. government's finding that all marine mammals face some risk of extinction and therefore deserve protection.[187]

Similar protections exist in Australia; there, the government has established the Australian Whale Sanctuary to protect all whales in Australian waters. Under the Environment Protection and Biodiversity Conservation Act 1999 (EPBCA), it is illegal to kill, injure, or even interfere with a dolphin or whale within the boundaries of the Sanctuary. The law requires permits for activities that might have some effect on whales within the Sanctuary.[188] An Australian case brought against a Japanese whaling company demonstrates one of the other problems with international laws—enforcement.[189] Despite an injunction granted in favor of the complaining party (Humane Society International), the court noted that unless the respondent entered Australian waters, it could escape any sanction even if it continued to violate the EPBCA.[190]

Mexico is a member of the IWC and has established an additional, separate structure of protection, indicating its dedication to the conservation of many cetaceans. These laws and agreements provide different protections than the IWC for a number of marine mammals, including the grey whale.[191] By way of example, Mexico is a party to the United Nations' Convention on the Law of the Sea (UN Convention). The UN Convention was intended to establish an "effective international regime over the seabed and the ocean floor beyond a clearly defined national jurisdiction."[192] Over fifteen years (1967–1982), representatives of more than 160 nations repeatedly convened in order to prepare the documents that comprise the Convention. Prior to its adoption, the "freedom-of-the-seas doctrine" allowed the world's nations and commercial interests to operate effectively without any controls. Because that practice was threatening the health of the oceans as well as the species living in it, the UN Convention's creators felt the need to organize some global agreements on the uses of international waters.[193]

In addition to those protections, Mexico has enacted substantial domestic legislation for the protection of whales.[194] The extent of these laws illustrates the need for broad coverage in many areas in order to protect wildlife like whales who are both valuable and vulnerable to the national community. Mexico has a "General Law of Ecological Equilibrium and Environment," as well as specific marine mammal protections,[195] criminal sanctions for violation of laws that protect cetaceans,[196] and official standards even for whale watching.[197] As noted by one commentator:

> Pursuant to Mexican Secretary of Environment's 2002 decree, [nine different whale] species become protected by Mexican law as soon as they enter into the "marine zones that form part of the national territory ... over which the Nation exercises its sovereignty and jurisdiction, including the territorial sea, the internal waters, the contiguous zone and the exclusive economic zone." The tenor of this decree earned international attention when it announced that Mexico had established the "world's largest whale sanctuary."[198]

The Mexican sanctuary established by the 2002 decree includes over 3 million square kilometers of ocean.[199] Whales have now received protection through the Mexican Constitution, federal statutes, and various special presidential decrees and agreements.[200]

This description of other international and domestic laws in covering whales simply highlights the fact that international animal law—to the extent it provides protections to a given species—can and should involve multiple layers of protection, through different international organizations as well as domestic legislatures. As always is the case, animal advocacy groups, working through both legal and grass roots campaigns, may also play an important role. This has been the case with whaling issues, as many groups advocate for greater protections.[201]

Notes

1. M.J. Bowman, *The Protection of Animals Under International Law*, 4 CONN. J. INT'L LAW 487, 487–89 (1989).

2. So that all readers can appreciate the context of this chapter, we begin with this basic primer.

3. The International Court of Justice (ICJ) resolves legal disputes among United Nations member states and issues advisory opinions on issues of international law. However, there are two significant limitations on the ICJ's jurisdiction. First, only countries may submit disputes to the ICJ, not non-governmental organizations or individuals. Statute of the International Court of Justice art. 34, para. 1, June 26, 1945, 59 Stat. 1055, 3 Bevans 1153 (ICJ Statute). Second, the ICJ hears only disputes in which the parties have consented to the ICJ's jurisdiction. *Id.* art. 36, para. 1.

4. Article 38 of the Statute of the International Court of Justice is widely recognized as a statement of the basic sources of international law: "[1] international conventions, whether general or particular, establishing rules expressly recognized by the contesting states; [2] international custom, as evidence of a general practice accepted as law; [3] the general principles of law recognized by civilized nations; [4] judicial decisions and the teachings of the most highly qualified publicists of the various nations, as subsidiary means for the determination of rules of law." ICJ Statute, *supra* note 3, art. 38, para. 1.

5. Vienna Convention on the Law of Treaties, art. 53, Apr. 18, 1961, 23 U.S.T. 3227, 1155 U.N.T.S. 331; *see also* Christopher A. Ford, *Adjudicating Jus Cogens*, 13 WIS. INT'L L.J. 145 (1994).

6. For example, in the United States, torture is prohibited under 18 United States Code section 2340. The Universal Declaration of Human Rights banned all forms of torture in 1948. Universal Declaration of Human Rights art. 5, G.A. Res. 217A, U.N. GAOR, 3d Sess., 1st plen. Mtg., U.N. Doc. A/810 (Dec. 12, 1948).

7. *See, e.g.*, Mark Danner, *US Torture: Voices from the Black Sites*, N.Y. REV. BOOKS, Apr. 9, 2009, *available at* http://www.nybooks.com/articles/22530 (discussing confidential report from the International Committee of the Red Cross concluding that the Bush administration's interrogation techniques constituted torture under international law).

8. *See* Mark Allan Gray, *The International Crime of Ecocide*, 26 CAL. W. INT'L L.J. 215, 225 (1996) (discussing the potential customary norm against "ecocide," but acknowledging that rights for nature and animals "do not currently enjoy recognition under international law"). *But see* Michael J. Glennon, *Has International Law Failed the Elephant?*, 84 AM. J. INT'L L. 1, 30 (1990) (arguing that customary international law now requires the protection of endangered species); *see also* Michael Bowman, *"Normalizing" the International Convention for the Regulation of Whaling*, 29 MICH. J. INT'L L. 293, 459 ("[I]t is unquestionably legitimate, and arguably compulsory [under international law], to afford [animal welfare] due consideration in the development of policy regarding the exploitation of wild fauna of all descriptions."). Some theorists see the development of standard rules against animal exploitation as both imminent and necessary. *See* Anthony D'Amato & Sudhir K. Chopra, *Whales: Their Emerging Right to Life*, 85 AM. J. INT'L L. 21, 23 (1991) (arguing that the historical trajectory of whaling regulations and the developing international consensus

against whaling should provide whales with the right to life under customary international law); Kyle Ash, *Why "Managing" Biodiversity Will Fail: An Alternative Approach to Sustainable Exploitation for International Law*, 13 ANIMAL L. 209, 244–45 (2007) (discussing how existing principles of international law, including *jus cogens*, could be expanded to combat bias based on species alone).

9. *See, e.g.*, Melissa A. Waters, *Creeping Monism: The Judicial Trend Toward Interpretive Incorporation of Human Rights Treaties*, 107 COLUM. L. REV. 628, 635–36 (2007); *see also* Treaty Negotiation and Implementation in Canada, UNIVERSITY OF PENNSYLVANIA LAW SCHOOL, *available at* http://www.law.upenn.edu/bll/archives/ulc/igasloc/summary_english.htm (describing Canada's dualist approach to international law).

10. For a detailed examination of this question, see Harold Hongju Koh, *Why Do Nations Obey International Law?*, 106 YALE L.J. 2599 (1997) (book review).

11. CITES, Mar. 3, 1973, 27 U.S.T. 1087, 993 U.N.T.S. 243.

12. CITES, *Member Countries*, *available at* http://www.cites.org/eng/disc/parties/ index.shtml.

13. CITES' protected species consist of 5,000 animal species and 28,000 plant species. *The CITES Species*, CITES, *available at* http://www.cites.org/eng/disc/species.shtml. For a full listing of protected plant and animal species, see CITES, APPENDICES I, II, AND III (2008), *available at* http://www.cites.org/eng/app/E-Jul01.pdf.

14. 16 U.S.C. §§1531–1534 (2006).

15. *About IUCN*, INTERNATIONAL UNION FOR CONSERVATION OF NATURE, *available at* http://www.iucn.org/about/.

16. *See A Brief History of CITES*, CITES WORLD OFFICIAL NEWSLETTER OF THE PARTIES 2–3 (March 3, 2003), *available at* www.cites.org/eng/news/world/30special.pdf.

17. *Id.* at 3.

18. *Id.*

19. CITES, Preamble.

20. CITES, Article II, para. 1.

21. *Id.*

22. For a thorough and comprehensive discussion of CITES, *see* David S. Favre, INTERNATIONAL TRADE IN ENDANGERED SPECIES: A GUIDE TO CITES (1989).

23. Art. II, para. 1.

24. Art. II, para. 2(a).

25. Art. II, para. 3.

26. "Subspecies" and "population" refer to geographically distinct groups within a species that can interbreed, but are considered separate species because of their development apart from other species members.

27. *The CITES Species*, CITES, *available at* http://www.cites.org/eng/disc/species.shtml.

28. Art. III, para. 2.

29. Art. III, para. 3.

30. *World Wildlife Fund v. Hodel*, No. 88-1276, 1988 U.S. Dist. LEXIS 19409 (D.D.C. June 17, 1988) (memorandum opinion). Notably, the court did not invalidate the importation of the pandas, which had already occurred, but simply enjoined the zoo from charging an extra fee for the panda exhibit.

31. Art. VII, para. 4.

32. Art. II, para. 2.

33. Art. IV, para. 2. Appendix II species may receive additional protection from the exporting country if that country's Scientific Authority finds "that the export of specimens

of any such species should be limited in order to maintain that species throughout its range at a level consistent with its role in the ecosystems in which it occurs." Art. IV, para. 3. In such cases, the country may take "suitable measures" to reduce export permits for that species. *Id.*

34. Art. II, para. 3.

35. *Appendices I, II, and III,* CITES, *available at* http://www.cites.org/eng/app/appendices.shtml; *The CITES Species, supra* note 13.

36. *How CITES Works,* CITES, *available at* http://www.cites.org/eng/disc/how.shtml.

37. Art. V, para. 2.

38. Art. VIII, para. 3.

39. Art. XI, para. 2.

40. Julie Martin, Note, *The Price Of Fame: CITES Regulation and Efforts Towards International Protection of The Great White Shark,* 39 GEORGE WASHINGTON L. REV. 199, 206 (2007).

41. *Conference of the Parties,* CITES, *available at* http://www.cites.org/eng/disc/CoP.shtml.

42. *The CITES Secretariat,* CITES, *available at* http://www.cites.org/eng/disc/sec/ index.shtml.

43. *Id.*

44. Jolene Lin, *Tackling Southeast Asia's Illegal Wildlife Trade,* 9 S.Y.B.I.L. 191, 192 (2005) (Singapore Year Book of International Law). "Each year the World Wildlife Fund (WWF) proposes a list of species that have suffered the greatest detriment from unregulated trade. Nine out of ten of the most endangered species on the 2004 list are found in Asia." *Id.* at 195.

45. Julie Cheung, *Implementation and Enforcement of CITES: An Assessment of Tiger and Rhinoceros Conservation Policy in Asia,* 5 PAC. RIM L. & POL'Y J. 125 (1995); David Favre, *Debate within the CITES Community: What Direction for the Future?,* 33 NAT. RESOURCES J. 677 (1993).

46. *See* Claudia A. McMurray, *Wildlife Trafficking: U.S. Efforts to Tackle a Global Crisis,* 16 NAT. RES. & ENVIRONMENT 16 (Winter 2009); *What is ASEAN-WEN?,* ASEAN-WEN WILDLIFE ENFORCEMENT NETWORK, *available at* http://www.asean-wen.org/index.php?option=com_content&view=article&id=47&Itemid=55; Press Release, The ASEAN Ministerial Session on CITES (Oct. 11, 2004), *available at* http://www.asean.org/16468.htm.

47. *Id.*

48. Inés Arroyo-Quiroz *et al., Developing Countries and the Implementation of CITES: The Mexican Experience,* J. OF INT'L WILDLIFE L. & POLICY 8(1), 13–49 (2005).

49. Although captive-bred tigers would seem to fit in Appendix II, the CITES ban is on the transport and sale of all tiger parts that were not stockpiled prior to the ban. And while wild tigers are listed on Appendix I, there is an exception for trade in captive-bred tigers, generating much controversy over the propriety and value of the exception. *See, e.g.,* Joonmoo Lee, *Poachers, Tigers and Bears ... Oh My! Asia's Illegal Wildlife Trade,* 16 NW. J. INT'L L. & BUS. 497, 505 (Spring 1996); J. Santangelo, *Evading Extinction: A 21st Century Survey of the Legal Challenges to Wild Siberian Tiger Conservation,* 1 J. ANIMAL L. 109, 125–27 (2005).

50. *See, e.g.,* Andrew Jacobs, *Tiger Farms in China Feed Thirst for Parts,* N.Y. TIMES, Feb. 12, 2010, *available at* http://www.nytimes.com/2010/02/13/world/asia/13tiger.html; *Tiger Farms: A Ticket to Extinction,* WORLD WILDLIFE FOUNDATION (July 9, 2009), *available at* http://www.worldwildlife.org/what/globalmarkets/wildlifetrade/tigerfarms.html.

51. Products can be traded within a country's borders without violating CITES, because the Convention regulates only international trade.

52. *See, e.g., China Lobbies to Farm Tigers for Body Parts,* MSNBC (May 17, 2007), http://www.msnbc.msn.com/id/18720080/ns/world_news-world_environment/; *Tiger Farms: A Ticket to Extinction, supra* note 50.

53. *Id.*

54. *Id.*

55. *See, e.g.*, K. Nowell & X. Ling, *Taming the Tiger Trade: China's Markets for Wild and Captive Tiger Products Since the 1993 Domestic Trade Ban*, TRAFFIC EAST ASIA (2007); *see also Tiger Farms Undermining Conservation Efforts*, ECOLOGIST (July 30, 2009), *available at* http://www.theecologist.org/blogs_and_comments/commentators/other_comments/295015/tiger_farms_undermining_conservation_efforts.html.

56. Leigh Henry, Program Officer for TRAFFIC North America, quoted in Press Release, *Lifting Chinese Tiger Trade Ban a Death Sentence for Wild Tigers Say WWF and TRAFFIC* (March 13, 2007), *available at* http://www.worldwildlife.org/who/media/press/2007/WWFPresitem923.html.

57. *See, e.g.*, Laurel Neme, *Tiger Farming and Traditional Chinese Medicine* (July 27, 2010), *available at* http://news.mongabay.com/2010/0628-neme_tigers_ge_gabriel.html.

58. Holly Edwards, *When Predators Become Prey: The Need for International Shark Conservation*, 12 OCEAN & COASTAL L.J. 305 (2007). In the case of the elephant, CITES uses two monitoring tools to track poaching and assess policies for trade in elephant products. These are MIKE (Monitoring the Illegal Killing of Elephants) and ETIS (Elephant Trade Information System). Nigel Hunter & Tom Milliken, *Clarifying MIKE and ETIS*, 36 PACHYDERM 129 (2004). The two tools provide information that helps CITES members understand the trends behind the illegal killing of elephants in the member states. Before MIKE, there were no "means to provide a systematic and detailed assessment of the impact of [CITES] decisions to allow, restrict or suspend trade in a particular species." *Id.* MIKE established a monitoring system across the entirety of the African and Asian elephants' ranges in order to receive and transmit reliable information about elephant populations, illegal killings, and trade. However, MIKE does *not* work as an anti-poaching operation to stop the illegal killing of elephants. MIKE is solely a monitoring tool to make sure elephant populations maintain a sustainable level. Whereas MIKE focuses on tracking elephant populations and the illegal killing of elephants, ETIS focuses on recording and analyzing trends in the illegal trade of elephants and elephant parts. Like MIKE, ETIS does not affect poaching. It simply gathers information the Convention needs to support its decisions regarding elephants.

59. *See, e.g.*, Thaddeus McBride, *The Dangers of Liberal Neo-Colonialism: Elephants, Ivory and the CITES Treaty*, 19 B.C. THIRD WORLD L.J. 733 (1999) (book review) (describing CITES as a neo-colonial agreement that undermines the sovereignty of "developing" countries by forcing them to limit their economic opportunities to conform to Western conservation norms).

60. *See, e.g.*, Sam B. Edwards III, *Legal Trade in African Elephant Ivory: Buy Ivory to Save the Elephant?*, 7 ANIMAL L. 119 (2001).

61. Inés Arroyo-Quiroz *et al.*, *supra* note 48, at 13.

62. Shawn M. Dansky, *The CITES "Objective" Listing Criteria: Are They "Objective" Enough to Protect the African Elephant?*, 73 TUL. L. REV. 961 (1999).

63. *Id.* at 974–75; *see also* S. Wasser *et al.*, *Elephants, Ivory & Trade*, 327 SCIENCE 1331 (Mar. 12, 2010).

64. Dansky, *supra* note 62, at 974–75.

65. *Id.* at 969.

66. *African Elephant*, INTERNATIONAL FUND FOR ANIMAL WELFARE, *available at* http://www.ifaw.org/ifaw_international/save_animals/elephants/african_elephant.php; *See also Seventh Meeting of the Conference of the Parties*, CITES, *available at* http://www.cites.org/eng/cop/07/prop/index.shtml.

67. 16 U.S.C. §4201 *et seq.*; *see generally* A. M. Lemieux and R. V. Clarke, *The International Ban on Ivory Sales and its Effects on Elephant Poaching in Africa*, 2009 BRITISH J. OF CRIMINOLOGY 49(4):451.

68. Dansky, *supra* note 62, at 970.

69. *Id.* at 972; *see also* M. Del Baglivo, *CITES at the Crossroads: New Ivory Sales and Sleeping Giants*, 14 FORDHAM ENVT'L L. J. 279 (Spring 2003); J. Dernbach, *Reflections on Comparative Law, Environmental Law, and Sustainability*, 3 WIDENER L. SYMPOSIUM J. 279, 284 n.34 (Fall 1998).

70. Dansky, *supra* note 62, at 972.

71. *Id. See also* D. R. Downes *et al.*, *International Environmental Law*, 43 INT'L LAWYER 837, 849 (Spring 2009); S. B. Edwards III, *Legal Trade in African Elephant Ivory: Buy Ivory to Save the Elephant?*, 7 J. ANIMAL L. 119 (2001).

72. McBride, *supra* note 59, at 746, 751–53.

73. Art. XIV, para. 1(a).

74. *See generally* 16 U.S.C. §§1361 *et seq.*; 16 U.S.C. §1375 (MMPA violations); 16 U.S.C. §§1531 *et seq.*; 16 U.S.C. §1540(b)(1) (ESA violations). *See also United States v. Hayashi*, 22 F.3d 859 (9th Cir. 1993) (discussing penalties for MMPA). *But see* J. Parent, *Animal Salvage: Cost Effective Methods for the Preservation of Marine Life*, 14 BUFFALO ENVT'L L. J. 117, 142 (Fall 2006) (noting that actual enforcement and issuance of penalties for MMPA violations may be extremely rare despite ongoing violations).

75. FLA. STAT. ANN. §379.2431.

76. *Environmental Treaties and Resource Indicators (ENTRI)*, CENTER FOR INTERNATIONAL EARTH SCIENCE INFORMATION NETWORK, *available at* http://sedac.ciesin.org/entri/register/reg-045.rrr.html.

77. *Id.*

78. FAO Advisory Committee on Marine Resources Research Working Party On Marine Mammals, Mammals in the Seas, Vol. II: Pinniped Species Reports and Summaries on Sirenians 142, FOOD AND AGRICULTURE ORGANIZATION OF THE UNITED NATIONS (1979).

79. *What is the WTO?*, WORLD TRADE ORGANIZATION, *available at* http://www.wto.org/english/thewto_e/whatis_e/whatis_e.htm. See also Peter Stevenson, The World Trade Organisation Rules: A Legal Anaylsis of Their Adverse Impact on Animal Welfare, 8 ANIMAL L. 107 (2002).

80. E. Kwan Choi, *The Roots of the WTO*, IOWA STATE UNIVERSITY DEPT. OF ECONOMICS, *available at* http://www.econ.iastate.edu/classes/econ355/choi/wtoroots.htm [hereinafter Roots of the WTO].

81. *Id.*

82. *About the WTO: A Statement by the Director General*, WORLD TRADE ORGANIZATION, *available at* http://www.wto.org/english/thewto_e/whatis_e/wto_dg_stat_e.htm; *see also* Roots of the WTO, *supra* note 80.

83. *About the WTO: A Statement by the Director General, supra* note 82.

84. The relevant language under this provision, Article I, reads:

> With respect to customs duties and charges of any kind imposed on or in connection with importation or exportation or imposed on the international transfer of payments for imports or exports, and with respect to the method of levying such duties and charges, and with respect to all rules and formalities in connection with importation and exportation, and with respect to all matters referred to

in paragraphs 2 and 4 of Article III, any advantage, favour, privilege or immunity granted by any contracting party to any product originating in or destined for any other country shall be accorded immediately and unconditionally to the like product originating in or destined for the territories of all other contracting parties.

85. The pertinent language under Article III reads:

1. The contracting parties recognize that internal taxes and other internal charges, and laws, regulations and requirements affecting the internal sale, offering for sale, purchase, transportation, distribution or use of products ... should not be applied to imported products or domestic products so as to afford protection to domestic products.

2. The products of the territory of any contracting party imported into the territory of any other contracting party shall not be subject, directly or indirectly, to internal taxes or other internal charges of any kind in excess of those applied, directly or indirectly to like domestic products....

3. The products of the territory of any contracting party imported into the territory of any other contracting party shall be accorded treatment no less favourable than that accorded to like products of national origin.

86. Art. XI reads, in pertinent part:

No prohibitions or restrictions other than duties, taxes or other charges, whether made effective through quotas, import or export licenses or other measures, shall be instituted or maintained by any contracting party on the importation of any product of the territory of any other contracting party or on the exportation or sale for export of any product destined for the territory of any other contracting party.

87. For a thorough explanation of the WTO Dispute Settlement Body, see David Hunter *et al.*, International Environmental Law and Policy 1261–66 (1998).

88. *Id.* at 1261.

89. *The WTO in Brief*, World Trade Organization, *available at* http://www.wto.org/english/res_e/doload_e/inbr_e.pdf.

90. Preamble to Agreement Establishing the World Trade Organization, "The parties to this Agreement ... [recognize] that their relations in the field of trade and economic endeavor should be conducted ... while allowing for the optional use of the world's resources in accordance with the objective of sustainable development, seeking both to protect and preserve the environment and to enhance the means for doing so in a manner consistent with their respective needs and concerns at different levels of economic development." *See, e.g.*, http://www.wto.org/english/res_e/booksp_e/analytic_index_e/wto_agree_01_e.htm#p.

91. *See, e.g.*, Hunter *et al. supra* note 87, at 1240–46.

92. "While common law countries respect the tradition of *stare decisis*, where prior judicial decisions on a question of law are generally regarded as binding on later cases posing the same questions, civil law countries (such as those in continental Europe) generally treat each case as de novo, where courts are not constrained by earlier decisions. In theory, the principle of *stare decisis* does not apply to the WTO dispute settlement process." *Id.* at 1267.

However, the Appellate Body of the WTO Dispute Resolution process has actually accorded great weight to its past decisions even though *stare decisis* is not formally followed by international tribunals.... In public international law, past decisions may be persuasive, but not binding.... On occasion, the Appellate Body has reached decisions that seem inconsistent with precedent. However, in general previous decisions and doctrine are so highly persuasive in WTO jurisprudence,

> and their use is so central to the discourse of dispute settlement, that it may be said that the WTO observes de facto *stare decisis*.

Richard Steinberg, *Judicial Lawmaking at the WTO: Discursive, Constitutional, and Political Constraints*, 98 AM. J. INT'L L. 247, 254 (2004).

93. Report of the Panel, United States—Restriction on Imports of Tuna (Sept. 3, 1991), GATT B.I.S.D. (39th Supp.) at 155 (1993) (Tuna-Dolphin I). The facts of the case discussed below are also set out in James L. Anderson and Josué Martínez-Garmendia, THE INTERNATIONAL SEAFOOD TRADE 70 (2003); Dominic A. Gentile, *International Trade and the Environment: What is the Role of the WTO?*, 20 FORDHAM ENVTL. L. REV. 197 (2009).

94. 16 U.S.C. §§1361–1407.

95. *Committee for Humane Legislation v. Richardson*, 540 F.2d 1141, 1144 (D.C. Cir. 1976).

96. 16 U.S.C. §1361(2).

97. An exception to the MMPA for "incidental takes"—activities which affected or killed a small number of marine mammals—still exists. 16 U.S.C. §1371(a)(2).

98. American fishers were able to circumvent the constraints of the MMPA by either going outside of U.S. waters or using foreign vessels for their operations.

99. *See generally Animal Welfare Institute v. Kreps*, 561 F.2d 1002 (D.C. Cir. 1977).

100. *See Mexico etc. versus U.S.: 'Tuna-Dolphin'*, WORLD TRADE ORGANIZATION, http://www.wto.org/english/tratop_e/envir_e/edis04_e.htm.

101. HUNTER, *supra* note 87, at 1271. "From the environmentalist [or animal protectionist] perspective, two cans of tuna that are physically identical should not be 'alike' if one is produced using a process that kills dolphin and the other is not." *Id.* at 1273.

102. Tuna-Dolphin I, ¶5.31.

103. *Id.*

104. Report of the Panel, United States—Restrictions on Imports of Tuna, unadopted, DS29/R (June 16, 1994) (Tuna-Dolphin II).

105. A full description of the case is available in Gentile, *supra* note 93, at 207–09.

106. Art. XX.

107. *Id.*

108. Gentile, *supra* note 93, at 207.

109. *See* Appellate Body Report, United States-Import Prohibition of Certain Shrimp and Shrimp Products, WT/DS58/AB/R (Oct. 12, 1998); *see also* Panel Report, United States-Import Prohibition of Certain Shrimp and Shrimp Products, WT/DS59/R (May 15, 1998).

110. Appellate Body Report, United States-Import Prohibition of Certain Shrimp and Shrimp Products, Recourse to Article 21.5 of the DSU by Malaysia, WT/DS58/AB/RW (Oct. 22, 2001); Panel Report, United States-Import Prohibition of Certain Shrimp and Shrimp Products, Recourse to Article 21.5 of the DSU by Malaysia, WT/DS58/RW (June 15, 2001).

111. Gentile, *supra* note 93, at 221–22.

112. The Article XX chapeau reads:

> Subject to the requirement that such measures are not applied in a manner which would constitute a means of arbitrary or unjustifiable discrimination between countries where the same conditions prevail, or a disguised restriction on international trade, nothing in this Agreement shall be construed to prevent the adoption or enforcement by any contracting party of measures [exemptions a through j].

113. Council Regulation (EEC) No 3254/91 of 4 November 1991, *available at* http://eur-lex.europa.eu/smartapi/cgi/sga_doc?smartapi!celexplus!prod!DocNumber&lg=en&type_doc=Regulation&an_doc=1991&nu_doc=3254.

114. Council Decision 98/487/EC of 13 July 1998 (concerning the conclusion of an international Agreement in the form of an Agreed Minute between the European Community and the United States of America on humane trapping standards) [Official Journal L 219, 7.8.1998]; Council Decision 98/142/EC of 26 January 1998 (concerning conclusion of an Agreement on international humane trapping standards between the European Community, Canada and the Russian Federation and of an Agreed Minute between Canada and the European Community concerning the signing of said Agreement) [Official Journal L 42, 14.2.1998].

115. Sebastiaan Princen, *EC Compliance with WTO Law: The Interplay of Law and Politics,* 15 Eur. J. Int'l L. 555, 555–65 (2004).

116. *See* Gillian Dale, *The European Union's Steel Leghold Trap Ban: Animal Cruelty Legislation in Conflict with International Trade,* 7 Colo. J. Int'l Envtl. L. & Pol'y 441 (1996).

117. Princen, *supra* note 115, at 565–66.

118. *See, e.g.*, Gaverick Matheny & Cheryl Leahy, *Farm-Animal Welfare, Legislation, and Trade,* 70 Law and Contemporary Problems 325 (2007).

119. "Battery cages" and other forms of confinement agriculture practices that have become standard industry practice are discussed in more detail in Chapter 2. In short, battery cage production involves the confinement of thousands of chickens in a highly concentrated space, in an environment that causes a myriad of severe health effects on the animals, and subjects them to suffering and cruelty on a constant basis.

120. *See, e.g.*, S. Glassman, *Proposed Amendments to Multilateral Trading Agreements to Encourage U.S.-Mexico Trade in Biofuels,* 17 Univ. Baltimore J. Envt'l L. 107, 139 (Spring 2010); *see also Quality, Health & Safety—The Issue of PPMs,* Newcastle University, *available at* http://www.staff.ncl.ac.uk/david.harvey/AEF372/IssuesFile/PPM.html; *see also* http://www.iisd.org/trade/handbook/5_1.htm.

121. *See* Gentile, *supra* note 93, at 226–31.

122. *See, e.g.*, Scott D. Kraus *et al.*, *North Atlantic Right Whales In Crisis,* Science, July 22, 2005, at 561.

123. The IWC also addresses this issue and is discussed in the next section.

124. The moratorium, part of the IWC's rules, is discussed in the next section as well.

125. The Fisherman's Protective Act of 1967 or the Packwood-Magnuson Amendment to the Magnuson Fishery Conservation and Management Act, 18 U.S.C. § 1821, allows limits on fishing rights for countries "engaging in trade or taking which diminishes the effectiveness of the International Convention for the Regulation of Whaling." *Id.* § 1821(e)(2).

126. D'Amato & Chopra, *supra* note 8, at 23.

127. Convention for the Regulation of Whaling, Sept. 24, 1931, 49 Stat. 3079, TS No. 880, 155 LNTS 349; *see also* D'Amato & Chopra, *supra* note 8, at 31.

128. International Agreement for the Regulation of Whaling, June 8, 1937, 52 Stat. 1460, TS No. 933, 190 LNTS 79; *see also* D'Amato & Chopra, *supra* note 8, at 31.

129. International Convention for the Regulation of Whaling, Dec. 2, 1946, 62 Stat. 1716, TIAS No. 1849, 161 UNTS 72 [hereinafter ICRW]; *see also* D'Amato & Chopra, *supra* note 8, at 33–34.

130. ICRW Preamble, 62 Stat. at 1717.

131. *Id.* at 1716.

132. ICRW, art. IV, 62 Stat. at 1718.

133. ICRW, art. V, 62 Stat. at 1718–19.

134. ICRW, art. VIII, 62 Stat. at 1719–20.

135. D'Amato & Chopra, *supra* note 8, at 35.

136. Geneva Convention on Fishing and Conservation of the Living Resources of the High Seas Apr. 29, 1958, 17 UST 138, TIAS No. 5969, 559 UNTS 285.

137. D'Amato & Chopra, *supra* note 8, at 36 (quoting Res. V., *Humane Killing of Marine Life*, 2 UNITED NATIONS CONFERENCE ON THE LAW OF THE SEA, OFFICIAL RECORDS 144, UN Doc. A/CONF. 13/38, UN Sales No. 58 V.4, Vol. II (1958)).

138. D'Amato & Chopra, *supra* note 8, at 36, 38–45.

139. *Id.* at 38–39, 42.

140. *Id.* at 43.

141. *Id.* at 43–46.

142. A dispute exists over the IWC's authority to dictate management of smaller cetacean species. One view is that the IWC can only mandate hunting controls with respect to the large whales specifically named in IWC documents. Setting the issue of quotas aside, all seem to agree that the IWC Scientific Committee has the right to research and offer counsel on the small cetaceans' population dynamics and preservation. This has included comments on the concerns raised when small cetaceans are caught (and die) in fishing nets. For a discussion of the place of small cetaceans in international law, *see* Rachelle Adam, *The Japanese Dolphin Hunts: In Quest of International Legal Protection for Small Cetaceans*, 14 ANIMAL L. 133 (2008).

143. *Details for The International Whaling Commission's 62nd Annual Meeting in Agadir, Morocco*, 2010 INTERNATIONAL WHALING COMMISSION, *available at* http://iwcoffice.org/meetings/meeting2010.htm.

144. *See* Brettny Hardy, Note, *A Regional Approach to Whaling: How the North Atlantic Marine Mammal Commission is Shifting the Tides for Whale Management*, 17 DUKE J. COMP. & INT'L LAW 169 (2006).

145. Elizabeth M. Bakalar, *Subsistence Whaling in the Native Village of Barrow: Bringing Autonomy to Native Alaskans Outside the International Whaling Commission*, 30 BROOKLYN J. INT'L L. 601, 613 n.72, 624, 629–32 (2005).

146. ICRW, art. V, para. 3, 62 Stat. at 1719.

147. For a list of whales killed under objection to the moratorium, *see Catches Under Objection Since 1985*, INTERNATIONAL WHALING COMMISSION, *available at* http://www.iwcoffice.org/conservation/table_objection.htm.

148. *See Twelve Governments Protest Norway's Increased Whaling Quota,* ENVIRONMENTAL NEWS SERVICES, http://www.ens-newswire.com/ens/apr2006/2006-04-21-01.html; Catherine Stein, *Whaling Quota Draws Fire,* AFTENPOSTEN, Feb. 7, 2007, *available at* http://www.aftenposten.no/english/local/article2243265.ece.

149. *Id.*; *Norway Lowers Quota for 2009 Whale Hunt*, GUARDIAN, Dec. 13, 2008, *available at* http://www.guardian.co.uk/uslatest/story/0,,-8158113,00.html.

150. *Iceland and Commercial Whaling*, INTERNATIONAL WHALING COMMISSION, *available at* http://iwcoffice.org/conservation/iceland.htm.

151. *Id.*

152. D'Amato & Chopra, *supra* note 8, at 48 n.192.

153. A. Gillespie, *Iceland's Reservation at the International Whaling Commission*, 14 EUROPEAN J. INT'L LAW 977, 979 (Nov. 2003); *see also Iceland and Commercial Whaling,* INTERNATIONAL WHALING COMMISSION, *available at* http://iwcoffice.org/conservation/ iceland.htm.

154. B. Hodges, *The Cracking Façade of the International Whaling Commission as an Institution of International Law: Norwegian Small-Type Whaling and the Aboriginal Subsistence*

Exemption, 15 J. ENVT'L LAW & LITIG. 295, 312 (Fall 2000). Norway also left the Convention, for the same reasons, the same year. *Id.* at 314.

155. International Whaling Commission, *Iceland and Her Re-adherence to the Convention After Leaving in 1992*, *available at* http://iwcoffice.org/_documents/_iceland.htm.

156. *See, e.g.*, *Iceland Dissatisfied with U.S. Whaling Demand*, ICELAND REVIEW ONLINE, April 9, 2010, *available at* http://icelandreview.com/icelandreview/daily_news/?cat_id=16539&ew_0_a_id=360507; Lowana Veal, *Whaling Profitable but Bad for Iceland's Image*, IPS NEWS, April 16, 2010, *available at* http://ipsnews.net/news.asp?idnews=51067; *Germany Delivers an Ultimatum to Iceland on Whaling*, SEA SHEPHERD CONSERVATION SOCIETY, June 16, 2010, *available at* http://www.seashepherd.org/news-and-media/news-100616-3.html.

157. Richard Black, *Iceland Begins Commercial Whaling*, BBC NEWS, Oct. 17, 2006, *available at* http://news.bbc.co.uk/2/hi/science/nature/6059564.stm. In 2008, Iceland exported its whale meat to Japan to sell in its markets. Richard Black, *Japan Sells Icelandic Whale Meat*, BBC NEWS, Dec. 5, 2008, *available at* http://news.bbc.co.uk/2/hi/science/nature/7767716.stm.

158. Gladys Fouché, *Bankrupt Iceland Pins Its Hopes on Whaling—But Will It Work?*, GUARDIAN, Feb. 24, 2009, *available at* http://www.guardian.co.uk/environment/2009/feb/24/whaling-iceland. The decision to increase the quota was made by the outgoing administration and could be overturned by the incoming fisheries minister. *Id.*

159. D'Amato & Chopra, *supra* note 8, at 46–47.

160. ICRW art. VIII, 62 Stat. at 1719–20.

161. *See, e.g.*, JAPANESE MINISTRY OF FOREIGN AFFAIRS, JAPAN'S POSITION ON SCIENTIFIC RESEARCH WHALING 4 (2008), *available at* http://www.cl.emb-japan.go.jp/doc/2008 04 Japan's Position (revised ver).pdf.

162. *Catches Taken: Under Scientific Permit*, INTERNATIONAL WHALING COMMISSION, *available at* http://www.iwcoffice.org/conservation/table_permit.htm.

163. Tatjana Rosen, *Whaling for Scientific Research Purposes*, (Washington, D.C.: Environmental Information Coalition, National Council for Science and the Environment).

164. For a defense of Japanese scientific whaling under international law and the IWC, *see* Eldon V.C. Greenberg, Paul S. Hoff & Michael I. Goulding, *Japan's Whale Research Program and International Law*, 32 CAL. W. INT'L L.J. 151 (2002).

165. ICRW, art. VIII, para. 2, 62 Stat. at 1720.

166. *See, e.g.*, R. Ackerman, *Japanese Whaling in the Pacific Ocean: Defiance of International Whaling Norms in the Name of "Scientific Research," Culture, and Tradition*, 25 BOSTON COLLEGE INT'L COMP. L. R. 323 (Spring 2002); D. Vice, *Implementation of Biodiversity Treaties: Monitoring, Fact-Finding, and Dispute Resolution*, 29 N.Y.U. J. INT'L. LAW & POLITICS 577, 595 (Summer 1997); *see also Monitoring of Whaling and Trade in Endangered Species*, OREGON STATE UNIVERSITY CETACEAN CONSERVATION GENETICS LAB, *available at* http://mmi.oregonstate.edu/ccgl/research/monitoring.

167. Rosen, *supra* note 163.

168. *See, e.g.*, *U.S. Role in 57th Annual Meeting of the International Whaling Commission*, 99 AM. J. INT'L. L. 911 (Oct. 2005) (resolution rejecting Japan's proposal to expand whaling program); Howard Schiffman, *Scientific Research Whaling in International Law: Objectives and Objections*, 8 ILSA J. INT'L AND COMPARATIVE L. 473, 478 (Spring 2002) (discussing 2001 Resolution 2001-7 in which IWC urged Japan to stop killing minke whales until scientific assessment performed); Rachelle Adam, *The Japanese Dolphin Hunts: In Quest of International Legal Protection for Small Cetaceans*, 14 J. ANIMAL. L. 133 (2008) (dolphins and porpoises).

169. *See, e.g.*, Karla J. Black & Greg Domareki, *A Review of Developments in Ocean and*

Coastal Law 2000, 6 OCEAN AND COASTAL L. J. 233, 245 (2001) (discussing Japan's justifications for whaling program).

170. Schiffman, *supra* note 168, *Scientific Research Whaling in International Law: Objectives and Objections*, at 479.

171. *See generally* Reuben B. Ackerman, *Japanese Whaling in the Pacific Ocean: Defiance of International Whaling Norms in the Name of "Scientific Research," Culture, and Tradition*, 25 B.C. INT'L & COMP. L. REV. 323 (2002); Atsushi Ishi & Ayako Okubo, *An Alternative Explanation of Japan's Whaling Diplomacy in Post-moratorium Era*, J. OF INT'L WILDLIFE L. & POLICY, Vol. 10, No. 1, 55–87 (2007).

172. *Id.*

173. *See* Alyson Decker, *Save the Whales—Save the Whales—Wait, Just Save the International Whaling Commission: A Fresh Look at the Controversy Surrounding Cultural Claims to Whale*, 16 S. CAL. INTERDISC. L.J. 253 (2006); Richard Kirk Eishstaedt, *"Save the Whales" v. "Save the Makah": The Makah and the Struggle for Native Whaling*, 4 ANIMAL L. 145 (1998); Russel C. D'Costa, *Reparations as a Basis for the Makah's Right to Whale*, 12 ANIMAL L. 71 (2005).

174. "Under current IWC regulations, aboriginal subsistence whaling is permitted for Denmark (Greenland, fin and minke whales), the Russian Federation (Siberia, gray and bowhead whales), St Vincent and The Grenadines (Bequia, humpback whales) and the USA (Alaska, bowhead and gray whales). It is the responsibility of national governments to provide the Commission with evidence of the cultural and subsistence needs of their people. The Scientific Committee provides scientific advice on safe catch limits for such stocks." *Aboriginal Subsistence Whaling*, INTERNATIONAL WHALING COMMISSION, *available at* http://www.iwcoffice.org/conservation/aboriginal.htm. Aboriginal subsistence whaling accounts for the deaths of approximately 300 to 400 whales annually. *Catches Taken: ASW*, INTERNATIONAL WHALING COMMISSION, *available at* http://www.iwcoffice.org/conservation/table_aboriginal.htm.

175. *Aboriginal Subsistence Whaling*, *supra* note 174.

176. United States law defines "take" as "harass, hunt, capture, or kill, or attempt to harass, hunt, capture or kill any marine mammal." 16 U.S.C. §§ 1362(13).

177. *See, e.g.*, *Anderson v. Evans*, 371 F.3d 475 (9th Cir. 2004) ("[T]akes by the Tribe ... must be considered in light of the MMPA through its permit or waiver process. The MMPA will properly allow the taking of marine mammals only when it will not diminish the sustainability and optimum level of the resource for all citizens. The procedural safeguards and conservation principles of the MMPA ensure that marine mammals like the gray whale can be sustained as a resource for the benefit of the Tribe and others."); *Whaling in the North Atlantic—Economic and Political Perspectives*, Ed. Gudrun Petursdottir, University of Iceland, 1997. Proceedings of a conference held in Reykjavik on March 1st, 1997, organized by the Fisheries Research Institute and the High North Alliance; *see also Whaling in the North Atlantic—Economic and Political Perspectives*, Ed. Gudrun Petursdottir, University of Iceland, 1997. Proceedings of a conference held in Reykjavik on March 1st, 1997, organized by the Fisheries Research Institute and the High North Alliance, *available at* http://www.highnorth.no/library/publications/iceland/ic-wh-in.htm.

178. CHRISTOPHER D. STONE, SUMMING UP: WHALING AND ITS CRITICS, TOWARD A SUSTAINABLE WHALING REGIME (Robert L. Friedheim ed., 2001).

179. *Japan Blocks Indigenous Whaling*, BBC NEWS, May 23, 2002, *available at* http://news.bbc.co.uk/2/hi/asia-pacific/2003658.stm.

180. The 1855 Treaty of Neah Bay, in which the United States government settled its differences with the Makah Tribe (a Native American nation), included a promise to the Makah people to allow their whaling practices to continue. Russel C. D'Costa, *Reparations as a Basis for the Makah's Right to Whale*, 12 Animal L. 71, 85–90 (2005).

181. *Id.*

182. Details for The International Whaling Commission's 62nd Annual Meeting in Agadir, Morocco, *supra* note 143.

183. *International Whaling Commission Puts Decision on Whaling Moratorium on Hold Another Year: Native Greenlanders Get Extended Whaling Rights*, Los Angeles Times, June 25, 2010, *available at* http://latimesblogs.latimes.com/unleashed/2010/06/international-whaling-commission-puts-decision-on-whaling-moratorium-on-hold-another-year-native-gre.html (statement of the American Whaling Commissioner Monica Medina).

184. *See* Hardy, *supra* note 144, at 177–78.

185. *Commission Information*, International Whaling Commission, *available at* http://www.iwcoffice.org/commission/iwcmain.htm#nations.

186. United States law defines "take" as "harass, hunt, capture, or kill, or attempt to harass, hunt, capture or kill any marine mammal." 16 U.S.C. §§1362(13).

187. *See Committee for Humane Legislation v. Richardson*, 540 F.2d 1141, 1144 (D.C. Cir. 1976); 16 U.S.C. 1361(2).

188. EPBCA §229-229D.

189. Several decisions were rendered in the case, the first being *Humane Society International, Inc. v. Kyodo Senpaku Kaisha, Ltd.*, 212 ALR 551 (2004), and the last 165 FCR 510 (2008).

190. *Id.* 165 FCR 510, 523 (2008).

191. *See* Jorge Vargas, *The California Gray Whale: Its Legal Regime Under Mexican Law*, 12 Ocean & Coastal L.J. 213 (2007). Grey whales complete one of the longest yearly migrations of any animal species. *Id.* at 214. Every year they travel from the freezing Arctic seas where they feed to the warmer waters off the coast of Mexico where they breed. *Id.* at 214–15. At one time in history, there were three different populations of grey whales. The northern Atlantic grey whale has since become extinct; the north-western Pacific grey whale is currently endangered. *Id.* at 218. The north-eastern Pacific grey whale is the only population whose numbers have recovered to anywhere near the original population size.

192. *The United Nations Convention on the Law of the Sea*, United Nations, *available at* http://www.un.org/Depts/los/convention_agreements/convention_historical_perspective.htm.

193. *Id.*

194. *See, e.g.*, M.J. Spalding & J.E. Blumenfeld, *Legal Aspects of Whale Watching in North America*, prepared for Legal Aspects of Whale Watching (Nov. 17–20, 1997), *available at* www.puertovallartawhalewatching.org/pdf/Legal-Aspects.pdf.; *see also* http://www.abc.net.au/news/scitech/2002/05/item20020525122228_1.htm.

195. Ley de Pesca, artículo 3, fracción V.

196. Código Penal Mexicano, artículo 254 bis.

197. *Id.*

198. J. Vargas, *supra* note 190, at 215–16.

199. *Id.*

200. *See, e.g.*, *Mexican Lagoons*, California Grey Whale Coalition, *available at* http://www.californiagraywhalecoalition.org/mexicanlagoons.shtml.

201. Thom Kuehls, Beyond Sovereign Territory: The Space of Ecopolitics 37 (1996); David S. Ardia, *Does the Emperor Have No Clothes? Enforcement of International Laws Protecting the Marine Environment*, 19 Mich. J. Int'l L. 497, 497–98, 560–64 (1998). In the whaling context, the Sea Shepherd Conservation Society engages in a number of practices, including following and confronting whaling vessels and their crew members. Sea Shepherd claims it takes its action pursuant to its right to enforce the United Nations' World Charter for Nature in order to protect whales from hunters. *See* United Nations World Charter for Nature, G.A. Res. 37/7, U.N. Doc. A/RES/37/7, art. III, para. 21, 24 (Oct. 28, 1982); *International Laws and Charters*, Sea Shepherd Conservation Society, *available at* http://www.seashepherd.org/who-we-are/laws-and-charters.html ("Sea Shepherd cooperates fully with all international law enforcement agencies and its enforcement activities comply[] with standard practices of law and policing enforcement. Sea Shepherd adheres to the utilization of non-violent principles in the course of all actions and has taken a stand[] against violence in the protection of the oceans."). For an analysis of Sea Shepherd's practices, see Joseph Elliott Roeschke, Comment, *Eco-Terrorism and Piracy on the High Seas: Japanese Whaling and the Rights of Private Groups to Enforce International Conservation Law in Neutral Waters*, 20 Vill. Envtl. L.J. 99 (2009); *see also* Raffi Khatchadourian, *Neptune's Navy: Paul Watson's Wild Crusade to Save the Oceans*, New Yorker, Nov. 5, 2007, *available at* http://www.newyorker.com/reporting/2007/11/05/071105fa_fact_khatchadourian ("When I described [Sea Shepherd leader Paul] Watson's use of the charter to David Caron, the co-director of the Law of the Sea Institute, at the University of California at Berkeley, he said, 'Clearly wrong. There is no ambiguity.'").

Index